Ancient Memory

Trends in Classics – Supplementary Volumes

Edited by
Franco Montanari and Antonios Rengakos

Associate Editors
Stavros Frangoulidis · Fausto Montana · Lara Pagani
Serena Perrone · Evina Sistakou · Christos Tsagalis

Scientific Committee
Alberto Bernabé · Margarethe Billerbeck
Claude Calame · Jonas Grethlein · Philip R. Hardie
Stephen J. Harrison · Stephen Hinds · Richard Hunter
Christina Kraus · Giuseppe Mastromarco
Gregory Nagy · Theodore D. Papanghelis
Giusto Picone · Alessandro Schiesaro
Tim Whitmarsh · Bernhard Zimmermann

Volume 119

Ancient Memory

Remembrance and Commemoration
in Graeco-Roman Literature

Edited by
Katharine Mawford and Eleni Ntanou

DE GRUYTER

ISBN 978-3-11-126773-9
e-ISBN (PDF) 978-3-11-072879-8
e-ISBN (EPUB) 978-3-11-072892-7
ISSN 1868-4785

Library of Congress Control Number: 2021936640

Bibliographic information published by the Deutsche Nationalbibliothek
The Deutsche Nationalbibliothek lists this publication in the Deutsche Nationalbibliografie;
detailed bibliographic data are available on the Internet at http://dnb.dnb.de.

© 2023 Walter de Gruyter GmbH, Berlin/Boston
This volume is text- and page-identical with the hardback published in 2021.
Editorial Office: Alessia Ferreccio and Katerina Zianna
Logo: Christopher Schneider, Laufen
Printing and binding: CPI books GmbH, Leck

www.degruyter.com

Preface

This volume has its origin in a two-day conference held at the University of Manchester in June 2018, the Annual Meeting of Postgraduates in Ancient Literature, which brought together forty international speakers presenting topics on a wide range of aspects of memory and commemoration in ancient literature. The papers presented over the course of the conference provoked a great deal of discussion and inspiration, the spirit of which we hope to have captured with the wide range of papers compiled in this volume, many of which began life in the conference.

The papers collected here deliberately cover a wide range of approaches and texts, and a wide span of time; the volume also brings together a fittingly wide range of viewpoints from international authors at various stages of their academic lives. The chapters are loosely grouped by approach and will benefit from being read not only independently but in dialogue with other chapters; it is our hope that the reader will find and enjoy the many threads running through these pages – an exercise in memory itself.

This volume benefits not only from the productive atmosphere of AMPAL 2018 and its theme of 'Memory and Commemoration', but also from what Galinsky (*Memoria Romana*, Ann Arbor, 2014: 3) has termed the 'memory boom', and the wave of scholarly interest of recent years into the threads of memory and forgetting which were woven through Graeco-Roman literature and cultures. The papers presented here showcase a range of approaches building on this scholarly background; we hope that the reader finds these discussions thought-provoking and that they may inspire and prompt more work in the future.

Contents

Preface —— V
Acknowledgements —— IX

Katharine Mawford and Eleni Ntanou
Introduction —— 1

Part I: The Mechanics of Memory

Sophia Papaioannou
Taking a Walk through Rome…: Comedic Itineraries and Early Republican Spatial Memory —— 19

Maria Haley
Quoting from Memory? Shared Knowledge in Cicero's Book Fragments of Accius' *Atreus* —— 41

Part II: Collective Memory

Kate Cook
Memories of Glory: Poetry, Prose, and Commemoration in the *Heraclidae* —— 71

Andreas N. Michalopoulos
Ovid's Poetics of Memory and Oblivion in his Exilic Poetry —— 89

Elinor Cosgrave
The Memory of Marcus Regulus and Cannae in Plautus' *Captivi* —— 103

Katarzyna Kostecka
Divine Memories and the Shaping of Olympus in the *Iliad* —— 123

Part III: Female Memory

Katharine Mawford
The Manipulation of Memory in Apollonius' *Argonautica* —— 145

Sophie Ngan
Bound to Break Boundaries: Memory and Identity in Seneca's *Medea* —— 165

Eleni Ntanou
***Audita mente notaui*: (Meta)memory, Gender, and Pastoral Impersonation in the Speech of Ovid's Galatea** —— 193

Part IV: Oblivion

Hannah Burke-Tomlinson
Ovid's Labyrinthine *Ars*: Pasiphae and the Dangers of Poetic Memory in the *Metamorphoses* —— 219

A.D. Morrison
Divine Memory, Mortal Forgetfulness and Human Misfortune —— 247

Carlos Hernández Garcés
Forgetfulness as a Narrative Device in Herodotus' *Histories* —— 267

Part V: Further Thoughts

Richard Hunter
Memory and its Discontents in Ancient Literature —— 293

List of Contributors —— 309
Index Rerum et Nominum —— 313
Index Locorum —— 315

Acknowledgements

It would not have been possible to bring this volume to life without the support of many colleagues and friends. We would like to thank first of all the contributors to the volume for their confidence, enthusiasm and (not least) their patience during this process. This volume would not exist but for the excellent papers and productive atmosphere of AMPAL 2018, so we would like to thank the rest of the organising committee, Julene Abad Del Vecchio, Serena Cammoranesi, Laura Chambers, and Matt Ingham, for their help with running the conference, and everyone who attended and participated in the conference and its many discussions. Both editors (and, indeed, the conference itself!) found ourselves at home in the department of Classics, Ancient History, Archaeology, and Egyptology at the University of Manchester over many years, so we would also like to extend our thanks to the whole department for their years of support. Parts of this volume were also completed during a stay in the wonderful environment of the Fondation Hardt in March 2019, so our thanks go to the people (and library) of the Fondation.

Our thanks also go to the *Trends in Classics* team at De Gruyter, and particularly to those who have supported us at each stage of this volume's publication. We would like to thank in particular Marco Michele Acquafredda, Anne Hiller, and Katerina Zianna for their support with this process.

In putting together this volume, from the initial proposal to assembling its introduction and structure, we benefitted greatly from the encouragement and advice of colleagues in Manchester, so our final, heartfelt thanks go to Andrew Morrison, Alison Sharrock, Jenny Bryan, Ruth Morello, Matt Ingham, Julene Abad Del Vecchio, Alexandra Wilding, and Katherine Molesworth.

Katharine Mawford and Eleni Ntanou
Introduction

The multiform nature of memory within ancient literature cannot be overstated. As the collection of chapters brought together in this volume attest, there exists a multitude of facets of memory, commemoration, remembering, and forgetting, which are woven through the body of Graeco-Roman literature, demanding the memory of its audiences, authors, and characters, and speaking to the establishment of cultural and social mores and responses. In the *Odyssey*, a product of oral composition and therefore inextricably linked with memory, the ultimate goal of Odysseus' epic journey – reunion with Penelope and Telemachus, and reintegration into Ithacan society – relies on Penelope's successful recognition of her husband after his extended absence, a feat which is itself enabled by the appearance of recognition tokens dependent on memory, most notably Odysseus' knowledge of their bed:[1]

> οὕτω τοι τόδε σῆμα πιφαύσκομαι· οὐδέ τι οἶδα,
> ἤ μοι ἔτ' ἔμπεδόν ἐστι, γύναι, λέχος, ἦέ τις ἤδη
> ἀνδρῶν ἄλλοσε θῆκε, ταμὼν ὕπο πυθμέν' ἐλαίης.
> ὣς φάτο, τῆς δ' αὐτοῦ λύτο γούνατα καὶ φίλον ἦτορ,
> σήματ' ἀναγνούσῃ τά οἱ ἔμπεδα πέφραδ' Ὀδυσσεύς·
> *Od.* 23.202–6

> Thus I present to you this token (σῆμα), but I don't know whether the bed is still inside, wife, or whether some man has at some point cut it from its olive stem and moved it. So he spoke; at this, her knees went weak and her heart softened, as she recognised the clear tokens Odysseus had declared.

This in turn finds an echo in folktale,[2] where such tokens function as aides-mémoire to characters within a narrative system characterised and transmitted through cultural memory. However, it is memory which also threatens Odysseus with failure: the spectre of Agamemnon haunts the narrative, reminding the audience – along with Telemachus and Odysseus – of the potential for disaster waiting in the wings.[3] When Odysseus literally meets the ghosts of his past in

---

[1] A further significant recognition token is Eurycleia's recognition of Odysseus' scar (19.467–75), a 'clear sign' (σῆμα ἀριφραδές, 23.75) of his identity which she relates to Penelope.
[2] Odysseus' return belongs to the Aarne-Thompson-Uther story-type ATU 974 *The Homecoming Husband*, Uther (2004). See Hansen (2002) 202–10 and Ready (2014).
[3] *Od.* 11.404–56; even as Agamemnon tells Odysseus that he need not fear death at Penelope's hands (ἀλλ' οὐ σοί γ', Ὀδυσεῦ, φόνος ἔσσεται ἔκ γε γυναικός, 11.444, 'but, Odysseus, there will

the underworld, he is confronted not only with remembered events and relationships (in meeting his mother and Ajax) but also with the subject of his epic's poetic memory, the failed return of Agamemnon. If Agamemnon's ghost represents the continuation of memory, a non-living reminder of the potential for failure, the Lotus presented to Odysseus' men in Book 9 is, in a sense, his opposite, entailing a blissful (if ultimately detrimental to epic itself) respite from memory and from the hardships which the Ithacan's long-distant memory of home will ultimately bring.[4]

In the *Odyssey*, then, memory operates not only on an individual or social level, nor is it an entirely beneficial or detrimental force; rather, the epic interweaves these different aspects, rendering memory essential to Odysseus' journey while simultaneously relying on and prompting the audience's memory of Agamemnon's demise as means of exploring the threat which Odysseus faces – that history and memory may repeat.

Similar patterns underpin Latin literature: in one of the most iconic closures of a book of poetry, so iconic indeed that it was reprised by Ovid at the end of the *Metamorphoses*,[5] Horace brings the monumentality of his finished poetic work centre stage:

> Exegi monumentum aere perennius
> regalique situ pyramidum altius,
> quod non imber edax, non aquilo impotens
> possit diruere aut innumerabilis
> annorum series et fuga temporum.
> non omnis moriar multaque pars mei
> uitabit Libitinam; usque ego postera
> crescam laude recens, dum Capitolium
> scandet cum tacita uirgine pontifex.
>
> Hor. *Carm*. 3.30.

I have completed a monument longer lasting than bronze, taller than the royal structure of the pyramids, which neither greedy rain nor the ungovernable Aquilus can destroy, nor countless turns of the year, nor the flight of time. I shall not altogether die, and a great part of me will avoid the goddess of death. I shall continue to grow, fresh with the praise of posterity, as long as the priest climbs the Capitol with the silent virgin.

---

be no murder arranged for you by your wife'), he advises the returning hero to return to Ithaca in secret, since 'there is no longer any faith in women' (ἐπεὶ οὐκέτι πιστὰ γυναιξίν, 11.456), undermining his reassurance.

4 *Od.* 9.82–97; Benardete (1997) 66.

5 On Ovid's reworking of this Horatian *sphragis*, see Hardie (2002) 95–6; Ingleheart (2015) 296–300; Smith (1997) 23–4; Solodow (1988) 167–8.

In these lines from *Carmen* 3.30, it is poetry which will prevent Horace from perishing and leaves at least a part of him unscathed for posterity. The assimilation of the poetic work to a monument construes poetic memory in terms of physical durability and concreteness. Similar ideas permeate the ancient world, which anticipate and literalise Nora's famous conceptualisation of *lieux de mémoire*, the material and non-material sites of collective memory.[6] In being reworked in Ovid's *Metamorphoses*, the prophecy of memory is fulfilled:[7]

> Iamque opus exegi, quod nec Iouis ira nec ignis
> nec poterit ferrum nec edax abolere uetustas.
> cum uolet, illa dies, quae nil nisi corporis huius
> ius habet, incerti spatium mihi finiat aeui;
> parte tamen meliore mei super alta perennis
> astra ferar, nomenque erit indelebile nostrum;
> quaque patet domitis Romana potentia terris,
> ore legar populi, perque omnia saecula fama,
> (siquid habent ueri uatum praesagia) uiuam.
> Ov. *Met.* 15.871–9

> Now I have completed a work that neither the wrath of Jupiter nor fire nor sword nor the devouring passage of time will be able to efface. When it wants, let that day that has power over nothing except over this body end the span of my uncertain time; still, in my better part I will be borne perennial over the lofty stars, and my name will be indestructible; and wherever Roman power extends over the conquered lands, I shall be read by the mouth of people, and through all ages (if the prophecies of the bards have any truth) in fame I shall live.

Like Horace before him, Ovid constructs his poetic work as a mnemonic space which defies mortality. The memorialisation of poetry sets up the social dimension of memory. It is made to address an audience, to preserve and excite the memory of its readers. As Gertz argues, such literary mnemonic spaces allow for meetings between readers and writers:

> they [writers and readers] "meet" in the space between memory and memorials, a space that…encourages individual reflection and stimulates echoes, a space that resembles the *locus* where Phaedrus and Socrates decide to settle for a while, one in which nothing yet is set in stone.[8]

---

[6] See Nora (1989).
[7] See Ingleheart (2015) and Michalopoulos in this volume, who suggest that Ovid reprises the end of the *Metamorphoses* in his exilic poetry and directly associates exile with poetic monumentality.
[8] Gertz (2003) 15.

The idea of mutability not only goes hand in hand with the Ovidian metamorphic epic but also with the mnemonic processes involved in the writing and reading of poetry. Alongside and perhaps contrary to the notions of concreteness conveyed by the physical memorial, the reperformance and the changes of the Horatian opus in Ovid's text thematise the malleability of memory and creativity as an essential part of creating new wholes, of re-membering.[9] Ovid's poetry, filled with 'echoes and reflections', sets the parameter of the fickleness and of memory as a creative, a truly poetic process.[10]

The brief exploration of the *Odyssey* and the Horatian and Ovidian endings through the lenses of memory offered above exemplifies the vast tradition of striving towards, working with, and problematising memory in antiquity. Whether social, individual, civic, or poetic, the different manifestations of memory are not isolated but typically co-exist and collaborate in literary frameworks. These varied and yet interconnected manifestations of memory, employed by the contributors, give unity to this volume. In each of the chapters collected here, memory is explored as working within a specific framework, be it spatial, temporal, generic, and/or socio-political. The purpose of this volume is to present a range of new perspectives on memory in Graeco-Roman literature which span genre and time period, showing the rich and multifaceted nature of literary memory, from its role in the construction of poetry or the individual memory of specific characters, to memory as a social function, informing and informed by cultural events and the reaction of its audience. Each perspective offered in this volume builds on the rich body of theoretical approaches to memory studies, while the volume itself has been prompted not only by a desire to bring together Classics and memory studies but also to revisit these issues in light of our modern fascination with memory.

The exploration and problematisation of memory and forgetfulness gave rise to questions which pervaded the Graeco-Roman world: Who and what should be remembered or celebrated? How does memory function? Why do we forget? Memory fuelled the production of the most serious literary genre of the ancient world, epic: the poet-bard was, at least in theory,[11] required to remember a narrative, and the performance of such a narrative demanded responsive-

---

9 Nora (1989) 18 attributes similar contrasting features to the *lieux de mémoire*, which are described as 'simple and ambiguous, natural and artificial, at once immediately available in concrete sensual experience and susceptible to the most abstract elaboration'.
10 We are borrowing the phrase here from the title of Gertz (2003).
11 For the fictionalisation of orality in Hellenistic and Latin epic poems, see Fulkerson & Stover (2016) 3–8, Papaioannou (2007) 189–95; Albis (1996) 1–16.

ness on the part of the audience – awareness and memory of the surrounding tradition, and the ability to respond to cues and references, being no small part of this.[12] Performed memory and memory of performance are integral to many of this volume's chapters, as together they consider its multifaceted nature which informs poetic invocations of memory and the Muses in order to initiate and situate their poetic *oeuvres* (ἄνδρα μοι ἔννεπε, μοῦσα, *Od.* 1.1, 'tell me, Muse, about the man'; μνήσομαι οὐδὲ λάθωμαι Ἀπόλλωνος ἑκάτοιο, *Hom. Hymn Ap.* 1, 'I will remember and not forget far-shooting Apollo').[13] Of course, awareness of memory is not limited solely to the poet-bard, but such awareness is also exhibited by their characters who at times show a metapoetic understanding of their role as objects of and in memory, such as Helen's famous assessment of the Trojan War in the *Iliad*:

> οἷσιν ἐπὶ Ζεὺς θῆκε κακὸν μόρον, ὡς καὶ ὀπίσσω
> ἀνθρώποισι πελώμεθ' ἀοίδιμοι ἐσσομένοισι.
> *Il.* 6.357–8

On us Zeus has placed a dreadful fate, so that in the future we may be songs for people to come.

The intersection between the requirement of the spectators' personal memory with the simultaneous reference to and formation of shared memory called for a dialogue between the epic poem, the bard, and audience. Thus, the social function was at the heart of memory in the ancient world, just as it is today. In our digital age, these social and performative functions of memory are perfectly encapsulated by the role of social media in spearheading the spread of information and prompting us individually to share memories and thoughts. This emphasis on the sharing of memories raises the question of whether acts not publicly documented are truly valid, while we rely increasingly less on our own memories as we store ever more information on phones, computers, and in the cloud. Simonides' mnemotechnic of spaces of memory, the famous *loci memoriae* (Cic. *de Or.* 2.353–4), have been literalised in our hard drives and storage.

---

[12] Bonifazi (2008) 41 notes that 'a significant cognitive part of remembering deals with the way in which characters, details, scenes, and moves are introduced not only "on the stage" but also to the mind of the performer on the one hand, and to the attention of the listeners on the other'.
[13] As Fearn (2018) 104 points out, 'the *Odyssey* provided foundational testimony for an archaic Greek text's ability to figure its own memorability'. The repercussions of the divine origin of the Mnemonides Muses are discussed by Morrison in this volume.

In constant tension with memory is forgetting. The fear of oblivion is more relevant than ever, as there is a continuous growth of degenerative brain diseases which severely affect memory, according to the World Health Organisation (WHO).[14] Ancient people were concerned with the preservation of memory in their day-to-day lives: the use of mnemotechnics and other mnemonic devices shows that memory loss and failure of memory was just as much a fear then as it is today, a topic discussed by Richard Hunter in the present volume. The ancient concern over the workings of memory and processes of memorialisation looks forward to the modern evolution of cognitive studies. Inversely, of course, cognitive studies have been successfully applied to the study of ancient literature, offering a way into 'reading the minds' of everyone involved in an artistic performance, and are repeatedly employed alongside other theories by contributors of this volume.[15] One famous example of ancient mnemotechnics is that of Simonides' aforementioned theory of mentally retracing visualised spaces of memory, as described by Cicero (*de Or.* 2.353–4). Such mnemonic devices were often associated with the preservation of shared, cultural memory in a world that heavily rested upon the oral (re)construction and transmission of knowledge. The Muses, repeatedly called upon to initiate and inspire epic poetry and commemoration, were figured as the daughters of Mnemosyne (or 'Memory'). Even after the development of writing, the Muse's aid in reminding the poet of the narrative that is about to unfold had been crystallised as a *topos*, gesturing towards mnemotechnics and the oral beginnings of poetry.[16] In an explicit mention of memory shortly after the opening of the *Aeneid*, the anonymous Muse is prompted to remind the epic poet of the causes driving the *telos* of the poem, *Musa, mihi causas memora* (1.8, 'Remind me of the causes, Muse'); memory thus has a double purpose here and is central to the conception of literature: it not only drives the creation of oral poetry but does so also and explicitly for written poetry, and allows Virgil to work within the epic tradition. It is this centrality of memory to the very conception of ancient poetry (its genesis and its purpose) that is the central topic of our volume, in which all approaches to memory are consistently viewed against the backdrop of genres and literary tradition. Epic, tragedy, comedy, elegy, rhetoric, epitaphs, historiography, and

---

14 See World Health Organization (September 2019) '10 Facts on Dementia'. Retrieved July 2020 from https://www.who.int/features/factfiles/dementia/en/.
15 Here, we borrow the title of Easterling & Budelmann (2010) 'Reading Minds in Greek Tragedy'. For a relevant approach in tragedy, see Budelmann (2010) and Easterling & Budelmann (2010). In the present volume, Haley and Ntanou employ notions of cognitive theory by discussing 'shared knowledge' and the 'malleability of memorisation' respectively.
16 See above, n. 10.

epistolography all employ memory as a central trope in markedly different ways, as the contributors of this volume demonstrate.

Although the prominence of memory in the ancient world is often acknowledged by Classical scholars, and despite the recent 'memory boom'[17] gaining increasing interest across different disciplines, there has been relatively little by way of a systematic exploration of ancient memory. Even less has been written regarding the theoretical consequences of memory studies as a critical tool for delving into ancient literature. The present volume provides just such an approach, theorising the use of memory studies in Graeco-Roman thought and literature and coming at the topic from four main perspectives, considering the mechanics of memory, collective memory, the memory of individual characters, and the role of oblivion. Between these different approaches there exist a range of links which cross these section boundaries, thus showcasing the interrelation between the many different aspects of memory.

Three recently published works, Galinsky (University of Michigan Press, 2014) *Memoria Romana*, Popkin (CUP, 2016) *The Architecture of the Roman Triumph: Monuments, Memory, and Identity*, and Castagnoli and Ceccarelli (CUP, 2019) *Greek Memories: Theories and Practices*, explore memory in the study of ancient thought and literature. But while Castagnoli and Ceccarelli (2019) focus on memory from a philosophical perspective and Galinsky (2014) and Popkin (2016) investigate ancient Rome primarily from a historical viewpoint, the present volume examines memory as literary practice, applied in both the writing and the reading of literature.

The close connection between memory, intertextuality, and the literary tradition has been the focus of a good number of influential works, among the most notable being Conte's (1974) *Memoria dei poeti e sistema letterario*. Building on Conte, Hinds argues that memory in literature often functions as a trope of allusion.[18] This theoretical underpinning has inspired more recent works on memory, such as Seider's exploration of memory as a frame for reading the *Aeneid*.[19] Building on these significant works, the present volume combines literary theory with memory studies and employs interdisciplinary memory concepts as perspectives through which to explore ancient literature. It brings together contributions from scholars who examine memory both as a theme and as a methodology, in order to enrich our understanding of ancient memory and

---

17 Galinsky (2014) 3.
18 Hinds (1998). See Lachmann (2008), who suggests that literary texts often stage acts of memory, thus functioning as 'fictions of memory'.
19 See Seider (2013).

offer new approaches to the study of Graeco-Roman thought and literature. The volume also extensively explores the interplay between memory and genre and the use of memory as a generic trope, deployed and altered to fit different generic and cultural frameworks.

Civic memory (Papaioannou, Cook, Haley), memoryscapes (Michalopoulos, Papaioannou, Haley), and women's memory (Mawford, Ngan, Ntanou) are some of the concepts of modern memory studies applied by the contributors of the volume in order to theorise memory in Classics. Memory is a cognitive phenomenon, informed by our experiences, understanding, and knowledge.[20] As neuroscience and cognitive studies have shown in recent decades, recollections are not fixed: far exceeding a mere record of a sum of recollections, the phenomenon of memory is defined by malleability and creativity.[21] No memory, however, is purely personal, as all recollections depend on a specific socio-cultural framework.[22] Aside from being a biological, cognitive process, memory also performs a fundamental cultural role, thereby affecting all spheres and perspectives of human activity and life. Erll explains how the conceptualisation of collective memory stems from the transposition of the cognitive process of remembering onto the level of a community: similar to the individual, societies (re)create a shared past through a process of selection of memories, which is open to alterations and 're-readings' depending on their needs.[23] First theorised by Halbwachs' famous concept of *mémoire collective*,[24] the research of collective memory has arisen as an interdisciplinary field in its own right.[25] In recent years, significant collective volumes (Erll, Nunning & Young (2008)) and separate works (Assmann (1995), Nora (1989)) have promoted the study of cultural memory, thereby offering an advanced toolbox for the examination of memory across all disciplines. In the present volume, Kate Cook and Elinor Cosgrave extensively discuss how cultural practices were preserved and altered to fit new circumstances through public performances of memory.

Closely related to cultural memory is civic memory. The latter underpins the discussions by Kate Cook, Katarzyna Kostecka, Andreas Michalopoulos, Sophia Papaioannou, and Maria Haley in this volume. Cook analyses the emergence of

---

[20] See Bakker (2008) 65.
[21] See Welzer (2005); Siegel (2006); Keightley & Pickering (2012) *passim*, esp. 1–10.
[22] See Bloch (1992); Kõresaar, Lauk & Kuutma (2009). However, as Erll (2008) 4 rightly points out, the mental aspect is not to be completely disassociated from cultural memory in the wider conception of the term 'cultural'.
[23] See Erll (2008) 5.
[24] See Halbwachs (1950).
[25] For the evolution of cultural memory, see Russell (2006).

the *epitaphios* as a genre stemming from a need to construct and control civic memory. This is not limited to real societies, but may also be explored in relation to literary or mythic constructs, as Kostecka demonstrates in her examination of the role of memory in the structure of the Olympian hierarchy in the *Iliad*. Desire for memory and commemoration both on the level of the individual and of the community was promoted in various ways in the Graeco-Roman world, including the construction of memorials and the engendering of literary memorabilia. This desire informed the composition and performance of epic poetry and its concern with *kleos* or renown, as well as epinician odes and epigrams: forgetting functions both within and without epic narratives as the death of epic poetry.[26] Civic memory was substantially promoted through public events, rituals, and even buildings installed in key locations in a city.[27] This in turn leads to the generation of 'memoryscapes', which could be used to promote and construct a shared understanding of citizenship. Memoryscapes are a complex notion, theorised by Pierre Nora in his famous *lieux de mémoire*.[28] These vary from the purely concrete, such as buildings and structures, to the deeply abstract and symbolic, although there is significant overlap between the two notions.[29]

In both the Greek and the Roman worlds, the cityscape was strategically turned into a memorial of civic identity, which participated in the generation of the shared understanding of citizenship. It is thus no coincidence that being erased from the collective memory of the city was for Romans one of the harshest forms of punishment.[30] The destruction of the houses of those condemned to *damnatio memoriae* was a way to remove them from the physical fabric and the 'memoryscape' of Rome; Michalopoulos discusses exile as a further form of physical and symbolic removal from the city's memory. Haley and Papaioannou explore how drama, tragedy and comedy respectively, is set against the background of civic identity and the cityscape of Rome. In particular, Papaioannou

---

[26] Encapsulated, for instance, in the effect of the Lotus-Eaters in *Odyssey* 10: those who ingest the Lotus no longer wish to complete their *nostos*, an effect which threatens the essential function of the epic and which is explicitly figured as an act of forgetting: νόστου τε λαθέσθαι, 10.97. Compare however the effect of Helen's drug of forgetting (φάρμακον ... ἐπίληθον, *Od.* 4.220–1) which in fact *allows* for storytelling: μύθοις τέρπεσθε, 4.239. See also Morrison in this volume.
[27] As Dagger (1997) 164 notes, 'civic memory is related to citizenship in the same way that memory is related to personality: it is its foundation'. See also Davies (2017).
[28] See Nora (1989).
[29] See Nora (1989).
[30] See Flower (2006).

shows that by alluding to its Republican and even Greek counterparts the imagined cityscape of Augustan Rome becomes a palimpsest of civic identity. Although the chapters included in this volume span a substantially long period of time, including both Greek and Latin works, extending from Homer to Seneca, and covering a range of literary genres, they are linked by a multitude of such unifying themes, including literary genre, gender, and politics. Their collection, therefore, invites a side-by-side examination of the many different aspects of the multifarious concept of memory.

Outline of chapters

As mentioned above, four main approaches (the mechanics of memory, collective memory, female memory, and oblivion) underpin the collection of chapters included in this volume. These approaches inform the volume's structure, allowing the volume to move from the fundamentals of memory to its use, and from social memory to personal memory, before finally considering the absence or failure of memory. Nonetheless, these chapters are in dialogue with one another and therefore the reader will be able to locate a number of threads (both thematic and methodological), which cross these section boundaries. Fittingly enough, there is some self-referentiality involved in the reading of the volume at hand, as the process of reading it rests on just such a creative mnemonic process.[31]

The exploration of the cognitive performance of memory played against the backdrop of literary works and mental stimuli offered by literary tradition are the main topics of Sophia Papaioannou's and Maria Haley's chapters, which both look at Roman drama and together form the first section of the volume. Interest in the study of cognition in ancient literature has increased over the last years, particularly with regard to the genre of tragedy.[32] In the present volume, Papaioannou explores the ways in which memory is triggered through fictional and real visual stimuli in the comedies of Plautus and Terence. She argues that the process of selecting and synthesising topographical memories of the Roman landscape may have political ramifications and reads the Plautine and Terentine recreations of the memory of sojourning across Rome as political and cultural commentaries. Building on a cognitive approach which has been already

---

[31] A central concept of intratextuality, about which see Sharrock (2000; 2018).
[32] See Budelmann (2010); Easterling & Budelmann (2010).

fruitfully explored in Classics, *viz.* 'Reading minds' in literature,[33] Haley explores Cicero's memory of Accius' *Atreus* in the Ciceronian corpus. By looking at how Cicero remembers tragedy and how he reminds his reader of it in the different genres of his work, Haley discusses how Roman tragedy affected contemporary thought and ultimately disputes the misreading of Roman tragedy as a mere translation of a Greek original. Furthermore, Haley examines the concern with and theorising of mnemonic strategies in Cicero's *De Oratione* and the pseudo-Ciceronian *Rhetorica ad Herennium*.

Moving on from mnemonic theory to the praxis of memory within a community, the second section focuses on collective memory.[34] Collective memory is intertwined with the notions of identity and belonging, and it crosses into the main spheres of shared experience, such as politics, religion, and literature.[35] In her chapter, Kate Cook explores the construction of shared memory in classical Athens, as depicted in Euripides' *Heraclidae*, and shows how this play engages in problematising the commemoration of political acts and the agents of this process. Cook associates the politics of commemoration in the *Heraclidae* with the emergence of a new genre, the *epitaphios*, and suggests that Euripides projects the genre of tragedy as a more appropriate means of commemoration because of its fuller inclusion of memories both desirable and problematic. The social role of memory may be viewed not only temporally but also spatially. Andreas Michalopoulos suggests that memory may act as a mechanism tightening social relations between people separated by the burden of distance. In his *Epistulae ex Ponto*, Ovid repeatedly declares his continuing memory of and devotion to his friends in Rome. All the same, Michalopoulos argues that memory functions as a surrogate for physical presence and real social interactions. The cultural framework of Rome is mentally imprinted into the inhospitable surroundings of Tomis and the fictional recreation of Rome's world and its people makes life tolerable for the poet. In effect, by subverting – to a certain degree – the emperor's exilic conviction and the separation of Ovid from Rome, memory acquires significant political dimensions.

Elinor Cosgrave explores how Plautus' *Captivi* brings out the development of attitudes towards and representation of captive-taking. Cosgrave suggests that Plautus' representations of captives should be viewed in tandem with his audiences' preoccupation with the memories and concept of captivity at the time and their shared memory of the Punic Wars. Katarzyna Kostecka shows

---

[33] See above, n. 14.
[34] For an exploration of collective memory, see Olick, Vinitzky-Seroussi & Levy (2011).
[35] For such an approach to the shared memory of Rome, see Galinksy (2014).

how the shared memory of human communities is matched with divine collective memory in the *Iliad*, and explores why gods refrain from realising their threats of harming one another within Homer's epic narrative. She studies the interrelation between the violent divine past which is the subject of various gods' recollections, and the narrative present of the *Iliad*, in which threats made by the gods are never enacted to the same extent. Kostecka argues that the gods' abstention from physically harming other gods may only be understood when viewed against their shared cultural memories, which are glimpsed through relevant narrative digressions. In effect, the shared divine memories solidified their power-dynamics in the present time of the main narrative of the *Iliad*.

Within the notion of collective memory there exist subcategories which involve smaller or distinct groups; women's memory is one such category, and it is this which informs the next section of this volume. Eleni Ntanou, Sophie Ngan, and Katharine Mawford approach the depiction of women remembering and being remembered, exploring the extent to which memory is key to the shaping of transgressive female characters. Scholars of modern memory studies have addressed the frequent marginalisation or even exclusion of female perspectives in 'official sites of public memory'.[36] This phenomenon can be found just as clearly in ancient memorial practices. The marginalisation of female memories ties into the overall scarcity of female voices in ancient literature, in which the narration of a story filtered through a female character's memory often appears as challenging established male-centred sites of memory.[37]

Mawford and Ngan discuss the role of memory in the construction of Medea's identity in Apollonius and Seneca respectively. Mawford explores the characterisation and development of Medea in Apollonius' *Argonautica* in terms of memory, suggesting that Medea changes from being the victim of remembrance into becoming an active user and manipulator of memory. Becoming a perverse double of male epic heroes, Medea is concerned with her afterlife fame and acquires a more active role through crimes in a grim attempt to gain epic *kleos*. Ngan suggests that Medea's attempt to reshape her reputation to match that of a male epic hero is revisited in Seneca's *Medea*. The established gender hierarchies, however, ultimately prevent Medea from manipulating shared

---

36 For the quotation, see Dubriwny & Poirot (2017) 199. See Hamber & Palmary (2009), Jacobs (2008), Kõresaar, Lauk & Kuutma (2009) 16. For the gendering of memory mainly from the perspective of neuroscience rather than that of cultural memory, see Hill, Laird & Robinson (2014); Kramer *et al.* (2003).
37 See e.g. Jarratt (2002); Reading (2016; 2019).

memory and reconstructing her intra- and extra-dramatic identity, leading her to a repetition of her monstrous crimes.

The challenging of a male poetic agenda through the act of memory is also explored in Ntanou's chapter. Ntanou looks at the Galatea, Polyphemus, and Acis episode in Ovid's *Metamorphoses* 13 and suggests that the Ovidian epic offers an unprecedented account of the story through the voice and the memory of a female character. Galatea becomes for the first time the narrator and controller of the memory of her story. The nymph's extensive memory, enclosed in a seemingly stern-epic narrative, that of Aeneas' wanderings, pushes the typically male-centred scope of epic memory as well as revising the memory of the story's pastoral precedents in the poem.

Next, we move into the processes and impact of forgetting for three further chapters. The first of these, Hannah Burke-Tomlinson's chapter, bridges the gap between this section and the previous, as she explores the phenomenon of oblivion in the figure of Pasiphae in Ovid's *Metamorphoses*. Burke-Tomlinson argues that Pasiphae is persistently construed as a character who should be forgotten, but, nonetheless, ultimately succeeds in escaping oblivion, becoming an absent presence in the Ovidian epic.[38] The famous assimilation of the Ovidian epic to a labyrinth thus not only rests in its bewildering narrative structure but also extends to function as a prison: like the mythical structure crafted by Daedalus, the poem contains and appears as trying to captivate dangerous monuments to female sexual *furor* ('madness', 'passion').

The consequences of forgetting are the subject of A.D. Morrison and Carlos Hernández Garcés' chapters. Morrison suggests that, like remembering, forgetting is also tantamount to the construction of shared identity in ancient Greek thought and texts. He argues that oblivion is critical in the conceptualisation of the notions of humanity and mortality in early Greek texts. As a natural human failing, forgetting can incur the blame of the gods. Remembering is often associated primarily with privileged groups of gods' favourites, such as bards; however, their acts of memorialisation in song can (perhaps paradoxically) bring about a positive kind of forgetting, that of one's cares, achieved through the recollection of the sufferings of figures from the mythic past.

Hernández Garcés explores the use of oblivion as a narrative device in Herodotus' *Histories*, and discusses the intricate and eclectic process involved in the work of Herodotus as a historian, who ultimately decides on what is and is not worthy of being remembered through the means of observation, inquiry, and sound judgment. He suggests that the control of what should be forgotten

---

38 For absent presences in Ovid's *Metamorphoses*, see Hardie (2002).

corroborates the historian's authority over the (re)construction of the past; functions as another mechanism for characterisation in historical works; and underscores the sway that making adequate use of the faculty of memory held within the Greek worldview.

Finally, Richard Hunter's synoptic concluding essay steps back to consider a broader picture of the interrelations between memory and Classical studies, and explores potential avenues for future developments at the intersection between Classics and modern memory studies.

These thirteen chapters participate in the developments and growing interest in memory and together theorise a new approach to memory in Classics, informed by the interdisciplinary developments in memory studies. The volume deals with a wide range of genres as well as a great span of time, thus providing a much-needed and in-depth picture of the various functions of memory, commemoration, and forgetting in ancient literature, which benefits from overlapping themes in an unprecedented series of papers on memory across Graeco-Roman literature. The authors showcase the use of memory as a reading method against the background of different genres and as part of their generic repertoire. Ancient memory is a theme that can be integrally and eternally reprised, altered, and reconstructed; we hope that the theorisation of ancient memory presented here will inspire more relevant work in Classics in the future.

Bibliography

Albis, R.V. (1996), *Poet and Audience in the* Argonautica *of Apollonius*, Lanham.
Bakker, E.J. (2008), "Epic Remembering", in A. Mackay (ed.), *Orality, Literacy, Memory in the Ancient Greek and Roman World: Orality and Literacy in Ancient Greece*, Vol. 7, Leiden/Boston: 65–77.
Benardete, S. (1997), *The Bow and the Lyre*, Lanham/London.
Bloch, M. (1992), "Internal and External Memory: Different Ways of Being in History", *Suomen Antropologi* 1: 3–15.
Bonifazi, A. (2008), "Memory and Visualization in Homeric Discourse Markers", in A. Mackay (ed.), *Orality, Literacy, Memory in the Ancient Greek and Roman World: Orality and Literacy in Ancient Greece*, Vol. 7, Leiden/Boston: 35–64.
Budelmann, F. (2010), "Bringing Together Nature and Culture: On the Uses and Limits of Cognitive Science for the Study of Performance Reception", in E. Hall & S. Harrop (eds.), *Theorizing Performance: Greek Drama, Cultural History, and Critical Practice*, London: 108–22.
Budelmann, F./P. Easterling (2010), "Reading Minds in Greek Tragedy", *G&R* 57: 289–303.
Dagger, R. (1997), *Civic Virtues: Rights, Citizenship, and Republican Liberalism*, Oxford.

Davies, P.J.E. (2017), "Constructing, Deconstructing and Reconstructing Civic Memory in Late Republican Rome", in K. Sandberg & C. Smith (eds.), *Omnium Annalium Monumenta: Historical Writing and Historical Evidence in Republican Rome*, Leiden/Boston: 477–511.

Dubriwny, T.N./K. Poirot (2017), "Gender and Public Memory", *Southern Communication Journal* 82 (4): 199–202.

Erll, A. (2008), 'Cultural Memory Studies: An Introduction', in A. Erll & A. Nünning (eds.), *Cultural Memory Studies: Media and Cultural Memory*, Berlin/New York: 1–16.

Fearn, D. (2018), "Materialities of Political Commitment? Textual Events, Material Culture, and Metaliterality in Alcaeus", in F. Buldelmann & T. Phillips (eds.), *Textual Events: Performance & the Lyric in Ancient Greece*, Oxford: 93–114.

Flower, H.I. (2006), *The Art of Forgetting: Disgrace and Oblivion in Roman Political Culture*, Chapel Hill.

Fulkerson, L./T. Stover (eds.) (2016), *Repeat Performances: Ovidian Repetition and the Metamorphoses*, Madison/London.

Galinsky, K. (ed.) (2014), *Memoria Romana*, Ann Arbor.

Gertz, S.K. (2003), *Echoes and Reflections: Memory and Memorials in Ovid and Marie de France*, Amsterdam/New York.

Halbwachs, M. (1950), *La mémoire collective*, Paris.

Hamber, B./I. Palmary (2009), "Gender, Memorialization, and Symbolic Reparations", in R. Rubio-Marin (ed.), *The Gender of Reparations: Unsettling Sexual Hierarchies while Redressing Human Rights Violations*, Cambridge: 324–380.

Hardie, P. (2002), *Ovid's Poetics of Illusion*, Cambridge.

Hansen, W.F. (2002), *Ariadne's thread: a guide to international tales found in classical literature*, Ithaca/London.

Hill, A.C./A.R. Laird/J.L. Robinson (2014), "Gender differences in working memory networks: A BrainMap meta-analysis", *Biological Psychology* 102: 18–29.

Hinds, S. (1998), *Allusion and Intertext: Dynamics of Appropriation in Roman Poetry*, Cambridge/New York.

Ingleheart, J. (2015), "*Exegi monumentum*: Exile, Death, Immortality and Monumentality in Ovid, *Tristia* 3.3", *CQ* 65: 286–300.

Jacobs, J. (2008), "Gender and Collective Memory: Women and Representation at Auschwitz", *Memory Studies* 1 (2): 211–225.

Jarratt, S.C. (2002), "Sappho's Memory", *Rhetoric Society Quarterly* 32 (1): 11–43.

Keightley, E./M. Pickering (2012), *The Mnemonic Imagination: Remembering as Creative Practice*, London.

Kõresaar, E./E. Lauk/K. Kuutma (2009), "The Twentieth Century as a Realm of Memory", in E. Kõresaar, E. Lauk and K. Kuutma (eds.), *The Burden of Remembering: Recollections & Representations of the 20th Century*, Helsinki: 9–34.

Kramer, J.H. et al. (2003), "Age and gender interactions on verbal memory performance", *Journal of the International Neuropsychological Society* 9 (1): 97–102.

Lachmann, R. (2008), "Mnemonic and Intertextual Aspects of Literature", in A. Erll & A. Nünning (eds.), *A Companion to Cultural Memory Studies*, Berlin/New York: 301–10.

Nora, P. (1989), "Between Memory and History: Les Lieux de Mémoire", *Representations* 26: 7–24.

Olick, J.K./V. Vinitzky-Seroussi/D. Levy (eds.) (2011), *The Collective Memory Reader*, Oxford.

Papaioannou, S. (2007), *Redesigning Achilles. 'Recycling' the Epic Cycle in the 'Little Iliad' (Ovid, Metamorphoses 12.1–13.622)*, Berlin/New York.

Reading, A. (2016), *Gender and Memory in the Globital Age*, London.
Reading, A. (2019), "The Female Memory Factory: How the Gendered Labour of Memory Creates Mnemonic Capital", *European Journal of Women's Studies* 26: 293–312.
Ready, J.L. (2014), "ATU 974 The Homecoming Husband, The Returns of Odysseus, and the End of *Odyssey* 21", *Arethusa* 47 (3): 265–285.
Russell, N. (2006), "Collective Memory before and after Halbwachs", *The French Review* 79: 792–804.
Seider, A. (2013), *Memory in Vergil's Aeneid: Creating the Past*, Cambridge.
Sharrock, A. (2000), "Introduction", in A. Sharrock & H. Morales (eds.), *Intratextuality. Greek and Roman Textual Relations*, Oxford/New York.
Sharrock, A. (2018), "How Do We Read a (W)hole?: Dubious First Thoughts about the Cognitive Turn", in S. Harrison/S. Frangoulidis/T.D. Papanghelis (eds.), *Intratextuality and Latin Literature*, Trends in Classics 69, Berlin/New York: 15–32.
Siegel, D.J. (2006), "Entwicklungspsychologische, interpersonelle und neurobiologische Dimensionen des Gedächtnisses. Ein Überblick", in H. Welzer & H.J. Markowitsch (eds.), *Warum Menschen sich erinnern können. Fortschritte in der interdisziplinäre Gedächtnis*, Stuttgart: 19–49.
Smith, A. (1997), *Poetic Allusion and Poetic Embrace in Ovid and Virgil*, Ann Arbor.
Solodow, J.B. (1988), *The World of Ovid's Metamorphoses*, Chapel Hill.
Uther, H.-J. (2004), *The Types of International Folktales: A Classification and Bibliography* I, Helsinki.
Welzer, H. (2005), *Das kommunikative Gedächtnis. Eine Theorie der Erinnerung*, Munich.

Part I: **The Mechanics of Memory**

Sophia Papaioannou
Taking a Walk through Rome...: Comedic Itineraries and Early Republican Spatial Memory

Abstract: The application of memory studies to the exploration of Classical antiquity has advanced the view of the image of Roman topography as a work in progress, alike in literary imagination and architecture. These approaches focus on the texts of the Augustan age and the Early empire, when the memory of the Roman past is both revisited and canonized. Drawing on this discussion, I focus on reminiscences of journeys through Middle Republican Rome as transcribed in Roman comedy, and I explore them from a variety of perspectives working in correlation. Sojourning across the Roman landscape in Roman comedy is a multi-layered self-conscious composition that reflects contemporary politics and cultural trends. The texts I analyze include the Choragus' description of the Forum in Plautus' *Curculio* and Demea's fool's errand in Terence's *Adelphoe*. In my analysis these travelogues serve, in their peculiar ways, as witnesses to the transformation of the Roman cultural identity in the aftermath of the Roman expansion eastwards and of the image (or memory) of the civic landscape of the capital as a result of the building activity in the posthannibalic era. In the Choragus tour, Plautus offers an impressionable, lasting overview of the early 2nd c. Republican Forum, and underscores its Italian character by associating landmarks with comic types originating in the Italian comic tradition. Demea's fool's errand in the *Adelphoe*, on the contrary, traces an itinerary that is deliberately vague, communicating the different ways in which different individuals mentally read space narratives in a geographically pre-canonized society.

The study of Roman 'urban memory' – defined as the way Romans remember their experience of their city or record their memory of the city for others to see

---

I would like to thank Eleni Ntanou and Katharine Mawford for inviting me to contribute to this exciting project; texts throughout are quoted from the editions of the authors in the OCT series; translations of Plautus and Terence follow those of De Melo (2011) and Barsby (2001), respectively, in the Loeb series, while I have used Small (1997) for the passages quoted from the *Rhetorica ad Herennium*; the remaining translations are mine.

(actually or mentally through auditing or reading these recordings) – through descriptions of civic space rendered in literary writing, is an elusive task for literary landscapes are compositions filtered through aesthetics. This elusiveness however has generated the publication of a steadily growing number of scholarly readings in recent decades, which approach literary descriptions of Roman landscape as dynamic interfaces – complex culturally determined narratives.[1] To this may have contributed the significant rise in memory studies in the past century,[2] and a similar trend among modern artists to identify the appreciation of their work with a walk through landscape, directing the viewers' understanding of the work through the artist's visual or written documentation of a walking tour.[3] More recently, scholarship in the Classics has advanced illuminating approaches of the topographic descriptions in poetic texts as aesthetically determined narratives, allegorical depictions of poetic compositions, rather than actual memoirs,[4] and also as narratives that employ mnemonic topographical descriptions as metaphors subject both to a metaliterary and a cultural interpretation.[5]

My contribution profits from these interpretative trends as it tries to explore the visual memory of Rome in the earliest surviving poetic transcripts of journeys through the city, recorded in the plays of Plautus and Terence, from a variety of perspectives that work in correlation. I will demonstrate that the comedic recordings of sojourning across the Roman landscape are multi-layered self-conscious compositions that work as commentaries on contemporary cultural and political

---

[1] Important recent studies on Roman topography and cultural/historical memory, including the manipulation thereof, include Edwards (1996); Edwards and Woolf (2003) 1–20; Woolf (2003) 203–21; Galinsky (2014), especially the chapters by Favro (2014) and Hughes (2014); also Galinsky and Lapatin (2016).
[2] These stem from the views of Maurice Halbwachs (1925), who approaches memory as a socially determined construction, dictating that even individual memories have a social dimension.
[3] British artist Richard Long is one such case of a walking artist; on Long and other artists of this genre, including novelists, such as Jane Austen, who craft the artistry of walking through their heroes, see Solnit (2001); Long is discussed on pp. 267–76. On identifying and studying literary walking in Latin literature, see O'Sullivan (2012).
[4] See notably (on the topography of Horace's Sabine farm), Thomas (1982) 8–26; Jaeger (1995) 177–91; and Johnson (1993); and (on Martial's numerous descriptions of the civic landscape of Flavian Rome) Fowler (1994) 31–58; Harrison (2002) 40–57 (on the topography in Apuleius).
[5] On Horace: Dang (2010); Bowditch (2001). On Rome as memorialized in the topographical descriptions recorded in the texts of the Late Republican and Augustan authors, see the papers by Hammar (2015) 75–88, Corbeill (2015) 89–98, Spencer (2015) 99–110 and O'Sullivan (2015) 111–22, in Östenberg, Malmberg and Bjørnebye (2015). Also Davies (2017) 477–512.

forces. My discussion will comprise a detailed analysis of the Choragus' description of the Roman Forum in Plautus' *Curculio* and Demea's fool's errand in Terence's *Adelphoe*.

The comedic travelogues presently under study acknowledge the employment of literary artistry as a means to transmit widely socio-political commentary and as a memory tool. The transformation of the Roman cultural identity in the aftermath of the Roman expansion eastwards and of the image of the civic landscape of the capital as a result of the building activity in the posthannibalic era, prompt the demiurges of the *palliata* to capture in-performance and comment in a variety of ways on contemporary cultural and political reality. Roman comedy as a rule is set in the Greek world, but Roman reality invades too often and too conspicuously – and the politics of topography accommodates the reality of present-day Roman cultural activity into the make-believe Greek world of the comic stage and brings to the fore the various trends that were transforming the memory of old Rome.[6]

There are two important reasons for the suitability of the *palliata* as the literary space par excellence to address the development of civic memory in Rome at the turn of the 3rd c. BCE: a) the location of the Roman stage was movable and subject to relocation from festival to festival. The Plautine Choragus tour has inspired many studies on the politics of realizing stage performances at the Roman *ludi*;[7] and Demea's route has been considered potentially visible depending on the setting of the stage and the audience;[8] b) even if they reproduce an actual site accurately, topographical descriptions in Plautus and Terence are literary constructions, which enables us to consider them as conditioned compositions and as part of the playwrights' literary program.[9] Literary topography in the *palliata* in particular involves two interconnected aspects: foremost, the way in which

---

[6] E. Cosgrove in this volume addresses the ways in which the representation of captives in Plautus' *Captivi*, a play thought to have been produced soon after 193 BCE, reflects the Roman audience's cultural/historical memory of captive-taking as formed in the aftermath of the Punic Wars.

[7] See most recently Goldberg (2018); note especially the following remark: "Experienced actors with talent and imagination can perform almost any kind of script in any kind of place: it would be most unwise to argue that this script must have been written for this space and performed in this way" (p. 142).

[8] Frank (1936).

[9] Similarly, in his Exile poems Ovid, who enjoys revisiting Rome mentally aided by his memory, builds an edited topographical description of the capital, that includes his favorite spots; see the discussion in Michalopoulos in this volume.

certain geographical locations described in the Roman comedies look back to significant literary sources, and the way in which, in several plays, toponyms and their associations interact with themes and ideas of notable importance in the comedy. The lack of most of the Greek originals and most of contemporary (to Plautus and Terence) Latin literature, makes it hard to trace the influence of earlier works on the Roman playwrights with satisfactory comprehensiveness. The surviving Greek plays do not include topographical accounts, while the itinerary of a journey to Sicily in Lucilius' satires suggests that literary topography might have been at play more broadly in early Latin poetry.[10] Then, topographical descriptions are associated internally with persons, physical objects, or themes, and with the narrative backgrounds each of them carries. This association adjusts and expands their meaning as well as the way they are meant to be recorded in the audience's memory. Plainly speaking, topographical memory is always contextualized, and the context usually directs the politics of landscape representation. Also, it depends upon a script or text (the topographical synthesis) and a set of directions on how to read and decode it – a process often challenging because each member of the audience may contextualize differently the same synthesis in light of their own personal memories of the individual monuments in the synthesis in question.[11]

---

10 Breed (2018) 57–78, proposes a comparable metaliterary reading of topographical itineraries in Lucilius' satire, focusing on the poet's famous journey to Sicily in the third book of his *Satires*. For Breed, the narrative description of the journey and the emphasis on the distance between Sicily and Rome map the distance between author and reader, as well as establishing the essence of satire as a genre created in the city and for an urban audience. Satirical travelogues, further, are political, because they map "Rome's authority over its province and the space in between, which may also be manifested in one Roman's distant control over, and obligations to, his property" (69).

11 Daniels and Cosgrove (1988) 1: "A landscape is a cultural image, a pictorial way of representing, structuring or symbolising surroundings. [...] They [landscapes] may be represented in a variety of materials and on many surfaces – in paint on canvas, in writing on paper, in earth, stone, water and vegetation on the ground. A landscape park is more palpable but no more real, nor less imaginary, than a landscape painting or poem. [...] And of course, every study of a landscape further transforms its meaning, depositing yet another layer of cultural representation". The concept of a topographical synthesis as a directed way of seeing has been analyzed through metaphors coming from the domains of spectacle, theater, textual analysis, veil and gaze; see Daniels and Cosgrove (1993) 57; Wylie (2007) 56. On Roman literary landscapes as texts directing their audience to cultural self-awareness and self-fashioning, see Spencer (2010).

1 Roman comedy and Roman civic identity in Choragus' tour through the Forum

At Plautus, *Curc.* 462, the Choragus, an extradramatic character who provides the accessories (costumes, etc.) for the comic performance, breaks the dramatic illusion and takes the stage.[12] Seemingly in search of the parasite Curculio, he soon turns to the audience and offers to guide them through the Roman Forum (466–86) – even though the play is set in Epidaurus.

```
                        sed dum hic egreditur foras,
    commonstrabo, quo in quemque hominem facile inveniatis loco,
    ne nimio opere sumat operam si quem conventum velit,
    vel vitiosum vel sine vitio, vel probum vel improbum.
    qui periurum convenire volt hominem ito in comitium;              470
    qui mendacem et gloriosum, apud Cloacinae sacrum,
    ditis damnosos maritos sub basilica quaerito.
    ibidem erunt scorta exoleta quique stipulari solent,
    symbolarum collatores apud forum piscarium.
    in foro infimo boni homines atque dites ambulant,                 475
    in medio propter canalem, ibi ostentatores meri;
    confidentes garrulique et malevoli supera lacum,
    qui alteri de nihilo audacter dicunt contumeliam
    et qui ipsi sat habent quod in se possit vere dicier.
    sub veteribus, ibi sunt qui dant quique accipiunt faenore.        480
    pone aedem Castoris, ibi sunt subito quibus credas male.
    in Tusco vico, ibi sunt homines qui ipsi sese venditant,
    [in Velabro vel pistorem vel lanium vel haruspicem]
    vel qui ipsi vorsant vel qui aliis ubi vorsentur praebeant.       485
    [ditis damnosos maritos apud Leucadiam Oppiam.]
```

In the interim and until he comes back, I'll show in which place you can easily find which sort of person, so that no one strives too laboriously if he wants to meet someone, be it a man of vice or a man without vice, be it worthy or a worthless character. Anyone who wants to meet a perjurer should go to the assembly place. Anyone who wants to meet a liar and a braggart must look for him at the temple of Venus Cloacina, and anyone who wants to meet rich and married wasters must look below the colonnaded hall. In the same place there will also be grown-up prostitutes and men who ask for formal guarantees from prospective debtors. Those who contribute to shared meals are on the fish market. At the lower end of the market decent and wealthy people stroll around; in the middle part of the market next to the open drain are the mere showoffs. Arrogant, garrulous and malevolent people are above the Lake, ones who boldly insult their neighbor for no good reason and who have enough

---

12 On the issue of the actor-audience relationship in Plautus' plays see Moore (1998) 8–23.

that could in all truth be said about themselves. Below the Old Shops there are those who give and receive on interest. Behind the temple of Castor there are those whom you shouldn't trust quickly. In the Tuscan Quarter there are the people who sell themselves. In the Velabrum you can meet the miller or the butcher or the soothsayer or those who turn or give others the opportunity to turn. [Rich and married wasters at the house of Leucadia Oppia]. [Trans. De Melo (2011), with minor changes]

The Choragus identifies eleven individual locations in the Forum, though not all of them are in use or identified with precision in Plautus' day, and the deictics in the description have been employed to endorse two different arguments on determining the exact position of the stage and the spectators' seats in the Roman Forum. Timothy Moore[13] argues that the Choragus faces east, the stage stands where the Augustan rostra later were set, and the audience before him fills the Forum. The lofty vantage point of the actor enacting the Choragus part allows him to have a comprehensive overview of the topography of the entire Forum spreading out in front of him and beyond the heads of the spectators. According to Marshall,[14] the spectators are positioned in the western part of the Forum and so the Choragus would face in that direction: he gesticulates behind and beside himself to locations and buildings which the spectators are able to see (in full or partially, depending on how lofty their own vantage position is) beyond the stage.[15] Both arguments, however, converge on the identity of the monuments reported, though some of them are not specified; these are eleven in total:

1. The *Comitium*, which is the convention point of perjurers (470, *periurum*)
2. The temple of Venus Cloacina, the hangout place for liars and braggarts (471, (*mendacem et gloriosum*).[16]
3. The/a basilica, where afflicted husbands and prostitutes are found (472–3, *damnosos maritos; scorta exoleta, quique stipulari solent*).

---

[13] Moore (1991) 359. Refined in Moore (1998) 131–9; 219–22, which identify additional parts in Plautus' plays where Roman topography and Roman life disturb and blend the boundaries separating the world of the spectators from the Greek reality of dramatic time.
[14] Marshall (2006) 40–5.
[15] The most detailed analysis to date of the topography in the Choragus' tour is Sommella (2005); Goldberg (2018), the most recent study on the inconclusiveness regarding a fixed or preferable position for the setting of theatrical performances prior to the construction of a permanent theater in Rome, shows the strengths and the limitations of the studies of Moore and Marshall.
[16] The reference to the temple of Venus Cloacina is the earliest one attested in Latin literature; see Sommella (2005) 77–8, who further points out that the shrine was destroyed in another fire that broke out in Rome at 178 BCE but was restored and, unlike the *tabernae* in its vicinity, was not relocated.

4. The *Forum Piscarium* ('fish market'); this both Moore and Marshall identify with the *Macellum*, the main food market area northeast of the Forum; according to Choragus it is the hangout for dining-club members (474, *conlatores symbolarum*).
5. The lower part of the Forum (475, *foro infumo*), where wealthy and noble citizens gather (*boni homines atque dites*).
6. Mid-way through the culvert of the *Cloaca maxima* (476, *in medio propter canalem*) one may find individuals who like to show off (*ostentatores*).
7. The area 'beyond' the Lake (*supra lacum*), according to both Moore and Marshall, Lake Curtius (a problematic identification as will be shortly discussed), where an assortment of sinister characters are found (*confidentes, garrulique et malevoli*, 'confident, chatterboxes and ill-willed'; 477–9).
8. The veterae tabernae, where bankers are located (480, *qui dant quique accipiunt faenore*).
9. The temple of Castor (481, *aedes Castoris*), a place frequented by people with bad credit (*quibus credas male*).
10. The *vicus Tuscus*, the Etruscan quarters, which is presented as yet another location in the Forum favored by prostitutes (473, *homines qui ipsi see venditant*).
11. Finally, the Velabrum, where merchants prone to cheat are found – bakers, butchers and soothsayers (484, *vel pistorem vel lanium vel haruspicem*).

The tour concludes with a mention of Leucadia Oppia, an anthroponym that has traditionally puzzled critics.

The Choragues offers simultaneously a topographical overview of the Forum and an overview of the *palliata*. Regardless of where stage and audience are located, how many buildings are identified, and how many of them are actually visible to the audience (and to the Choragus himself), Moore has convincingly argued that the Choragus' itinerary invites the spectators to imagine the Forum as an area populated with comedic types, further noting that the Choragus traces an itinerary "both restricted and orderly. It includes only places in the immediate vicinity of the forum, east of the western end of the *comitium*";[17] while Marshall suggests to visualize the chorus master gesticulating (as a pantomime might do) and guiding the audience's gaze along a series of locations beside and behind the Choragus – a series that traces a nearly perfect S route.[18]

---

[17] Moore (1998) 137.
[18] Marshall (2006) 41–2.

While acknowledging the powerful metapoetics in the effort of Moore's Choragus to employ the denizens of the literary universe of the *palliata* to claim the Forum, the signature space of Roman identity, back into their Greek world, I will briefly point out that the Romans comprehended geography and travelling itineraries much differently than we do today. For them, movement in space was a complex cognitive process, aptly described by Bekker-Nielsen as "cognitive mapping", and defined as "the mental image of the physical environment which may, or may not, conform with the image produced by conventional cartography". Cognitive maps are 'broad' and 'comprehensive', meaning that they define the location of a site in relation to all the other sites in its closer or more distant vicinity, and that they diligently include numerous topographical details; modern or conventional maps are 'route' and 'strip' maps, concerned primarily with tracing routes of communication between sites, and with linear, clearly defined itineraries, while paying little attention to topography that affects little the realization of the itinerary; "mental maps of the 'strip' type are formed, indicating how to get to different places but giving no clear idea of the location in relation to each other".[19] Should we agree that the Choragus verbalizes a comprehensive map, it is easy to understand why the S-shaped route that Marshall maps out is problematic and gives a rather hazy idea of geographical direction and of the relative locations of the various buildings and sites involved (or not involved) in the process. And it explains why the chorus master has included the house of Leucadia Oppia, a well-known prostitute,[20] as a building of reference for finding one's whereabouts in the Forum with relation to other locations!

In light of this knowledge of the Roman cognitive understanding of geographical space, I would like to advance a new reading of this memory journey through the early Forum and argue that Plautus' Roman Forum is not as accurately described as it is generally believed, and that this inaccuracy is deliberate, because it is a tongue-in-cheek commentary on the impending transformation of the Roman civic landscape, which in a few decades will redefine the greater area of the Forum from an area of private and commercial activity to one of public, political significance. I will additionally point out that the Choragus' pairing of sites and *palliata* characters constitutes the earliest application of mnemotechnics in Roman literature, and results into attaching distinct, poetically defined markers on sites and monuments shortly about to receive a new significance

---

19 Bekker-Nielsen (1988); the quote is from p. 153.
20 On the identity of the Leucadia Oppia and the humor involved in her inclusion in the Forum tour, see Goldberg (2018) 163–4 with n. 55.

within the transformed socio-political framework of the 2nd century BCE Republican Forum.

As each location in the Forum is recorded to the audience's memory foremost through its ties to a particular group of comedic individuals, its contextualization is determined by the identity of these individuals. The instructive process of constructing selectively a mentally visualized synthesis (a landscape, an itinerary, or a pictorial composition) and describing it in a way that would in turn enable the receptors of this description to visualize it themselves, might well be inspired by the methodology of a mnemonic system that is based on the architecture or geography of space. Roman orators and those among the Roman elite trained in oratory in order to be able to deliver from memory complex and long arguments, had received special training on how to enhance the faculties of their memories to recall in detail visual impressions. As a result of methodical training, visually received impressions could be held in the mind with vividness resistant to the passage of time. The Roman process of artificial memory, structured around the premise that the process of remembering meant the retrieval of information stored in the mind, identified certain places where the memories judged worthy for preservation could be securely stored. The places to store these memories were arranged in the mind in a way as to be readily traversable once the need for the recollection of a series of memories arose; an architecture of orderly synthesized physical spaces and mental imagery.[21] The construction and the operational management of these structures that would be imagined best as houses is ideally described in the anonymous rhetorical treatise known as *Rhetorica ad Herennium* dating from the middle 80s BCE, the first systematic effort in Rome to describe and assess artificial memory training.[22] For the author of the *Ad Herennium*, this synthesis is best visualized mentally as a familiar space, like a housing complex, with multiple compartments in terms of architectural features inside; memories would be located in orderly fashion on each of these compartments:

---

[21] On artificial memory the reference study is Yates (1966); pp. 1–49 discuss the theories on artificial memory in ancient Rome (1–26) and Greece (27–49); other studies on artificial memory in antiquity with special emphasis on the pioneering contribution of Roman oratory to the cultivation and professionalization of the architectonics of memory, see Small (1997), esp. 85–103 and 156–77 (on artificial memory in Ancient Rome).

[22] *Ad Herennium* 3.16–24 is the section devoted to the description and training of artificial memory; full discussion of the views on mnemotechnics introduced in the *Ad Herennium*, in Yates (1966) 4–16.

> Constat igitur artificiosa memoria ex locis et imaginibus. Locos appellamus eos qui breviter, perfecte, insignite aut natura aut manu sunt absoluti, ut eos facile naturali memoria conprehendere et amplecti queamus: ut aedes, intercolumnium, angulum, fornicem, et alia quae his similia sunt.
>
> Ad Herennium 3.16
>
> Artificial memory consists of physical places and mental images. We call places those things which by nature or by artifice are for a short distance, totally and strikingly complete, so that we can understand and embrace them easily with natural memory – such as a house, an intercolumniation, a corner, an arch, and other things which are similar to these. [Trans. Small (1997), with minor adjustments]

The memories would be captured as images (*imagines*) and impressed on these specific locations (*loci*) according to some order readily recalled by the individual (an orator) interested in recalling them in the future in the very state they had been originally stored and in the particular order that facilitated their personal recollection process: *imagines eorum locis certis conlocare oportebit*, 'it will be necessary to set the mental images of them [the different information which needs remembering] in specific places'.[23]

Comic actors were no less keen on memorizing than orators, being themselves professional performers who had to memorize scripts by hearing. The Choragus' arrangement of architectural monuments and physical locations in association with individuals of distinct social/professional classes, portrays the Roman Forum as a proto-memory palace – only in this synthesis monumental architecture does not necessarily work as the memory house: the *imagines* help identify and memorize the *loci* inasmuch as the *loci* direct to the correct *imagines*, and their interaction reflects the fluidity of the Roman civic landscape at the turn of the 3rd c. BCE – a landscape under construction.

In the year 210 BCE a great fire broke out on the north side of the Roman Forum, where a series of shops (*tabernae*), including the bankers' shops, the *tabernae argentariae*, were located. Livy offers a detailed description of the catastrophe (26.27.1–4):

> a fire [...] broke out in several places at once about the Forum. At the same time the seven shops (*tabernae*) which later were five, and the bankers' offices (*tabernae argentariae*), now called Tabernae Novae, caught fire; then private houses (*privata aedificia*) took fire – for there were no basilicas then – the quarries [*lautumiae*; a stone-quarry district on the east

---

[23] M. Haley in the present volume similarly recourses to the ancient theory and practice of mnemonics as recorded in the treatise *Ad Herennium* in order to discuss the ways in which Cicero and his audience "remember" specific passages and dramatic moments of Accius' tragedy *Atreus*, because of their performance by the famous actor Aesopus.

slope of the Capitoline], and the Fish Market [*forum piscatorium*; located behind the *tabernae* and north of the Forum] and the *Atrium Regium*. The Temple of Vesta was saved with difficulty chiefly by the aid of thirteen slaves, who were purchased by the state and manumitted.

The destruction offers the opportunity for rebuilding, and rebuilding rewrites and reinterprets space. Several of the locations identified in the Choragus' tour were affected and underwent reconstruction in the years immediately following the catastrophic fire of 210.

Since the early days of the Republic, the Forum was a space of memory, in which Romans celebrated the heroes of their past and the virtues they embodied, and built monuments that would help them remember these heroes. The primary space within the Forum dedicated to political activity was restricted to the area of the Comitium, the more or less round-shaped area defined by the Curia to the north and the Rostra to the south, with the Via Sacra serving as a boundary between the primarily political and the primarily commercial parts of the Middle Republican forum.[24] During the first half of the 2nd century BCE the landscape of the Forum began to change drastically:[25] on the one hand, political activity spread southwards beyond the Comitium, on the other, the larger Forum area was increasingly perceived as a prime space for publicly displaying (and advertising) Romanness to the increasingly higher numbers of foreign dignitaries who were visiting Rome on diplomatic trips in the aftermath of the Second Carthaginian war, and as Rome was expanding its political influence and territory eastwards. These delegations had to cross the Forum as they entered through the Via Sacra, in order to reach the *graecostasis*, the area designated for them before the Senate house – they ought to be impressed. Over the fifty years following the fire of 210, a set of new constructions gradually transformed the Forum from an area with an assortment of shops randomly situated next to temples, sites and monuments

---

24 Varro nicely grafts into their respective etymologies the primary function of the Comitium (*comitium ab eo quod coibant eo comitiis curiatis et litium causa* – 'the Comitium is so called because people come together there for the meetings of the curiate assemblies and for lawsuits'; *Ling.* 5.155) and the area of the wider Forum, which expands beyond the politically determined section of the Comitium (*quo conferrent suas controversias et quae venderentur vellent quo ferrent, forum appellarunt* – 'the place where they collected their arguments and where they carried what they wished to sell, they called "forum"'; *Ling.* 5.145).
25 On the transformation of the Roman Forum into a politically determined public space during the 2nd and the 1st centuries BCE, and the various cultural and social changes as a result in Roman everyday life, see Russell (2015), esp. 43–95 (discussing the changes in the architecture of the Forum in the 2nd century BCE).

reminiscent of the great heroes of the early days of the Republic, into a finely defined rectangular open space, lined along the three sides by impressive porticoes, namely the basilica Aemilia along the north side of the forum (built in 189), the basilica Sempronia along the south side just opposite the basilica Aemilia (built in 169), and the colonnade extending from the temple of Saturn, past the Senate house, and on to the Curia (built in 174, the same year the clivus Capitolinus was paved as well).[26]

More changes followed: the construction of the basilica Aemilia, only a few years after the staging of the *Curculio*, caused the demolition of the *tabernae novae*, the shops and bankers' stalls that stood in that area and had been rebuilt after they had been originally destroyed by the fire of 210. The rebuilt *tabernae* followed a different orientation that brought them into line with the basilica Aemilia and the new orientation of the forum rectangle. The various open-air markets were gathered together into a covered complex that was constructed on the north-east side of the basilica Aemilia in 179 BCE by M. Fulvius Nobilior, the very consul who had initiated the construction of the basilica, as well. According to Varro, this new market absorbed the *forum piscarium*, the *forum cuppedinis*, and other markets of specialized products which until then were scattered in nearby locations (*Ling.* 5.146–7). Shoppers now still crossed the Forum, but the piles of merchandise, the commotion and noises involved in the supply process and the transactions, were not seen or heard by those moving around in the Forum piazza. The *forum piscarium* had already been relocated away from the Forum area and down by the banks of the Tiber right after the fire of 210 (Varro *Ling.* 5.146, the *forum piscarium* is *secundum Tiberim ad <Por>tunium*), which suggests that it is out of the Choragus' sight during his description of the Forum tour.

Interestingly, this is not the only topographical inaccuracy in the Choragus' Forum tour. Certain locations on the Choragus map are vague and thus impossible to identify. I believe this topographical indeterminacy was deliberate. As noted, the Choragus identifies eleven locations (plus the residence of Leucadia Oppia). The precise location of three of them, the basilica, the fish market and the *lacus* (in the order they are mentioned by the Choragus) is impossible to determine. First, the *basilica*: none of the oldest known Republican basilicas (Porcia

---

[26] Livy 41.27.7: *et clivom Capitolinum silice sternendum curaverunt, et porticum ab aede Saturni in Capitolium ad senaculum, ac super id curiam.* ('They also undertook the paving of the ascent from the Forum to the Capitol with flint and the construction of a colonnade from the temple of Saturn to the Capitol, and then on to the *senaculum*, and beyond that to the senate-house').

or Fulvia [known later as Fulvia et Aemilia]) had been built at the time.[27] We could assume that some sort of basilica was present, or at least some building that served the same function, which may have borne the nick-name 'basilica' as a result.[28] Another possibility may be to identify the basilica with the *Regia* (or *atrium regium*), the residence of the *Rex sacrorum*; in this case Plautus could be making a clever interlingual pun, according to which a 'basilica' does not mean the architectural construction known as such in later decades but would be the literal translation in Greek of the Latin term *Regia*, 'the court of the king (*rex*)' or αὐλὴ βασιλική.[29] Still, this identification is not without problems: the basilica is tied to afflicted husbands and prostitutes of the worst kind – it would be unlikely that the space near the Regia and the house of the Vestals attracted such a lowly crowd. Further, the same part of the Forum is called 'lower forum' (475, *foro infumo*) by the Choragus and is considered a hangout for 'wealthy and noble citizens' (*boni homines atque dites*) – a very different crowd.

The problematic location of the fish market has already been discussed. Its identification with the *macellum* complex NE of the basilica Fulvia/Aemilia is an anachronism as is its presence in the Forum after 210 BCE – unless of course a proposal supporting the construction of a *macellum* complex in the NE part of the Forum was introduced already in the aftermath of the fire, which Plautus may echo in that case – a proposal that materialized eventually a couple of decades later.

Finally, the location of the so-mentioned 'lacus' poses another question: it may be the Lacus Iuturnae or the Lacus Curtius, with Plautus deliberately not specifying which one he means, because he wants to play with both possibilities: the Lacus Curtius would be the one most likely to come to mind (as indeed has happened with modern critics – most identify 'lacus' with the Lacus Curtius).[30] Still, the Lacus Iuturnae might be a stronger candidate: its waters were renowned

---

27 Should we accept a date of ca. 193–1, or at least prior to 188–7, for the play; on the date of the *Curculio* see Paratore (1958) 5ff.; Monaco (1969) 11; Slater (1987). The Basilica Porcia was built a little later, in 184 (Livy 39.44), and the Basilica Fulvia was contracted in 179 BCE (Livy 40.51).
28 This is the suggestion by Sommella (2005) 84, who further notes that this is the earliest attestation of the term 'basilica' as a term of monumental architecture. From a different perspective, it is always probable to consider the verse an interpolation, from a reproduction of the play at a later time.
29 An identification favored by Sommella (2005) 86–7. The identification was first proposed in Steinby (1987) 174–6. See also Richardson (1992) 42; Goldberg (2018) 162.
30 Sommella (2015) 88–90; Marshall (2006) 40 n. 109; Moore (1998) 136–7.

for their healing qualities throughout the Classical period (and likely also in Plautus' era),[31] and until the construction of the first aqueduct in 312 BCE, only a few years prior to the staging of the *Curculio*, the Lacus Iuturnae supplied the Romans with fresh water, hence it must have been a frequently visited spot. The healing properties of the Lacus Iuturnae designate the particular location a fitting one for a play that is set in Epidaurus and whose action is situated right next to the temple of Aesculapius, the medicine god.[32] Not least, the emergence of the pimp Cappodox from the temple of Aesculapius a few hundred lines earlier in the play makes the characterization of the Lacus Iuturnae as a place near which the corrupt and evil characters are to be found (*confidentes garrulique et malevoli supra lacum*, 476), temptingly appropriate.

In light of the above, it is plausible to assume that the audience observing the Choragus' guiding gestures realize that he is not offering them an exact topographical guide of the area – only a nearly exact one, and that this imprecise recollection of reality is part of his performance as *director* or tour-guide (a pun on the false etymology of his name from *chōros*, 'space', and *agein*). The Choragus invites his audience to memorize a 'comprehensive' map of the Forum (and he employs the technology of artificial memory in order to assist them to do so) and at the same time he exposes certain problems that may inhibit them from doing so. The impossibility of locating the basilica, the problematic location of the *forum piscarium*, and the predilection for the Lacus Iuturnae not just revises the S-shaped route of the Choragus' tour as proposed by Marshall, but in essence makes this route erratic and imprecise – confusing and impossible to trace if one follows a modern 'route' map thereof, instead of a traditional 'comprehensive' map. The Choragus employs mnemotechnics in order to prompt his audience to capture in their memories the current image of the lower forum, a shapeless space that is ever evolving in the comic imagination – an image soon to disappear in light of the sweeping architectural changes that will transform it in the following

---

31 On the healing powers of the waters of the Lacus Iuturnae, see Varro L.5.71; Prop. 3.22.26; Frontin. *Aq.* 4; Serv. Ad *Aen.* 12.139: *cum enim naturaliter omnis aqua noxia sit extraneorum corporibus, hic omnibus saluberrimus fons est*; cf. Boni (1901) 77.

32 The close association between Iuturna and Aesculapius is attested by the statue of Aesculapius, dating from the imperial period, that was found in the sanctuary next to the Lacus Iuturnae in the Forum; see Renberg (2006/2007) 120 with n. 139; Campbell (2012) 16–17; Boni (1901) 114–6. Boni believes that Aesculapius might even have had a sanctuary in the forum next to that of Iuturna; archaeological evidence does not support this. Goldberg (2018) 162 (with n. 49) points to sources that strengthen the salubrious nature of the waters of the Lacus Iuturnae: Castor and Pollux (their temple located right next to the Lacus Iuturnae) were said to have refreshed themselves there after the Battle of Lake Regillus, set by tradition in 496 BCE.

decades into a well-defined, fixed and controlled rectangle. The Choragus capitalizes on this dynamic fluidity of mnemonic topography that enables him to form and reform Roman topography and Roman daily life at will, along with the scripts of his *palliatae*, and makes a covert political statement that is recorded in an unparalleled, to our knowledge, breach of dramatic illusion.

2 On a fool's errand around the Capitol with Terence

Terence embraces a different approach in his study of the interaction of memory and Roman topography. The following excerpt from *Adelphoe* 572–85 is reminiscent of the Plautine itinerary in the *Curculio* but also markedly different in structure. In several of his comedies Terence orders various characters off stage and on some wild goose chase through the streets of Rome, but none is more closely tied to the topography of Rome than the itinerary offered to old Demea in *Ad.* 572ff, as he is directed by the cunning slave Syrus on how to find his son:[33]

SY.   Ad nomen nescio
   illius hominis, sed locum novi ubi sit. DE. Dic ergo locum.
SY. Nostin porticum apud macellum hac deorsum? DE. Quid ni noverim?
SY. Praeterito recta platea sursum hanc: ubi eo veneris,
   clivos deorsum vorsum est: istac praecipitato; postea   575
   est ad hanc manum sacellum: ibi angiportum propter est,
DE. Quanam? SY. Illi ubi etiam caprificus magna est. DE. Novi. SY. Hac pergito.
DE. Id quidem angiportum non est pervium. SY. Verum hercle: uah,
   censen hominem me esse? erraui: in porticum rursum redi:
   sane hac multo propius ibis et minor est erratio.   580
   scin Cratini huius ditis aedes? DE. Scio. SY. Vbi eas praeterieris,
   ad sinistram hac recta platea; ubi ad Dianae veneris,
   ito ad dextram: prius quam ad portam venias, apud ipsum lacum
   est pistrilla, ei exaduorsum fabrica: ibist. DE. Quid ibi facit?
SY. Lectulos illi salignis pedibus faciundos dedit.   585
                                                        Ad. 572–85

---

33 In the *Hecyra*, Young Pamphilus sends his slave Parmeno on a fool's errand to the Acropolis, allegedly to find a man named Callidemides – in truth, Pamphilus, like Syrus in the *Adelphoe*, is trying to keep Parmeno away and off stage so that he cannot interfere with his affairs. Notably, Terence varies the, let us call it, 'meandering theme': Parmeno is instructed not on the itinerary to Callidemides' place but on the latter's physiognomy (*Hec.* 439–43).

SYRUS. I do not know the name of the man, but I know the place where he is.
DEMEA Tell me the place then.
SYRUS Do you know the porticus down this way, near the market?
DEMEA Of course I do.
SYRUS Go straight past it, right up that street; when you arrive there, there is a downward hill in front: go straight down that. After that, there is a sanctuary, on this side there: close by there is an alley.
DEMEA Which one?
SYRUS Where there is a large fig-tree.
DEMEA I know it. SYRUS Go past that----
DEMEA But the alley is not a thoroughfare!
SYRUS Indeed, by Hercules! Ah, would you believe that I am only human? I made a mistake. Go back to the porticus. Truly you will go a lot closer, and there is less going wandering. Do you know the house of Cratinus, the rich man?
DEMEA I know it. SYRUS When you have passed it, go to the left, straight down the street. When you come to the Temple of Diana, turn to the right. Before you come to the gate, just by that pond (lacus), there is a bakery, and opposite to it a craftsman's shop. There he is.
DEMEA What is he doing there?
SYRUS He has given some couches to be made, with oaken legs, for use in the open air.

Trans. Barsby (2001)

Syrus' proposed itinerary, vague as to adhere to an itinerary through the streets below and about the Acropolis of Athens, and yet temptingly applicable to an actual tour in the sight of the Roman Capitol, is no less artfully crafted. Already in 1936 Tenney Frank tried to trace Demea's errand with an actual route through the city of Rome, by assuming that the play was presented in a theater that stood on the west slope of the Capitoline, above the temple of Apollo Medicus. From the particular vantage point, Terence's spectators, like Plautus' spectators attending the *Curculio*, would observe Demea's itinerary and envision his errand.[34]

Metapoetics would interpret Syrus' recollections as alternative scripts of a character who acts the part of the *servus currens* in different plays while bearing the same name, Syrus, and possibly even enacted by the same actor, who nonetheless every time traverses a different route, leading him in the case at hand to confusion. It is possible, too, to extract a more nuanced reading of Demea's route

---

[34] Frank (1936) 470–2. Frank describes an actual route up the Capitol hill and then downwards to a shrine next to the fig tree of the *Comitium*; and later a different route past the temple of *Diana in circo* and to a craftsman's shop next to a *lacus*. Frank further attributes the absence of specifically identified Roman locations to the playwright's desire to maintain for the audience the illusion that the play is set in Athens, even though only a few lines earlier the same critic has noted the unusualness of this insertion of Romanness in Terence's as a rule seamlessly Greek comic universe: "the passage is interesting in that it reveals the dramatist's willingness to abandon the original in order to hold the interest of the spectator by using recognizable details" (471).

in light of the model proffered by Plautus' Choragus and his embrace of the dynamics offered by the transformation of the cartographic understanding of space in the context of Roman comedy. The itinerary Demea is directed to follow takes him away from the Forum and sets him off from a *porticus* near an unidentified downhill (*deorsum*) – open-air? – market place (*macellum*), which certainly is not the *macellum* complex, which by Terence's time was firmly in place behind the basilica Aemilia. The hill Demea supposedly descends must be, according to Frank, the Capitoline. Then the hero passes through some street (*platea*) up and then down another hill (*clivos*), and reaches a shrine (*sacellum*) and past it an alley (*angiportum*)[35] next to a fig-tree (*caprificus*). At this point, Demea, who is tracing the itinerary in his head, realizes that this route leads to a dead end. Syrus admits so, goes back to the starting point, the *porticus*, and offers an alternative, much shorter itinerary (580), that mentally takes Demea to the house of a certain wealthy Cratinus (*Cratini ditis aedes*) and from there on the left (*ad sinistram*) and directly down a street (*platea*) to some shrine of Diana (*ad Dianae*) on the right (*ad dextram*), and then to the desirable destination which is located next to a pond (*lacus*) and a bakery (*pistrilla*), and right before one of the city gates (*porta*).

Unlike Plautus' itinerary, Terence's only two specific locations are the house of the wealthy Cratinus and the so-defined temple of Diana – or are they? Frank believes that Terence here refers to the temple of Diana in the Circus Flaminius, a shrine dedicated in 179 BCE, but the name Cratinus is certainly not a Roman name, and unlikely to belong to an actual resident of the Roman suburbs. In the present reading both landmarks are markers on Terence/Syrus' fluid topographical memory. The house of Cratinus operates similarly to the residence of Leucadia Oppia in the Plautine Choragus' mental map: it is a landmark of importance for the comprehensive map that defines everyday movement about Rome. The precise location of both sites is nowhere on a route map because it does not belong therein.

Still, the name Cratinus is certainly a Greek name, and a name particularly reminiscent of Greek comedy (Cratinus was one of the best-known comic poets of Old Comedy). This Cratinus promptly transports the itinerary to an Athenian landscape. On its part, the temple of Diana could potentially evoke some Attic shrine, e.g. the temple of Artemis Agrotera, which likewise was associated with the outskirts of the city of Athens. Demea's itinerary, in short, could describe a territory alike in Greece and in Rome, and this topographical openness trans-

---

[35] A site temptingly charged with metapoetics, being the space on the *scaena* particularly welcoming to characters eager for eavesdropping.

forms Terence's wayfinding travelogues into 'open itineraries', fluid compositions determined in their particular details by the individual viewer / listener and their particular memories. Since the understanding of moving through and reading space differs, occasionally substantially, from individual to individual, as different people interact with their surrounding space in different ways, Terence's *Adelphoe* 572–84 dramatizes the cognitive process through which spatial information was conveyed, a process that was decidedly personal even when the space narrative to be committed to memory included topographical landmarks widely known (the temple of Diana and the house of Cratinus may serve as such in Syrus' narrative of space). In this respect, Terence's memory sojourn through streets and alleys of the city is hardly different from Plautus' quasi-nostalgic commemoration of the architecturally fuzzy Middle Republican Forum. Both playwrights express the spirit of the everyday Roman denizen and their subjective, synesthetic relationship with space – a relationship that the architectural regularization and monumentalization of the Forum (and to a considerable extent also the areas around it) in subsequent decades, regularized and canonized, controlling it as much as mirroring it.

3 Conclusion

Throughout Graeco-Roman antiquity topography and memory are interconnected and mutually determined. The art of memorization is imagined as the placement of images in various parts of the house, and the art of remembering is the act of walking through this imaginary house, and retrieving the images as one passes by – a setting best known as a Palace of Memory, a label this imaginary house received from humanist Matteo Ricci.

A walk through Rome was not an ordinary walk. In later centuries, in the Augustan and especially the Imperial eras, taking a walk through the *Urbs*, an endless course of buildings and monuments, each having its own multiple histories and associations, equaled a mental tour in time as well as space: a review of the similarly layered history of the city and, given the numerous imported monuments and the structures built under the influence of foreign architecture, an overview of the geography of the empire controlled by Rome. Aeneas' tour of proto-Rome under the guidance of King Evander in *Aeneid* 8 is the best-known example of politically and culturally determined description of Roman topography in Classical Literature. Aeneas' political visit to Pallanteum becomes an opportunity for Vergil to introduce, seemingly before the eyes of Aeneas, the ancestor of the Romans, and also for his contemporaries, a description of Rome that is historically accurate, but truly for neither of the two audiences. For Aeneas, the Rome he traverses is a projection to the future, while for Vergil's contemporaries it corresponds with a site that does not exist anymore.[36] For the latter, Aeneas' travelogue serves as a point of reference to highlight the grand expansion of the city and especially the thorough transformation under Augustus that is in progress during the time Vergil composes his epic.

This understanding of the power of topography to fashion and control civic memory and by extension reinforce Roman identity is first understood and developed upon by Plautus and Terence. The two comic playwrights were witnesses to the changes on the landscape of Rome and of the Roman expansion eastwards, and the first to understand that Rome's intrinsic value does not lie in its land, but in its geography. Their plays are conscious literary constructions that comment not just on the transformation of Romanness in the cultural and political reality of the late 3rd century Rome but more specifically, as I hope to have shown in this study, on the palimpsestic character of the topography of posthannibalic Rome throughout the 2nd century BCE, both culturally and visually – a phenomenon readily comprehensible to the people who attended the *palliatae*.

The Choragos' tour of the Forum maps a fluid cityscape. Some of the buildings and sites mentioned are there, but some are under construction, others will soon be gone, and there may be certain ones whose construction has not begun yet. The audience is invited to 'see' them mentally and build the image of the city each wishes to experience visually. The association of each monument and site with a particular group of comic characters not only transforms the Roman Forum into a comedic stage but from a civic perspective also accentuates the Roman identity of the landscape, for several of these comic figures are distinct types of the *palliata* and the Roman mime, not of Menandrian comedy. In this respect, the Choragus' tour is both aesthetically and socio-politically self-conscious, with poetics and contemporary reality working together towards mutual assertion. Demea's fool's errand offers an alternative expression of the interfusion of poetics and cultural politics. His itinerary is deliberately vague, communicating the different ways in which different individuals mentally read space narratives in a geographically pre-canonized society. This is true not only for Demea, the country man whose distancing from the city lifestyle has subjected him to a culture that understands and memorizes space and interacts with the environment differently than an urbanite does, but also for the slave Syrus, who presumably has lived his

---

36 Cf. Spencer (2010) 50: "The route… remains surprisingly difficult to visualize. Evander's back-to-the-future lecture tour of the future site of Rome configures space as a synchronous sequence of tagged landmarks: a hypertext".

entire life in the streets of the city, and even has composed and memorized his own mapping routes thereof, in his potential performances as a running slave in other plays.

Bibliography

Bekker-Nielsen, T. (1988), "*Terra Incognita*: The Subjective Geography of the Roman Empire", in A. Damsgard-Madsen, E. Christiansen and E. Hallager (eds.), *Studies in Ancient History and Numismatics Presented to Rudi Thomsen*, Århus: 148–161.
Boni, G. (1901), "Il sacrario di Giuturna", *Notizie degli Scavi*: 41–144.
Bowditch, P.L. (2001), *Horace and the Gift Economy of Patronage*, Berkeley/Los Angeles.
Breed, B. (2018), "Lucilius' Books", in B. Breed, E. Keitel, and R. Wallace (eds.), *Lucilius and Satire in Second Century BC Rome*, Cambridge: 57–78.
Campbell, J.B. (2012), *Rivers and the Power of Ancient Rome*, Chapel Hill.
Corbeill, A. (2015), "'A Shouting and Bustling on All Sides' (Hor. *Sat.* 1.9.77–8): Everyday Justice in the Streets of Republican Rome", in I. Östenberg, S. Malmberg and J. Bjørnebye (eds.), *The Moving City: Processions, Passages and Promenades in Ancient Rome*, London: 89–98.
Daniels, S./D. Cosgrove (eds.) (1988), *The Iconography of Landscape. Essays on the Symbolic Representation, Design and Use of Past Environments*, Cambridge.
Daniels, S./D. Cosgrove (1993), "Spectacle and Text: Landscape Metaphors in Cultural Geography" in J. Duncan & D. Ley (eds.), *Place/Culture/Representation*, London: 57–77.
Dang, K. (2010), "Rome and the Sabine 'Farm': Aestheticism, Topography and the Landscape of Production", *Phoenix* 64: 102–127.
Davies, P.J. (2017), "Constructing, Deconstructing and Reconstructing Civic Memory in Late Republican Rome", in K. Sandberg & C. Smith (eds.), *Omnium Annalium Monumenta: Historical Writing and Historical Evidence in Republican Rome*, Leiden: 477–512.
Duncan, J./D. Ley (eds.) (1993), *Place/Culture/Representation*, London.
Edwards, C. (1996), *Writing Rome: Textual Approaches to the City*, Cambridge.
Edwards, C./G. Woolf (eds.) (2003), *Rome the Cosmopolis*, Cambridge.
Favro, D. (2014), "Moving events: Curating the memory of the Roman triumph", in K. Galinsky (ed.), *Memoria Romana: Memory in Rome and Rome in Memory*, Ann Arbor: 85–103.
Fowler, D. (1994), "Martial and the book", *Ramus* 24: 31–58.
Frank, T. (1936), "The Topography of Terence, *Adelphoe* 573–85", *AJP* 57: 470–472.
Galinsky, K. (ed.) (2014), *Memoria Romana: Memory in Rome and Rome in Memory*, Ann Arbor.
Galinsky, K./K. Lapatin (eds.) (2016), *Cultural Memories in the Roman Empire*, Los Angeles.
Goldberg, S.M. (2018), "Theater without Theaters: Seeing Plays the Roman Way", *AJP* 148: 139–172.
Halbwachs, M. (1925), *Les cadres sociaux de la mémoire*, Paris.
Hammar, I. (2015). "Rolling Thunder: Movement, Violence and Narrative in the History of the Late Roman Republic", in I. Östenberg, S. Malmberg and J. Bjørnebye (eds.), *The Moving City: Processions, Passages and Promenades in Ancient Rome*, London: 75–88.
Harrison, S.J. (2002), "Literary Topography in Apuleius' *Metamorphoses*", in M. Paschalis & S. Frangoulidis (eds.), *Space in the Ancient Novel*, Groningen: 40–57.

Hughes, J. (2014), "Memory and the Roman viewer: looking at the arch of Constantine", in K. Galinsky (ed.), *Memoria Romana: Memory in Rome and Rome in* Memory, Ann Arbor: 103–117.
Jaeger, M. (1995), "Reconstructing Rome: The Campus Martius and Horace *Ode* 1.8", *Arethusa* 28: 177–191.
Johnson, W.R. (1993), *Horace and the Dialectic of Freedom: Readings in Epistles 1*, Ithaca, NY.
Larmour, D./D. Spencer (eds.) (2007), *Sites of Rome: Time, Space, Memory*, Oxford.
Marshall, C.W. (2006), *The Stagecraft and Performance of Roman Comedy*, Cambridge.
Monaco, G. (1969), *Plauto: Curculio*, Palermo.
Moore, T. (1991), "*Palliata Togata*: Plautus, *Curculio* 482–86", *AJP* 112: 343–362.
Moore, T. (1998), *The Theater of Plautus: Playing to the Audience*, Austin.
Östenberg, I./S. Malmberg/J. Bjørnebye (eds.) (2015), *The Moving City: Processions, Passages and Promenades in Ancient Rome*, London.
O'Sullivan, T. (2012), *Walking in Roman Culture*, Cambridge.
O'Sullivan, T. (2015), "Augustan Literary Tours: Walking and Reading the City", in I. Östenberg, S. Malmberg and J. Bjørnebye (eds.), *The Moving City: Processions, Passages and Promenades in Ancient Rome*, London: 111–122.
Paratore, E. (1958), *Plauto: Curculio (=Il Gorgolione)*, Florence.
Renberg, G. (2006/2007), "Public and Private Places of Worship in the Cult of Aesculapius at Rome", *MAAR* 51/52: 87–172.
Richardson, L. (1992), *A New Topographical Dictionary of Ancient Rome*, Baltimore.
Russell, A. (2015), *The Politics of Public Space in Republican Rome*, Oxford.
Slater, N. (1987), "The Dates of Plautus' *Curculio* and *Trinummus* Reconsidered", *AJP* 108: 264–269.
Small, J.P. (1997), *Wax Tablets of the Mind: Cognitive Studies of Memory and Literacy in Classical Antiquity*, London.
Solnit, R. (2001), *Wanderlust: A History of Walking*, London.
Sommella, P. (2005), "La Roma Plautina (con particolare riferimento a *Cur.* 467–85)", in R. Raffaelli & A. Tontini (eds.), *Lecturae Plautinae Sarsinates VIII: Curculio*, Urbino: 69–109.
Spencer, D. (2010), *Roman Landscape: Culture and Identity*, Cambridge.
Spencer, D. (2015), "Urban Flux: Varro's Rome in Progress", in I. Östenberg, S. Malmberg and J. Bjørnebye (eds.), *The Moving City: Processions, Passages and Promenades in Ancient Rome*, London: 99–110.
Steiby, E.M. (1987). "Il lato orientale del Foro Romano", *Arctos* 21: 139–184.
Thomas, R.F. (1982), *Lands and Peoples in Roman Poetry: The Ethnographic Tradition*. Cambridge Philological Society, Suppl. 7. Cambridge.
Woolf, G. (2003), "City of letters", in C. Edwards & G. Woolf (eds.), *Rome the Cosmopolis*, Cambridge: 203–221.
Wylie, J. (2007), *Landscape*, London.
Yates, F.A. (1966), *The Art of Memory*, London/New York.

Maria Haley
Quoting from Memory? Shared Knowledge in Cicero's Book Fragments of Accius' *Atreus*

Abstract: Republican tragedies are considered forgotten theatre, surviving largely through quotations in Cicero's works. Recalling these lines allows Cicero to demonstrate his skill as a writer by using these quotations as cultural capital.

This study will examine the repeated quotations of Accius' *Atreus* and Ennius' *Thyestes* as a case study, to examine what Cicero's recollection of these extracts can tell us about their cultural caché and what impact the quotations have on Cicero's work in turn. Accius' *Atreus* tells the tale of Atreus feeding his brother Thyestes' children to him. Ennius' *Thyestes* deals with Thyestes' rape of his daughter to father an avenging son. Both are quoted in historiography, even in Seneca's own prose, to critique contemporary tyrants by analogy. As a result, the Thyestes tragedies provide a useful case study for comparing Cicero's recollection of the tragedies against others'.

First we will consider to what extent the mnemonics in *Rhetorica ad Herennium* are reflected in Cicero's recall of tragedy. Then we will examine if relative dating of quotations and performances can help us uncover whether Cicero quotes from a recent performance or a text. Finally, we will investigate how the repeated quotation of different Thyestean fragments creates intertext within Cicero's own work and with the work of other authors.

Ultimately by comparing Cicero's works and spotting trends in his quotation, this study will reveal how the book fragments of Republican tragedy once lived beyond the book, in the memory of initial audience members, Cicero himself and his own readership.

1 Introduction

Republican tragedies have often been treated as forgotten theatre, resigned to the footnotes of studies on either Seneca or Attic tragedy. In order to recover these lost plays, we rely largely on quotations in either Nonius Marcellus' grammar or Cicero's prose. Whereas Nonius focuses on linguistic anomalies, Cicero's texts provide the most useful reflection of the content of tragedies by quoting full lines, rather than individual words as the grammarians do.¹ Thus, Cicero provides a rich source for Republican tragedy, both quantitatively and qualitatively. Cicero is responsible for 78 of 180 fragments presumed to come from Republican tragedy,² 28 of which are from Accius' dramas.³ For the Thyestean tragedies in particular, Cicero not only preserves three of four extant fragments from Ennius' *Thyestes* and thirteen of twenty fragments from Accius' *Atreus*, but also appropriates these lines to illustrate his own arguments, problematically providing *his interpretation* of their original context.⁴

As a result, scholars have noted Cicero's tendency to quote Accius' *Atreus* in particular, which makes it a fruitful case study to determine how Cicero remembers tragedy, because for him, this story is most memorable.⁵ Unlike the Greek *Thyestes* fragments, Accius' *Atreus* clearly reflects Thyestes' crime, because frr.6–8 provide a detailed monologue, attributed to Atreus by Cicero, wherein Atreus describes his brother's affront:⁶

> at id ipsum quam callide, qui regnum adulterio quaereret—⁷
> adde (inquit) huc quod mihi portento caelestum pater
> prodigium misit, regni stabilimen mei,
> agnum inter pecudes aurea clarum coma
> quem clam Thyestem clepere ausum esse e regia;
> qua in re adiutricem coniugem cepit sibi.

> But how cunningly is this done, by the very one who sought to gain the kingdom by adultery—
> What is more (he [Atreus] says) the father of the heavens by portent
> Sent me a prodigy, an assurance for my realm,—
> Among my sheep shone a ram with a Golden Fleece
> Which Thyestes dared to steal in secret from the palace;
> From where he took my wedded queen as his accomplice.
> Accius 8 Ribbeck

---

[1] Cf. Manuwald (2010) 28.
[2] Schierl (2015) 45.
[3] Dueck (2009) Table 1, 315.
[4] Steiner notes how popular Accius' *Atreus* is in Cicero's prose, amongst all mythological texts (1968) n. 4.
[5] Shackleton Bailey (1983) 245, Steiner (1968) n. 4 cf. Laidlaw (1960) 62.
[6] Accius 6 Ribbeck *apud* Cic. *Nat. D.* 3.26.68.
[7] Here I accept the introductory line from Warmington's 1936 Loeb, which had not yet been included in the 1871 *TrGF*.

The fragment tells the story of Thyestes seducing his brother Atreus' wife Aërope and claiming the Golden Fleece.[8] Traditionally, this crime provokes Atreus to kill Thyestes' sons and feed them to him. Therefore, it is no surprise that the Atreus story was a *zeitgeist* in Cicero's lifetime, given the relevance of tyranny, betrayal and infighting to contemporary politics, as Petrone has well noted.[9]

As a result, Cicero quotes *Atreus* more than any other play of Accius, and later both Seneca and Suetonius accuse their own tyrants of speaking lines from the tragedy.[10] The fragments we will consider are frr. 3, 5, 9, 16 and 18 in Ribbeck's first edition shown in Table 1. However, as Manuwald has pointed out, Cicero's quotation of Republican tragedy poses challenges when trying to reconstruct the plays themselves. For example, Cicero and his reader appreciated the quotations as part of a whole, Cicero manipulates fragments to suit his own narrative and he does not always cite the tragedian he quotes by name.[11]

For these fragments, it is Cicero's repeated quotation that allows us to attribute them to Accius through cross-reference to occasions where Cicero names Accius, or quotes them in conjunction with other known Accius fragments. This persistent recollection of Accius' *Atreus* in Cicero's prose suggests the play itself was memorable. But this study will first examine how memory is at work in Cicero's quotations by considering whether Cicero quotes from the memory of either Accius' text or a performance of it, or whether Cicero refers to a text of Accius' *Atreus* to quote directly. This will lead to a discussion of how and why Cicero recalls tragedy differently not only in particular time periods but also in different genres of his work. Considering how Cicero remembers tragedy and reminds his reader of it in the different genres of his work will help us to determine how Roman tragedy contributed to contemporary thought and further distance ourselves from the misconception that Roman tragedy merely translated a Greek original.

To consider how and why Cicero recalls Accius' *Atreus*, we will first deal with the role of mnemonics in Cicero's work by comparing the art of memory in the pseudo-Ciceronian *Rhetorica ad Herennium* to that of Cicero's *De Oratore*. Then, we will read across Cicero's prose works to determine whether repeated quotations of Accius' *Atreus* indicate a possible re-performance date when the play could have been fresh in Cicero's memory. Having considered how Cicero remembers Accius' *Atreus*, attention will then turn to how Cicero reminds his readers of the tragedy, by using Atreus' *oderint dum metuant* as a meme, "a cultural element

---

8 Cf. Abbott (1907) for the political resonance of Republican tragedy indicated in Cicero's prose.
9 Petrone (2002) 246.
10 Cf. Shackleton Bailey (1983) 244–5, Suet. *Tiber.* 59.2, Sen. *De. Ir.* 1. 20. 4–5; *De Clem.* 2.2, 12.4.
11 Manuwald (2010).

or behavioural trait whose transmission and consequent persistence in a population, is considered as analogous to the inheritance of a gene."[12] Finally, we will consider how Cicero frames his quotations of Accius as shared memory to exploit the cultural caché of Roman drama.

2 Cicero's Memory? Remembering Cicero: *Rhetorica ad Herennium*

When considering Cicero's use of memory, it is impossible to ignore the *Rhetorica ad Herennium*, historically attributed to Cicero from the Middle Ages. The authorship of the work is contested, with many suggesting that Cornificius (*fl.* 35 BC) is the author.[13] However, as Adamik points out, *Rhetorica ad Herennium* is similar to Cicero's *De Inventione* in style and phrasing. This leads Adamik to suggest that Cicero referred to *Rhetorica ad Herennium* 4 when writing *De Inventione* 2, prompting his argument that *Rhetorica ad Herennium* was widely-known in antiquity, though unlikely to be Ciceronian.[14]

Most interestingly, Adamik identifies the overlap between Quintilian's discussion of the *ars memoriae* in his *De Oratore* and the *Rhetorica ad Herennium*, which, like Cicero's own *De Oratore*, describe memory as a "treasury" of eloquence and invention for orators:

> neque inmerito **thesaurus** hic **eloquentiae** dicitur
>
> It is not without good reason that it has been called the treasury of eloquence.
>
> Quintilian *De Or.* 1

---

12 s.v. Meme *OED*.
13 Regius (1491) is the first to refute the attribution to Cicero, Victorinus (1553) is the first to suggest Cornificius as an author. These cases are largely based on Quintilian's references to Cornificius, which allude to the subject matter of *Rhetorica ad Herennium*, though Cornificius' text is unnamed. (Quint. *Inst. Or.* 3.1.21; 5.10 3; 9.2.27; 9.3.71; 9.3.89). E.g., Marx (1894) 7; Calboli (1969) 1–29; Achard (1989) 17–20 cf. Kennedy (1972) 126–37 or Caplan (1954) 9–15 for an appraisal of the differences between *Rhetorica ad Herennium* and *De inventione*, with which it has significant overlap and is thus originally in the mss attributed to Cicero. Shackleton Bailey (1983) 240 notes the overlaps between *Rhetorica ad Herennium* and *Cicero's De Oratione*, as does Hunter (2010) 27–57, but ultimately conclude that the work is not Ciceronian.
14 Adamik (1998) 274. N.b. Douglas (1960) 65 uses internal stylistic evidence to date the treatise to 86–82 B.C., a widely accepted date.

> nunc ad **thesaurum inventorum** atque ad omnium partium rhetoricae custodem, memoriam transeamus
>
> Now let us turn to the treasure-house of invention and to the guardian of all parts of rhetoric, memory.
>
> [Cic.] *Rh. Her* 3.16.28
>
> quid dicam de thesauro rerum omnium memoria?
>
> What should I say about the treasury of all things, memory?
>
> Cic. *De Or.* 1.5.18

This is not the only overlap between the *Rhetorica* and Cicero's *De Oratore* but is the most pertinent for our present study of mnemonics.[15] Therefore, despite the disputed authorship of the *Rhetorica ad Herennium*, it provides the earliest surviving classical treatise on memory written c. 55 BC, which was referred to in Cicero's treatise on oratory.[16] Thus, the *Rhetorica ad Herennium* provides a useful near-contemporary framework to discuss how Cicero remembers Accius' *Atreus* in his securely-attributed works. So, regardless of whether the *Rhetorica ad Herennium* is Ciceronian or not, there are enough similarities with *De Inventione* and *De Oratore* to show some similar thought patterns and establish an understanding of mnemonics in Cicero's lifetime.

Yates' landmark study *The Art of Memory* praises *Rhetorica ad Herennium* as an exemplar of "the art of classical memory,"[17] that is creating mnemonic strategies for recalling texts and speeches as an orator. The most pertinent extract of *Rhetorica ad Herennium* suggests that images are more memorable than text:

> si aliquas exornabimus, ut si coronis aut veste purpurea, quo nobis notatior sit similitudo; aut si qua re deformabimus, ut si cruentam aut caeno oblitam aut rubrica delibutam inducamus, quo magis insignita sit forma, aut ridiculas res aliquas imaginibus adtribuamus, nam ea res quoque faciet ut facilius meminisse valeamus.
>
> if we dress some of them with crowns or purple cloaks, for example, so that the likeness may be more distinct to us; or if we somehow disfigure them, as by introducing one stained with blood or soiled with mud or smeared with red paint, so that its form is more striking, or by

---

15 See, for example, Winkel (1979) 327–8 on the repetition of *imprudentia* across these works (1979). Cf. Vatri (2015) 751. For an alternative view of mnemonics in the Augustan period see Michalopoulos (above) on Ovid.
16 Cf. Winkel (1979).
17 Yates (1966) 5., cf. Small (1997) 82.

assigning certain comic effects to our images, for that, too, will ensure our remembering them more readily.

[Cic]. *Rhet. Her.* 3.22.37

To illustrate the memorability of images the author of *Rhetorica ad Herennium* uses theatrical elements suggesting that performance was considered more memorable than text.[18] In particular the imagery suggests tragic production such as "crowns or purple cloaks" of royal characters and the "red paint" used to dramatize blood on stage. Therefore, *Rhetorica ad Herennium* indicates that theatrical production, be it imagined or recalled, aids the memory of tragic dialogue.

Not only does this extract evidence the memorability of theatrical performance in Cicero's time, but as den Boer suggests, this pseudo-Ciceronian passage anticipates Cicero's own suggestion in *De Oratore* that images are more memorable than words:

sed verborum memoria, quae minus est nobis necessaria, maiore imaginum varietate distinguitur; multa enim sunt verba quae quasi articuli connectunt membra orationis quae formari similitudine nulla possunt; eorum fingendae nobis sunt imagines quibus semper utamur; rerum memoria propria est oratoris; eam singulis personis bene positis notare possumus ut sententias imaginibus, ordinem locis comprehendamus.

But a memory for words, which for us is less essential is given distinctness by a greater variety of images; for there are many words which serve as joints connecting the limbs of the sentence, and these cannot be formed by any use of simile—of these we have to model images for constant employment; a memory for things is the special property of the orator— this we can imprint on our minds by a skilful arrangement of the several masks that represent them, so that we may grasp ideas by means of images and their order by means of localities.

Cic. *De Or.* 2.359[19]

Like the pseudo-Cicero of *Rhetorica ad Herennium*, Cicero describes mnemonics, here the art of remembering *images*, in theatrical terms by referring to masks. Thus, I suggest that theatrical performances are not only remembered by Cicero, but are also part of his methodology for recalling dialogue as an orator and, by extension, reminding his reader of pertinent dramatic scenes.

As Fantham has suggested, readers of tragedy would imagine its production, and as Cicero himself claims in *De Oratore*, visualizations of tragedy are more memorable.[20] Thus the task remains: to determine whether Cicero's quotations of

---

18 See, for example, evidence of stage blood at Suet. *Nero*. 12.2.
19 Cf. den Boer (2008) 19–20 and Small (1997) 96.
20 Fantham (1982) 48–9.

Accius' *Atreus* recall a near-contemporary performance, or whether Cicero reminds the reader of the tragic lines by using the memory of a performance to make his own quotation memorable. To do so I will first compare the texts across which the same quotes of Accius' *Atreus* are repeated, in order to consider the dating and genre of the works in which the quotations appear, and what point these serve to illustrate in each case.

3 Repetition & Relative Dating: Aesopus as Accius' *Atreus* (Ribbeck 3, 5, 9, 16 and 18)

Repeated quotations provide a useful litmus test for quoting from memory because they are used as illustrative examples in different contexts. As Dueck points out, Cicero professes to memorise texts to illustrate his arguments:

> cuius edidici etiam versus et lubenter quidem, quos in secundo *De Consulatu* Urania Musa pronuntiat.

> I have learned by heart and with great pleasure the following words uttered by the Muse, Urania, in the second book of your poem entitled *On Consulship*.
> Cic. *Div.* 1.17 tr. Dueck 2009 p. 331

Thus, deliberately committing passages to memory was a point of pride and status, as indicated in the development of mnemonics in *Rhetorica ad Herennium* and *De Oratore*.[21] This practice is in evidence in the repeated quotations we shall examine. Of the thirteen fragments Cicero quotes from Accius' *Atreus*, seven are repeated across eight texts, including forensic oratory such as *Pro Sestio* and *Pro Plancio* (c. 56 BC), political oratory such as the *Philippics* (44–43 BC); rhetorical dialogue such as *De Oratore* (55 BC) and moral treatises such as *Tusculan Disputations* and *De Officiis* (45–44 BC).

The most obvious point to notice is the spread of dates, as the repeated quotations are clustered around 56–55 BC and 45–43 BC. Although Accius' *Atreus* was originally composed before the death of Pacuvius in 130 BC, this *terminus ante quem* is based on Accius' presentation of the script to Pacuvius, the renowned stage tragedian:

---

21 Fantham (2004) 138–46 on trends in Cicero's quotation of tragedy in *De Oratione* and (2013) 129–32 on Cicero's admiration of Ennius' *Thyestes* and Accius' *Atreus*.

> Accius tunc, haut parvo iunior, proficiscens in Asiam, cum in oppidum venisset, devertit ad Pacuvium comiterque invitatus plusculisque ab eo diebus retentus, tragoediam suam cui Atreus nomen est desideranti legit. tum Pacuvium dixisse aiunt sonora quidem esse quae scripsisset et grandia, sed videri tamen ea sibi duriora paulum et acerbiora.
>
> Then Accius, who was a much younger man, coming to Tarentum on his way to Asia, visited Pacuvius, and being hospitably received and detained by him for several days, at his request read him his tragedy entitled Atreus. Then they say that Pacuvius remarked that what he had written seemed sonorous and full of dignity, but that nevertheless it appeared to him somewhat harsh and rugged.
>
> Gell. *Noct. Atti.* 13.2.2[22]

This suggests that Accius was drafting a play for performance. Moreover, Cicero's distaste for Accius' posthumously produced *Clytemnestra* at the theatre of Pompey in 55 BC suggests that posthumous re-performance of Accius was possible.[23] Could it be, then, that Accius' *Atreus* was re-performed around 56–55 BC and again around 45–43 BC? Is Cicero remembering these productions when quoting the tragedy?

Goldberg warns against pinning Cicero's quotations of Accius' *Atreus* to performances because of the problem presented by relative dating of a particular performance and Cicero's recollection of it. Goldberg suggests that in 44 BC "Accius' *Atreus* was certainly fresh in Cicero's memory,"[24] pointing out that Cicero quotes Accius' *Atreus* (fr. 5) as though from performance in *Philippics*:

> quod videmus etiam in fabula illi ipsi qui "oderint, dum metuant" dixerit perniciosum fuisse.
>
> Even in the play we see that it was ruinous to the very character who said "Let them hate me, so long as they fear me."
>
> Cic. *Phil.* 1.34 = Accius 5 Ribbeck

Although Eigler considers fr. 5 to be quoted from a contemporary performance,[25] when compared to another quotation of Accius' *Atreus* (fr. 18) in the *Tusculan Disputations* published in the same year, Cicero's reference to the actor Aesopus compels Goldberg to date the performance ten years earlier than Cicero's texts:

---

22 Cf. Baldarelli "Jerome suggests the year to be 140/39 BC, Cicero suggests that 140 BC was when Accius and Pacuvius produced plays in the same year. Pacuvius then ended his career between 139–135 BC. He died in Tarentum in 132–131 BC, so in order to visit Pacuvius on his way to Asia, Accius must have visited him between 139–131 BC." (2005) 105–6.
23 Cic. *Ad. Fam.* 7.1.2.
24 Goldberg (2000) 127.
25 Eigler (2000) 619 n. 1.

cum iam rebus transactis et praeteritis orationes scribimus, num irati scribimus?
 ecquis hoc animadvertit? vincite!
num aut egisse umquam iratum Aesopum aut scripsisse existimas iratum Accium? aguntur ista praeclare et ab oratore quidem melius, si modo est orator, quam ab ullo histrione, sed aguntur leniter et mente tranquilla.

Again, after the trial is over and done with and I write my speeches out, surely you do not think that I am angry as I write?
 Does no one punish this? Seize him!
Surely one does not think Aesopus was ever angry when he played this part or Accius angry when he wrote it? Such parts are finely played and better indeed by the orator, if only he is an orator, than by any actor; but they are played without bitterness and with a mind at peace.

Cic. *Tusc. Disp.* 4.55= Accius 18 Ribbeck[26]

From this Goldberg concludes that since Aesopus retired after his performance in 57 BC: "Cicero's 'stage recollection' must therefore be over a decade old and is not specific: thus *videmus* rather than *vidimus*, *umquam* rather than *nuper*."[27] Though the terms are general, the actor is specified. Thus, I suggest that Cicero reminds the reader of Aesopus' delivery to illustrate the detachment from the creator/ performer and the creation/ production that he discusses here. Cicero refers to a famous bygone performance because the performer is well-known, a favourite of Cicero in fact,[28] and this allows him to detach Aesopus the actor from Atreus the character to better illustrate the distinction between roleplay, the performance, and reality, the actor's separate identity.

This complicates the issue of performance recall and relative dating, because the most memorable productions may not be the most recent ones, and productions are memorable for different reasons. As a result, Cicero reminds his reader of the *performance* that is most pertinent to his point, trusting that they will remember Aesopus as an outstanding actor and thus distinguish the actor from the character. But what is more, alluding to performance allows Cicero to appeal to a frame of reference anyone would understand. As Wiseman points out, drama productions enter "popular memory" because they can be accessed by the illiterate, and Cicero defined the audience of the games as the Roman people.[29] So although Cicero's reader must be literate, using theatre as a frame of reference allows him

---

26 Cf. 4.77 "hear Thyestes" (*audi Thyestem*), Eigler (2000) 633.
27 Goldberg (2005) 127.
28 Laidlaw outlines Cicero's alliance with Aesopus (1960) 57–8.
29 Cic. *Sest.* 106, 116–18, Wiseman (2014) 50–1.

to emphasise that the distinction between performance and actor is obvious to anyone, even a Roman *pleb*.

In short, Cicero may not remember a recent performance but instead remind his reader of a memorable one, in order to sharpen his point that a truly good actor can convey any emotion. Though we cannot accurately date dramatizations, what does arise from Goldberg's discussion of this quotation is a trend in Cicero's quotations of Accius' *Atreus*: the quotations cluster around two date ranges, c. 44 BC and c. 56 BC, which demands greater consideration.

Therefore, the repeated quotations I will now examine cluster around the two possible dates brought forth from Goldberg's discussion. I will include *Pro Sestio*, *De Oratore* and *Pro Plancio* clustered around 56 BC, shortly after the *terminus ante quem* date of Aesopus' performance in 57 BC, in addition to the *De Natura Deorum*, *Tusculan Disputations*, *De Officiis* and the *Philippics* clustered around 44 BC. Based on Goldberg's refutation of a 44 BC performance, I will compare and contrast 57 BC and 44 BC quotations of the same Accius' *Atreus* fragments to examine how Cicero remembers these lines and why he reminds his readers of them.

4 *Atreus* Again: Ribbeck 3 and 16

Turning to the repeated fragments themselves, Cicero's three quotations of *Atreus* fr. 3 point to different performances of the same lines. In *De Oratore* (55 BC) fr. 3 is quoted in full to contrast a tone of anger, most likely that of the vengeful Atreus, and energy, seemingly Thyestes:

> aliud enim vocis genus iracundia sibi sumat, acutum, incitatum, crebro incidens:
>> ipsus hortatur me frater ut meos malis miser
>> manderem natos ...
>> [...]
>
> aliud vis, contentum, vehemens, imminens quadam incitatione gravitatis:
>> iterum Thyestes Atreum attractatum advenit,
>> iterum iam aggreditur me et quietum exsuscitat.
>> maior mihi moles, maius miscendumst malum
>> qui illius acerbum cor contundam et comprimam.
>
> For one kind of tone must be taken by anger—shrill, hasty, with short abrupt clauses—
>> Why, my very brother bids me miserably masticate
>> My own sons...[30]

---

[30] Accius 16 Ribbeck.

> [...]
> Another denotes energy; this is intense, vehement, eager with a sort of impressive urgency:
>> Again Thyestes comes to grapple Atreus,
>> Again he approaches to disturb my peace.
>> More misery, more misfortune must I brew,
>> With which to check and crush his cruel heart.[31]
>
> Cic. *De Or.* 3. 58. 219

If we differentiate the characters by their two tones, as Cicero suggests, then the brothers cap each other in an *agon*, as Thyestes approaches and the delivery of the lines in performance is foregrounded by Cicero's emphasis on tone. Thus, it seems that Cicero remembers a specific performance, as the delivery of the lines is considered shared knowledge: the speakers' names are not provided but the alternation is made clear.

In *Tusculan Disputations* (45 BC), the final two lines of fr. 3 appear in contrast to the *stichomythia* between Agamemnon and Menelaus from an unknown tragedy and before another repeated fragment of Accius' *Atreus*, fr. 16:

> ira vero quae quam diu perturbat animum, dubitationem insaniae non habet, cuius impulsu exsistit etiam inter fratres tale iurgium:
>> quis homo te exsuperavit usquam gentium impudentia?
>> quis item malitia te?
>
> nosti quae sequuntur; alternis enim versibus intorquentur inter fratres gravissimae contumeliae, ut facile appareat Atrei filios esse, eius qui meditatur poenam in fratrem novam:
>> maior mihi moles, maius miscendumst malum,
>> qui illius acerbum cor contundam et comprimam.
>
> Next anger which so long as it disorders the soul undoubtedly implies unsoundness of mind, and starts a brawl like this even between two brothers:
>> What man in all the world in impudence have you ever surpassed?
>> Who have you surpassed in malice?
>
> You know what follows; the bitterest taunts are hurled from brother to brother in alternate lines, so that it is easy to see they are sons of the Atreus who plots an unheard of penalty for his brother:
>> More misery, more misfortune must I brew,
>> With which to check and crush his cruel heart.
>
> Cic. *Tusc. Disp.* 4. 36. 77 = Accius 3 Ribbeck

Cicero attributes both of these lines of fr. 3 to Atreus alone, before contrasting Thyestes' reaction:

---

31 Accius 3 Ribbeck.

> quo igitur haec erumpit moles? audi Thyestem:
>> ipsus hortatur me frater, ut meos malis miser
>> mandarem natos...

> Which way then is this mass to crash? Listen to Thyestes:
>> Why, my very brother bids me miserably
>> masticate my sons...[32]

>> Cic. *Tusc. Disp.* 4. 36. 77= Accius 16 Ribbeck

So whereas in *De Oratore* Cicero quotes fr. 3 as *stichomythia*, in *Tusculan Disputations* Cicero presents fr. 3 as Atreus' monologue in contrast to the *stichomythia* of Agamemnon and Menelaus, to then present the outcome of Atreus' plot: Thyestes' recognition of the cannibalistic feast in fr. 16. Cicero thus remembers, or perhaps misremembers, the delivery of these lines and uses that performance context to remind his reader of how to perform emotion.

Similarly, in the *De Natura Deorum* of the same year (45 BC), Cicero quotes the same final two lines of fr. 3 and introduces them to present Atreus' rational *psychomachia* in comparison to Medea's "most unnatural murder of her kin" (*familiari pareret parricidio*):

> huic ut scelus sic ne ratio quidem defuit. quid? ille funestas epulas fratri conparans nonne versat huc et illuc cogitatione rationem?

> Thus, this was a crime that did not lack reason. Again, does not the hero plotting the direful banquet for his brother turn the design this way and that in his thoughts?
>> Cic. *Nat. D.* 3. 26. 68

Thus the final lines of fr. 3 are attributed to Atreus as a speaker wavering in his thoughts. The consistency of the lines need not suggest that Cicero refers to a text, since only the alliterative lines of fr. 3 are recalled twice in the texts of 45 BC (*meos malis miser | mandarem natos*), suggesting that they are the most memorable and thus are quoted from memory. Therefore, I suggest that Cicero recalls two *possible* performances of fr. 3: the *agon* is suggested in *De Oratore* in 55 BC, whereas in 45 BC only the final lines of fr. 3 are quoted and assigned to Atreus. So either Cicero is representing two possible ways of attributing these lines to make his point, or is misremembering a performance when quoting in 45 BC.

Given that in 45 BC, Cicero quotes less of the dialogue, this suggests that his memory of an early performance has faded. Thus it seems more likely that in *De Oratore* of 55 BC Cicero was recalling a recent performance of the passage, given

---

32 Again, for Seneca's reception of this line, see Baldarelli (2004) 258–9.

his focus on its delivery and the contrasting tones of the speakers. Moreover, Cicero's quotation in 55 BC scarcely postdates the end of Aesopus' career in 57 BC, who as Goldberg points out, is praised by Cicero for playing Atreus in *Tusculan Disputations* when he quotes fr. 18. Thus a performance in the 50's BC would be far fresher in Cicero's memory, when he quotes fr. 3 most fully.

When we return to the texts of 45 BC the final lines of fr. 3 are recalled to discuss anger and reason in the philosophical treatises. Thus the content of Atreus' crime is more emphasised than the tone of delivery, when compared with Cicero's recollection of Agamemnon and Menelaus in *Tusculan Disputations* and Medea in *De Natura Deorum*. When we examine the repeated quotation of fr. 3, Goldberg's suggestion seems plausible; perhaps Cicero is remembering a performance in the 50s BC to remind the reader of how to perform emotively, and by 45 BC is only recalling two alliterative lines of fr. 3 for thematic purposes. By this point, Cicero may quote more succinctly to make thematic points as he is less interested in the delivery of speech.

Returning to *De Oratore* (55 BC), Cicero again quotes Accius' *Atreus* fr. 16 to emphasise performance:

> aliud enim vocis genus iracundia sibi sumat, acutum, incitatum, crebro incidens:
> > ipsus hortatur me frater ut meos malis miser
> > manderem natos ...
>
> et ea quae tu dudum, Antoni, protulisti:
> > segregare abs te ausu's ...
>
> et
> > ecquis hoc animadvertit? vincite ...
>
> et Atreus fere totus.

> For one kind of tone must be taken by anger—shrill, hasty, with short abrupt clauses—
> > Why, my very brother bids me miserably masticate
> > My own sons...[33]
>
> and the line you quoted some time ago, Antonius...
> > You dared to separate yourself...[34]
>
> and
> > Will no one mark this? Put in chains...[35]
>
> and almost the whole of Atreus.
>
> > Cic. *De Or.* 3. 58. 217

---

[33] Accius 16 Ribbeck.
[34] Pacuvius 12 Ribbeck = Telamon in *Teucer* cf. Erasmo (2004) n. 21.
[35] Accius 18 Ribbeck.

Whereas ten years later in *Tusculan Disputations* Cicero quotes fr. 16 to present a consequence to Atreus' plot in fr. 3, here, as elsewhere in *De Oratore*, Cicero focuses on the delivery of the lines. Moreover, in *De Oratore* Cicero trusts his reader to apply the themes of frr. 16 and 18 to "the whole of *Atreus*" and even quotes fr. 12 of Pacuvius' *Teucer* second-hand from Antonius to draw on Teucer's father Telamon "bereft of sons" (*indigem liberum*) after Teucer fails to return the body of his half-brother Ajax.[36] In *De Oratore*, fr. 18 appears after fr. 12 to denote anger; in *Tusculan Disputations* Cicero suggests that this anger was imitated by the writer Accius and the actor Aesopus who, as Goldberg points out, positions the performance of Accius' *Atreus* before 57 BC: a performance I suggest Cicero recalls to quote Accius' *Atreus* from memory in the *De Oratore* of 55 BC.

5 *Oderint dum Metuant*: Memory and Accius' Meme Ribbeck 5, 9 and 9a

So, we can see that Accius' *Atreus* enjoys special status in Cicero's discourse, who regularly quoted it to convey a message to his reader through shared memory. In *De Oratore* (55 BC) Cicero quotes *agon* as though from a recent performance to contrast forms of delivery. In *Tusculan Disputations* (45 BC), Cicero recalls a bygone performance made memorable by the actor Aesopus who had retired in 57 BC, to illustrate the distinction between performance and reality.[37] Having examined the repeated quotations in *De Oratore* (frr. 3, 16,18), *Natura Deorum* (fr. 3) and *Tusculan Disputations* (frr. 3, 16, 18), we must now turn to the most memorable fragment of Accius' *Atreus*: the *oderint dum metuant* maxim (fr. 5).

As we know, Goldberg uses fr. 5 to illustrate Cicero's familiarity with the play and cites the latest quotation of fr. 5 in the *Philippics* of 44–43 BC.[38] Indeed, as Shackleton Bailey points out, Cicero's *Phillipics* scarcely quote tragedy when

---

[36] *Segregare abs te ausus aut sine illo Saliminem ingredi, | Neque paternum aspectum es ueritus quom aetate | exacta indigem | Liberum lacerasti orbasti extinxti, neque fratris necis | Neque eius gnati parui, qui tibi in tutelam est traditus?* (You dared to separate yourself, even went to Salamis without him,| Nor did you fear your father's sight; whom spent in years, bereft of sons you have wounded, made childless, and wiped out | Nor did you think of a brother's death nor of his infant son who was entrusted to your safe keeping.) Accius 12 Ribbeck tr. Erasmo (2004) n. 21.
[37] Cicero's quotations in the work tend to be illustrative paraphrases cf. Salamon, on Cicero's quotation of both philosophy and drama to elucidate his points in *Tusculan Disputations* (2004) 140–2.
[38] Goldberg (2005) 127.

compared to Cicero's other works.³⁹ Yet here in Cicero's invective against Marc Antony, he introduces fr. 5 as follows to contrast Marc Antony's tyranny against Republican values:

> carum esse civem, bene de re publica mereri, laudari, coli, diligi gloriosum est; metui vero et in odio esse invidiosum, detestabile, imbecillum, caducum. quod videmus etiam in fabula illi ipsi qui "oderint dum metuant" dixerit.
>
> It is glorious to be a citizen dear to the community, to deserve well of the Republic, to be praised and courted and esteemed. But to be feared and hated carries ill-will, execration, weakness, insecurity. Even in the play we see that it was ruinous to the very character who said: "Let them hate, so long as they fear."
>
> Cic. *Phil.* 1. 14. 34

In Cicero's earlier quotations of fr. 5, he uses the line to illustrate similar points on the danger and repugnance of tyranny, but does so in combination with the quotation of other *Atreus* fragments. Thus Cicero, as promised in *De Oratore*, reminds his reader of the idea of the tragic tyrant "by means of images" to illustrate his point, and is careful to remember the "order" of the dialogue "by means of localities," in conjunction with other quotations form Accius' *Atreus*.⁴⁰

In *De Officiis* (44 BC) for example, Cicero juxtaposes Atreus' plotting in fr. 5 against the outcome of Thyestes' feast in fr. 14 to underscore Atreus' characterisation:

> sed tum servare illud poetas, quod deceat, dicimus, cum id, quod quaque persona dignum est, et fit et dicitur; ut, si Aeacus aut Minos diceret:
>   oderint dum metuant
> aut:
>   natis sepulchro ipse est parens,
> indecorum videretur, quod eos fuisse iustos accepimus; at Atreo dicente plausus excitantur; est enim digna persona oratio.
>
> Now, we say that the poets observe propriety, when every word or action is in accord with each individual character. For example, if Aeacus or Minos said
>   Let them hate, so long as they fear,⁴¹
> or:
>   The father is himself his children's tomb,⁴²

---

[39] Shackleton Bailey (1983) 243.
[40] Cic. *De Or.* 2.359.
[41] Accius 5 Ribbeck.
[42] Accius 14 Ribbeck.

that would seem improper, because we are told that they were just men. But when Atreus speaks those lines, they call forth applause; for the sentiment is in keeping with the character.

Cic. De Off. 1. 28. 97

Though here in Cicero's moral treatise he focuses on "what is suitable and proper for all – even for the bad" (*etiam vitiosis quid conveniat et quid deceat*),[43] he does so by contrasting Atreus against "just men" recalling the political injustice associated with fr. 5 in *Philippics*. To emphasise this, Cicero quotes fr. 5 in tandem with the repulsive cannibalism of fr. 14. So, Cicero reminds the reader of tragic performance to emphasise the extreme emotions of the genre, whilst writing in the year of Caesar's assassination, a crime against tyranny; just as Atreus punishes Thyestes for attempting to seize the throne. Yet, in *Atreus* the protagonist becomes a tyrant to oust a tyrant by killing his nephews to punish his brother.

Tracing back to Cicero's earliest quotation of fr. 5 in *Pro Sestio* (56 BC), he quotes a wider range of lines from Accius' *Atreus* to contrast the good and bad lessons to be taken from the tragedy. Cicero exults the jurors to follow the examples of those such as Marcus Scaurus, who steadfastly resisted revolutionaries. In so doing, Cicero uses frr. 9, 9a and 5 of Accius' *Atreus* to set up an expectation of morality:

> fateor:
>   multae insidiae sunt bonis
> verissime dictum est; sed te
>   id, quod multi invideant multique expetant, inscitia est,
> inquit,
>   postulare, nisi laborem summa cum cura ecferas.
> Nollem idem alio loco dixisset, quod exciperent improbi cives:
>   oderint, dum metuant;
> praeclara enim illa praecepta dederat iuventuti.

> Most truly has it been said,
>   Many snares are set for the good,[44]
> but the poet adds:
>   What many envy, many strive to win,
>   For you to claim is foolishness, unless
>   You summon all your toil and all your care
>   To win it.[45]

---

43 Cic. *De Off.* 1.28.97. Cf. Petrone (2002) 247 on character and propriety in this passage compared to Seneca's use of the myth.
44 Accius 9 Ribbeck.
45 Accius 9a Ribbeck.

> I could wish that the same poet had not elsewhere used words for evil-minded men to lay hold of:
>> Let them hate, so long as they fear;[46]
> for in those others he had given the young excellent advice.
>
> Cic. Pro Sest. 48. 102

Fragments 9–9a are pitched as admirable advice, whereas fr. 5 is again deplored as "words for evil-minded men to lay hold of," which provides a clue as to how these lines are recalled. It is clear that in the earliest text, *Pro Sestio* (56 BC), Cicero recalls the fullest account of Accius' *Atreus*, including three fragments and in the case of fr. 9 an extended quotation with little verbal repetition to make it memorable. Shackleton Bailey suggests that this quotation is owed to the fact that Cicero would remember Accius "personally", from performances.[47] But Shackleton Bailey overlooks the way in which Cicero indicates the quotation of fr. 5 outside of his own work, as Cicero himself indicates it is used outside the theatre. Thus Cicero suggests that fr. 5 becomes dislocated from Accius' tragedy and is remembered not from *Atreus* per se, but from the appropriation and application of the line to denote tyrannical behaviour: a trend which, as Spahlinger notes, Cicero has initiated here in writing.[48] According to Cicero, his contemporaries recall *oderint dum metuant* outside of what Cicero might call its "locality", as the line develops its own cultural significance.[49]

Cicero's fear that "bad men" will appropriate the tyrannical sentiment of fr. 5 is fulfilled in Imperial Roman historiography, where this fragment functions as a meme. So although Manuwald suggests that generally the tragic fragment of tragedy for Cicero's reader "the quoted piece was not 'a fragment', but rather a passage from a complete text," on this occasion *oderint dum metuant* takes on its own cultural caché, as a quotation from the original text, a standalone phrase and finally a quotation that creates intertext between the works in which it is quoted.[50]

As Gotoff has suggested, ancient writers used memorable sayings, or apothegms, to illustrate a point.[51] Unfortunately, no ancient work on apothegms predating Cicero survives, but the *Memorable Doings and Sayings* written by Valerius

---

46 Accius 5 Ribbeck.
47 Shackleton Bailey (1983) 242.
48 Spahlinger (2005) 231.
49 For the overlap between performance and cultural memory in Roman comedy, see Cosgrave in this volume.
50 Manuwald (2015) 2.
51 Described in the original as ἐρωτεθεὶς εἶπε or *obiter dictum* (Gotoff (1981) 294–5).

Maximus (fl. AD 30) illustrates the relevance of such phrases in the ancient world. Cicero's repeated quotation of *oderint dum metuant* not only recalls Accius' *Atreus*, but also Cicero's quotation of it elsewhere as we see in the table below, alluding to a variety of contexts. This fragment is eventually used as a "cultural element" to denote the "behavioural trait" of tyranny in the Imperial period, as it is quoted by Seneca and Suetonius to describe contemporary rulers: thus, it surpasses a popular apophthegm to become a meme that recalls its previous quotation contexts, each time distancing the quote from its original dramatic context.[52]

Therefore, Cicero quotes Accius' *Atreus* most fully in *Pro Sestio* (56 BC), written near the retirement of Aesopus (*pre*-55 BC), the actor who is later credited with both having played Atreus and thus having spoken fr. 5 on stage in Cicero's *Tusculan Disputations*.[53] For although in the texts of 44 BC Cicero positions the maxim in a performance context, he uses the present habitual to suggest that Atreus' words excite applause (*plausus excitantur*) in *De Officiis*, just as Goldberg points out the use of *videmus* in *Philippics*.[54] Thus fr. 5 is quoted alone in *Philippics* and with the brief fr. 14 in *De Officiis* as an example of moral repugnance, which eventually becomes a hallmark of the quotation outside the play itself under Sulla and Caligula. Overall, Cicero's use of the fragment to denote tyranny, though remembered in context, sets up the use of fr. 5 as a meme: the very form of recall Cicero fears in *Pro Sestio*.

Moreover, Cicero's multiple quotation of Accius' *Atreus* fragments in *Pro Sestio* (frr. 9, 9a, 5) alludes to Aesopus' performance of *Atreus*, given that the quotations are written close to Aesopus' retirement, suggesting a production in the 50s BC. In *Pro Sestio* Cicero himself maps out the different modes of quotation "proclaimed in common talk" (*haec fama celebrantur*) and "committed to the records of history" (*monumentis annalium mandantur*), claiming that fr. 9 in particular must be "handed down to posterity" (*posteritati propagantur*). Indeed, Cicero quotes fr. 9 again with the same advisory tone in his *Pro Plancio* (55 BC):

> quin etiam, ne forte ille sibi me potius peperisse iam honores quam iter demonstrasse adipiscendorum putet, haec illi soleo praecipere (quamquam ad praecepta aetas non est gravis) quae ille a Iove ortus suis praecipit filiis:
> > vigilandum est semper: multae insidiae sunt bonis;
> > id quod multi invideant...

---

[52] Sen. *Clem.* 2.2, 12.4, *De Ir.* 1. 20.4; Suet. *Calig.* 30; *Tiber.* 59.2. Cf. Zwierlein (1983) 120–2 and Baldarelli (2004) 193–9 on Seneca's reception of Accius 5.
[53] Reference to Aesopus' retirement is made in Cicero's letter on the opening of Pompey's theatre in 55 BC (Cic. *ad Fam.* 24.3).
[54] Goldberg (2005) 127.

> Lest he should think that rather than showing him the way to win honours in the future I have already won his honours for him, I am accustomed to give him the advice (though advice is somewhat beyond him at his present years) which that king who was himself sprung from Jupiter gave to his sons:
> Be cautious always: for many snares are set for the good,[55]
> but the poet adds:
> What many envy...
>
> Cic. Pro Planc. 24.59

Here Cicero uses fr. 9 more fully than in *Pro Sestio*, adding *id quod multi invideant* to warn against the dangers of relying on social status rather than merit, to suggest that the defendant Plancius is the target of envy. The quotation of fr. 9 is thus only repeated as advice in forensic speeches shortly after Aesopus' retirement in 57 BC. This not only suggests that the quotations reflect a performance, but also introduces another key theme found in Cicero's recollection of the passages: the use of shared memory, as Cicero expects the jurors to remember the context of fr. 9 in order to apply it to the case at hand.

Thus far, studying Cicero's repeated quotation of Accius' *Atreus* fragments indicates that the fullest quotations and the passages with the most quotations in succession cluster around 56 BC. Fr. 3 is quoted in full in *De Oratore* of 55 BC, whereas only the last two alliterative lines of fr. 3 are recalled in the texts of 44 BC, *Tusculan Disputations* and *Natura Deorum*.

The *oderint dum metuant* meme of fr. 5 is quoted alongside frr. 9 and 9a in *Pro Sestio* of 56 BC where Cicero emphasises the quotability of fr. 5 for "bad men" (*improbi cives*), which he reiterates in the texts of 44 BC by quoting fr. 5 alone in the *Philippics* and alongside fr. 14 in *De Officiis*.

6 Shared Memory: Ribbeck 3, 4, 5, 8, 9, 14 and 18

So far, the pattern of repeated quotations places the most extensive quotation from Accius' *Atreus* in the texts of 56 BC shortly after Aesopus, who performed as Atreus, had retired. But the repeated quotations of Accius' *Atreus* across these texts reveal another pattern. Cicero remembers fewer lines in the later texts but he also recalls the tragedy differently depending on the genre in which he is writing: thus we must reconcile Cicero's memory of the tragedy in these different time frames with his manipulation of memory in different genres.

---

55 Accius 9 Ribbeck.

If we return to Cicero's quotation of fr. 9 in *Pro Plancio*, we find that Cicero relies on shared knowledge with the jurors to convince them that his friend Plancius is not guilty of electoral fraud, but a victim of his rival's envy, having won a position as *aedile*:

> vigilandum est semper: multae insidiae sunt bonis;
> id quod multi invideant...
>
> nostis cetera. Nonne, quae scripsit gravis ille et ingeniosus poeta, scripsit non ut illos regios pueros, qui iam nusquam erant, sed ut nos et nostros liberos ad laborem et laudem excitaret.

> Be watchful always, many snares are set for the good.
> What many men do envy...
>
> No doubt you recall the rest of the passage. These lines were written by an earnest and gifted poet, whose object in writing them was to kindle the spirit of industry and ambition, not in those young princes who were merely the figments of his imagination, but in us and in our children.

Cic. Pro Planc. 24.59

The fragment illustrates Plancius' defence: that the charges against him have been trumped up by the jealous M. Iuventus Laternis, who stood as a candidate for aedileship as well but had lost.

Moreover, despite the fact that trends in Cicero's repeated quotations indicate a performance in the 50s BC, here the emphasis falls on the written record of fr. 9. Cicero imposes authorial intent, claiming that fr. 9 holds contemporary relevance for "us and our children" (*nos et nostros liberos*) to align himself with the jurors. Just as Cicero had highlighted the didactic function fr. 9 in *Pro Sestio*, he emphasises the record and dissemination of these lines to jurors in *Pro Plancio*: he invites his well-read addressees to remember the text and not the performance. As Geffcken points out, Cicero's manipulation of dramatic texts is not unusual, using the tragic character Medea to defame his contemporary Clodia.[56] Thus, the close dating of the forensic speeches to Aesopus' career (*pre* 57 BC) may point to a near-contemporary performance, but in a defence speech context where the precision of expression is key and the role of literacy is used to engage an exclusive few, Cicero focuses on the tragic text to create a shared reading of the text and thus ingratiate the jurors.

Returning to fr. 18, where one brother calls for the seizure of the other (*vincite...*) we find that earlier in *De Oratore* Cicero reflects that "almost the whole of Atreus" (*et Atreus fere totus*, 3.58.217) is written and performed in the same spirit of anger.

---

[56] Geffcken (1973).

Thus, in his treatise on speech and delivery Cicero is able to rely on the reader's memory of not only the lines in Accius' Atreus but also the manner in which they were performed. This is consistent with Cicero's expectations of an orator's memory expressed elsewhere in *De Oratore*: Cicero prefers a "memory for images" to a "memory for words."[57]

Therefore, in *De Oratore* Cicero emphasises visual and conceptual recall over the ability to quote from memory, thus the anger that *Atreus* is charged with and the masks that represent it are more important to his illustration than the exact quotation. Cicero's quotation is not just a question of remembering, but a question of *recollecting*; of both his memory of the performance at the time and his narrative posturing in his prose.

We find a similar emphasis on performance in the later philosophical treatises to align the reader with the shared experience of viewing a performance. *Tusculan Disputations* in particular cuts off the quotation fr. 3 with "You know what follows" (*Nosti quae sequuntur*) before discussing performance, bidding his reader "Listen to Thyestes" (*audi Thyestem*), or recalling both Aesopus' enraged performance of fr. 18 (*Vincite...*). So although Cicero uses the present habitual to discuss performances in general rather than using the past tense to pinpoint a particular performance of Aesopus, he presents his quotations in a production context to make the reader imagine the energetic delivery of the speech.

Similarly, in *De Officiis* Cicero draws in the reader with "we say" (*dicimus*), "we see" (*videmus*) in a similar conspiring tone when introducing frr. 5 and 14 as lines befitting Atreus. Again, Cicero refers to performance to conspire with his reader by claiming that the lines "excite applause" (*plausus excitantur*). Thus, allusion to performance allows Cicero to apply the point he is illustrating to a theatre audience including illiterate classes, underscoring the wider relevance of the drama to his literate readership who would also know the lines from the tragic text.

7 Conclusion

Overall, the two date ranges put forward by Goldberg of performance before 57 BC and quotation in 44 BC are not so polarised as they first appear. The fragments of Accius' *Atreus* that are repeatedly quoted occur in texts around both dates,

---

[57] See p. 43 above. For the use of shared memory in Roman comedy see Papaioannou in this volume.

with an absence of quotations in the intervening decade. The earlier texts examined here, *Pro Sestio*, *Pro Plancio* (56–55 BC) and *De Oratore* (55 BC), quote fragments more fully and often in combination to give a snapshot of the dramatic action of Accius' *Atreus*. Yet in these texts Cicero also establishes expectations as to how the tragedy is to be remembered: guarded for posterity (fr. 9) and misquoted by "bad men" (*improbi cives*) (fr. 5) in the forensic speeches, yet remembered as an overall performance for orators (fr. 18). As a result, the forensic speeches treasure the tragic lines as a text accessible to literate jurors and their sons, despite the proximity to a possible performance by Aesopus.

In the later texts, the moral treatises *Tusculan Disputations* and *De Officiis* (45–44 BC), Cicero *does* focus on performance, despite writing over a decade after the Aesopus performance (pre-57 BC) that he recalls in the *Philippics* (44–43 BC). Yet we consistently find that Cicero uses the present habitual and uses features of performance to emphasise the enraged delivery of Atreus' lines (frr. 3, 16, 18) in his moral treatises and demonstrate the wide appeal of his analogy by recalling a performance for the masses (fr. 5). The structural patterns in quotation suggest that in the earlier texts Cicero remembers quotations from a 50s BC performance by Aesopus, but Cicero's specific recollection of the quotations from either text or performance better reflect what he wants to remind his reader of rather than what Cicero remembers himself.

The primary objective of this study was to determine whether Cicero remembers a specific performance of Accius' *Atreus*, or uses performance to improve his readers' recall of the lines. Yet this discussion has highlighted other aspects of memory when considering Cicero's recall of tragedy. First, it showed that at least one of the mnemonic techniques set out in the spurious *Rhetorica ad Herennium* can be found in Cicero's *De Oratore*, which suggests that Cicero used theatrical contexts to make his recollections of tragedy memorable for his readership. Secondly, Cicero's use of *oderint dum metuant* (fr. 5) to disparage Marc Antony leads to the line being dislocated and recalled as a meme in Imperial historiography, only to be commemorated in Seneca's own *Thyestes*.[58] Thus having attempted to recapture Cicero's natural ability to remember a performance of Accius' *Atreus*, this study has uncovered Cicero's artificial memory, or mnemonics, and his incidental establishment of fr. 5 as a meme.

Ultimately, Accius' *Atreus* is not a forgotten drama but survives through the distorted memories of Cicero the advocate, the orator and the philosopher. The

---

58 Sen. *Thy.* 211–15.

tragedy clearly had a strong contemporary relevance in Cicero's time. Cicero's repeated quotations demonstrate that the play *was* angry, energetic, political and *is* now frustratingly fragmentary: "the whole of Accius' *Atreus*" is like that.

Tab. 1: Accius' *Atreus* in Cicero's Texts.

Fragment	Cicero's Quotation
Again Thyestes comes to grapple Atreus, Again he approaches to disturb my peace. More misery, more misfortune must I brew, Wherewith to check and crush his cruel heart **Accius 3 Ribbeck**	*De Or.* 3. 58. 219. For one kind of tone must be taken by anger—shrill, hasty, with short abrupt clauses—Another denotes energy; this is intense, vehement, eager with a sort of impressive urgency: **Accius 3 R follows**
As with frr. 16 and 18 below, attributed to Accius on the basis of Cicero's reference to the title *Atreus* in *De Oratore* and based on the logic that these fragments clearly apply to the feast, which owing to Accius' title *Atreus*, suggest that his play dealt with the same episode as these fragments.	*Tusc. Disp.* 4. 36. 77. You know what follows; the bitterest taunts are hurled from brother to brother in alternate lines, so that it is easy to see they are sons of the Atreus who plots an unheard of penalty for his brother **Accius 3 R follows** (Close to quotation of fr. 16 below) *Nat. D.* 3. 26. 68. Medea was criminal, but also she was perfectly rational. Again, does not the hero plotting the direful banquet for his brother turn the design this way and that in his thoughts? **Accius 3 R follows**
Atreus: Let them hate me so long as they fear me. **Accius 5 Ribbeck**	*Pro Sest.* 48. 102. I could wish that the same poet had not elsewhere used words for evil-minded men to lay hold of: **Accius 5 R follows**
Only Accius is named in *Philippics*, not Ennius. Accius is repeatedly named in *De Officiis*. Fr. 5 is quoted in tandem with a fragment that clearly indicates the feast, suggesting a reference to Accius' *Atreus*, which dealt with the feast, whereas' Ennius' *Thyestes* dealt with Thyestes' exile after the feast.	*De Off.* 1. 28. 97. Now, we say that the poets observe propriety, when every word or action is in accord with each individual character. For example, if Aeacus or Minos said [...] Or "The father is himself his children's tomb," (Accius 14 R) **Accius 5 R follows** that would seem improper, because we are told that they were just men. But when Atreus speaks those lines, they call forth applause; for the sentiment is in keeping with the character.

Fragment	Cicero's Quotation
	Phil. 1. 14. 34. It is glorious to be a citizen dear to the community, to deserve well of the Republic, to be praised and courted and esteemed. But to be feared and hated carries ill-will, execration, weakness, insecurity. Even in the play we see that it was ruinous to the very character who said: **Accius 5 R follows**
[Thyestes:][59] Be watchful always, many snares are set for the good. **Accius 9 Ribbeck** Quoted in sequence with Accius fr. 5, securely attributed above.	*Pro Sest.* 48. 102. These examples are glorious, they are superhuman, they are immortal; they are proclaimed in common talk, are committed to the records of history, are handed down to posterity. It is a difficult task; I do not deny it. There are great risks; I confess it. Most truly has it been said— **Accius 9 R follows**. […] I could wish that the same poet had not elsewhere used words for evil-minded men to lay hold of: Let them hate, so but they fear **(Accius 5 R)**
	Pro Planc. 24. 59. So that he should not think that rather than showing him the way to win honours in the future I have already won his honours for him, I am accustomed to give him the advice (though advice is somewhat beyond him at his present years) which that king who was himself sprung from Jupiter gave to his sons: […] No doubt you recall the rest of the passage. These lines were written by an earnest and gifted poet, whose object in writing them was to kindle the spirit of industry and ambition, not in those young princes who were merely the figments of his imagination, but in us and in our children.
Thyestes: Why, my very brother bids me miserably masticate **Accius 16 Ribbeck**	*De Or.* 3. 58. 217. For one kind of tone must be taken by anger—shrill, hasty, with short abrupt clauses— **followed by Accius 16 R** (Close to quotation of fr. 18 below)
	Tusc. Disp. 4. 36. 77. Which way then is this mass to crash? Hark to Thyestes— **followed by Accius 16 R**

---

[59] Cf. Petrone (2002) 247–9 makes the case that Atreus speaks these lines to warn his sons against a retaliation from Thyestes after the feast, contrary to La Penna (1972) and Ribbeck (1871), who read this as Thyestes warning his son(s) as they return from exile, which subscribes to the Senecan model of Thyestes returning with his exiled son (Tantalus junior).

Fragment	Cicero's Quotation
Attributed to Accius on the basis of Cicero's reference to the title *Atreus* in *De Oratore*.	(Close to quotation of fr. 3 above)
Will no one mark this? Put in chains— **Accius 18 Ribbeck**	*De Or.* 3. 58. 217. and the line you quoted some time ago, Antonius—[...] and almost the whole of *Atreus*.
Attributed to Accius on the basis of Cicero's reference to this title *Atreus* in *De Oratore*.	(Close to quotation of fr. 16 above)
	Tusc. Disp. 4. 25. 55. Again, after the trial is over and done with and I write my speeches out, surely you do not think that I am angry as I write? [...] Surely one does not think Aesopus was ever angry when he played this part or Accius angry when he wrote it?

Bibliography

Abbott, F.F. (1907), "The Theatre as a Factor in Roman Politics under the Republic", *TAPA* 38: 49–56.
Achard, G. (1989), *Rhétorique à Herennius*, Paris.
Adamik, T. (1998), "Basic Problems of the *Ad Herennium*: Author, Date, its Relation to the *De Inventione*", *Acta Ant. Hung.* 38: 267–85.
Auvray-Assayas, C. (1998), "Relectures philosophiques de la tragédie: les citations tragiques dans l'oeuvre de Cicéron", *Pallas* 49: 269–77.
Baldarelli, B. (2004), *Accius und die vortrojanische Pelopidensage*, München.
Calboli, G. (1969), *Rhetorica ad C. Herennium*, Bologna.
Caplan, H. (1954), *[Cicero] Ad. C Herennium: De Ratione Dicendi*, London.
Denard, H. (2009), "Lost Theatre and Performance Traditions in Greece and Italy", in D.M. MacDonald & M. Walton (eds.), *Cambridge Companion to Greek and Roman Theatre*, Cambridge: 136–60.
den Boer, P. (2008), "Loci Memoriae- Lieux de mémoire", in A. Eril & A. Nünnig (eds.), *A Companion to Cultural Memory Studies*, Berlin: 19–27.
Dueck, D. (2009), "Poetic Quotations in Latin Prose Works of Philosophy", *Hermes* 137: 314–34.
Douglas, A.E. (1960), "Causulae in the *Rhetorica ad Herennium* as Evidence of its Date", *The Classical Quarterly* 10 (1): 65–78.
Duffalo, B. (2007), *The Ghosts of the Past: Latin Literature, the Dead and Rome's Transition to a Principate*, Ohio.
Eigler, U. (2000), "Cicero und die römische Tragödie. Eine Strategie zur Legitimation philosophischer Literatur im philosophishen Spätwerk Ciceros", in E. Stärk & G. Vogt-Spira (eds.), *Dramatische Wäldchen. Festschrift für Eckhard Lefèvre zum 65*: 619–36.
Erasmo, M. (2004), *Roman Tragedy: Theatre to Theatricality*, Austin.

Fantham, E. (1982), *Seneca's* Troades, Princeton.
Fantham, E. (2004), *The Roman World of Cicero's* De Oratore, Oxford.
Fantham, E. (2013), *Roman Literary Culture: From Plautus to Macrobius*, Baltimore.
Favorini, A. (2008), *Memory in Play: From Aeschylus to Sam Shephard*, New York.
Geffcken, K.A. (1973), *Comedy in the* Pro Caelio, Leiden.
Gildenhard, I. (2007), *Paideia Romana: Cicero's Tusculan Disputations*, Cambridge.
Goldberg, S.M. (2000), "Cicero and the Work of Tragedy", in G. Manuwald (ed.), *Identität und Alterität in der frührömischen Tragödie*, Würzburg: 49–59.
Goldberg, S.M. (2005), *Constructing Literature in the Roman Republic*, Cambridge.
Gotoff, H.C. (1981), "Cicero's style for relating memorable sayings", *ICS* 6: 294–316.
Hölkeskamp, K.-J. (2014), "In Defense of Concepts, Categories, and Other Abstractions; Remarks on a Theory of Memory (in the Making.)", in K. Galinsky (ed.), *Memoria Romana: Memory in Rome and Rome in Memory*, Ann Arbor: 63–70.
Hunter, A.G. (2010), *Cicero's Art of Quotation: Poetry in the* Philosophica *and* Rhetorica. Diss., University of Cornell.
Kennedy, G. (1972), *The Art of Rhetoric in the Roman World*, Princeton.
Kubik, J. (1887), *De M. Tulli Ciceronis poetarum Latinorum studiis. Dissertationes philologae Vindobonenses*, Leipzig. 1: 239–348.
La Penna, A. (1972), "Atre e Tieste sulle scene romane (il tiranno e l'atteggiamento verso il tiranno)", *Studi classici in onore di Q. Cataudella, Catania* 1: 357–71.
Laidlaw, W.A. (1960), "Cicero and the Stage", *Hermathena* 94: 56–66.
Marx, F. (1894), *Incerti auctoris De ratione dicendi ad C. Herennium libri IV*, Leipzig.
Manuwald, G. (2010), *Roman Drama: A Reader Theatre*, London.
Manuwald, G. (2011), *The Roman Republican Theatre*, Cambridge.
Manuwald, G. (2015), "Editing Roman (Republican) Tragedy: Challenges and Possible Solutions", in G.W.M. Harrison (ed.), *Brill's Companion to Roman Tragedy*, Leiden: 3–24.
Michel A. (1983), "Cicéron et la tragédie: les citations de poètes dans les livres II-IV des Tusculanes", *Helmantica* 34: 443–54.
Morello, R. (2013), "Writer and addressee in Cicero's letters", in C. Steele (ed.), *Cambridge Companion to Cicero*, Cambridge: 196–214.
Petrone, G. (2002). "L'Atreo di Accio e lle passioni del potere", in S. Faller & G. Manuwald (eds.), *Accius und seine Zeit*, Würzburg: 245–53.
Regius, R. (1491), *Vtrum ars rhetorica ad Herennium Ciceroni falso inscribebatur*, Venetiis.
Ribbeck, O. (1871). *Tragicorum Romanorum Fragmenta*, Leipzig.
Salamon, G. (2004). "Les citations dans les Tusculanes: quelques remarques sur les livres 1 et 2", in C. Darbo-Peschanski (ed.), *Le citation dans l'Antiquite: acte du colloque di PARDA Lyon, ENS LSH 6–8 novembre 2002*, Grenoble: 135–46.
Schierl, P. (2015), "Roman Tragedy – Ciceronian Tragedy? Cicero's Influence on Our perception of Republican Tragedy", in G.W.M. Harrison (ed.), *Brill's Companion to Roman Tragedy*, Leiden: 45–63.
Shackleton Bailey, D.R. (1983), "Cicero and Early Latin Poetry", *ICS* 8: 239–49.
Small, J.P. (1997), *Wax Tablets of the Mind: Cognitive Studies of Memory and Literacy in Classical Antiquity*, London.
Spahlinger, L. (2005), *Tulliana simplicitas. Zu Form und Funktion des Zitats in den philosophischen Dialogen Ciceros*, Göttingen.
Victorinus, P. (1553), *Variarum lectionum libri XXV*, Florentiae.

Ward, J.O. (2015), "What the Middle Ages Missed of Cicero, and Why", in W.H.F. Altman (ed.), *Brill's Companion to the Reception of Cicero*, Leiden: 307–26.
White, P. (2010), *Cicero in Letters: Epistolary Relations in the Late Republic*, Oxford.
Wiseman, T.P. (2014), "Popular Memory", in K. Galinsky (ed.), *Memoria Romana: Memory in Rome and Rome in Memory*, Ann Arbor: 43–62.
Winkel, L.C. (1979), "Some Remarks on the Date of *Rhetorica ad Herennium*", *Mnemosyne* 32: 327–32.
Wright, F.W. (1931), *Cicero and the Theatre*, Northampton.
Yates, F. (1966), *The Art of Memory*, London.
Zillinger, W. (1911), *Cicero und die altrömischen Dichter*, Würzburg.
Zwierlein, O. (1983), "Der Schluß der Tragödie 'Atreus' des Accius", *Hermes* 11: 121–5.

Part II: **Collective Memory**

Kate Cook
Memories of Glory: Poetry, Prose, and Commemoration in the *Heraclidae*

Abstract: The early description of the *Heraclidae* as one of the 'political' Euripidean plays has had a substantial impact on its interpretation. Yet the *Heraclidae* does not simply engage in political questions of how to act, either as an individual or as a state. It also raises questions as to how such actions should be commemorated, and who should be involved in their commemoration. Its engagement with a range of discourses for memorialisation, both poetic and prose, brings it into direct dialogue both with the cultural, poetic heritage of tragedy, and with the new genre of the *epitaphios*.

Yet, at the same time, the *Heraclidae* is distinctly different to an *epitaphios*, not least in its inclusion of problematic elements in what is usually a common myth featured in the *epitaphios*. Furthermore, the Heraclidae engages persistently with the language of commemoration and celebration of past deeds – including by incorporating some of the language and themes of the *epitaphios* itself. At the same time, however, the Heraclidae maintains a strongly poetic tone, with both characters and the chorus drawing on poetic discourses of praise and commemoration as much as they do the prose *epitaphios*. As a result, the *Heraclidae* draws not only the *epitaphios* into connection with tragedy, but, via tragedy, draws archaic praise poetry into connection with the *epitaphios*. In so doing, it demonstrates the value of both approaches to commemorating Athens' past glories, and shows how the genre of tragedy can have a particularly valuable memorialising function in contemporary Athens.

The unpopularity among scholars of the *Heraclidae*, along with accusations of its being 'mutilated', has led to this work being somewhat neglected in modern scholarship.[1] Its early inclusion as one of the 'political' plays of Euripides has also shaped much interpretation,[2] and it has most fully been considered in terms of what it says about the city of Athens, her relationships with other Greek states, and the ideals of democracy, particularly in connection with other 'suppliant'

---

[1] I am convinced by Zuntz (1947) that the *Heraclidae* is not missing substantial parts or whole scenes. Arguments on both sides are extensive: see Allan (2001) 35–37.
[2] See particularly Zuntz (1955), but as Mendelsohn (2002) 2 notes, this approach to the *Heraclidae* dates to its recent reception.

dramas.³ Yet there is a further aspect to the *Heraclidae* which existing discussion has not fully acknowledged – partly due to the lack of attention given to the *Heraclidae's* chorus.⁴ The *Heraclidae*, as I shall argue here, does not simply engage in political questions of how to act, either as an individual or as a state. It also raises questions as to how such actions should be commemorated, and who should be involved in their commemoration. Its engagement with a range of discourses for memory and glory, both poetic and prose, brings it into direct dialogue with the cultural, poetic heritage which tragedy developed in classical Athens, and with the new genre of the *epitaphios*.⁵ Yet, at the same time, the *Heraclidae* is distinctly different to an *epitaphios*, not least in its inclusion of problematic elements in what is usually a common myth featured in the *epitaphios*.⁶ As a result, the *Heraclidae* represents tragedy's ability to commemorate Athens' glories more fully than other genres – both in encompassing both poetic and political prose forms of commemoration, but also in the scope of its 'memory' of the deeds portrayed.

As Loraux has shown, the *epitaphios*, a new, state-organised genre for commemorating the war dead in Athens, had grown out of and to some extent superseded older poetic genres for the same purpose.⁷ Archaic poetry had, to some extent, shared the speech's function of commemoration – in providing *kleos*, it could provide an immortal record of an individual's deeds. As Detienne has shown in an influential study, the *kleos* which results from archaic poets speaking praise and blame was considered essential for establishing the "memory" of a warrior, which would ensure that he and his worth to society were not forgotten after death.⁸ Similarly, the *epitaphios* aims at providing a memory of those dead

---

3 e.g. Tzanetou (2012) or Grethlein (2003).
4 Henrichs (1996) is the only recent study of the *Heraclidae* to treat the chorus *qua* chorus at length, and many recent works do not discuss the play's chorus at all.
5 Dating the origin of the *epitaphios* is difficult – see Loraux (1986) 58–61, but given Pericles' apparent claim to be taking part in an already existing tradition in 430 (Thuc. 2.35.1–3), it seems reasonable to assume the speech existed by the time of this play's first performance (usually dated to 430–26 – see Allan (2001) 54–56).
6 Athens' acceptance of the Heraclidae is celebrated widely in Athenian oratory e.g. Lys. 2.11–16, Isoc. 4.54–60, 5.33–4, 10.31, 12.194, Dem. 60.8–9, Plat. *Menex.* 239b. See also Aristotle, *Rhet.* 1396a. Steinbock (2013) 57–58 argues that the orators often draw on this myth (and others) already familiar as *topoi* for celebration in the funeral orations. Grethlein (2003) 381–82 notes the myth's relative unpopularity in tragedy earlier than its taking up by the *epitaphioi*, and suggests that the myth itself became more widely disseminated with its use in these speeches.
7 Loraux (1986) 86–90.
8 Detienne (1996) 45–51. Similarly Nagy (1979) esp. chaps. 6 & 12 has explored epic poetry's ability to convey κλέος ἄφθιτον – a *kleos* that, with its connection to memory, can never perish, and

Memories of Glory: Poetry, Prose, and Commemoration in the *Heraclide* — **73**

in Athens' wars for generations to come.[9] Both tragedy and the *epitaphios* also share a key role in establishing Athenian views of Athens, particularly via the establishment of shared or social memories of Athens' legendary past.[10] Yet the *epitaphios* was substantially different to the poetic praise genres already existing – it commemorated a community rather than individuals, it was somewhat secular in its handling of Athens' more distant past, and it was spoken by an orator appointed by the city.[11] At the same time as the *epitaphios* was emerging as a central Athenian discourse for memorialisation, however, tragedy continued to operate as its poetic counterpart – a poetic performance organised by the city, aimed at a wide audience of the city, and often concerned with the past, so that it regularly enacted 'remembered' myths.

Generally, the two genres coexist separately, not least as a result of their substantial differences. Tragedy is obviously persistently concerned with myth and ritual in a way which the *epitaphios* is not, it is concerned with the fates of individuals and families, and it is often associated with non-Athenian subjects such as Theban families. However, in the *Heraclidae*, a close relationship between *epitaphios* and tragedy is developed. The *Heraclidae*, in dramatising the story of Athens' welcome to the children of Heracles, takes up a myth which was itself a common theme of the funeral speech – one of the mythical instances which could be used in that genre to celebrate Athens' unique qualities as a city. Furthermore, the *Heraclidae* engages persistently with the language of commemoration and celebration of past deeds – including by incorporating some of the language and themes of the *epitaphios* itself. At the same time, however, the *Heraclidae* maintains a strongly poetic tone, with both characters and the chorus drawing on poetic discourses of praise and commemoration as much as they do the prose *epitaphios*.[12] As a result, the *Heraclidae* draws not only the *epitaphios* into connection with tragedy, but, via tragedy, draws archaic praise poetry into connection with the *epitaphios*.[13] In so doing, it demonstrates the value of both approaches to commemorating Athens' past glories, and shows how tragedy, by incorporating both,

---

Segal (1998) 114–15 discusses the same overcoming of forgetfulness by memory associated with *kleos* in the songs of Pindar. For more on the connections between memory and song see Morrison in this volume.
9 Loraux (1986) 26–27.
10 Steinbock (2013) 49–65.
11 Loraux (1986) 86–92.
12 Pozzi (1993) argues for the *Heraclidae* as a rehabilitation of Heracles' *kleos*, but as I shall argue here, the play's concerns with *kleos* and renown are broader in scope.
13 While scholars have discussed the *Heraclidae* in terms of a Euripidean *epitaphios* (Wilkins (1990) 337), particularly as regards its praise of Athens (Butts (1947) 105–6 gives an especially

and by linking both to Athens throughout its performance, can have a particularly valuable memorialising function in contemporary Athens.¹⁴

The importance of memory and the commemoration of deeds to the *Heraclidae* is made clear early on, in the introduction of Iolaus. Iolaus' concern is primarily with *kleos* (glory), the epic and poetic form for remembering heroic deeds. When Iolaus first introduces himself to the chorus, he draws on *kleos* to do so, describing himself by reference to his most famous companion, Heracles, before claiming:

οὐ γὰρ σῶμ' **ἀκήρυκτον** τόδε

For this body does not go unproclaimed! (89)¹⁵

The reference to himself as being regularly 'proclaimed', literally, by a herald, evokes the context of epinician victors, whose names and victories were similarly proclaimed by a herald, and whose proclamation was often then repeated in the epinician celebrations of their victory.¹⁶ Iolaus associates himself with praise and celebration again in his introduction to Demophon, telling him:

πόλει μὲν ἀρκεῖ· καὶ γὰρ οὖν ἐπίφθονον
λίαν ἐπαινεῖν ἐστι, πολλάκις δὲ δὴ
καὐτὸς βαρυνθεὶς οἶδ' ἄγαν αἰνούμενος.

That's enough (said) to the city, for indeed it is hateful to praise too much, and I myself know that I have often been depressed by being praised excessively. (202–4)

The risks of being over-praised are a common trope of epinician poetry, so that Iolaus again associates himself and his past history with one of poetic praise.¹⁷ As with his introduction to the chorus, the praise he invokes here is a feature of his

---

useful list of patriotic readings of the play, an approach which he then supports), few scholars have engaged with the concern for *poetic* memory and memorialisation which the play reveals.

14 An interest in tragedy's potential for memorialisation is recognised as a key feature of Euripidean tragedy by Segal (1993) (esp. 22–4), who sees Euripides as interacting particularly with the poetic tradition of commemoration in his tragedies, but does not address the *Heraclidae* and how it too, as I show here, engages with this potential function of tragedy.

15 The texts used for the Greek is from the Loeb edition. Translations are my own.

16 e.g. Pindar *Pyth.* 1.30–3. Pindar's use of the herald's announcement has been most fully explored by Nash (1990). Mendelsohn (2002) 69 notes the epinician echoes here.

17 e.g. Pindar *Pyth.* 1.41–5, 8.32 & 10.1–4, *Nem.* 7.66–7, 7.71–5 & 10.20, *Ol.* 2.95–6, etc. The same concern about the risks of over-praising is shown in Thucydides' account of Pericles' funeral oration: 2.35.2.

past experiences, reflecting the earlier commemoration of his deeds with Heracles that has, by implication, taken place, and enabling him to claim his current status through that commemoration.[18] At the same time, in a pattern which will be particularly noticeable in the choral odes, Iolaus associates the city of Athens too with a history of poetic praise, by applying this epinician trope of excessive praise to the city as well as himself.

Similarly, Iolaus associates Demophon at length with poetic praise as a way of commemorating his deeds, once Demophon has agreed to protect the children of Heracles and rejected the Argive herald's attempt to assault them. There are epic echoes in the language Iolaus uses to praise Demophon's nobility via praising generally the 'finest honour' a man can have (297–8),[19] and Iolaus follows these with a lengthy promise of further praise for Demophon:

ἐγὼ δὲ καὶ ζῶν <εὐγενῆ σ' οὐ παύσομαι
πᾶσιν προφαίνων,> καὶ θανών, ὅταν θάνω,
πολλῷ σ' ἐπαίνῳ Θησέως ἐστὼς πέλας
ὑψηλὸν ἀρῶ καὶ τέκνοισιν ἤρεσας
τοῖς Ἡρακλείοις, **εὐκλεὴς** δ' ἂν' Ἑλλάδα
σῴζεις πατρῴαν δόξαν, ἐξ ἐσθλῶν δὲ φὺς
οὐδὲν κακίων τυγχάνεις γεγὼς πατρός,
παύρων μετ' ἄλλων· ἕνα γὰρ ἐν πολλοῖς ἴσως
εὕροις ἂν ὅστις ἐστὶ μὴ χείρων πατρός.

So I, while I am alive, <will not stop proclaiming your nobility to all>,[20] and when I die and am among the dead, I shall stand by Theseus and exalt you with praise, and gladden him with this story: how you took in Heracles' children from kindness, and how now you enjoy excellent *kleos* throughout all Hellas, and preserve your father's reputation, and how while you are born of noble stock, you turn out to be not less noble than your father – something

---

18 Iolaus' age in this play is unexpected – usually he is Heracles' nephew, so is of the same generation as Hyllus. In Pindar (*Nem.* 3.36–7) he is present with Heracles at the first sack of Troy, and is often associated with youth and athletics, including games (Paus. 5.17.11 & 9.23.1, Pind. *Ol.* 9.98–9, Diod. 4.24.4). The innovation of making Iolaus older not only allows for the unusual rejuvenation story (Allan (2001) 27–28), it also associates him with a past 'heroic age' which (perhaps) returns with his rejuvenation (Mendelsohn (2002) 65. Fitton (1961) 460 argues for the play's 'reversion' to that heroic age). As a result, however, it also makes commemoration more significant – Iolaus cannot rely on his current strength (23, 632, 636, and the chorus at 75), so must rely on the *past* praise he has received to help convince the chorus and Demophon of his worthiness to receive help.
19 For the epic echoes here see further Mendelsohn (2002) 72–73.
20 Kovacs' (1995) supplement is attractive for the purposes of this argument, but not required, as Iolaus' following speech continues along very similar lines.

said of few others, for only one out of many men can be found who is equal & not worse than his father. (320–28)

The praise Iolaus gives Demophon here has to some extent a motivating force – Iolaus wishes to further encourage Demophon's support of his cause.[21] Again Iolaus focuses on the probability of Demophon being widely praised and remembered, by the emphasis on his reputation across Greece. Simultaneously, the promise that Iolaus will talk of Demophon's reputation in the underworld suggests a memory of Demophon's deeds which extends even beyond death. Once again it is a term connected specifically to poetic praise and *kleos*, εὐκλεὴς, which describes that memory. Further epic praise tropes are found in the following lines; Iolaus promises to praise Demophon to his father in death,[22] and congratulates Demophon on living up to his father's example, an epic trope.[23] The final lines of his comment neatly recall Athena's words to Telemachus at the start of the *Odyssey*,[24] and the promise to praise Demophon to the dead Theseus similarly recalls the conversations between Achilles, Agamemnon and Odysseus about their sons, and their desire to hear them praised.[25] As such, Iolaus promises Demophon the kind of praise in return for his help which leads to one having 'good *kleos*', that is, praise established via poetry, and then explicitly draws on existing epic parallels as part of enacting that poetic praise. Demophon's response to this praise shows that Iolaus is not alone in valuing praise as a method of memorialising the deeds committed by individuals – indeed he explicitly recognises the value of being remembered (μνημονεύσεται, 335) in return for his 'favour' to the Heraclidae. As the situation then worsens, Iolaus even expresses his understanding of Demophon's refusal to sacrifice an Athenian girl in terms of praise, despite

---

[21] Both the chorus (329–332) and Demophon (333–5) recognise this aspect, and respond to it, as they both reaffirm the correctness of Demophon's choice to support the suppliants. It is also notable that Iolaus' initial speeches to Demophon are unusually convincing – Carter (2013) 49–50 notes the rarity of successful persuasion via an *agon*.

[22] That Demophon is king and Theseus dead (thus enabling this conversation) appears to be a Euripidean innovation. Usually the *Heraclidae* are welcomed to Athens by Theseus (Grethlein (2003) 381–82). See also Wilkins (1990) 332–33 on the educative role of the exemplar fathers this leads to.

[23] e.g *Il.* 4.364–418, 6.206–11.

[24] 2.276–7.

[25] *Od.* 11.457–64, 11.492–3, 11.504–541. Achilles' 'joyful' reaction to Odysseus' extensive praise of Neoptolemus in particular indicates what sort of reward Iolaus' promise may be to both Demophon and Theseus, and implies a similar scene which sets Iolaus and Theseus in parallel with the two paramount epic heroes, Odysseus and Achilles. As Avery (1971) 547 notes, this scene also draws connections between Theseus, Heracles, and their respective children.

the fact that his own language demonstrates the potential difficulty of such a description:

> ... αἰνέσαι δ' ἔχω
> **καὶ** τἀνθάδ·'
>
> I **even** have words of praise for this event here... (436–7)

It is in this context that Macaria's sacrifice then takes place.²⁶ Both Demophon and Iolaus have demonstrated a shared agreement with the importance of praise as a motivator for fine deeds, and the memory of that praise, in the form of a good reputation, as a reward for their accomplishments. Iolaus, in particular, has also connected that praise persistently with its poetic vehicles, epic and epinician, both older forms of praise poetry by the time of the tragedy's performance. Macaria's sacrifice is similarly connected with rewards of praise for her behaviour – she herself describes it as dying εὐκλεῶς (534), i.e. with 'good *kleos*', and uses a line reminiscent of epic poetry to describe herself as 'worthy' of her father (563),²⁷ just as Demophon's reputation is associated with his father's via epic echoes. Iolaus further associates Macaria's death with the strongly epic praise term ἄριστος (554).²⁸ Macaria also explicitly connects her deed to the need for appropriate memorialisation, when she requires her brothers to 'remember' the correct burial, with all honours, which should be due to her (588–9). The chorus further elaborate the connection between praise and the memory of Macaria's sacrifice, when they promise Iolaus,

> οὐδ **ἀκλεής** νιν
> δόξα πρὸς ἀνθρώπων ὑποδέξεται·
>
> She will receive a not un-glorious reputation among men. (623–4)

The chorus' lyric comment here means that their promise of *kleos*, poetic praise, for Macaria is in fact enacted by their singing; they assure Iolaus that her reputation will be made glorious in song, just as they themselves sing about her glory.

---

26 She is simply παρθένος in Euripides' text – Macaria is a name attached to this character later. The character herself is likely a Euripidean invention (along with the rest of Heracles' daughters). See further Wilkins (1993) xvi, xix–xx, and Mendelsohn (2002) esp. 17–20.
27 See similar language at *Il.* 14.113.
28 On the importance of the judgement ἄριστος to epic praise discourses, see especially Nagy (1979).

It is therefore a particularly forceful comment on the potential of poetry to memorialise fine deeds; both Iolaus and, more importantly, the audience, can see not only the promise of memorialisation but the fulfilment of that promise enacted before them.

This vocabulary of praise poetry does not cease after the sacrifice of Macaria; it is reiterated in the description of Iolaus' victory and miraculous youth. The messenger describing the event to Alcmene calls him (and the rest of the Heraclids) "εὐκλεεῖς" (792), making use of the same, *kleos*-associated term as that used by Macaria to celebrate her sacrifice. At the point of his youthful transformation, Iolaus is described by the messenger as κλεινός (859), a further term from the same root as *kleos*,[29] and the monument to victory they build is described as "καλλίνικον" (937) – a term used frequently in Pindar's epinician, and associated with Heracles as an epithet in praise poetry and tragedy.[30] Here this poetic language is directly associated with a further form of memorialisation, in the building of a monument to remain after the victory.[31] Iolaus is therefore persistently associated with the language of *kleos* and the language of praise poetry, both in the memory of his earlier deeds, and in the active description and memorialisation of the deeds he undertakes over the course of the play.

Thus throughout the *Heraclidae* multiple characters, including Demophon, Macaria, messengers, and particularly Iolaus, draw on the language of praise po-

---

29 κλεινός is not uncommon in tragedy, particularly in Euripides – indeed most of its extant classical uses are tragic. It also features in Bacchylides' *epinicia*, as at 2.6, 5.14 & 182, and 11.78.
30 Swift (2010) 132–3 with notes. καλλίνικος also occurs as a cult title for Heracles – see Sourvinou-Inwood (2003) 363; Stafford (2012) 90, 176, so that the term here strengthens the connection with the divine Heracles created by the rejuvenation of Iolaus. Its use in tragedy is rare, especially outside of Euripidean tragedy.
31 The potential for complex interactions between monuments or inscriptions and lyric poetry as methods of memorialisation is discussed well in Fearn (2013). Athanassaki (2016) 23 similarly notes the Pindaric competition between monuments and poetry as a form of memorialisation. Given the potential for competition between archaic lyric poetry and stone monuments as a form of commemoration, Euripides' combination of the poetic term with the material memorial being built by Iolaus and Demophon seems to allow tragedy to encompass *both* types of memorial – as it similarly encompasses both poetry and the *epitaphios* (see further below). Torrance (2013) 172–74 notes a similar use of writing in Euripides' *Suppliants*, in the inscription of the Argive-Athenian oath, as being part of Euripides' engagement with myth-making and the authoritative voice of tragedy, and see also n. 122 on the connection between poetry, writing and memorialisation in Euripides. Especially given the many similarities between the *Suppliants* and the *Heraclidae*, it is not unreasonable to see a similar type of authority being attached to tragedy in the *Heraclidae* in the reference to the monument here.

etry to celebrate their own deeds, to commemorate those deeds which have already happened, or to promise commemoration of those undertaken during the play. However, the associations between poetic praise and memory are not limited to the concerns of individual characters. The *Heraclidae* also draws a persistent association between the city of Athens itself, and the significance of poetic praise for memorialising good deeds. This association is particularly, although not exclusively, emphasised by the chorus of the *Heraclidae*. Two aspects of the chorus make this connection between Athens and poetic memory most effective. The first is the chorus' own connection with Athens – as a group of Athenian citizens, they demonstrate a persistent relationship with the city throughout their odes.[32] At the same time, the chorus repeatedly emphasise their role *as* chorus, and in so doing also frequently associate the city of Athens with such choral performances.

The chorus' very identity as men of Marathon connects them closely to the deme in which the tragedy is set, and to Athens itself.[33] The choice of local men for the chorus also presents a sharp contrast with the other 'political play' of Euripides, the *Suppliant Women*, in which the eponymous Argive women make up the main chorus. In that play, the chorus' foreign nature sets them at odds with Theseus on multiple occasions, whereas in the *Heraclidae*, both the chorus and the king, Demophon, can represent the 'Athenian' viewpoint. This connection between Athens and the chorus is not solely a matter of their identity, however, as the chorus frequently demonstrate the importance of their connection to the city in their speech. They are originally introduced on to the stage in response to Iolaus' cry to "τὰς Ἀθήνας δαρὸν οἰκοῦντες χρόνον" 'inhabitants of Athens since long ago' (69), such that their association with Athens is not only immediately established, but strengthened by the historic aspect Iolaus gives to his description. They defend the land's sovereignty in their insistence that the Argive herald should speak to its ruler before attempting to abduct Iolaus and the Heraclidae (111–3), and then go on to explain the situation to Demophon in such a way as to

---

32 Zuntz (1955) 38 sees the chorus as 'representative of that Athens which takes pity on the unfortunate and successfully upholds the rule of *nomos*'. Similarly Avery (1971) 550 claims that as citizens of Athens the chorus represent 'the whole of Athens', and Fitton (1961) 450 claims that they represent the 'ordinary moral consciousness of the 'folk'' and help to strengthen the association between audience and Athens. It is not simply the identity of the chorus which build this connection, however, but also the language of their odes (below).

33 Similarly, the use of men of Colonus for the chorus of Sophocles' *Oedipus at Colonus* has the effect of strengthening the connection between the setting, the Athenian audience, and the action of the play. Wilkins (1990) 330 argues for a religious significance to the setting of Marathon, suggesting a further similarity with the *Oedipus at Colonus*.

establish cordial, respectful relationships between the king of Athens and themselves (120–29).³⁴ Following the acceptance of Iolaus and the Heraclidae, the chorus further associate themselves with Athens, to the point of representing themselves as able to voice the land's "desire" to 'side with justice and help the weak' (ἀεί ποθ' ἥδε γαῖα τοῖς ἀμηχάνοις / σὺν τῷ δικαίῳ βούλεται προσωφελεῖν, 329–30). This particular formulation is a common trope of Athenian self-presentation and self-praise, often found in the funeral oration itself.³⁵ As a result, the chorus not only associate themselves with the mythical Athens of the play, but also with the contemporary Athens in which the play is being performed, through their use of contemporary political rhetoric. When Athens' rescue of the suppliants is thrown into doubt by the news of the necessary sacrifice, the chorus continue to demonstrate a strong association between themselves and the city by protesting against Iolaus' potential reproach of Athens (461), asking him not to say that "ξένους προυδώκαμεν" – '**we** betrayed strangers' (463). In the final scenes of the play, they again represent the Athenian view to Alcmene by advising her not to kill Eurystheus (1018–9).³⁶

The chorus' association with Athens is further strengthened in the choral odes, and it is here that the chorus also begins to engage in self-referential speech which simultaneously associates Athens with choral performance. In the ode immediately following Demophon's exit to prepare for war with Argos, the chorus swear that they, as Athens, will not be daunted by the herald's boasting (353–356), and talk with confidence of Athens' strength with which she will resist Argos (362–380). At the same time, they describe Athens as "καλλιχόροις" (359) – 'with beautiful dancing grounds' – drawing a link between Athens and choral performances.³⁷ Similarly, in their ode to Athena before the battle, the chorus remind her that,

... οὐδὲ λά-
θει μηνῶν φθινὰς ἁμέρα
νέων τ' ἀοιδαὶ **χορῶν** τε μολπαί.

---

34 The relative equality of status between this chorus and Demophon is demonstrated in their willingness to instruct and reprove him (271, 273), and represents a further difference between the choruses of *Heraclidae* and *Suppliants*.
35 Isoc. 14.1 represents the Plataeans as reflecting precisely this self-image, and in 4.57 connects this kind of protection with Athens as 'leader'. See Steinbock (2013) 54, Tzanetou (2012) 22–23 on this self-presentation in relation to suppliants.
36 Their resistance here is rather limited – such that some scholars have suggested that this is meant to throw doubt on the praise of Athens otherwise found in the play – e.g. Burian (1977) 19–20.
37 This is also a Homeric epithet – see Henrichs (1996) 51.

ἀνεμόεντι δ' ἐπ' ὄχθῳ
ὀλολύγματα παννυχίοις ὑπὸ παρ-
θένων ἰαχεῖ ποδῶν κρότοισιν.

... Nor do we forget the songs of young men, or the day of the waning moon, or the dances of choruses. And on the windy hill loud shouts of joy sound all night long accompanying the beat of maiden feet. (778–83)

Once again, the chorus draw strong associations between multiple aspects of the city and choral performance. The city's patron goddess and protector, Athena, is associated with the performances as their recipients, and the chorus simultaneously recall the citizens' role in performing dances and choral song in her honour. These lines also recall the Panathenaea, a central Athenian religious celebration, which would have particular resonance for the audience in associating contemporary Athens with the mythical Athens of the world of the play which the chorus describes.[38] The mention of both young men and young women in this context widens the range of citizenry associated with these performances, encompassing a greater selection of Athens' population. The specifically choral vocabulary further has the effect of making the description somewhat self-referential, in that the chorus refer *in* a choral performance *to* choral performance.[39] This self-referential aspect to the chorus' comments is then further strengthened in their final ode, where the chorus do not simply discuss choral performances, but associate *themselves* specifically with choral performance:

ἐμοὶ **χορὸς** μὲν ἡδὺ καὶ
λίγεια λωτοῦ χάρις ἀμφὶ δαῖτα·

(Dancing in) the chorus is sweet to me, and so is the delightful high voice of the flute at feasts. (892–3)

As the ode goes on, they again draw strong connections between themselves, now irrevocably associated with choral performance, and the city, which they address directly at 901, and continue to praise and advise (902–9). They also make further reference to Athena in celebrating her connection with Heracles, and the connection between her people, and his children (919–27).

---

38 Henrichs (1996) 52–53.
39 The term 'choral self-referentiality' comes from the essential study of Henrichs (1994). As he notes (58), its occurrence in tragedy is relatively rare, and so its presence should demand particular attention.

As a result, two unusual aspects of the *Heraclidae's* chorus become clear: their persistent close association with Athens, and their self-referential discussion of choral performance. In their combination of these elements, they also draw a close connection between Athens (including her patron goddess Athena), and choral performance. Through the use of self-referentiality to refer to their own ongoing, present, choral performance, and through the allusion to contemporary events such as the Panathenaea, the chorus simultaneously draws the contemporary Athens of the audience into the web of connections, rather than limiting their associations to the mythical Athens present in the internal world and time of the play. Yet as noted above, this self-referential, very Athenian chorus takes a key role in celebrating and commemorating the sacrifice undertaken by Macaria, and connect themselves to the discourse which draws heavily on archaic praise poetry to participate in this kind of commemoration. In so doing, they demonstrate the ability of such choral performances to have a memorialising, celebratory function.

Yet at the same time, the *Heraclidae* engages fully with the new genre of praise speech which had replaced poetic praise in Athenian discourse – the *epitaphios*.[40] The dramatisation of the return of Heracles' children is itself already an engagement with the material of the *epitaphios*, but there are further significant echoes in the language of the characters and chorus. Demophon's and Iolaus' emphasis on Athens as a *free* city, and the connection between this freedom and their obligation to help the suppliants (198, 244–5) is a popular topic of rhetoric celebrating Athens, including the *epitaphios*.[41] Similarly, Macaria's description of her own sacrifice not only makes linguistic reference to praise poetry, but she also draws on the prose genre to describe her actions and its consequences. Her original promise to sacrifice herself is given as a promise literally to *stand by* the sacrifice, "παρίστασθαι σφαγῇ". Yet the language here also evokes the promise to 'hold the line' phrased in precisely the same way by contemporary speakers to describe hoplite warfare.[42] Her appeals to the nobility of her father as motivating

---

[40] n. 6 above.
[41] e.g. Lysias 2.18, Thuc. 2.37.2. On freedom in this play Tzanetou (2012) 76–80, and for its use in the *epitaphios* Loraux (1986) 248–50. Burnett (1976) 21 convincingly argues that the action of the play ensures this freedom, making it more than simply a claimed virtue.
[42] On the hoplite echoes of this phrase see further Mendelsohn (2002) 96–98, Tzanetou (2012) 94. Grethlein (2003) 391 also notes the traces of the term 'hoplite', unusual in tragedy, found in this play.

her actions (510–11, 513), as well as having epic echoes, echo the connections between Athenians and their ancestors celebrated in the funeral orations.⁴³

An additional connection is built in the *Heraclidae* between the *epitaphios*, praise poetry and choral performance in Athens, through the shared praise for the city itself found in both genres. As Loraux has noted, a key aspect of the *epitaphios* was not simply its praise for the (communal) dead, but also its function in praising the city of Athens.⁴⁴ The poetic praise and performances in the *Heraclidae* both by individual characters and by the chorus frequently diverge from praise of individuals into praise of Athens. Iolaus describes Athens as "κλεινῶν" in his prologue speech, so that the city is associated with his language of praise poetry as soon as it is introduced. Similarly, he attempts to praise Athens by favourable comparison with other cities where the suppliants have not been protected (191–94), and draws on the same epinician trope of avoiding excess praise in praising Athens as he uses to identify himself (202–3). In the same way, when Iolaus celebrates Demophon's acceptance of the suppliants, he connects this to praise of Athens, claiming that they are "ἄξιοι δ' ὑμῖν σέβειν" ('worthy of your reverence/praise', 315).⁴⁵ The chorus similarly evoke Athens' "ἀρετᾷ" ('excellence', 776) as a reason why Athena should protect the city in the new war, and praise their association with justice once the war is won (901–8). Furthermore, much of their connection between Athens and choral performance, as discussed above, takes the form of praise – Athens is associated, for example, with *beautiful dancing-grounds* in the term "καλλιχόροις" (359). As a result, the *Heraclidae* can be seen to join the *epitaphios* in its function not only of commemorating the rescue of the suppliants, and those who sacrifice themselves for the city (in this case Macaria), but also in its direct praise *for* Athens, and thus the commemoration of Athens' own glory.⁴⁶

---

43 cf. Lys. 2.3–19 & 20–66, Dem. 60.3–11 & 27–31, Plat. *Menexenus* 237b3–c5. Ziolkowski (1981) 94 n. 11 argues for a similar passage in Gorgias' oration.
44 Loraux (1986) 26–27.
45 The usual translation for σέβω is 'revere' or 'respect', but it is connected to a specific idea of praising someone in tragedy when the chorus of the *Agamemnon* use it in their address to him on his return (784–6) – and specifically, invoke the epinician idea of not over-praising in this address, with language of 'overshooting', drawing similarities with Pindar *N*. 6.26–8, or *Ol*. 2.83, 89–90. The use of the term in this context, in which Iolaus immediately follows with his promise to 'praise' Demophon to Theseus, therefore has similar connotations of praise rather than simply respect.
46 In this regard, while a description of the *Heraclidae* as a 'panegyric' may be somewhat oversimplified, it can be seen that it is not entirely unreasonable.

Thus the *Heraclidae* takes up and makes use of the language of two types of commemoration in its depiction of Macaria's sacrifice and the events of the play. It exploits the praise poetry of the archaic world, both epic and epinician, associated with the commemoration of aristocratic or 'heroic' figures, and incorporates the new form of praise and commemoration most strongly connected to the city of Athens, the *epitaphios*.[47] It is also significant to note here that, as Rehm has shown, the *Heraclidae* is staged with the young boys, the children of Heracles, on stage throughout the play,[48] so that all of this commemoration takes place in a doubly public space – the internal audience of the boys, as well as the external Athenian audience, constantly witness the celebration and commemoration both of past deeds and those deeds occurring over the course of the play. As a result, the audience(s) are invited to witness both the poetic and *epitaphios* traditions as working together to memorialise both the glorious deeds of Athens, and the glory of Athens herself, throughout the play.

The question of how best to commemorate the dead, and the role of the *epitaphios* in remembering the suppliant myths, is not one which Euripides concluded in the *Heraclidae*.[49] In his *Suppliant Women*, a later play,[50] the issue is re-imagined in the conflict between the mourning, lamenting mothers of the chorus and the state-sanctioned speeches of praise which Adrastus gives at Theseus' request.[51] In that play, the older poetic forms are made problematic, both in the uncontrollable impression of female grief and lament given, and in the problematic

---

[47] Tragedy's allusion to and manipulation of epinician poetry is not infrequent (see further Swift (2010) 104–18 and Carey (2012)), nor is its use of epic (Garner (1990) on direct allusions; or Herington (1985) 133–36) – but the combination of both of these genres and the rhetoric and functions of the prose *epitaphios* is the striking feature here.

[48] Rehm (1988) 304.

[49] Given Euripides' seeming interest in the topic of praise & commemoration, it is tempting to find further demonstration of this interest in the writing of an epinician for Alcibiades, although the attribution of this poem to Euripides is not uncontested. See further Bowra (1960), or Gribble (2012) 65 and n. 93, who is more sceptical about the attribution. Even if Euripides wrote no such poem, the later connection between him and this type of praise-poetry does perhaps suggest some recognition of the interest in such questions which his 'political' plays show.

[50] The *Suppliant Women* was first performed in 423 BC, putting it most likely a few years after the *Heraclidae*.

[51] Loraux (1986) 156–58 demonstrates how, despite its individual focus, the speech of Adrastus about the Seven can still be read as an *epitaphios*. Foley (2001) 36–44 represents Theseus' and Adrastus' commemoration of the dead as a replacement of the (archaic) female lament with this political speech. See similarly Vinh (2011) 331–32.

attempts made by Evadne to re-purpose poetic praise for her own glory, especially with her suicide.⁵² In the *Heraclidae*, however, the mediation between genres was still possible, and in many ways is shown to be positive. Within the world of the play, both those who hold to the 'traditional' approach to praise and praiseworthy deeds and the proponents of the *epitaphios* find success. Iolaus' memory for *kleos* and valuing of its ability to identify a man can be seen as vindicated in his rejuvenation – in which the enduring memory of his earlier deeds, associated by him with their commemoration in praise poetry, becomes 'live' once more, and even leads to the committing of further heroic actions in his capture of Eurystheus.⁵³ Similarly, Macaria's sacrifice, which marries both the hoplite, self-sacrificing rhetoric of the *epitaphios* and the poetic praise of the chorus, contributes directly to Athens' victory in her war against the Argives.⁵⁴ Tragedy, with its ability to marry democratic contemporary ideas and older poetic genres can be seen therefore as combining both the new genres of praise and commemoration and the old, in a format which demonstrated the most successful way of commemorating the glorious myths of Athens for its citizens. The older poetic forms are here not forgotten, ignored, or problematised, but instead successfully reincorporated into this contemporary Athenian genre, to work alongside it. Indeed the success of this tragic reincorporation may even be seen in the later reception of Euripidean tragedy and its relationship with the *epitaphios*. In the fourth century, as Hanink has shown, the assimilation between *epitaphios* and Euripidean tragedy is treated as almost complete by Lycurgus and many of his contemporaries, such that Euripidean tragedy is seen as working alongside the *epitaphios* to commemorate the Athens' glories for its citizens.⁵⁵

---

52 Mendelsohn (2002) 197–218 is particularly interesting on the problems of Evadne's glory-seeking suicide, and the praise vocabulary she uses of it.
53 Daneš (2015) 370–71 argues that this is part of a broader pattern in the play showing that Iolaus' values are demonstrated to be right by the action.
54 Wilkins (1990) 185–90 claims that, despite the problematic nature of human sacrifice for its Greek audience, Macaria's sacrifice is not meant to be seen as problematic, partly due to its close connections to the patriotic rhetoric of Athens and to existing rituals for other self-sacrificing heroines. Conversely, Henrichs (2000) 184–86 argues that the close combination of 'normal' ritual language around animal sacrifice and the resulting *human* sacrifice is a problematic aberration.
55 Hanink (2014) 37–40. Hanink particularly connects the *Erectheus* with the funeral oration as a celebration of Athenian glory, suggesting that this may be a third of Euripides' plays to explore these themes.

At the same time, however, the *Heraclidae* raises the question not just of *how* Athens' glories should be commemorated, but also *which* glories should be commemorated – or, more specifically, which content is or is not appropriate for celebration. In their celebration of Macaria's sacrifice, the chorus begins to enact the commemoration which they promise. For an Athenian audience, this episode therefore becomes part of their city's 'remembered' mythical history, celebrated here before their eyes.[56] Yet this episode may not have been a part of Athens' 'history' before Euripides' play.[57] Similarly, Alcmene's final action of the play, killing Eurystheus, seems to have been attributed to Iolaus or Hyllus in the earlier tradition, making this either an innovation of Euripides, or, if it reflects a less common tradition for Eurystheus' death, the deliberate selection of a more problematic facet of the myth for dramatisation.[58] The *Heraclidae* therefore moves beyond the *epitaphios* in completeness, by including problematic aspects in its version of the myth along with the glorious, and thus ensuring that both are remembered.[59] This completeness may also be aimed at demonstrating some of the problematic results that may come from the attitudes espoused in the early parts of the play, and, if these are connected to Athenian values and ideals, the problems or extremes that may result from these.[60]

Whether or not the *Heraclidae* has such a strong message about Athenian ideology, however, it is clear that in this "political" play Euripides engages with not simply the ideas of democracy, but the language for celebrating and remembering them. In combining poetic commemoration with state prose commemoration, Euripides' play argues for the ability of tragedy as a genre to transcend them, and provide a fuller, more successful account than either alone. As such, the *Heraclidae* demonstrates tragedy's capacity to be a state genre of commemoration, associated fully with Athens, just as the *epitaphios* was.

---

[56] In the process Macaria's sacrifice joins a collection of other famous examples of mythical girls sacrificing themselves for Athens, some of which were also commemorated in tragedy – such as the daughters of Erectheus (Eur. *Erech.*). Other examples include Aglauros, and possibly the daughters of Leos (see further Larson (1995) 102–3).
[57] Wilkins (1993) xvi, xix–xx, and Mendelsohn (2002) esp. 17–20.
[58] It is likely that this is a Euripidean invention (Allan (2001) 28–29), and is possibly even marked in Euripides' language as such – see further McDermott (1991) 128–29. Wilkins (1993) xvi however suggests that Euripides may be drawing on Aeschylus or other sources for this myth.
[59] Loraux (1986) 271 argues similarly in relation to the *Supp.* that, as Euripides includes additional details of democracy in the speeches, not usually found in an *epitaphios*, tragedy provides a more 'faithful' representation of democracy.
[60] Burian (1977) 21 suggests that the *Heraclidae* is designed to set up and then undermine an ideology.

Bibliography

Allan, W. (2001), *Euripides: The Children of Heracles* (1 edition), Warminster.
Athanassaki, L. (2016), "Political and Dramatic Perspectives on Archaic Sculptures: Bacchylides' Fourth Dithyramb (Ode 18) and the Treasury of the Athenians in Delphi", in V. Cazzato & A. Lardinois (eds.), *The Look of Lyric: Greek Song and the Visual* (Studies in Archaic and Classical Greek Song, vol. 1), Leiden/Boston: 16–49.
Avery, H.C. (1971), "Euripides' *Heracleidai*", *AJP* 92: 539–65.
Bowra, C.M. (1960), "Euripides' Epinician for Alcibiades", *Historia* 9: 68–79.
Burian, P. (1977), "Euripides' *Heraclidae*: An Interpretation", *CPh* 72: 1–21.
Burnett, A. (1976), "Tribe and City, Custom and Decree in *Children of Heracles*", *CP* 71: 4–26.
Butts, H.R. (1947), *The Glorification of Athens in Greek Drama*, Iowa.
Carey, C. (2012), "The Victory Ode in the Theatre", *BICS* 55: 17–36.
Carter, D.M. (2013), "Reported Assembly Scenes in Greek Tragedy", *ICS* 38: 23–63.
Daneš, J. (2015), "AMHXANIA IN EURIPIDES' *HERACLIDAE*", *CQ* 65: 366–71.
Detienne, M. (1996), *The masters of truth in archaic Greece*, tr. J. Lloyd (with introduction by Pierre Vidal-Naquet), Cambridge, MA.
Fearn, D. (2013), "*Kleos* versus stone? Lyric poetry and contexts for memorialization", in P. Liddel & P. Low (eds.), *Inscriptions and their uses in Greek and Latin literature.* (Oxford studies in ancient documents), Oxford/New York: 231–53.
Fitton, J.W. (1961), "The Suppliant women and the *Herakleidai* of Euripides", *Hermes* LXXXIX, 430–61.
Foley, H.P. (2001), *Female acts in Greek tragedy*, Princeton, N.J.
Garner, R. (1990), *From Homer to tragedy: the art of allusion in Greek poetry*, London.
Grethlein, J. (2003), *Asyl und Athen: die Konstruktion kollektiver Identität in der griechischen Tragödie* (M & P Schriftenreihe für Wissenschaft und Forschung 21), Stuttgart.
Gribble, D. (2012) "Alcibiades at the Olympics: Performance, Politics and Civic Ideology", *CQ* 62: 45–71.
Hanink, J. (2014) *Lycurgan Athens and the Making of Classical Tragedy*, Cambridge Classical Studies, Cambridge.
Henrichs, A. (1994) "'Why should I dance?': choral self-referentiality in Greek tragedy", *Arion* 3: 56–111.
Henrichs, A. (1996) "Dancing in Athens, dancing on Delos: some patterns of choral projection in Euripides", *Philologus* 140: 48–62.
Henrichs, A. (2000), "Drama and Dromena: Bloodshed, Violence, and Sacrificial Metaphor in Euripides", *HSCP* 100: 173–88.
Herington, J. (1985), *Poetry into drama. Early tragedy and the Greek poetic tradition*, Berkeley.
Larson, J. (1995), *Greek Heroine Cults*, Madison.
Loraux, N. (1986), *The invention of Athens. The funeral oration in the classical city*, Cambridge, MA.
McDermott, E.A. (1991), "Double Meaning and Mythic Novelty in Euripides' Plays", *TAPA* 121: 123–32.
Mendelsohn, D.A. (2002), *Gender and the city in Euripides' political plays*, Oxford.
Nagy, G. (1979), *The best of the Achaeans: concepts of the hero in archaic Greek poetry*, Baltimore/London.
Nash, L.L. (1990), *The Aggelia in Pindar*, New York.

Pozzi, D.C. (1993), "Hero and antagonist in the last scene of Euripides' *Heraclidae*", *Helios* 20: 29–41.
Rehm, R. (1988), "The Staging of Suppliant Plays", *GRBS* 29: 263–307.
Segal, C. (1993), *Euripides and the poetics of sorrow: art, gender, and commemoration in Alcestis, Hippolytus, and Hecuba*, Durham, N.C.
Segal, C. (1998), *Aglaia*, Lanham, Md.
Steinbock, B. (2013), *Social Memory in Athenian Public Discourse: Uses and Meanings of the Past*, Ann Arbor.
Swift, L. (2010), *The hidden chorus: echoes of genre in tragic lyric*, Oxford.
Torrance, I. (2013), *Metapoetry in Euripides*, Oxford/New York.
Tzanetou, A. (2012), *City of suppliants: tragedy and the Athenian empire*, Austin.
Vinh, G. (2011), "Athens in Euripides' Suppliants: ritual, politics, and theatre", in D.M. Carter (ed.), *Why Athens? A Reappraisal of Tragic Politics*, Oxford: 325–44.
Wilkins, J. (1990a), "The state and the individual: Euripides' plays of voluntary self-sacrifice", in A. Powell (ed.), *Euripides, women and sexuality*, London: 177–94.
Wilkins, J. (1990b), "The Young of Athens: Religion and Society in *Herakleidai* of Euripides", *CQ* 40: 329–39.
Wilkins, J. (1993), *Heraclidae*, Oxford.
Ziolkowski, J.E. (1981), *Thucydides and the Tradition of Funeral Speeches at Athens*, New York.
Zuntz, G. (1947), "Is the *Heraclidae* Mutilated?", *CQ* 41: 46–52.
Zuntz, G. (1955), *The political plays of Euripides*, Manchester.

Andreas N. Michalopoulos
Ovid's Poetics of Memory and Oblivion in his Exilic Poetry

Abstract: In this paper I explore the role of memory and oblivion in Ovid's *Tristia* and *Epistulae ex Ponto*. I analyze Ovid's language of memory and oblivion, I focus on what Ovid remembers or chooses to forget, and I investigate how his memories shape his exilic identity. Memory appears to be Ovid's sole companion at Tomis, covering for the absence of his wife and his loved ones. It becomes a substitute for physical presence. Although Ovid is not allowed to live in Rome physically, his memory enables him to travel to Rome mentally. It is Ovid's mental bridge and connection with his homeland, a surrogate for the senses arousing strong emotion for the poet's precious faces and places. Through memory Ovid struggles to keep on living his previous life. Memory is a way for him to rebuild his familiar world and to create a haven among the inhospitable, dangerous and barbaric Tomitans.

Augustus' decision to banish Ovid in 8 CE came as a severe blow to the poet. His departure from Rome – the center of the world and his own life – and his separation from his family and friends, was tantamount to death.[1] The situation for Ovid became even worse due to the place of exile, Tomis, on the Black Sea, on the most remote northeastern border of the empire. For the poet, writing poems and letters and sending them back to Rome was a vital psychological outlet and unfortunately the only way to communicate and keep in touch with his loved ones back in the capital.

Memory and oblivion are pervasive themes in Ovid's poetry from exile, and their presence is felt throughout the *Tristia* and the *Epistulae ex Ponto*. In this paper I explore what one might call Ovid's "poetics of memory and oblivion", focusing on selected elegies from his exilic corpus. I discuss the function and

---

[1] The *topos* 'exile = death' dominates Ovid's exilic poetry: *Tr.* 1.2.65–66, 1.2.71–72, 1.3.21–24, 1.3.89–98, 1.4.28, 3.3, 5.9.19, *Pont.* 1.8.27, 1.9.17, 4.9.74, 4.16.51. See Owen (1902) 99 on *Tr.* 1.2.72, Wistrand (1968) 6–26, Nagle (1980) 22–35, Doblhofer (1987) 166–178, Helzle (1988) 78, Williams (1994) 12f., Claassen (1996) 576–585, *eadem* (1999) 239–241 with n. 37, *eadem* (2008) 44, 196–199, Gaertner (2005) on *Pont.* 1.5.86, *eadem* (2007) 160 with n. 26. See also Gaertner (2007) 159 with n. 24 on the wordplay *exilium-exitium* in Ennius and on the possibility that the association of exile and death is of Latin origin.

https://doi.org/10.1515/9783110728798-005

form of memory and oblivion in the *Tristia* and the *Epistulae ex Ponto*, and how they contribute to the formation of Ovid's exilic identity.

1 Forget me not

An ideal first case study on the multi-dimensional role of memory and oblivion in Ovid's exile poetry is elegy 2.4 of the *Epistulae ex Ponto*, addressed to Atticus.[2] This is how the poem begins (*Pont.* 2.4.1–10):

> accipe colloquium gelido Nasonis ab Histro,
> Attice iudicio non dubitande meo.
> ecquid adhuc **remanes memor** infelicis amici
> deserit an partis languida cura suas?
> non ita di mihi sint tristes ut credere possim
> fasque putem iam te non meminisse mei.
> **ante oculos** nostros posita est tua semper **imago**
> et videor vultus **mente** videre tuos.
> seria multa mihi tecum conlata **recordor**
> nec data iucundis tempora pauca iocis.
>
> Let Ovid speak to you from the icy Danube, Atticus, / you who, in my opinion, should not be doubted. / **Do you still think of** your wretched friend at all, / or has your love played its part, and weakened? / The gods are not so harsh to me that I'd believe, / or think it reasonable, that **you've forgotten me already.** / **Your image** is always **in front of my eyes,** / and I seem to see your features **in my mind.** / **I remember** many deep talks you and I had, / and more than a few hours of playful fun.[3]

By the conventions of epistolography, in his opening couplet the sender mentions his name (*Nasonis*), his location (*gelido ab Histro*), and addresses the letter's recipient by name (*Attice*). He also refers to his letter as a *colloquium*, picking up

---

[2] The dates of publication of Ovid's exilic works, according to Syme (1978) 37–47, are as follows: *Tristia* (5 books) 9–12 CE, *Epistulae ex Ponto* (Books 1–3 in 13 CE, Book 4 perhaps posthumously c. 17–18 CE). Claassen (1986) section 4.1 investigates in detail the dating of composition and publication of Ovid's exile poetry. Her findings are summarized in Claassen (1987) 32. On the chronology of Ovid's career see more recently Harrison (2017). More specifically for the dating of the *Epistulae ex Ponto*, see Galasso (2009) 195–196.
[3] All translations of the *Tristia* and the *Epistulae ex Ponto* are by Tony Kline (slightly adapted): [available at: https://www.poetryintranslation.com/PITBR/Latin/Ovidexilehome.php (accessed: 19/03/2021)].

a traditional aspect of correspondence, namely that a letter is one half of a conversation, a *colloquium absentis*.⁴

Then, Ovid moves on to his primary concern: he is worried that Atticus may have forgotten him and wants to make sure that this is not the case. The memory of his friend is crucial to Ovid,⁵ who devotes two couplets on the matter (3–4, 5–6).⁶ Particularly notable is the phrase *memor infelicis amici*: with these three words Ovid essentially assigns roles and identities both to himself and to his friend. He employs memory as a method of constructing individual identity:⁷ on the one hand, the designated role and identity of Atticus and Ovid's other friends back in Rome should be *memores Ovidi*.⁸ As for himself, Ovid chooses the identity of the *infelix amicus*.⁹ He wants his friends in Rome to remember him as an unhappy man and to work continuously for his return. Most tellingly, Ovid associates the *memoria* of his friends with their love and care for him (*deserit an partis languida cura suas?*, line 4). In other words, *cura* is a necessary prerequisite for *memoria*, and, vice versa, *cura* is nourished by *memoria*: those who love, they remember, and those who remember, they love.

In lines 5–6 (*non ita di mihi sint tristes ut credere possim / fasque putem iam te non meminisse mei*) Ovid essentially invests memory with a religious dimension. He strikingly associates the memory of his friends with the gods and claims, more or less, that remembering him is what the gods want his friends to do, whereas forgetting him (*non meminisse*), oblivion, is a *nefas*, it is unholy and

---

4 For correspondence as a form of conversation and dialogue – a commonplace of ancient epistolographic theory – see Dem. *Eloc.* 223ff. Cicero (*Phil.* 2.7) calls letters the '*amicorum colloquia absentium*' and Seneca (*Epist.* 40.1) states that letters '*vera amici absentis vestigia, veras notas adferunt*'. Cf. also Cic. *Fam.* 12.30.1, Sen. *Ep.* 75.1. Ovid repeatedly likens his letters to a *colloquium* (*Tr.* 4.4.2, *Pont.* 1.2.6, 2.4.1 etc). See also Cazzaniga (1937) 1–6, Peter (1965) 19–20, Thraede (1970) 19–24, 39–47 (on Cicero), 52–61 (on Ovid), Schindler (1989) 14, Gaertner (2005) 7, 25–6, 32, Michalopoulos (2006) Ov. *Her.* 16.3, Gaertner (2007) 169, Roussel (2008) 44–8. For the letter as a bridge between two people see Rosenmeyer (2001) 116. For Ovid's letters from exile as *sermo absentis* but also for the caution with which one needs to approach them bearing in mind that they differ from actual prose letters see Claassen (1999) 110–114.
5 For *memoria* as a *topos* and an element of the ἐπιστολαὶ φιλικαί see Helzle (2003) on *Pont.* 1.4.55–6 and Helzle (1989) 19.
6 Ovid's question using the accusative neuter indefinite pronoun *ecquid* indicates his anxiety. See Pinkster (2015) 334. On the style of *ecquid* see also Helzle (2003) on *Pont.* 1.1.37–8.
7 On literature as closely interwoven with the thematic complex of memory and identity see Neumann (2008) 334.
8 The idea is underscored by the etymological wordplay *remanes memor*. Varro (*LL* 6.49) states: *memoria a manendo ut manimoria potest esse dicta*.
9 For Ovid as *infelix* see also *Tr.* 1.2.62, 1.7.14, *Pont.* 2.3.38, 2.7.48.

it runs contrary to divine laws. This gains added significance in light of the fact that the man who banished Ovid, the divine Augustus, is constantly portrayed in Ovid's exilic poetry as a god, as Jupiter on earth.[10]

Right after these two couplets, in which Ovid wishes to be the object of Atticus' remembrance, he refers to his own memory. He claims that the image (*imago*) of his friend is always before his eyes (*ante oculos*).[11] The vividness and clarity of memory substitutes for physical presence and proper vision: Ovid can see his friend mentally (*videor mente videre*).[12] Memory, which is a purely mental process, functions as a surrogate for the senses. The exiled Ovid cherishes affectionate remembrances of his life in Rome and remembers the past through his mental vision. He is able to visit Rome and his friends with the power of his *oculi mentis*, the 'eyes of his mind'.[13]

Ovid closes the introductory part of his letter by fondly evoking the experiences and moments he shared with his friend, Atticus. This time he uses

---

10 In both the *Tristia* and the *Epistulae ex Ponto* Augustus is constantly portrayed as a god, as Jupiter. See e.g. *Tr.* 1.1.20, 1.2.3–4, 12, 1.3.37–40, 1.5.77–78, 2.37–40. See Owen (1924) 79–81, Scott (1930) 52–58, Green (2005) xxxii–xxxiii and on *Tr.* 4.3.63–70, Claassen (1999) 227, *eadem* (2001) 36–39, *eadem* (2008) 29–33, 125–126, 177–183, Ciccarelli (2003) on *Tr.* 2.33–8, Gaertner (2005) 14, McGowan (2009) ch. 3, Ingleheart (2010) on *Tr.* 2.33–42. Warde Fowler (1915) discusses the development in time and the changes in Augustus' presentation as Jupiter in Ovid's exile poetry. For Augustus as a *laesus deus* in Ovid's exile poetry see Helzle (2003) on *Pont.* 1.4.43–44. Ovid's most defiant statement about Augustus is *Tr.* 3.7.47–52 on the emperor's inability to control the poet's mind, talent, and reputation. See Evans (1983) 17–19 and 182 n. 20 for bibliography. For possible interpretations of the poet's bold irreverence towards the emperor see Claassen (2008) 38.
11 On *ante oculos* see Helzle (2003) on *Pont.* 1.9.7–8. Cicero feels that the addressee of his letters is standing in front of him (*Fam.* 15.16.1): *fit enim nescio qui, ut quasi coram adesse videare, cum scribo aliquid ad te*. For the so-called "παρουσία-Motiv" see Thraede (1970) 44, 52. Through his letters Ovid tries to be close to his friends in Rome (e.g. *Tr.* 5.1.79–80, *Pont.* 3.5.29–30).
12 The polyptoton *videor-videre* strengthens the idea. This polyptoton is an Ovidian favourite, see Wills (1996) 295–8.
13 This is a proverbial metaphor, see Evans (1983) 186 n. 13. The etymological link between *mens* and *meminisse* highlights memory, which is the central concept of *Pont.* 2.4.1–10. Isidore (*Orig.* 11.1.12) states: *mens...vocata...quod meminit*. For the motif of 'mental vision and travel' – which Ovid may have borrowed from Cicero's *Ad familiares* – see Nagle (1980) 35, 91–9, 169 n. 1, Doblhofer (1987) 146–147, Claassen (1999) 299 n. 77, Gaertner (2005) on *Pont.* 1.2.48. On the role of imagination in Ovid's exile poetry see Helzle (2003) on *Pont.* 1.8.31–32. For Ovid's mental travels back to Rome and his simultaneous presence in and absence from both Rome and Tomis see also Williams (2002a) 237–238 and Hardie (2002) 6. Gaertner (2007) 158 notes that the motif of the exile's mental journey to his faraway home has a close parallel already in a simile in Apollonius (*Arg.* 2.541–7). On walks through Rome as mental tours in time and space see Papaioannou in this volume.

another *terminus technicus* for the process of memory, the verb *recordari*,[14] which is linked in folk etymology with *cor* 'the heart'.[15] Ovid's goal is to get his friend to help him. One way of doing this is by obliging Atticus and making him feel bad in case he stops remembering the exiled poet, especially since Atticus is always (*semper*) on his mind, as Ovid makes sure to stress (7–8: *ante oculos nostros posita est tua semper imago / et videor vultus mente videre tuos*).

Perhaps the most telling passage regarding Ovid's mnemonic abilities, mental vision (the eyes of the mind), and the terminology of memory that he employs in his exilic poetry is elegy *Pont*. 1.8.31–8:[16]

> nam modo vos **animo**,[17] dulces, **reminiscor**, amici,
> nunc mihi cum cara coniuge nata **subit**,[18]
> aque domo rursus pulchrae loca vertor ad Vrbis
> cunctaque mens oculis pervidet illa suis.
> nunc fora, nunc aedes, nunc marmore tecta theatra,
> nunc **subit** aequata porticus omnis humo,
> gramina nunc Campi pulchros spectantis in hortos
> stagnaque et euripi Virgineusque liquor.

> For **I recall in thought** my sweet friends sometimes, / sometimes **I think of** my dear wife and daughter: / and I revisit the sites of the lovely city from my home, / and **my mind surveys it all with its own inward eye**. / Now the fora, now the temples, now the marbled theatres, / now **I think of** each portico with its levelled grounds. / Now the grassy Campus that faces the lovely gardens, / the ponds and the canals, and the Aqua Virgo.

Ovid longingly evokes Rome and his beloved persons, with whom he can connect only through his letters. The word order *a-b-a-b* in line 31 (*animo-dulces-reminiscor-amici*), the use of the compound *pervidere*[19] instead of *videre*,[20] the

---

14 Nagle (1980) 93 considers the verb *recordor* as "more prosaic".
15 Varro (*Ling*. 6.46): *recordare rursus in cor revocare*. Cf. Cassiod. in psalm. 77,42 l. 573 A: *recordari...dictum est, revocare ad cor*.
16 Green (2005) 311 dates the poem, by lines 27–8, to the late autumn of 12 CE, since the Pleiads' rising took place towards mid-October, and Ovid had witnessed this four times since his exile, beginning in 9 CE.
17 Gaertner (2005) *ad loc*. rightly notes that *animo* points to the poet's memory (*OLD* s.v. 5c, *TLL* s.v. 95.20–56).
18 Gaertner (2005) *ad loc*.: "*subit*: 'comes to mind' (cf. 1.2.59n.)".
19 Gaertner (2005) *ad loc*. notes that *mens pervidet / mente pervidere* is unparalleled, while *oculis pervidere* is used by Horace (*S*. 1.3.25) and Valerius Maximus (7.3.6).
20 *OLD* s.v. 1 "to see fully or comprehensibly".

tautology[21] *oculis pervidet...suis*, and the repetition of the verb *subire*[22] (32, 36), all highlight the concept of memory which is dominant in this passage. Ovid's memory is a form of nostalgia arousing strong emotion for his precious faces and places.[23] Thanks to memory he can escape from his miserable exile and visit Rome whenever he wishes.[24] Augustus has no control whatsoever over Ovid's imagination and cannot hinder his mental journeys. Memory enables the poet to defy the emperor's autocratic power and secures the intellectual freedom of the artist.[25]

2 Half a world away

At the beginning of elegy *Pont.* 2.11 Ovid again touches on memory and oblivion (1–6):

> hoc tibi, Rufe, brevi properatum tempore mittit
> Naso, parum faustae conditor Artis, opus,
> ut, quamquam longe toto sumus orbe remoti,
> scire tamen possis **nos meminisse tui**.
> nominis ante mei venient **oblivia** nobis,
> pectore quam pietas sit tua pulsa meo.

> Naso, the author of the unfortunate *Ars Amatoria* / sends you this effort, Rufus, rushed off in a hurry, / so that though we're separated by a whole world's / width, you can still know that **I remember you**. / I'd sooner come to **forget** my own name, / than let your loyalty be driven from my heart.

---

21 Helzle (2003) *ad loc.*
22 *OLD* s.v. 12: "(of a mental image, object of thought etc.) to suggest itself (to a person, his mind etc.)".
23 On Ovid's nostalgic (but repetitive) evocation of Roman landmarks cf. *Tr.* 3.1.2, 19–22 and 27–36, Green (2005) on *Pont.* 1.8.31–9. On writing poetry in exile as consolation for Ovid see Stevens (2009) 169–171. On correspondence as consolation see Dem. *Typ. Epist.* 5, Ps. Libanius 25, Cic. *Fam.* 4.13.1, *Att.* 8.14.1, cf. Nagle (1980) 99–105.
24 On Ovid's 'Vorstellungskraft' see Helzle (2003) *ad loc.*
25 The struggle between poetry and political power, Ovid and the *princeps*, is a staple theme of Ovid's exile poetry. See among others Evans (1983) 17–19 and 182 n. 20 with bibliography, Williams (2002a) 240, Boyle (2003) 11, McGowan (2009) 203ff. This struggle has played a decisive role to Ovid becoming the embodiment of the conflict between art and authoritarian regimes, see Michalopoulos (2011) 280 with n. 20.

Like he did in *Pont.* 2.4, Ovid keeps to the fundamental epistolographic conventions: he addresses the recipient of the letter by name (*Rufe*)[26] and then introduces himself as the sender (*Naso*) and as the creator of the *Ars amatoria*. He had previously introduced himself as *infelix amicus*, and now he introduces himself as the writer of an unfortunate work (*parum faustae conditor Artis*).

Ovid presents this letter – and presumably the whole book, since this is the final poem of the book – as tangible evidence that he still remembers his friend. In this case Ovid is the agent, not the object of memory.[27] He associates memory with distance (*quamquam longe toto sumus orbe remoti*) and takes them to be inversely proportionate: the longer the distance, the weaker the memory. Distance is expected to cause oblivion; however, this is not the case with Ovid and his friend, as Ovid takes pains to confirm. Memory helps bring the two friends together, although they are half a world away from each other.[28] The hasty writing of a letter in *brevi tempore*[29] is enough to join two loving friends separated by *toto orbe*. This proves the close association of poetic composition and memory; memory inspires poetic composition and is also preserved by it.[30] This is a straightforward process with two stages: a) Ovid remembers his friend and writes him a letter; b) Ovid's friend reads the letter and instantly recalls Ovid in his memory.

Ovid's discussion about memory automatically brings to the foreground its direct opposite, oblivion (*oblivium*). Through a striking exaggeration[31] – "I'd sooner come to forget my own name than...your loyalty" – Ovid pronounces his eternal friendship and devotion to his friend. He finds himself in a weak spot and wants to renew his bonds with Rufus. He assures Rufus that he remembers him, hoping that in this way he will make Rufus remember him back. At the same time, Ovid's remembrance of Rufus is a reward for Rufus' *pietas* and *fides* towards

---

26 This is the uncle of Ovid's third wife, see Helzle (2003) 403.
27 On the distinction between active and passive memory, between one's own memory and one's position in the memory of others, see Mawford in this volume.
28 On life at the edge of the world see Helzle (2003) on *Pont.* 1.3.49–50.
29 Ovid frequently writes about the careless composition of his poems in exile, the quality drop of his poetry, and the sterility of his creative *ingenium*: e.g. *Tr.* 1.1.35–48, 1.11.35–36, 3.14.27–30, 33–6, 43–50, 5.1.69–72, 5.7.55–8, 5.12.21–22, *Pont.* 1.5.3–8, 15–18, 3.4.11, 4.2.15–20, 4.8.65–66. Hinds (1985) 14 rightly notes that Ovid's insistence on this issue makes the reader reasonably suspicious about his sincerity. Luck (1961) has convincingly shown that Ovid's diction in the *Tristia* is not inferior to the diction of his pre-exilic works. Williams (1994) 50–51 writes about Ovid's 'pose of poetic decline', cf. Gaertner (2005) 305–306. See also Nagle (1980) 171, Harrison (2002) 89, Williams (2002a) 238, *idem* (2002b) 354–60, Green (2005) 350, Tissol (2014) 113.
30 On the connections between writing with memory see Morrison in this volume.
31 For parallels see Helzle (2003) *ad loc.*

him.³² In other words, memory joins two people who are thousands of miles apart and is a vital catalyst for friendship; memory is an essential mechanism tightening social relations and creating the need for reciprocity.

This is clearly stated in one of Ovid's last elegies from exile, *Pont.* 4.6.³³ Lines 45–50 read:

> et prius hic nimium nobis conterminus Hister
> in caput Euxino de mare vertet iter,
> utque Thyesteae redeant si tempora mensae,
> Solis ad Eoas currus agetur aquas,
> quam quisquam vestrum qui me doluistis ademptum
> arguat ingratum non meminisse sui.
>
> The Danube, all too close, will sooner turn its course / back from the Euxine shore towards its source, / the chariot of the sun be driven to the Eastern sea, / as if the age of Thyestean banquets were returned, / than any of you who've grieved at my exile / shall denounce me as **ungrateful, un-remembering**.

Closing his elegy,³⁴ Ovid uses two *adynata*³⁵ and declares that he will always remember those who remember him; a few lines above he stated that he would forget those who forgot him. Ovid highlights the reciprocity of both memory and oblivion. He will exact his revenge on those who have forgotten him using the same weapon, oblivion³⁶ (4.6.41–4):

---

32 For the letter as a gift (δῶρον) and as a service of friendship (φιλοφρόνησις) see Gaertner (2007) 169, who cites Dem. *Eloc.* 224, [Isoc.] 1.2. Cf. Ov. *Tr.* 4.4.11, *Pont.* 1.1.19–20, 3.6.53–8, 4.12.1–6. Williams (1994) 116–128 discusses the close relationship between letters and *amicitia*, while Labate (1987) 114–128 notices the close relationship of Ovid's *Tristia* with Horace's *Epistulae* as lessons on the proper management of *amicitia*. Nagle (1980) 103, discussing *Tr.* 1.5, points out that consolation of a friend in distress is an *officium* of friendship and an expression of *pietas* and *fides*. In elegy *Tr.* 5.4 Ovid promises to his unnamed friend that he will always remember and be loyal to him. Memory again plays the role of a gift in return for a friend's good services (*Tr.* 5.4.43–6). Cf. also *Tr.* 5.9.3–4.
33 Most likely composed in late 14 CE, see Helzle (1989) 135.
34 It is perhaps of some significance that references to memory and/or oblivion tend to appear at focal points of poems, i.e. the beginning or the end.
35 Akrigg (1985) on *Pont.* 4.6.45–50 notes that by adding a personal detail (*hic nimium nobis conterminus Hister*) Ovid makes the *adynaton* reflect his own circumstances.
36 Cf. *Tr.* 4.5.17–20, where Ovid asks his friend to be happy because the poet still remembers his loyalty: *quod licet et tutum est, intra tua pectora* **gaude** / **meque tui memorem** *teque fuisse pium,* / *utque facis, remis ad opem luctare ferendam,* / *dum veniat placido mollior aura deo.* "This you can do (and it's safe): delight in this inwardly, / that I've remembered you and you've been loyal, / and, as you have, bend your oars to bring me help, / till there's a softer breeze and the god's

> hoc ego praecipue sensi, cum magna meorum
> notitiam pars est infitiata mei.
> **inmemor illorum**, vestri non inmemor[37] umquam
> qui mala solliciti nostra levatis ero.

> I felt this most of all when the larger part of my friends denied all knowledge of me. **Them I'll forget**, you I'll never forget, you who ease the anxiety of my ills.

We have seen thus far that typically Ovid worries he may be forgotten by his friends back in Rome. Nevertheless, there are also cases in which oblivion can be desirable and profitable for him. Such is the oblivion regarding Ovid's *culpa*, the *error* which cost him his banishment (*Tr.* 3.11.65–8):

> utque meae famam tenuent **oblivia** culpae,
> facta **cicatricem** ducere nostra sine
> humanaeque **memor** sortis, quae tollit eosdem
> et premit, incertas ipse verere vices.

> And allow a **scar** to form, over my actions, / so **forgetfulness** might lessen knowledge of my fault: / **remember** mortal fate that lifts a man and crushes him, / and fear the uncertainties of change yourself.

This is a tough problem for Ovid to solve: on the one hand, he does not want to be forgotten by his friends, but on the other, he wants everyone to forget about his *error*.[38] Oblivion cuts both ways, and so does memory, depending on Ovid's strategy. Particularly interesting is Ovid's application of medical terminology in this passage: his *culpa* is likened to an open wound, and oblivion is likened to a scar (*cicatricem*) which forms over it as it heals.[39] This is a witty oxymoron.

---

appeased." Again, memory strengthens the bond between two friends. Cf. also *Tr.* 5.4.43–6, 5.9.3–4, 20, 33–34.

37 Akrigg (1985) *ad loc.*, on the repetition of *immemor* at lines 43, 44, notes Tarrant's observation about a similar epanalepsis at Hor. *Ep.* 1.11.9 *oblitusque meorum, obliviscendus et illis*.

38 On Ovid's major concern for his poetic fame and immortality in his exilic poetry (e.g. *Tr.* 3.7.51–53, 4.9.19–24, 4.10.127–128) see Ciccarelli (2003) 114–115, McGowan (2009) with n. 34, 213 with n. 28, Ingleheart (2010) 103, Kyriakidis (2013) 11–12, *idem* (2014) 173–176, Michalopoulos (2016). Ovid declares his craving for poetic glory already at *Rem.* 393: *nam iuvat et studium famae mihi crevit honore*. He then voices his certainty for poetic immortality in his famous epilogue to the *Metamorphoses* (15.871–879). Cf. also *Am.* 1.3.25–26, 1.15.7–8, *Ars* 2.740, *Rem.* 363. On the experience of forgetting and how it contributes to conceptions of humanity and morality see Morrison in this volume.

39 Gaertner (2007) 162–163, citing Langslow (1999) and Zanker (1987) 124–7, rightly notes that the use of medical formulations such as *cicatricem ducere* is not a sign of Ovid's more prosaic

Oblivion is associated with absence (of memory); however its presence in the form of a scar is needed to heal Ovid's *culpa* (which is an open wound). In other words, in this case, oblivion – the oblivion of his *culpa* – has therapeutic qualities: it is the medicine that cures Ovid's illness. On the other hand, when oblivion concerns Ovid himself, it can be lethal, because it cuts off his lifeline with Rome.[40]

3 Gifts from the edge

Elegy *Pont.* 3.8 is addressed to Ovid's friend, Fabius Maximus.[41] It is a gift poem attached to a present that Ovid is sending to him from Tomis (*Pont.* 3.8.1–4):

> quae tibi quaerebam **memorem** testantia **curam**
> dona Tomitanus mittere posset ager.
> dignus es argento, fulvo quoque dignior auro,
> sed te, cum donas, ista iuvare solent.
>
> I was wondering what gift the land of Tomis / might send you as witness to my **thoughtful affection**. / You deserve silver, even more so yellow gold, but you used to find more joy in those when you were the giver.

Ovid wants to show Fabius Maximus that he always remembers him in exile. This time the token of memory will be a particular gift from Tomis. Although the poet would have preferred to send something precious (made of gold or silver), in the end he is sending the most emblematic gift from Tomis, Scythian arrows in their quiver (*Pont.* 3.8.19–22):

> clausa tamen misi Scythica tibi tela pharetra
> hoste, precor, fiant illa cruenta tuo.
> hos habet haec calamos, hos haec habet ora libellos,
> haec viget in nostris, Maxime, Musa locis!

---

style in his exilic poetry, and that technical diction, particularly medical, already appears in Ovid's previous works and originates in Hellenistic poetry.
40 Interestingly, in the next couplet (67–68) Ovid warns his unnamed enemy to remember the mutability of the human fate (*humanaeque memor sortis*). Memory here does not concern the poet or some other particular person, but the condition of mortals in general.
41 On the identification see Green (2005) 347 in his introductory note to the elegy.

> Still I've sent you Scythian arrows sheathed in a quiver: I pray they might be stained by your enemies' blood. Such are the pens of this shore: such are the books, such is the Muse, Maximus, that flourishes in this place!

Memory gets objectified, it acquires physical presence and particular form, and of course is still meant to point directly back to Ovid.[42] The objective value of the gift is not important; besides, precious metals lose their value, even though they can withstand the passing of time. What matters for Ovid is that his gift will be a constant reminder to Fabius Maximus of a wretched friend who lives at the edge of the world. In effect, Ovid intends to oblige Fabius Maximus;[43] once again *cura* and *memoria* are closely tied together, and memory functions as a cohesive social bond, as already seen above (*Pont.* 2.4.1–4).[44]

Memory is again linked with a specific object in elegy *Tr.* 4.3. Among his anxious questions about whether his wife still loves him, Ovid's mind turns to their marital bed which they had shared before his relegation (*Tr.* 4.3.23–24): *tunc **subeunt** curae, dum te lectus locusque / tangit et **oblitam non sinit esse mei**.* "Do cares rise, while you touch my place in the bed, / that does not allow you to forget me." The bed acts as a constant reminder of Ovid to his wife. An object – in fact, not any random object, but the couple's own bed – substitutes for Ovid's physical presence and keeps his memory alive. Odysseus and Penelope are of course at the back of Ovid's mind here.

To conclude: Ovid's banishment by Augustus was a major turning point in the poet's life and work. Ovid struggled to keep his channel of communication with Rome alive, so that he might survive in his semi-barbaric place of exile. Memory and oblivion (denoted by various terms, such as *recordari, reminisci, subire, oculi mentis, mente videre, venire in mentem, inmemor esse, oblivisci, oblivium*) are key aspects of Ovidian exilic poetics and perform many different but interdependent and complementary functions.

Memory is one of Ovid's few companions in exile, compensating for the absence of his wife and loved ones. Through memory Ovid strives to keep on living his previous life. Memory is Ovid's mental bridge with his homeland, and a surrogate for the senses arousing strong emotion for his precious faces and

---

[42] On the link between memory and physical objects see Orlin (2016) 116–120, 139–140, Hölkeskamp (2016) 193–194, 203–204.
[43] Evans (1983) 123 notes that the double meaning of *calamos* – "arrows" as well as "reed pens" – reinforces the irony of Ovid's final request, that Fabius may accept this modest gift as representative of life in Tomis. According to Green (2005) 347 Fabius will use the Scythian arrows, which were dipped in venom, against his own (line 20) and Ovid's enemies.
[44] On the social and collective dimensions of memory in antiquity see Morrison in this volume.

places. Memory joins people who are thousands of miles apart. Ovid can see his friends with the eyes of his mind (*Pont.* 2.4). Although he is not allowed to live in Rome physically, he manages to live in Rome mentally, breaking the ban imposed by the emperor. Augustus cannot control Ovid's memory and imagination, nor can he prohibit his mental journeys. Thanks to memory the poet secures his intellectual freedom (*Pont.* 1.8).

Furthermore, memory is closely associated with poetry; memory inspires poetry and is also preserved by it (*Pont.* 2.11). Writing poems in exile is not merely about preserving Ovid's poetic fame, it is also about his biological survival. Memory keeps Ovid alive back in Rome. He can hope for a return only if he is remembered. If he is forgotten, he will die helplessly at Tomis. To that end, Ovid employs memory as a method of constructing individual identity (*Pont.* 2.4): he is the *infelix amicus* at Tomis, whom his friends back in Rome should always remember (*memores Ovidi*). Memory nourishes and is nourished by their love for him (*Pont.* 2.4, 3.8). Memory is an essential mechanism that tightens social relations and forges ties of reciprocity between Ovid and his friends (*Pont.* 2.11, 3.8, 4.6).

Bibliography

Akrigg, G.M. (1985), *The Last Poems of Ovid: a New Edition, with Commentary, of the Fourth Book of the Epistulae Ex Ponto*, Diss., Univ. of Toronto.
Boyle, A.J. (2003), *Ovid and the Monuments: A Poet's Rome*, Bendigo.
Cazzaniga, A. (1937), *Elementi retorici nella composizione delle lettere dal Ponto di Ovidio*, Venegono.
Ciccarelli, I. (2003), *Commento al II libro dei Tristia di Ovidio*, Bari.
Claassen, J.-M. (1986), *Poeta, Exsul, Vates: A Stylistic and Literary Analysis of Ovid's Tristia and Epistulae ex Ponto*, Diss. Univ. of Stellenbosch.
Claassen, J.-M. (1987), "Error and the imperial household: an angry god and the exiled Ovid's fate", *AClass* 30: 31–47.
Claassen, J.-M. (1996), "Exile, Death and Immortality: Voices from the Grave", *Latomus* 55: 571–90.
Claassen, J.-M. (1999), *Displaced Persons: the literature of exile: from Cicero to Boethius*, London.
Claassen, J.-M. (2001), "The singular myth: Ovid's use of myth in the exilic poetry", *Hermathena* 170: 11–64.
Claassen, J.-M. (2008), *Ovid revisited. The poet in exile*, London.
Doblhofer, E. (1987), *Exil und Emigration: Zum Erlebnis der Heimatferne in der römischen Literatur*, Darmstadt.
Evans, H.B. (1983), *Publica carmina: Ovid's books from exile*, Lincoln/London.

Gaertner, J.F. (2005), *Ovid Epistulae ex Ponto, Book 1*. Edited with Introduction, Translation, and Commentary, Oxford.
Gaertner, J.F. (2007), "Ovid and the 'poetics of exile': how exilic is Ovid's exile poetry?", in J.F. Gaertner (ed.), *Writing exile. The discourse of displacement in Greco-Roman antiquity and beyond*, Leiden/Boston: 155–72.
Galasso, L. (2009), "*Epistulae ex Ponto*", in P.E. Knox (ed.), *A Companion to Ovid*, Chichester: 194–206.
Green, P. (2005), *Ovid: The Poems of Exile*, London.
Hardie, P. (2002), *Ovid's Poetics of Illusion*, Cambridge.
Harrison, S. (2002), "Ovid and genre: evolutions of an elegist", in P. Hardie (ed.), *The Cambridge Companion to Ovid*, Cambridge: 79–94.
Harrison, S. (2017), "The chronology of Ovid's career", in A.N. Michalopoulos, S. Papaioannou, and A. Zissos (eds.), *Dicite, Pierides: Classical studies in honour of Stratis Kyriakidis*, Newcastle upon Tyne: 188–201.
Helzle, M. (1988), "Ovid's Poetics of Exile", *ICS* 13: 73–83.
Helzle, M. (1989), *Publii Ovidii Nasonis Epistularum ex Ponto liber. IV: a Commentary on Poems 1 to 7 and 16*, Hildesheim.
Helzle, M. (2003), *Ovids Epistulae ex Ponto. Buch I-II Kommentar*, Heidelberg.
Hinds, S.E. (1985), "Booking the Return Trip: Ovid and *Tristia* 1", *PCPhS* 31: 13–32.
Hölkeskamp, K.-J. (2016), "In the web of (hi-)stories: *memoria*, monuments, and their myth-historical interconnectedness", in K. Galinsky (ed.), *Memory in ancient Rome and early Christianity*, Oxford: 169–213.
Ingleheart, J. (2010), *A Commentary on Ovid* Tristia *Book 2*, Oxford.
Kyriakidis, S. (2013), "Ovid's *Metamorphoses*: The text before and after", *LICS* 11.1, 1–16 [http://lics.leeds.ac.uk/2013/201301.pdf].
Kyriakidis, S. (2014), "Musa iocosa: το παιχνίδι με τις λέξεις στα *Tristia* του Οβιδίου", in M. Voutsinou-Kikilia, A.N. Michalopoulos and S. Papaioannou (eds.), *Rideamus igitur: humour in Latin literature*. Proceedings of the 9th Panhellenic Symposium of Latin Studies, Athens: 170–77.
Labate, M. (1987), "Elegia triste ed elegia lieta. Un caso di riconversione letteraria", *MD* 19: 91–129.
Langslow, D.R. (1999), "The Language of Poetry and the Language of Science: The Latin Poets and Medical Latin", in J.N. Adams & R.G. Mayer (eds.), *Aspects of the Language of Latin Poetry*, (*Proceedings of the British Academy* 93), Oxford: 183–225.
Luck, G. (1961), "Notes on the language and text of Ovid's *Tristia*", *HSPh* 65: 243–61.
McGowan, M.M. (2009), *Ovid in exile. Power and Poetic Redress in the Tristia and Epistulae ex Ponto*, Leiden/Boston.
Michalopoulos, A.N. (2006), *Ovid Heroides 16 and 17: Introduction, Text and Commentary*, Cambridge.
Michalopoulos, A.N. (2011), "Ovid's last wor(l)d", in J. Ingleheart (ed.), *Two thousand years of solitude. Exile after Ovid*, Oxford: 275–88.
Michalopoulos, A.N. (2016), "*Famaque cum domino fugit ab urbe suo*: Aspects of Fama in Ovid's Exile Poetry", in S. Kyriakidis (ed.), *Libera Fama: An Endless Journey*. Pierides, 6. Newcastle upon Tyne: 94–110.
Nagle, B.R. (1980), *The Poetics of Exile: Program and polemic in the "Tristia" and "Epistulae ex Ponto" of Ovid*, Brussels.

Neumann, B. (2008), "The Literary Representation of Memory", in A. Erll, A. Nünning and S.B. Young (eds.), *Cultural Memory Studies: An International and Interdisciplinary Handbook*, Berlin/New York: 334–43.
Orlin, E. (2016), "Augustan reconstruction and Roman memory", in K. Galinsky (ed.), *Memory in ancient Rome and early Christianity*, Oxford: 115–44.
Owen, S.G. (1902), *Ovid's Tristia Book 1*. 3rd ed. (1st ed. 1885), Oxford.
Owen, S.G. (1924), *P. Ovidi Nasonis Tristium Liber Secundus*, Oxford (repr. Amsterdam 1967).
Peter, H. (1965), *Der Brief in der Römischen Literatur*, Hildesheim.
Pinkster, H. (2015), *Oxford Latin Syntax: Volume 1: The Simple Clause*, Oxford.
Rosenmeyer, P.A. (2001), *Ancient Epistolary Fictions. The Letter in Greek Literature*, Cambridge.
Roussel, D. (2008), *Ovide épistolier*, Collection Latomus Vol. 314, Brussels.
Schindler, W. (1989), "*Speculum animi* oder das absolute Gespräch", *AU* 32: 4–21.
Scott, K. (1930), "Emperor Worship in Ovid", *TAPA* 61: 43–69.
Stevens, B. (2009), "*Per gestum res est significanda mihi*: Ovid and Language in Exile", *CPh* 104: 162–83.
Syme, R. (1978), *History in Ovid*, Oxford.
Thraede, K. (1970), *Grundzüge griechisch-römischer Brieftopik*, Munich.
Tissol, G. (2014), *Ovid: Epistulae ex Ponto Book I*, Cambridge.
Warde Fowler, W. (1915), "Note on Ovid, *Tristia* III.6.8 (Augustus et Juppiter)", *CR* 29: 46–47.
Williams, G.D. (1994), *Banished voices: readings in Ovid's exile poetry*, Cambridge.
Williams, G.D. (2002a), "Ovid's exile poetry: *Tristia, Epistulae ex Ponto* and *Ibis*", in P. Hardie (ed.), *The Cambridge Companion to Ovid*, Cambridge: 233–45.
Williams, G.D. (2002b), "Ovid's exilic poetry: worlds apart", in B.W. Boyd (ed.), *Brill's Companion to Ovid*, Leiden: 337–81.
Wills, J. (1996), *Repetition in Latin Poetry: Figures of Allusion*, Oxford.
Wistrand, E. (1968), *Sallust on Judicial Murders in Rome: A Philological and Historical Study*, Studia Graeca et Latina Gothoburgensia XXIV, Gothenburg.
Zanker, G. (1987), *Realism in Alexandrian Poetry. A Literature and its Audience*, London.

Elinor Cosgrave
The Memory of Marcus Regulus and Cannae in Plautus' *Captivi*

Abstract: Plautus' *Captivi* is thought to have been first produced sometime between 193 and 189 BCE, within memory of captive-taking incidents during the First and Second Punic Wars. In scholarship on Roman theatre, there has been an acknowledgement that the Romans' 'rich oral-performance culture', of which the theatre was a component, is crucial for the study of 'cultural' memory (Wiseman, 2014). However, within Plautine studies, previous scholars have either dismissed (Gruen, 2001), or not fully explored the memory and impact of events in Roman history on Plautus' *Captivi* (Richlin, 2018, Stewart, 2012). In this paper, I consider the extent to which the memory of two specific events, namely the capture of Marcus Regulus (255 BCE) and the Battle of Cannae (216 BCE), influenced the representations of captives and captive-taking in the *Captivi*. In turn, this shows Plautus' consideration of the concerns of his contemporary audiences, which were ultimately shaped by their shared memory of events in Roman history.

I begin by outlining the *exempla* which derived from captive-taking in the Punic Wars, events within the audiences' shared cultural memory. Having established the composition of Plautus' audiences, I address their expectations of captive-taking as presented in the *exempla* and *Captivi*. I continue by exploring the implications of the cultural memory of captive-taking in the Punic Wars on the themes and representation of captives in Plautus' *Captivi*. This involves challenging the notion that *Captivi*'s key theme is slavery, rather than the transitional nature of 'captivity', of which enslavement was just one outcome. Such a theme has repercussions on Plautus' portrayal of such issues as the captives' social and financial worth, and the way in which the captives' oaths, sacrifices and inherent nobility are presented. Ultimately, I demonstrate that the cultural memory of captive-taking resulting from the Punic Wars is inextricably linked to Plautus' representations of captives, which reflects the audiences' preoccupation with the memories and concept of captivity at the time.

1 Introduction

Plautus' *Captivi* was produced in the 2nd century BCE, within memory of captive-taking events during the First and Second Punic Wars. An adaptation of a now-lost Greek original, *Captivi* hails from a genre known as *fabula palliata*. The genre chiefly comprised light dramas, originating from Greece and which remained set in Greek city-states, adapted for the Roman audience.[1] *Fabula palliata* became increasingly popular during the 3rd century BCE as a result of Roman imperialism,[2] including the experiences of members of the Roman military in Greece,[3] and the subsequent cultural exchanges which were perpetuated by captive persons.[4] Despite its Greek origins, *Captivi*'s plot would only have been relevant to Roman audiences if it reflected a Roman understanding of how captives were viewed within society,[5] and how such attitudes were shaped by events within the audiences' collective memory. As such, the play, which is thought to have been produced sometime between 193 and 189 BCE,[6] is useful in exposing middle-Republican attitudes towards captive-taking, including the memory of specific events related to captive-taking. Such attitudes to captive-taking, shared with other Mediterranean societies,[7] were shaped by inherent cultural values, and the memory of Rome's wars against Carthage and other nations during the 3rd and 2nd centuries BCE. This paper explores how the captive-taking of Roman soldiers by Carthaginian forces, including incidents within the audiences' shared cultural memory,[8] such as the Battle of Cannae, should not be underestimated in the study of Plautus' *Captivi*.

---

[1] Manuwald (2011) 144–5.
[2] Richlin (2014) 174.
[3] Chalmers (1965) 23.
[4] Cameron (2011) 169–209.
[5] Chalmers (1965) 22; Moore (1998) 50–52; Gruen (2001) 84; Richlin (2018) 213–240.
[6] De Melo (2011) 503, Franko (1995) 155–156. The production certainly took place after the recovery of the Cannae captives in 196 BCE, given references to the Porta Trigemina market which was built in 193 BCE. De Melo and Franko suggest that *Captivi* was first performed in 189 BCE, after Rome defeated the Aetolians.
[7] Garcia Riazia (2015) 15–41.
[8] I refer to audiences throughout as Plautus alludes to the socio-economic differences between his audience at large, thus suggesting that different groups were essentially different audiences, e.g. enslaved or free, elite or non-elite. Please see further below.

Previous scholarship has not fully addressed the memory of events in Rome's history on Plautus' plays.[9] Gruen suggests that such conjecture is irrelevant to discussions of Plautus' works, or may simply reflect Plautus' desire to keep his audience guessing as to his allusions to recent events,[10] which would have inevitably existed within the audiences' shared cultural memory. Granted, there are no direct references to public affairs within Plautus' works.[11] However, Stewart in *Plautus and Roman Slavery* explores the impact of historical events on the presentation of slavery in Plautus' *Rudens*, and argues that scenes within the play refer to specific events relating to Cannae.[12] Richlin, who briefly addresses the cultural memory of Cannae in *Captivi*, argues that the comedic tone within *Captivi* differs from Plautus' other works, as it was a 'black comedy' which reflected the interests of the audience who had been directly affected by the captive-taking at Cannae.[13]

Wellesley, Grimal and Lefèvre have acknowledged that recent captive-taking events in Roman history would have inevitably had an impact on the production and themes of *Captivi*, but have primarily focussed on trying to date the first production of the play.[14] Furthermore, Leigh has conducted the most comprehensive study of contemporaneous concerns within *Captivi*, building upon Lefèvre's work on Plautus.[15] Leigh argues that previous scholarship, often relating to Roman law and slavery, has 'habitually raided Plautus for allusions to contemporary legal principles and procedures.'[16] Leigh conducts an in-depth study of the implications *Captivi* has on our understanding of Roman social and legal practices, including *postliminium*, the process of social and legal reintegration after captivity.[17] However, this paper does not seek to address specific legalities, but rather consider how the societal impact of captive-taking on the Roman people was reflected in Plautus' *Captivi*.

As previously stated, Gruen dismisses the value of identifying the impact of historical events on Plautus' works, but comments on the themes within Plautus'

---

9 Dean *et al.* (2015) 12. Dean *et al.* suggest that an underestimation of the usefulness of theatre as an historical source links to the West placing a higher value on written or material documentation over performances representations of the past.
10 Gruen (2001) 83–4.
11 Gruen (2001) 83–4, 86–7.
12 Stewart (2012) 136.
13 Richlin (2018) 226, (2017) 372, cf. Leigh (2004) 96.
14 Wellesley (1955) 298–305; Grimal (1969) 413; Lefèvre (1998) 33–36, cf. Leigh (2005) 59.
15 Lefèvre (1998) 33–36.
16 Leigh (2005) 59.
17 Leigh (2005) 57–97.

work which reflect trends within Roman society at the time.[18] Arguably, such trends would have been reflective of events and issues which were present within the audiences' shared memory, or such references would have failed to have an impact on the audience. As such, recent events did have a great impact on Roman culture, with the Punic Wars having a lasting effect on the Roman people and their society.[19] Wiseman argues that the Romans' 'rich oral-performance culture', of which the theatre was a component, is crucial for the study of 'collective' or 'cultural' memory.[20] Furthermore, Dean *et al.* consider how theatre has the potential to not only to 'reshape elements of the past', but also to capture 'a fragment of its own historical moment for posterity'.[21] As such, we cannot ignore the impact and memory of specific historical events on Plautus' works.[22] Therefore, the representations of captives in *Captivi* embody the audiences' concern for the process of re-integration into Roman society, after capture by a foreign enemy, which would have been present in the cultural memory of Plautus' audiences.

In this paper, I will initially outline the *exempla* which derived from captive-taking during the Punic Wars, including such incidents as the capture of Marcus Regulus and the Cannae soldiers, which would have existed in the audiences' shared memory. Having established the plot of *Captivi* and the make-up of Plautus' audiences, I will continue by exploring the implications of the cultural memory of captive-taking on the themes and representation of captives in *Captivi*. This includes addressing such issues as the social and financial value of captives, oaths, sacrifices and inherent nobility. Ultimately, I will show that the cultural memory of captive-taking during the Punic Wars is inextricably linked to Plautus' representations of captives which reflects the audiences' shared preoccupation with, and recollections of, captivity at the time.[23]

---

[18] Gruen (2001) 83–94.
[19] Gruen (2001) 84.
[20] Wiseman (2014) 62. Wiseman further suggests that theatre could be used to convey myth as historical fact, cf. Wiseman (2014) 56; Richlin (2017) 355–7.
[21] Dean *et al.* (2015) 8.
[22] On the impact of changes to Rome's urban landscape and how such changes were commemorated in Plautus' works, see Papaioannou in this volume.
[23] On the importance of theatre as a tool to explore shared experiences, particularly in the writings of Cicero, see Haley in this volume.

2 Captive-taking in the Punic Wars in the Audiences' Collective Memory

Before proceeding to discuss *Captivi*, we need to outline the events involving captive-taking which would have been within the audiences' collective memory. As stated, *Captivi* was produced *circa* 189 BCE, mere decades after the conclusions of the First and Second Punic Wars (264–241 BCE and 218–201 BCE, respectively). As such, the events of these two wars would have been within the audiences' shared memory. Much of what we know about captive-taking in this period derives from these conflicts, and it largely survives in *exempla* (moral anecdotes). *Exempla* are powerful as they portray pivotal societal concerns,[24] presenting idealised behaviour and individuals which could be used to evoke a collective response from those who understood them.[25] Two *exempla* involving captive-taking are used by later sources to compare the appropriate behaviour of Roman citizens should they be captured by the enemy, and these *exempla* reflect Roman expectations of captive-taking which are also evident in Plautus' *Captivi*. The first *exemplum* concerns Marcus Regulus, a former consul and Roman commander captured by Carthaginian forces during the First Punic War. Following his capture at Tunis in 255 BCE, Regulus was sent as an envoy to the Roman senate, swearing an oath that he would return to his Carthaginian captors. Regulus convinced the senate not to ransom him or his men, which ensured that the Carthaginians did not benefit financially or politically.[26] Despite the senate's protests, Regulus was intent on keeping his oath and returned to the Carthaginians, who subsequently executed him.

Writing two centuries later, Cicero uses this *exemplum* in contrast with that of the captives taken during the Second Punic War at the Battle of Cannae in 216 BCE, thus demonstrating that the two incidents were linked in Roman cultural memory.[27] The Battle of Cannae, which took place in south-eastern Italy, is of note as it was a crushing defeat for the Romans, enabling the Carthaginians to capture thousands of Roman soldiers.[28] In a panicked response, concerned with the army's diminished population after this significant loss, the Roman senate

---

24 Bell (2008) 1–4.
25 Hölkeskamp (2013) 25.
26 Polybius 1.35.1–10; Dio 11 = Zonaras 8.13–15; Flor. *Epit.* 1.8.23–26.
27 Cic. *de off.* 3.32.
28 Livy 22.57.17; App. *Hann.* 4.

bought enslaved people and enlisted them into the army,[29] promising them freedom after two years of service.[30] The cost of purchasing such a large number of enslaved people was so prohibitive that, when Hannibal offered to ransom the Roman captives taken at Cannae, the senate was faced with a dilemma.[31] Hannibal's offer was delivered to the senate by a number of captives, bound by oath to return to their Carthaginian masters.[32] In the end, the senate refused to ransom the captured Roman soldiers, citing the captives' supposed cowardice and the expense of the enlisted enslaved people as the reasons for their refusal.[33] In reality, the senate's concern may have been to limit Hannibal's financial acquisitions through the ransom of the Roman captives.[34] The Roman people were enraged by the senate's decision,[35] and at least one of the messengers attempted to return home, thus breaking the oaths they had sworn to their new masters. The senate ordered the messengers' return to the Carthaginians, not wishing for the Romans to appear as oath-breakers.[36] The Roman captives being held by the Carthaginians were subsequently sold into slavery, but some were recovered by Gaius Flaminius in 196 BCE and appeared in his triumph of 191 BCE, wearing caps of freedom.[37] The triumph was a public event which attracted vast crowds,[38] and Flaminius would therefore have returned the captives to the public eye, two decades after their initial capture. As a result, Lefèvre suggests that *Captivi* was first performed during the celebrations which followed Flaminius' triumph, arguing that the adaptation of the play from the Greek original is evidence of Plautus responding to the concerns of his audience regarding the return and reintegration of prisoners of war into society.[39] Unfortunately, the specific dating of the first

---

29 In line with recent scholarship on transatlantic slavery, I have chosen to use the terms 'enslaved person' or 'enslaved attendant' rather than 'slave'. I have used 'master', rather than enslaver, to more succinctly convey the nature of the relationship between the enslaved person and individuals 'who held people in slavery', cf. Foreman (2019). For further discussion on the language of slavery, cf. Foreman (2019); Dugan (2019) 62–87.
30 Livy 22.57.11, 24.14.1–8, 24.18.12.
31 Livy 22.58.4.
32 Livy 22.59.1–19.
33 Livy 22.60.6–24.
34 Livy 22.57.12.
35 Livy 22.61.1–8.
36 Livy 22.61.7–8.
37 Plut. *Flam.* 13.5–6. Plutarch claims that only 1200 were recovered by Flaminius.
38 Beard (2007); Östenberg (2009).
39 Lefèvre (1998) 33–36.

production of *Captivi* is highly speculative.⁴⁰ Nevertheless, given the chronological proximity of the Cannae captives' return to the play's production, it is likely that Plautus and his audience were still conscious and affected by the memory of recent captive-taking events of which Cannae and, by association, Regulus were the most prominent.⁴¹

3 The Memory of Cannae and its Impact on Roman Society

Given that the play was adapted and performed within years of events resulting from the Battle of Cannae, the captives' return was probably still a concern within Roman society, and it would certainly have been within the audiences' shared memory. It should be noted that most of what we know of Cannae and Regulus derives from later sources, such as Livy and Cicero, who were writing more than a century after the events in question. However, as Richlin argues, the development of the Cannae stories into *exempla* suggests that these events were within the audiences' collective memory from the time of their historical origins to well into the Republican period.⁴² As a result, the impact of the Battle of Cannae on Romans at the time cannot be underestimated. It was a crisis, which, as Libourel shows, was apparent in the inclusion of enslaved people within the military.⁴³ Evidently, the Battle of Cannae had social and political implications on the Romans which lasted for decades after the battle itself, and would have been remembered by Plautus' audiences. Despite the historical uncertainties surrounding the Cannae captives and their fate, there was no doubt a widespread awareness of the captive-taking resulting from the battle, and this would have been highly emotive for the audiences.

---

40 As a case in point: Wellesley and Grimal suggest that the *Captivi* can be linked to the detention of 43 Aetolian prisoners of war in the Lautumiae, tufa quarries, near Rome in 190 BCE. Wellesley argues that the play was therefore first performed at the *Ludi Romani* in September 189 BCE, cf. Wellesley (1955) 298–305; Grimal (1969) 413.
41 The parallels between the Cannae and Regulus *exempla* are likely to have been drawn at an early stage, given their later use by Cicero, cf. Cic. *De Off.* 3.21–32; *Pro Sest.* 127.
42 Richlin (2018) 226. The ransom of the soldiers at Cannae continued to be a point of contention until the 1st century BCE, with Cicero claiming that Greek philosophers still discussed the incident, *cf.* Cicero, *De Or.* 3.109; Cicero, *De Off.* 1.13. Richlin's comments can also be applied to the Regulus *exemplum*.
43 Libourel (1973) 119.

Plautus may have chosen to adapt the Greek original of *Captivi* because of this awareness, particularly as theatrical performances acted as a forum for the public to express their feelings towards political developments.[44] Richlin argues that theatre was a means by which the playwright and the audience, as components of society at large, could explore traumatic events which they had directly or indirectly been affected by.[45] As a result, theatre was used as a means of conveying and exploring socio-political concerns, which ultimately derived from events within the Romans' collective memory.[46]

4 The Plot of *Captivi*

Having established the *exempla* pertaining to captive-taking in the Punic Wars, we should consider *Captivi*'s plot before exploring its themes and how they relate to the audiences' memory of past events. *Captivi* centres on Hegio, a nobleman from Aetolia who buys captives taken during conflict with a neighbouring enemy state, Elis. The captives in question, Philocrates and his enslaved attendant Tyndarus, are two of many bought by Hegio with a view to exchange them for his son, who is being held captive by the enemy Eleans.[47] After ascertaining through questioning that Philocrates belongs to a noble family,[48] Hegio decides to send the other captive, whom he believes to be the enslaved person, to the enemy with a message offering the exchange of his son for Philocrates. By this time, Tyndarus and Philocrates, the enslaved person and the master respectively, have secretly exchanged places so that Philocrates can return home in the guise of the messenger. Philocrates leaves and Tyndarus' identity as the enslaved person, not the nobleman's son, is revealed when Hegio introduces another captive who transpires to be an acquaintance of Philocrates' from Elis. The captive recognises Tyndarus and reveals him to be an enslaved person. Angered by Tyndarus' deceit, Hegio sends Tyndarus to carry out hard labour in the quarries. Sometime later, Philocrates returns with Hegio's son who reveals that an enslaved person in Hegio's household stole Hegio's other son as a child and sold him to the household of Philocrates' father. The enslaved person in question is Tyndarus, who is quickly recalled from the quarries and reinstated as Hegio's son. The play concludes with

---

44 Cic. *Att.* 2.19.3; *Pro Sest.* 106–26, cf. Martin (2007) 49–53.
45 Richlin (2017) 355–6, cf. Dean *et al.* (2015) 16.
46 Chalmers (1965) 21.
47 Plaut. *Capt.* 23–24, 126–128.
48 Plaut. *Capt.* 251–450.

a 'happy ending', as the main characters return to their appropriate social positions: Philocrates is ransomed for Hegio's son, returning to his free status; Tyndarus is returned to his father as a free man; and the devious enslaved person who sold Tyndarus is placed in chains.[49]

5 Plautus' Audience and their Impressions of Captive-taking

Next, let us consider who was present in the audience of Plautus' plays, as the audiences' diversity indicates that Plautus' works addressed issues and events which concerned, or were remembered by, the whole of Roman society.[50] Plautus' audiences consisted of individuals from across Rome's social classes, including the senatorial elite and enslaved people.[51] This is evident in the opening lines of *Captivi* in which Plautus deliberately draws the attention of the audience to the standing position of the two chained captives, addressing his remarks to audience members stood at the back of the theatre.

> hos quos uidetis stare hic captiuos duos,
> illi quia astant, hi stant ambo, non sedent.
>
> Plaut. *Capt.* 1–2

> Those two prisoners you can see standing here, they're both standing, not sitting, because the people back there are standing.[52]

That Plautus chose to address those standing, and 'those on the censor's list', i.e., those with property, is significant as it directly alludes to the class distinctions within Roman society.[53] The opening lines have often been used within scholarship to suggest a form of seating plan for the theatre. Moore argues that remarks within the prologue are aimed at different parts of the audience, which was formally separated by social class from 194 BCE,[54] with those with property seated

---

49 Plaut. *Capt.* 1018–1028.
50 On the different classes present at theatrical productions during the late Republic, see Haley in this volume.
51 Richlin (2017) 89.
52 All translations in this paper, unless stated otherwise, are by De Melo (2011).
53 Moore (1994) 118–9; Rei (1998) 92–108.
54 Livy 3.54.3–8; Val. Max. 2.4.3, cf. Moore (1994) 122–3.

and those without made to stand at the back of the theatre.⁵⁵ Following this logic, the prologue's direct address to the Roman audiences enables Plautus to cast the play, despite its Greek origins, as being Roman in nature, with Roman social conventions referenced within the opening lines. Thus, the captive-taking traditions alluded to within the play are Roman, and recall events within the Romans' shared cultural memory which involved captive-taking.

Within the prologue, Plautus stresses expectations of captive-taking which his audience would have recognised, and understood from the memory of past events. The primary expectation was that the outcome of defeat in warfare was captivity.⁵⁶

> Ut fit in bello, capitur alter filius.
> Plaut. *Capt*. 25
>
> His [Hegio's] other son's taken prisoner, as so happens in war.

As a result, those within the standing audience could have been the real-life counterparts of the captives standing on-stage. It is also possible that the actors themselves were former captives.⁵⁷ From the outset, the prologue places the audience and actors in the social hierarchy in which they lived, essentially making the audience and actors aware of their own social position. Furthermore, references to captives on stage may have encouraged the audience to recognise that they were participants, whether active or passive, of captive-taking as they directly benefitted from seeing former captives as actors onstage.⁵⁸ In addition, given the return of captives to Rome and the captive-taking carried out during the Punic Wars by Rome, it is likely that the audience were witnessing on-stage representations of events they either recalled from their culture memory, or had encountered off-stage through Roman captive-taking and slavery on a domestic level.

It is also thought that Plautus was enslaved or of lower-class origins, and that he may have encountered captives during his work in the theatre or in his supposed employment as a manual labourer.⁵⁹ However, that is not to suggest that Plautus was attempting subversive dissension and we know from the onset of the

---

55 Plaut. *Capt*. 1–2, 10–13.
56 Cf. Richlin (2018) 214.
57 Richlin (2018) 213–217.
58 Dufallo (2018) 23.
59 Gellius, *NA* 3.3.14, cf. Gruen (2001) 84.

play that the issues will be resolved, with the characters returning to their appropriate social positions. As a result, Plautus' play explores issues of captivity, status, and contemporary social concerns, which were developed by and evocative of events in Rome's recent history. Ultimately, as Chalmers argues, through a play set in Greece and adapted from a Greek original, Plautus could 'allude to contemporary events and conditions with less inhibitions than he might have felt had the scene of his plays been set in Italy.'[60]

Furthermore, Plautus' career depended upon his plays being enjoyed by both the audience and the aediles in charge of financing public performances.[61] This links to the funding for the *ludi* (games), in which theatrical performances usually took place.[62] References to the purchase of the captives from quaestors' spoils (*praeda*),[63] and the retention of enslaved people by the state,[64] may have been deliberately included by Plautus, as spectacles and performances were often financed *ex manubiis*, effectively from the funds raised from the sale of wartime captives or spoils.[65] The term is often referenced on inscriptions adorning later public buildings,[66] but it is also likely that funds deriving from the sale of spoils and captives were used to fund performances and the creation of their temporary venues.[67] Given Plautus' references to spoils, it is likely that the audience recognised, without Plautus offering any extensive explanation, the relationship between captive-taking and financial gain.

Such issues link to the financial and, by extension, social considerations of purchasing or ransoming captives, as evident in *postliminium*. There is some debate surrounding *postliminium* centring on whether or not those who ransomed the captives effectively became the captives' masters.[68] Here, the concern was that even those who were freed from enemy captivity were essentially still captive, and in the 'custody' of their fellow Romans until the ransom was repaid.[69]

---

60 Chalmers (1965) 24.
61 Manuwald (2010) 16; Chalmers (1965) 23.
62 Martin (2007) 49.
63 Plaut. *Capt.* 34, 111, 453.
64 Plaut. *Capt.* 333–4.
65 Shatzman (1972) 177–205.
66 The Colosseum, on which construction began in 70 CE, is the most famous example of a building funded by *manubiae*. An inscription on the building states that the amphitheatre was funded by 'the spoils of war', and although the war is not specified, it was likely funded using the loot, including captives, taken during the First Jewish Revolt, cf. *CIL* 6.40454a in Millar (2005) 118.
67 Beacham (1991) 56.
68 Levy (1943) 159–176.
69 Levy (1943) 159–176.

Romans who paid the ransoms of their fellow citizens were often praised for their generosity,[70] and this may be indirectly referenced by Plautus when Hegio relays that he has been congratulated by his fellow citizens for arranging the recovery of Aetolian citizens.[71] This may relate to Plautus claiming that *Captivi* was intended to be a moralising play, demonstrating '*pudicos mores*' (pure morals).[72] As a result, it is possible to consider the idealised expectations of captive-taking within the Roman world, based on the memory of incidents in Roman history involving captive-taking, namely that it was accepted that captives were taken during warfare and that it was considered shameful to be forced into a captive status which was considered to be a form of slavery, or akin to enslavement. Captives could be ransomed, but there were financial and social ramifications which the Romans had to consider before deciding whether they would pay a captive's ransom. This concern largely centred on the social position of the captive in question, and may have been a particularly poignant topic for certain members of the audience, given the events of Cannae mere decades before the play's production. We shall address this issue shortly, but we must first acknowledge the issue of 'captivity', its role in Plautus' *Captivi* and the associations with the audiences' memories of Regulus and Cannae.

6 The Social Value of Plautus' Captives and the Cannae Returnees

The issue of 'captivity' is significant for Plautus' *Captivi*, as scholarship tends to label its key themes as being 'slavery' and 'freedom'.[73] However, with the exception of Tyndarus' condemnation to the quarries, the captives are never actively employed in any form of work which we could identify as being akin to slavery whilst in Hegio's custody.[74] Even when Philocrates is employed as a messenger, he is secretly acting in his own interests, rather than those of his new master.[75] Furthermore, Philocrates utilises the 'double-speak' commonly found in enslaved characters in order to convince Hegio of his lowly status.[76] Tyndarus,

---

70 Cic. *de off.* 2.16, 3.29.
71 Plaut. *Capt.* 598.
72 Plaut. *Capt.* 1029.
73 Moore (1998) 181–5; Duncan (2006) 165–6; Richlin (2017) 236.
74 Bodel (2011) 312–3.
75 Plaut. *Capt.* 271–3.
76 Richlin (2014) 175–9.

whom Hegio assumes to be a member of the free elite, is kept in captivity and appears to be at liberty, but for one guard, within Hegio's household.[77] This relative freedom is symbolised by the removal of his chains.[78] That chains were a symbol of both captivity and slavery is evident in art and later literature,[79] but also in *Captivi* when Tyndarus returns from the quarries in chains, a 'dress that does not suit his worth' (*ornatus haud ex suis uirtutibus*).[80] The symbolic change in status links to Richlin's comments on the fluidity of Roman society, and how the Roman audience had witnessed and understood the fact that individuals could transition between free, enslaved person, and freedman with relative ease.[81] I would argue that *Captivi* explores the state of captivity itself, particularly the transition between the aforementioned statuses, rather than the nature of slavery as a whole. For instance, as we have seen in the justification for the senate's refusal to ransom the Cannae soldiers, captives were considered to be cowards. This is reflected in the play when Hegio is told, by Philocrates, that he and Tyndarus are cowards, implying that Hegio's captured son also falls into the same category.[82] The language Plautus uses in this exchange does not allude to slavery, but rather to captivity, with Hegio's son being described as guarded (*servor*) and captured (*capior*) in the following lines:

> Philocrates: nec pol tibi nos, quia nos seruas, aequom est uitio uortere, nec te nobis, si abeamus hinc, si fuat occasio.
> Hegio: ut uos hic, itidem illic apud uos meus seruatur filius.
> Philocrates: captus est?
>
> Plaut. Capt. 259–262

> Philocrates: It wouldn't be fair of us to blame you for guarding us; and it wouldn't be fair of you to blame us if we clear out from here if we get a chance.
> Hegio: My son's being guarded there at your place, just as you are here.[83]
> Philocrates: Has he been captured?

Interestingly, Hegio does not correct him, thus suggesting that this view was commonplace within Roman society and was not something Plautus intended to challenge within his work.[84]

---

77 Plaut. *Capt*. 393.
78 Plaut. *Capt*. 393.
79 Hope (2003) 79–97; De Souza (2011) 40.
80 Plaut. *Capt*. 995–7. For further discussion of chains in Plautus' works, cf. Richlin (2017) 95–6.
81 Richlin (2014) 208, (2017) 236, 234–5.
82 Plaut. *Capt*. 264.
83 I have adjusted De Melo's translation to reflect the significance of the word *servo* in this line.
84 Plaut. *Capt*. 264.

In addition, within the play, the two captives retain their social status throughout.[85] Both Philocrates and Tyndarus are captives, reduced to the status of slaves, yet Philocrates' status is kept relatively intact, with the man Hegio assumes to be his enslaved attendant being sent to negotiate his ransom. The issues surrounding the captives' social status are where much of the humour of the play lies, namely in the dramatic irony, with the audience knowing of Tyndarus' true identity as Hegio's free-born son.[86] Despite their mutual reduction in status upon their capture, the valueless nature of the enslaved person is indicated by Hegio's decision to not send a separate messenger offering the return of the master and slave. From this, Plautus may have expected the audience to understand that the socially superior master was of more value in terms of negotiating and was also a social equal of Hegio's captured son. The discrepancy between the treatment of the former master and his enslaved attendant would also account for the relative comfort which Tyndarus, acting in the stead of Philocrates, is kept in until his deceit is revealed. As punishment for the deception, Tyndarus is condemned to hard labour in the quarries. Hard labour was a typical punishment assigned to disobedient enslaved people by their masters.[87] In this respect, there does appear to be differentiated treatment between the enslaved person and the nobleman, even though they now have the same standing as they are both captives enslaved by Hegio, a situation they both recognise and address.[88] Ultimately, this demonstrates that captives of different classes held different worth to their captors and were treated accordingly. Furthermore, given the difference in social class between Marcus Regulus and the Cannae soldiers, the audience would have recognised the connection between a captive's value to society, as understood by the political elite, and their financial worth as a captive set for enslavement.

7 Captives, Financial Worth and Recollections of Cannae

The social position of the captives before their capture also links closely to financial considerations, both in the purchase of captives and their subsequent ran-

---

85 Duncan (2006) 168.
86 Plaut. *Capt.* 311–14, 318–20.
87 Juv. *Sat.* 8.180; Apul. *Met.* 9.12, cf. Millar (1984) 126; Groen-Vallinga & Tacoma (2015) 6.
88 Plaut. *Capt.* 241–2, 246.

som. In turn this aspect of *Captivi* links closely to the financial worth of the Cannae captives, an issue which would have been within the audiences' shared memory, given the captives' recent return to Rome in 191 BCE. Tyndarus alludes to this socio-economic connection when he acknowledges that his life is cheap in comparison to Philocrates'.[89] There may be an implication here about the discrepancy in cost between the sale of the two, with former enslaved people being cheaper than their former masters. However, that Hegio states that the two are kept in chains because they were expensive purchases suggests that they were both bought for high prices.[90] Here, Plautus may be further evoking the dramatic irony evident throughout the play as Tyndarus, despite being enslaved before his capture, is sold alongside a formerly free man and at a similar price, thus alluding to his freeborn status. Furthermore, there were certainly financial considerations for the ransom of captives, as we have seen with the captured soldiers at Cannae. However, captives of high social status were valued more highly, and there is the suggestion that their families could be exploited should the captor learn of their fortune. This is evident when Tyndarus, pretending to be Philocrates, suggests that Hegio should not take advantage of his father's wealth. He further claims that his father would prefer his son to live like an enslaved attendant in Hegio's house, rather than bankrupt the family to attain his freedom.

> ego patri meo esse fateor summas diuitias domimeque summo genere gnatum. sed te optestor, Hegio, ne tuom animum auariorem faxint diuitiae meae: ne patri, tam etsi sum unicus, decere uideatur magis, me saturum seruire apud te sumptu et uestitu tuo potius quam illi, ubi minime honestum est, mendicantem uiuere.
>
> Plaut. *Capt.* 318–323

> I do admit that my father has great wealth at home and that I come from a great family. But I entreat you, Hegio, do not let my riches make you greedier; otherwise it might seem more appropriate to my father that even though I'm his only son, I should be a well-fed slave at your place, nourished and clothed at your expense, rather than live as a beggar back there, where it would be most disgraceful.

Within the audiences' shared memory, we need to consider that the senate made the decision not to ransom the captured soldiers from Hannibal, thus condemning them to slavery. However, for the Roman senate, the possibility of providing Hannibal with much-needed financial resources by paying the ransom could have resulted in the metaphorical 'enslavement' of the entire populace.[91] As such,

---

89 Plaut. *Capt.* 229–30.
90 Plaut. *Capt.* 255–8, cf. Maurach (2011), 433.
91 Lavan (2013) 73–123.

whilst ransoming was preferable to Roman citizens being enslaved to foreign powers, there were other issues to consider for those weighing up the possibility of paying the ransom. Thus, Plautus may have been alluding to the issues of exploitation and the reality of captive-taking, including events within his audiences' collective memory. As the audience would have been aware from the fate of the Cannae captives before their recovery, captivity mostly resulted in captives being lost to enemies simply because the financial considerations overrode social mores.

8 Oaths, Sacrifice and Inherent Nobility in *Captivi* and the Memory of the Punic Wars

Another key theme of *Captivi* is the concept of oaths, which were essential within Mediterranean warfare, as international law did not exist in a ratified form.[92] The oath Philocrates swears to Tyndarus to return when they exchange places suggests that they are on a socially equal footing and conveys the innate nobility of Philocrates. The oath is essential for the humour of the play which, as Duncan outlines, relies upon Tyndarus' concern that he has been abandoned by his former master.[93] Tyndarus is also presented as being loyal to his former master,[94] even sacrificing himself for Philocrates, a characteristic which is often found in Plautus' stock enslaved characters.[95] Ideally, enslaved people would transfer their loyalties to their new masters, and Duncan argues that a depiction of a enslaved person's rebellion would have caused the audiences no small discomfort. However, this threat is neutralized by the audiences' knowledge that Tyndarus is a wrongly enslaved freeborn man.[96] As such, this also links to the Regulus *exemplum*, as Regulus continued to exhibit 'Roman' characteristics despite his guise as a person enslaved by the Carthaginians, and made the ultimate sacrifice for those to whom he remained loyal whilst keeping his oath.[97] Like Tyndarus, Regulus displayed his inherent nobility even during enslavement.[98] Regulus' *exemplum* is in direct contrast to the Cannae captives, particularly as at least one of the

---

[92] Bederman (2001) 89–90; *OCD*: Law, international.
[93] Duncan (2006) 165–6.
[94] Plaut. *Capt.* 241–2, 717–20.
[95] Duncan (2006) 167.
[96] Duncan (2006) 172–3.
[97] Cassius Dio 11 = Zonaras 8,15.
[98] Tipps (2003) 375–6.

Cannae captives attempted to return home, despite being obliged to serve their new masters. Similarly, by not being ransomed, the Cannae captives were ensuring that the Romans were not contributing towards the Carthaginian cause, a form of sacrifice in itself. However, with the Cannae examples, this was not done with the same nobility as Marcus Regulus, as they had to be returned to their captors by force. In a similar way to the *exemplum* of Regulus, Tyndarus' sacrifice shows his inherent nobility which derives from his status as a free man who had been sold into slavery under false pretences. Essentially, Plautus perpetuates the concept of inherent nobility, namely that a man who is noble cannot be made ignoble by his enslavement. This concept is illuminated in the following line, spoken by Tyndarus:

> qui per uirtutem periit, at non interit.
>
> Plaut. *Capt.* 690

> A man who dies as a result of his noble character does not perish.

This link to concerns, relating to the memory of recent events, which the Roman audiences may have had with regards to the status of the returning Cannae captives. However, Plautus' ending essentially provides the conclusion the audiences would most desire for the returning Roman soldiers, namely that the captives were freed.

9 Conclusion

Overall, although Plautus adapts a Greek play, he uses Roman features of captive-taking to ensure that the themes of captivity, freedom and status were directly relatable to the Roman audience through their memories of specific events. I have shown that there can be little doubt that the events of Marcus Regulus' return and the Battle of Cannae were still within the audiences' collective memory at the time *Captivi* was produced. Plautus' *Captivi* presents a view of captive-taking which inevitably would have brought the consequences of Cannae to the mind of the Roman audience, who may have undergone or witnessed the transition of their fellow Romans from soldiers to captives to free men. Given the parallels between the Cannae and Regulus *exempla*, it is fair to suggest that Plautus was acutely aware of the impact of the Punic Wars on his audiences and their concerns about captive-taking, which were inextricably linked to their shared memories. We can only guess as to Plautus' attitude towards the returning captives. However, as Plautus provides the captives in *Captivi* with a 'happy ending', it can be argued that he was aware of the public's desire to see a resolution for the on-stage counterparts of the Punic War captives. This links to Richlin's comments on the nature of playwriting as a form of 'communal history writing', enabling 'damaged groups [to] repair identities'.[99] As a result, Plautus' play may have been used to reflect and explore, using a distant setting, issues surrounding captivity and *postliminium* which would have been present within contemporary Roman society and its collective memory.

Bibliography

Beacham, R.C. (1991), *The Roman Theatre and Its Audience*, London.
Beard, M. (2007), *The Roman Triumph*, Cambridge, MA.
Bederman, D.J. (2001), *International Law in Antiquity*, Cambridge.
Bell, S. (2008), "Introduction: Role Models in the Roman World", in S. Bell (ed.), *Memoirs of the American Academy in Rome: Supplementary Volumes* 7, Rome: 1–39.
Cameron, C.M. (2011), "Captives and Culture Change: Implications for Archaeology", *Current Anthropology* 52/2: 169–209.
Chalmers, W.R. (1965), "Plautus and His Audience", in T.A. Dorey & D.R. Dubley (eds.), *Roman Drama*, London: 21–50.
Dean, D./Y. Meerzon/K. Prince (2015), "Introduction", in D. Dean, Y. Meerzon and K. Prince (eds.), *History, Memory, Performance*, Basingstoke: 201–18.
De Melo, W. (2011), "Introduction to *Captivi*", in W. De Melo (ed. trans.), *Plautus'* Captivi, Cambridge: 502–3.
De Souza, P. (2011), "War, Slavery and Empire in Roman Imperial Iconography", *BIC* 54/1: 31–62.
Dufallo, B. (2018), "The Comedy of Plunder: Art and Appropriation in Plautus' *Menaechmi*", in M.P. Loar, C. MacDonald, and D. Padilla Peralta (eds.), *Rome, Empire of Plunder: The Dynamics of Cultural Appropriation*, Cambridge: 15–29.
Dugan, K. (2019), "The 'Happy Slave' Narrative and Classics Pedagogy: A Verbal and Visual Analysis of Beginning Greek and Latin Textbooks", *The New England Classical Journal* 46/1: 62–87.
Duncan, A. (2006), *Performance and Identity in the Classical World*, Cambridge.
Foreman, P.G. (2019), "Writing about 'Slavery'? This Might Help." [Online]. Retrieved 5th September 2019 from https://naacpculpeper.org/resources/writing-about-slavery-this-might-help/
Franko, G.F. (1995), "Fides, Aetolia, and Plautus' *Captivi*", *Transactions of the American Philological Association* 125: 155–176.
Garcia Riazia, E. (2015), "Le protocole diplomatique entre paricularisme romain etc universalisme", in B. Grass & G. Stouder (eds.), *La Diplomatie Romaine sous la République Réflexions sue une Pratique*, Paris: 15–41.

---

99 Richlin (2017) 355–6, cf. Dean *et al.* (2015) 16.

Grimal, P. (1969), *Le modèle et la date des "Captivi" de Plaute*, Bruxelles.
Groen-Vallinga, M.J./L.E. Tacoma (2015), "Contextualising condemnation to hard labour in the Roman Empire", in C.G. de Vito & A. Lichtenstein (eds.), *Global convict labour*, Leiden: 49–78.
Gruen, E. (2001), "Plautus and The Public Stage", in E. Segal (ed.), *Oxford Readings in Menander, Plautus, and Terence*, Oxford: 83–94.
Hölkeskamp, K.J. (2013), "Friends, Romans, Countrymen: Addressing the Roman People and the Rhetoric of Inclusion", in C. Steel & H. Van Der Blom (eds.), *Community and Communication: Oratory and Politics in Republican Rome*, Oxford: 11–28.
Hope, V. (2003), "Trophies and Tombstones: Commemorating the Roman Soldier", *World Archaeology* 35/1: 79–97.
Larson, J.A.O./S. Hornblower (2003), "Law, international", in S. Hornblower & A. Spawforth (eds.), *The Oxford Classical Dictionary*, Oxford: 823.
Lavan, M. (2013), *Slaves to Rome: Paradigms of Empire in Roman Culture*, Cambridge.
Leigh, M. (2004), *Comedy and the Rise of Rome*, Oxford.
Levy, E. (1943), "Captivus Redemptus", *Classical Philology* 38/3: 159–176.
Libourel, J.M. (1973), "Galley Slaves in the Second Punic War", *Classical Philology* 68/2: 116–119.
Lowe, J.C.B. (1991), "Prisoners, Guards, and Chains in Plautus, *Captivi*", *The American Journal of Philology* 112/1: 29–44.
Manuwald, G. (2010), *Roman Drama: A Reader*, London.
Manuwald, G. (2011), *Roman Republican Theatre*, Cambridge.
Martin, R.P. (2007), "Ancient Theatre and Performance Culture", in M. McDonald & J.M. Walton (eds.), *The Cambridge Companion to Greek and Roman Theatre*, Cambridge: 36–54.
Maurach, G. (2011), "Anmerkungen ze Plautus' *Captivi*", *Hermes* 139/4: 431–442.
Millar, F. (1984), "Condemnation to Hard Labour in the Roman Empire, from the Julio-Claudians to Constantine", *Papers of the British School at Rome* 52: 124–147.
Millar, F. (2005), "Last Year in Jerusalem: Monuments of the Jewish War in Rome", in J. Edmondson, S. Mason and J. Rives (eds.), *Flavius Josephus and Flavian Rome*, Oxford: 129–144.
Moore, T.J. (1994), "Seats and Social Status in the Plautine Theatre", *The Classical Journal* 90/2: 113–123.
Moore, T.J. (1998), *The Theater of Plautus*, Austin.
Östenberg, I. (2009), *Staging the world: spoils, captives, and representations in the Roman triumphal procession*, Oxford.
Rei, A. (1998), "Villains, Wives and Slaves in the Comedies of Plautus", in D.R. Joshele & S. Murnaghan (eds.), *Women and Slaves in Greco-Roman Culture*, Oxford: 92–108.
Richlin, A. (2014) "Talking to Slaves in the Plautine Audience", *Classical Antiquity* 33/1: 174–226.
Richlin, A. (2017), *Slave Theater in the Roman Republic: Plautus and Popular Comedy*, Cambridge.
Richlin, A. (2018), "The Ones Who Paid the Butcher's Bill: Soldiers and War Captives in Roman Comedy", in J.H. Clark & B. Turner (eds.), *Brill's Companion to Military Defeat in Ancient Mediterranean Society*, Leiden: 213–240.
Shatzman, I. (1972), "The Roman General's Authority over Booty", *Historia* 21/2: 177–205.
Tipps, G.K. (2003), "The Defeat of Regulus", *The Classical World* 94/4: 75–385.
Wiseman, T. (2014), "Popular Memory", in K. Galinsky (ed.), *Memoria Romana: Memory in Rome and Rome in Memory*, Ann Arbor: 43–62.

Katarzyna Kostecka
Divine Memories and the Shaping of Olympus in the *Iliad*

Abstract: The gods in the *Iliad* are a conflicted community. They support different sides of the Trojan conflict and root for different heroes and, because of that, they constantly quarrel or plot against each other. In many scenes, the tension between them rises and the audience is made to think it will turn into violence – for instance when Hera incites the gods to revolt against her husband (*Il.* 8.205–207) or when Zeus threatens all the gods that he will suspend them high in the air ((*Il.* 8.18–26). The menace of aggression, however, never gets realized – at the last moments the gods restrain themselves and are able to achieve peace. The tension between them is often released with shared laughter. This duality of the divine reactions – violent anger on one hand and rational withdrawal on the other – is surprising. In this paper, I argue that this state can be truly understood if one considers it from the perspective of divine experiences. During the narrative, the gods share many memories of the past, which reveal a different and much more violent world of the past, when Zeus was a tyrannical ruler and the gods were rebellious subjects. Together these stories present a memory of the Olympians as a collective, which influences the way they behave and what they choose, often contrary to their initial impulses.

During the short period of the Trojan War presented in the *Iliad*, the Olympian gods quarrel endlessly.[1] Contrary to what we see in the *Odyssey* or in Hesiod's *Theogony*, in the *Iliad* Zeus does not manage his dominion in an orderly and calm way, nor are his divine subjects easy to placate.[2] After all, while Zeus is the ruler of the Sky, he has to share the power on Earth and Olympus with others (*Il.* 15.187–193) and this easily becomes a bone of contention. Oftentimes the divine hostility seems to head in a dangerous direction and the audience is given the impression that the confrontation will have grave consequences. Zeus threatens the gods that he will suspend them high in the air if they intervene one more time in the battle (*Il.* 8.18–26). When Patroclus dies and the Trojans press the

---

[1] The research on this article was supported by the National Science Centre grants number 2016/23/N/HS3/00838 (Mythical genealogies of aristocratic families in archaic and classical Greece).
[2] Grube (1951).

Achaeans, Athena arms herself and rushes towards Apollo on the battlefield – the audience is made to think that the two will clash in battle (*Il.* 7.17–21). Hera incites the gods to revolt against Zeus and leave him abandoned on Mount Ida (*Il.* 8.205–207). Poseidon wants to send Zeus rebellious words through Iris (*Il.* 15.184–200). These divine quarrels, especially compared to the human debates, seem aggressive and untamed and create a threat that violence will prevail on Olympus.

Yet however dangerous the situations appear to be, Homer always takes great care not to lead the gods too far and neither Zeus' threats nor any other bold declarations are realised.[3] In the end, the gods never harm each other – Apollo persuades Athena to make peace instantly (*Il.* 7.24–36), Hera's plan to abandon Zeus is mocked by Poseidon (*Il.* 8.209–211), Poseidon is advised by Iris to modify his message to Zeus to a milder one (*Il.* 15.201–2019) and Zeus' rage sooner or later ebbs away. Even the famous battle of the gods (*Il.* 20.5–108) is a spectacle orchestrated by Zeus rather than a serious strife.[4] The gods seem, after the initial outbursts, almost careless about what will happen. They may plot against each other and brawl, yet they will not sacrifice too much for men: their attitude is best summed up by Apollo's words:[5]

> οὐκ ἄν με σαόφρονα μυθήσαιο
> ἔμμεναι, εἰ δὴ σοί γε βροτῶν ἕνεκα πτολεμίξω
> δειλῶν

> you would have me be as one without prudence
> if I am to fight even you for the sake of insignificant
> mortals
> *Il.* 21.462–465[6]

Peace on Olympus is ultimately more important than the gods' individual goals.[7]

---

3 Heiden (2008) 180–181.
4 Louden (2006) 216.
5 Similarly, Hera restrains Hephaestus saying:

> Ἥφαιστε σχέο τέκνον ἀγακλεές: οὐ γὰρ ἔοικεν
> ἀθάνατον θεὸν ὧδε βροτῶν ἕνεκα στυφελίζειν

> Hephaistos, hold, my glorious child, since it is not fitting
> to batter thus an immortal god for the sake of mortals (*Il.* 21.379–380).

6 All passages from the *Iliad* as translated by Lattimore (1951).
7 Elmer (2013).

This duality of the reactions of the gods when things do not go their way, violent individual emotions on one hand, rational withdrawal and prioritizing community on the other, should make us wonder. How is it that the gods have the strong impulse to fight with each other so ardently and stand up for humans, yet know how to restrain themselves every time when the situations among their own company get overly tense? In this paper, I will argue that the duality of the divine behaviour presented in the *Iliad* becomes understandable in the light of their past and their social memory. In the poem, at various stages of the Trojan war, the gods become narrators and recall the times predating the Trojan War: the shaping of a younger Olympus.[8] They share the reminiscences they believe important in a given context, yet these considered together form a very coherent vision of the past and present the divine social memory of a chaotic and violent era.[9] I will argue that having in mind the consequences of past events, the gods rationally maintain a state of balance and relative peace,[10] which was not the "natural" order of Olympus. Further, I will show that Homer, using memories as a poetic device, presents an evolution of the reign of Zeus, a theme that interested many archaic poets.[11]

1 Memories and their function in the *Iliad*

Before inspecting the stories of the divine past in detail, I begin with a few notes on the use of memories as such in the Homeric poems and how they can be analyzed with narratological tools. Memory plays a significant role in the *Iliad* and the *Odyssey*.[12] Homer furnishes both the heroes and the gods with a form of memory – as Grethlein shows convincingly, the characters of the narrative have *Geschichtsbild* or an "idea of history", which is revealed in the stories of the past

---

8 Grethlein (2007). The stories of early Olympus appear only in the *Iliad* and never in the *Odyssey*, which to some point can be related to the generally different approach towards the gods in the *Odyssey* – there, Olympus is depicted as a more stable place and divine conflict, which appears in most memories in the *Iliad*, is generally absent from the poem.
9 Porter (2014).
10 Elmer (2013), Heiden (2008) 161–185.
11 Blickman (1987); Strauss Clay (1989; 2003; 2011).
12 Bakker (2008) 65–78; Strauss Clay (2011) 14–37.

they constantly refer to.¹³ The heroes focus on the adventures of the previous generations, which they either saw or of which they heard from others, while the gods reminisce on their own past.

Importantly, both in the *Iliad* and the *Odyssey*, remembering is usually presented as a social act. A rare example of a personal memory can be encountered in the *Odyssey*, when Eurycleia sees the scar of the disguised Odysseus, which makes her remember the time when he was wounded by a boar as a young boy, yet she does not share the memory with anybody and we only learn about it through the narrator (*Od.* 19.392–466).¹⁴ This, however, is an exception – principally, remembering is a form of communication. It is an act to be carried out in the social frame, meant to be heard by others and influence their decisions. The memories told by the characters present a social memory of the mythical communities, a collective set of shared knowledge and experiences from the past.¹⁵ The past is meant to affect the present, as both the heroes and gods use the memories mostly as paradigms.¹⁶ The gods and heroes are also surrounded physically by the past – the material objects are seen as reminders of the distant events.¹⁷ This social aspect of memory in the *Iliad* is important – telling stories of the past is not presented there as an occasional event, but a common way for the members of the community to orient themselves and others in various situations.

From the narratological point of view, the characters telling stories are secondary narrators and the memories they share are presented in external analepses or digressions. External analepses are a narratological tool used not only by Homer; similar digressions (especially paradigmatic) were used for instance in the *Epic Cycle*.¹⁸ Such digressions, once ignored or assumed to be left-overs of different traditions and poems, are now considered an important element of the narrative, crucial for its understanding.¹⁹ Many scholars argue that Homer uses these memories very intentionally in order to provide reflections on the human

---

13 Grethlein (2006). It is sometimes believed that the concept of time and its passing is not elaborated in the *Iliad* (Fränkel (1960), but as de Jong (2007) 15–18 rightly points out, the gods and heroes in their speeches they seem well aware both of the distant and close past and the future.
14 Minchin (2012).
15 Minchin (2012).
16 Kakridis (1930) 113–122; Kakridis (1949) 96–105; Willcock (1964) 141–154; Austin (1966) 295–313; Nagy (1996) 113–46; Grethlein (2006) 46–64.
17 Grethlein (2008).
18 Willcock (1964).
19 For paradigms see Kakridis (1930) 113–122; Kakridis (1949) 96–105; Willcock (1964) 141–154; and Austin (1966) 295–312. For genealogies see Alden (1996) 257–263 and Aronen (2002) 89–111. For objects, see Grethlein (2008) 27–51.

condition, foreshadow the fate of the Trojan War heroes, and mirror or contrast the crucial motifs of the story.[20] They are noted to have a twofold purpose within the narrative: as Andersen (1993) argues, they have both an "argument function" and a "key function". The "argument function" is the function the stories have for those who tell them – the secondary narrators want to communicate through them with other figures of the poem. The "key function" of the stories, on the other hand, is to provide a way of communication between the poet and his audience, to transmit information or perspectives that influence how the audience perceives the narrative and its characters. In the next section, I will show the role of each of the stories in their specific context and their argument function. Yet their key function should always be in the back of our mind – what those memories as a whole and the patterns that they share tell us about the divine relations, and how they can help us understand the gods' attitudes in the main narrative.

2 Remembering conflict

I will now present a catalogue of the memories of Olympus' past. I will note their contexts and the secondary narrators, but also what reality is presented through them: the common patterns and motifs that appear there, the attitudes and motivations of the different gods, and how they resolve the tensions that arise between them.

In the *Iliad*, ten digressions (representing eight different events), focus on the infra-divine relations on early Olympus (in order of appearance – the attack on Zeus by the gods Hera, Poseidon and Athena, *Il.* 1.395–407; the casting of Hephaestus from Olympus, *Il.* 1.585–594, 18.394–400; the building of Trojan Walls by Apollo and Poseidon by Zeus' order, *Il.* 7.446–454, 21.436–460; the conflict between Hera and Zeus over Heracles, *Il.* 14.242–262, *Il.* 15.14–33, 19.91–136; the division of power between Zeus, Poseidon, and Hades, *Il.* 15.184–200; the marriage between Thetis and Peleus imposed by Zeus, *Il.* 18.428–437).[21] The mythical chronology of the events cannot be defined very precisely, though most of them happened around one or two generations back – in the time of Heracles, Laomedon and Peleus, who feature in these stories.[22] Of the ten digressions, nine depict divine conflicts and miseries and they will be the core of this paper. Only one

---

20 Alden (1996; 2000; 2017), Andersen (1993; 1997), Grethlein (2006) 42–63.
21 Other stories of the past tell us more about the relations between men and gods, which were also violent (Grethlein 2006), they will not be the focus of this article.
22 Porter (2014).

presents an attempt at settlement: the already mentioned passage of the division of power between the three brothers, Poseidon, Hades and Zeus. The passage, however, is crucial to understand the conflicts and relations of the Olympians and can be thus a good introduction to the catalogue of the divine memories.

The story of the division of power is told by Poseidon, when Iris comes to him with an order from Zeus to stop fighting for the Achaeans and return to Olympus (*Il.* 15.184–200). Poseidon wants to remind Zeus that he should not impose his will on other gods too harshly. He recalls how in the past the three brothers received shares of power by lot – Hades received the Underworld, Poseidon the Sea and Zeus the Sky. The Earth and Olympus were to be shared by all, though it is unclear if Poseidon means all Olympians or just the three brothers. Whatever the interpretation, the passage gives us an important insight into the divine hierarchy. While in Hesiod's *Theogony* (71–74) Zeus divides the *timai* between all gods, Homer through Poseidon's words describes a very rough division of power done by lot and a shared space in which no god has the main say.[23] This lack of absolute power of Zeus given in the two realms, Olympian and human, has crucial consequences. Because of that, Zeus cannot impose his will without taking into account the other gods. What he needs to do is negotiate his decision with them as he does in the main narrative,[24] or fight, as he does in the majority of the divine memories, which will now be inspected.

The rest of the memories feature scenes of more or less violent conflicts, especially between Zeus and various gods. I will start my analysis with one of the most vivid stories – the conflict of Hera and Zeus over Heracles and the famous hanging of Hera by anvils. I will then continue through thematically, to capture the patterns crucial for the understanding of this divine era.

In the fourteenth Book of the *Iliad*, Hera comes up with a plan to help the Achaeans – she seduces Zeus and distracts him from the battlefield with the help of Hypnos, while Poseidon helps the Achaeans. During the episode, the gods recall her earlier insubordination against Zeus and its dangerous consequences twice. The story is told first by Hypnos who recounts it when he wants to dissuade Hera from acting against Zeus (*Il.* 14.242–262) and later Zeus recalls it to express his anger and reassert his power, when suspecting Hera's malevolence (*Il.* 15.14–33). The secondary narrators reveal how once Hera persuaded Hypnos to make Zeus sleep and then summoned strong winds to chase Heracles far away from his people, up to the island Cos. The past and present situations are to that point parallel – in both, we see Hera deceiving Zeus and intervening in the human

---

23 Heiden (2008) 181; Porter (2014).
24 Heiden (2008) 161–185; Elmer (2013).

world against Zeus' will with Hypnos' help. Their outcomes, however, differ crucially. In the main narrative, the reaction of Zeus to Hera's deceit is dual – he is infuriated at first, yet his anger quickly ebbs away and he does not punish Hera, Hypnos or Poseidon. To restore his will, he just sends Iris to Poseidon with an order to come back home (*Il.* 15.47–77). In the memories told by the gods, Zeus' reaction to Hera's insubordination was much more radical: he did not control his anger, but unleashed it on the Olympians. He chased Hypnos, Hera's ally, in an attempt to throw him out of the aether into the Sea. Hypnos managed to escape by taking refuge in Night's arms. Then Zeus punished Hera. He hung her in the sky with two anvils attached to her feet. Still, he did not stop there and chased all the gods who came near Hera and threw them out of Olympus: guilty or not. Zeus thus displays his immense power and strength and the gods are not only hurt but also humiliated, as Hera is hung up in the sky for all the gods to see. The acts that Zeus carried out against the other gods – binding and throwing away – were far from accidental. Since gods cannot be really killed (or hardly so) and they heal easily, both acts offer the best means to render the immortals powerless. Binding restrains a god's strength and power, and is a way of affirming one's supremacy, not only in Greek myths.²⁵ Throwing gods out of Olympus has a similar meaning – it is a brutal and humiliating act; it deprives the gods of their allotted space and of their honours connected to their physical presence position on Olympus, and it degrades them to the status of those who have to live on earth. Hypnos says that Zeus wanted to cast him to the deep so he would not be seen (ἄιστον) from the sky (*Il.* 14.257–258) – in other words, to become invisible even to the community of the gods. A related motif is used by Hesiod in his description of the Titanomachy, where the old gods are thrown away from Olympus to Tartarus (*Theog.* 713–721). In other words, Zeus' acts against the gods involve physical violence and have physical consequences for the victim (being unable to move or being far away from the place of power, Olympus), but also bear deep symbolic meanings connected to deprivation of honour.

This pattern of violence occurs in other stories, as I will show next; yet it is in these two memories describing one event that one can see the full extent of the individual power of Zeus. Through his aggressive behaviour Zeus shows the gods he can easily dominate them and that any opposition to his power will bring destruction to Olympus. His strength is so overpowering that it seems surprising that he never uses it in the main narrative to control the other gods – a crucial question I will come back to in the end. However, one should note an important detail. Even in this display of dominance, it is visible that there are things that

---

25 Eliade (1969) 92–124, Slatkin (1991) 66–69, Steiner (2001) 167–168.

even Zeus is scared of. Hypnos says that Night saved him, for even Zeus, at the peak of his anger, did not want to cross this primordial goddess (*Il.* 14.259–262).

Another story showing the brutal side of Zeus is presented by Hephaestus in the first Book, when he intervenes in the marital quarrel between Zeus and Hera over Thetis and the fate of the Achaeans (*Il.* 1.585–594). Hephaestus warns Hera not to engage the gods in another conflict with Zeus, and reminds her how in the past he tried to save her from Zeus. Physical violence against Hera is indicated again, since the goddess apparently needed saving from something. The reason for Zeus' brutality against Hera is not specified. It may be that Homer alludes here already to the quarrel over Heracles,[26] though one cannot rule out the possibility of yet another clash. What is crucial is that, as in the previous example, there is a parallelism between the present situation and the memory: in both Hephaestus attempts to help his mother during a conflict between her and Zeus. And again, the outcomes of the two are radically different. While in the main narrative both Zeus and Hera back off after Hephaestus' intervention, and all the gods soon laugh together and enjoy a shared feast, in the past the reaction of Zeus is violent. He threw Hephaestus away from Olympus down to the Earth, where he fell with little life left in him, though the god did nothing more than try to save his mother.

A similar motif can be found again in a story told by Agamemnon to the Achaeans (*Il.* 19.91–136). He recounts how Zeus wanted to make Heracles the king of the Argives, but, because of Hera's deceit, he had to agree for Eurystheus to take his place. Again, Hera is insubordinate against Zeus and her trick is a serious disregard of his will. Not only did she mingle with Zeus' primal sphere of influence (designating kings), but she also did that to debase his son. Zeus' reaction, as in the other episodes that we saw, is brutal. Agamemnon says that, believing that Ate blinded him, Zeus threw her by the head out of Olympus. We should note that this is the only story told in an entirely human context. By telling this narrative Agamemnon wants to minimize his faults towards Achilles: if the king of gods was fooled by Ate, a man could be misled as well. It is interesting to tackle the question of memory transmission. Contrary to the gods, Agamemnon could not have seen these events, but must have heard about them. He does not reveal his source, but Eurystheus, who appears in the story, was his uncle, which may point to an Argive oral tradition. Yet it is crucial that even in this transmitted memory we encounter a motif found in the personal memories of the gods – the escalation of conflict between Hera and Zeus and Zeus reacting to it by throwing a god out of Olympus.

---

26 Whitman (1970), Porter (2014).

Physical violence is not the only thing Zeus did to punish the gods. Poseidon remembers a conflict between himself, Apollo and Zeus, which took an interesting turn. Poseidon recounts the story twice. First, he refers to it only allusively while speaking to Zeus. He tells him that he is angry with the Achaeans for building their wall, fearful that their work will overshadow the Trojan Wall that he and Apollo had to build (*Il.* 7.446–454). He elaborates more on the story when he meets Apollo and tries to dissuade him from fighting for the Trojans (*Il.* 21.436–460). He reminds him how Zeus forced them to serve king Laomedon, who in the end did not even pay them for their work and even threatened to cut their ears off. The reason for their servitude is unclear; Poseidon tells him only that it was connected to Zeus' will (*Il.* 21.444).[27] Whatever their fault was, Zeus' choice of punishment is very surprising. He resorted here to methods other than violence: he punished the gods by humiliating them through the use of men. In a way this punishment is not so distant from casting the gods out of the sky – he still forces them to stay away from Olympus, but this time by locking them in the human society with the lowest status possible. The attitude of Zeus is even more striking if we bear in mind that, in the time of the Trojan War, Zeus is the guarantor of stability between the world of gods and man.[28] In this story, he willfully shakes this balance. Making the gods subject to a man and work as despicable labourers was not only a most humiliating punishment, but it also overturned and dangerously (even if for one year) the hierarchy of the divine and human worlds as the inaccessible gods suddenly became one man's subjects.

In the six memories that we saw, told by four different gods and one man, Zeus consequently appears to be a much different ruler than in the main narrative. He is tyrannical and chaotic, letting anger overtake him and fall on gods, whether their fault is real insubordination (as in the case of Hera) or an attempt of peaceful intervention (as in the case of Hephaestus). He treats the gods with no respect and humiliates them, even with the dangerous blurring of boundaries between men and gods. He uses strength as his main tool to shape authority and he does so quite effectively: the other Olympians are no physical match for him. The other gods are not, however, completely helpless, as we will now see.

Some divine memories show that the power of Zeus can be threatened. Even if the gods are physically weaker, they can do more than just refuse Zeus' orders

---

27 Porter (2014) 507–26 argues that the passage can be connected to Achilles' story of the revolt against Zeus and that the servitude is a punishment for Poseidon's planned attack. Apollo is not mentioned by Homer as one of the conspirators, but one of the scholiasts does include him in the list.
28 Lateiner (2002).

as Hera did when she harassed Heracles. A serious threat to Zeus' rule is alluded to in a dialogue between Thetis and Hephaestus after Achilles' wish to return to the battle. Both gods were once humiliated and put away from Olympus, but hold affection towards each other. Hephaestus, seeing Thetis, remembers how she took care of him when Hera, repulsed by his lameness, cast him away from Earth (*Il.* 18.394–410) – the motif of throwing away reappears there. Thetis, in turn, wants to gain his sympathy by recalling her own misery and reminds him how Zeus forced her against her will to marry Peleus (*Il.* 18.428–437). What the two passages have in common is that they are connected to a challenge to the power of Zeus: the problem of a dangerous heir. According to the *Homeric Hymn to Apollo* (*Hom. Hymn Ap.* 311–331), Hephaestus was produced by Hera in response to Zeus' giving birth to Athena by himself. He did not turn out to be powerful and Hera rejects him clearly in this passage. Homer does not include either the story of the more dangerous Typhaon, yet we can see that there is a tension between Hera and Zeus on this level.[29] The case of Thetis is even more significant – as Laura Slatkin has argued,[30] the fact that Zeus forces Thetis to marry Peleus can be understood in the light of the prophecy that Thetis would bear a son stronger than his father, which is a clear danger to the gods and Zeus especially. Thetis thus must be bound to the human world and produce a human child, Achilles: a fact that even Achilles seems to be aware of when he talks to his mother. The theme of the heir is rather alluded to than elaborated, yet it is important that the gods do have a potential weapon against Zeus and that Zeus has some reasons to be afraid. The gods may be weaker than him, but a new son may become stronger than him if he does not rule in a more controlled way.

But there is another, more clearly elaborated threat to Zeus' power. The king of gods may be all-powerful but he is not all-knowing. An important episode with which I want to end this catalogue of memories is the mutiny of gods presented in the first Book of the *Iliad*. It is also the very first memory of Olympus shared within the narrative. It is told by Achilles and the hero specifies he learned it before from Thetis herself. Achilles uses his mother's memory to convince her to talk to Zeus on his behalf (*Il.* 1.395–407). He reminds her how once she helped Zeus when other gods, Athena, Hera and Poseidon among them, put him in bonds. Zeus was not able to escape the trap by himself – he was susceptible to

---

[29] Yasumura (2011) 32–34, Lopez-Ruiz (2014).
[30] Slatkin (1986; 1991).

binding just like the other gods.³¹ It is only with the intervention of Thetis, an inconspicuous goddess in the main narration, that he was freed from the bonds.³² Thetis also brought Briareus to Olympus to guard Zeus.

The power of this story lies in its details. Binding is a weapon used by Zeus against Hera – in this story this dynamic is reversed. I want to stress that binding in this passage is especially significant as is a motif that in the archaic poetry is often connected to overthrowing divine regimes – it is used by Hesiod in his description of the Titanomachy.³³ Hesiod mentions that after Cronus' defeat he and the Titans were put in bonds (*Theog.* 718–720). We should also note the role played in this passage by the Hekatoncheiros Briareus, whom Thetis freed from Tartarus and called to Olympus to protect Zeus. This brings to mind the Titanomachy again – according to Hesiod, Zeus freed the Hekatoncheires (one of whom is named Briareus as well) and asked for their support, while fighting with the Titans (*Theog.* 617–675, 713–720). Taking those elements into account, the plan of the three (and possibly other) gods is clearly a dangerous, if failed, attempt to overthrow Zeus as a king and create a new divine order. What is important is that the plan could have succeeded – Zeus may be strong, but the gods did manage to bind him. He cannot predict every mutiny or plot done against him, and in the end he also needs the help of others – and similarly to the other Olympians, he gets it from outside, from older generations of gods, such as Thetis or Briareus.

With this story of a failed attempt to overthrow Zeus, our catalogue of memories of Olympus ends. As we have seen, while the stories present several different events, they are almost exclusively centered around the questions of violence (with recurring motifs such as binding or overthrowing), the radical imposition of power, and the will of subjugating others. The crucial question is – what is the function of such memories in the *Iliad*? How do they impact the gods' choices and attitudes in the main narrative? Can they change how we as an audience understand them? In the next sections, I analyze how the past influences the Olympic present and how the present becomes understandable with the past in mind.

---

31 Porter (2014).
32 Slatkin (1986).
33 Slatkin (1986, 1991), Yasumura (2011) 15–16. It is also interesting to note here another myth about an attempt to overthrow Zeus where the motif of binding and a divine helper are present – namely, the story of Typhaon' as presented by Apollodoros (*Bib.* 1.39–44). According to this version, Typhaon held Zeus in his coils (binding motif), and then deprived him of power even more by stealing his sinews and closing him in a cave. Zeus is freed by Hermes, who brings his sinews back. In earlier versions, however, Zeus defeated Typhaon in a regular fight with no help needed (as in Hesiod's *Theogony*, 820–868).

3 Memories – the personal and the collective

Homer makes the gods constantly turn to their past and reveal their background stories. In this section, I want to show that while the memories are told by individual gods to fit individual purposes, they also form together with a collective memory of Olympians that has the power to influence the gods as a community.

Let us start with the personal aspect of the memories. The stories are told by a range of narrators and each has his personal goal to share his story.[34] Most often, the secondary narrators use the memories as paradigms: to warn others and dissuade them from acting in a certain way (Hephaestus, Zeus, and Hypnos recall the old conflicts to prevent Hera from opposing Zeus) or to persuade them to make a specific decision (Poseidon tells the story of the Trojan Wall to make Zeus promise the destruction of the Achaean Wall, and to Apollo to dissuade him from fighting; Achilles reminds Thetis of Zeus' debt to make her intervene on his behalf on Olympus). It is, however, far from the only reason. Through the memories, the speakers also show affection (Hephaestus remembers how Thetis nurtured him), try to gain sympathy (Thetis presents to Hephaestus her misery from Zeus) or excuse their behaviour (Agamemnon explains his foolishness through the example of Zeus).

Furthermore, each narrator has his own perspective. While telling these stories, the gods act like anyone who remembers. They often talk allusively, omit many elements and highlight the ones that seem crucial to them at the moment. Because of that, the same episode can be shown differently by two different gods. Hypnos, remembering Hera's plot against Heracles, focuses on the anger of Zeus directed towards himself; Zeus, on the other hand, concentrates on his brutality towards Hera and other Olympians and presents the fate of his dear son more elaborately.

The memories have thus a strong personal aspect, but they are also meant to be communicative;[35] they help the gods find common ground. In most cases, both the secondary narrators and their audience participated in the remembered events, a fact which makes the memories of gods different from the digressions told by heroes, who usually focus there on the deeds of their predecessors. Because of that, the divine memories form a unique bridge of understanding based not only on an intellectual understanding of the lessons from the past, but also

---

34 Kakridis (1930) 113–122 (1949) 96–105; Willcock (1964) 141–154; Austin (1966) 295–313; Nagy (1996) 113–46; Alden (2000); Grethlein (2006) 46–64.
35 Minchin (2012).

on the feeling brought by the shared experiences. While Homer restricts emotional language in his narrative, he makes the secondary speakers emphasize them in their speeches.[36] Thus the gods present their memories with a mixture of anger, misery and fear that they can relive together.

Importantly, the memories of early Olympus are a way of communication that involves most of the gods of the narrative, in one way or another. They are told by five different gods (Poseidon, Hypnos, Zeus, Hephaestus, Thetis) and they have five different divine addressees (Hera, Zeus, Apollo, Hephaestus, Thetis and Iris). What is more, at least two of them (*Il.* 1.585–594, *Il.* 7.446–454) are told in front of the gathering of all Olympians. The events that the gods describe are also significant events in which many Olympians participated. Nine gods are mentioned by name (Hades, Hera, Hypnos, Zeus, Hephaestus, Poseidon, Apollo, Thetis, Athena; not counting Night and Briareus), and the gods as a collective are also implied, as in the memory of Hera hung in the sky:

σὺ δ' ἐν αἰθέρι καὶ νεφέλῃσιν
ἐκρέμω· ἠλάστεον δὲ θεοὶ κατὰ μακρὸν Ὄλυμπον
λῦσαι δ' οὐκ ἐδύναντο παρασταδόν·
Il. 15.20–21

You among the clouds and the bright sky
hung, nor could the gods about tall Olympos endure it
and stood about, but could not set you free

Finally, the past events left monumental material traces that can be seen by all gods. The Trojan Wall made by Poseidon and Apollo is impressive and can be a powerful reminder of past conflicts for the Olympians who know the story of its building.[37]

But most importantly, the memories the gods share are also very consistent: almost all of them are focused on conflict. Most of the gods participated in the brutality, either as victims or the perpetrators. Not accidentally, many of these stories are used to bring settlement to growing conflicts. The example of violence makes it easier to understand the value of peace. Yet even if the personal goal of the gods telling the story is different (for instance, to show affection), the memories still focus on violence. The gods certainly have other personal memories that they do not share during the narrative, but when they communicate, this is what they choose to concentrate on. We should bear in mind that the past is comprised

---

[36] Griffin (1986); de Jong (1988).
[37] Grethlein (2008).

of a variety of different events and Homer has at his disposal many stories about Olympus. What is remembered and shared is crucial – this is what the tellers decide to be especially impactful from their past. Interestingly, the reasons for the conflict are often mentioned allusively or sometimes not at all – we never know for instance why Hephaestus was cast out of Olympus or why Poseidon and Apollo were forced to work for Laomedon. The emphasis is put on the very fact of violence and the danger that the gods run into. The stories of the gods thus are not just a set of various personal reminiscences, but a social memory of past violence which affects the whole divine community.

4 The shaping of a community

The memories of the gods are an important point of reference to the gods both as individuals and as a community. But to what extent and how do they impact what the Olympians choose and how they act in the present? What in their attitudes and relations changes and why exactly?

In the narrative, the present and past of the Olympians are intertwined. Homer puts many of the stories in parallel moments, so we can see how the two eras are related, the similarities and differences between them. On some levels, the gods did not change. In both past and present, Zeus' reign is not absolute and he needs to exert effort to impose his will on the Olympians, who constantly try to undermine it. In both past and present the gods have strong emotional reactions to what happens on Olympus and Earth and the tensions between them rise often and quickly.

However, while the sources of conflict are similar, their outcomes are radically different: the gods in the past resolve their tensions with violence, which they never do in the main narrative. It is interesting that Zeus is the god who changes most profoundly. Porter argues that the passages showing the insubordination of gods explain the "authoritative reflexes" of Zeus.[38] He focuses especially on the story told by Achilles, where the three gods plan to overthrow Zeus. I want to note, however, that in the stories of the past the Olympians do not seem to be as bad subjects as Zeus is a bad ruler. In most memories shared by the gods it is Zeus who is shown using violence against other gods without much of a reason. He reacted to any, even minor insubordination (such as the gods' attempt to

---

38 Porter (2014).

help Hera), with uncontrollable anger. The divine community he wanted to establish was one under his total domination, which he hoped to impose by deeply hurting other gods in a physical and symbolic way, by binding, hanging, humiliating and throwing them away from the divine realm. In the main narrative, he may menace the gods, but his threats are only symbolic and never turn into anything more serious.[39] He also becomes very withdrawn and stops intervening personally in the world of man altogether – not even on behalf of his son Sarpedon.[40] The other Olympians change as well. In the main narrative they still are insubordinate at times, but easily become obedient when reprimanded, are able to de-escalate tense situations and never seriously consider a revolt against Zeus. What made the Olympians change? How are we to interpret the state of settlement that we see in the main narrative in the light of the violence that the gods remember?

To understand this, we need to recapitulate the effects the violence had for the Olympians. Zeus' method of imposing power and making it more absolute in the past was violence and aggression, which threatened the gods with mortal danger. However, the divine memories also show the limits of Zeus' power and the risks that the king of gods runs into. He may be the strongest of the Olympians, yet the gods could still threaten him. The problem of a dangerous heir is alluded to; but mostly, as indicated in the speech of Achilles, the gods could put Zeus at risk by using their guile and joining forces. Just as he put Hera in anvils, he had to suffer in bonds by the device of Hera, Athena and Poseidon. To manage such threats, not even Zeus could act alone but he needs help from others – it is, in the end, Thetis who saves him.[41] An important factor influencing the dynamic on Olympus is the primordial deities whom even Zeus fears, such as the Night, with whom the other Olympians might ally. In other words, the gods ultimately hold a balance of power and thus conflict in the past was destructive to all of them. The consequence of violence as a method of resolving divine tension was chaos and danger on a titanomachic scale and all the gods risked their eternal life in their strife.

If we look at the present from the perspective of this danger shared by all the gods we can better understand the new dynamics between the Olympians. Though they still struggle for influence and have a strong emotionality, their final

---

39 Heiden (2008) 180–181.
40 Lateiner (2002).
41 Slatkin (1986).

choices are different, because they gained experience – they know what happened in the past and the risks it brought on Olympus.[42] The gods are reminded of this brutal era on every occasion and it can influence them not only on an intellectual level as a lesson from the past, but also on an emotional level, as they vividly remember their misery.[43] This is why they can always take a step back each time situations get overly heated. In contrast to the community of men, where some powerful individuals such as Achilles still want to test the limits of their independence, they already know through experience that in the end, no god can act alone. It is no accident that one of the strongest threats that Hera makes is to leave Zeus abandoned on Ida (*Il.* 8.205–207).

5 Conclusions: Visions of early Olympus in archaic poetry

The gods in the *Iliad* form a specific community of powerful angry individuals, who are, however, able to cooperate. The specific dynamics between them become understandable when one looks at the past of the Olympians and how it affects them. Their emotional, yet safe outbursts of passion are indications of what they once were, but what they now know they cannot be anymore. In the past, they tested their limits and learned the consequences of violence, which make them consciously hold a state of balance. Thanks to the memories they share, the audience gets access to the motivations and thoughts that influence their behaviour. Knowing what they remember as a community, we may understand why in the main narrative Hera and Athena never risk an open conflict with Zeus and Zeus never realises his aggressive threats.

Through the digressions of Olympus past, Homer creates a vision of the growing of the Olympians as a community and Zeus as a ruler. The question of the beginnings of Zeus' reign is a recurring issue in the archaic poetry: it appears also in the *Homeric Hymns* and in Hesiod's *Theogony*. I want to end this paper with some remarks on how other archaic poets depict early Olympus and in what lies the uniqueness of Homer in his representation of this subject.

---

[42] On the question of how memory and manipulated remembering can influence decisions see Mawford in this volume.
[43] For the question of the emotional impact of memory see Hunter in this volume.

To a certain extent, the poets of the *Homeric Hymns* present early Olympus similarly to Homer in the *Iliad*. In the poems, during the times predating the Trojan War, many gods still struggle to gain the honour and a higher position on Olympus.[44] The hierarchy on Olympus is shifting and Zeus' power is often put into danger. In the *Hymn to Aphrodite*, Aphrodite endangers Zeus' position and humiliates him by forcing him to love human maidens (*Hom. Hymn. Ven.* 33–52).[45] In the *Hymn to Demeter*, Demeter's anger presents a real threat to the gods – should mortals die of hunger, the gods would stop receiving sacrifices (*Hom. Hymn. Dem.* 310–314).[46] The birth of new gods also creates problems of rivalry and finding a place for ambitious individuals. Yet contrary to the *Iliad*, in the *Hymns* there is no place for direct physical confrontations on Olympus. The gradual stabilization is an effect of negotiations of power and politics. Zeus does not use violence to manage the threats to the Olympic order, he makes his moves carefully from the very beginning – in the *Iliad* he needs experience to learn such an approach to ruling.

Homer's vision differs even more from that of Hesiod in *Theogony*. In the *Theogony* Zeus has challenges to face (such as the powerful Typhaon),[47] yet from the beginning he tries to establish a harmonious and deliberate distribution of roles and powers.[48] Even if he does not always act "justly", he does not use violence but guile to achieve his means (as when he swallows Metis, *Theog.* 886–900). Zeus' attitude towards the gods in the *Iliad* brings to mind rather the reign of the Hesiodic Cronus, characterized by primitive aggressiveness or the chaotic transition between the rules of the Titans and Olympians – there we encounter similar motifs such as binding, expelling the gods out of heaven, receiving aid from monstrous divinities. Thus while the Homeric Zeus learns from his own errors, the Hesiodic Zeus learns rather through his tyrannical predecessor's mistakes. Both authors present a scheme where aggressive domination is replaced by a rule taking into account the community, but in Homer's case this process is centred around one ruler who gains maturity.

But Homer also presents his vision of changes happening on Olympus in a different form than other poets. To create this image Homer adapts a poetic device typical for his genre – paradigmatic stories.[49] While the *Hymns* only concentrate

---

44 Strauss Clay (1989, 2011).
45 Segal (1974), Smith (1981), Strauss Clay (1989) 169–170.
46 Strauss Clay (1989) 233–245.
47 Ballabriga (1990), Blaise (1992), Yasumura (2014) 124–131.
48 Blickman (1987); Strauss Clay (2003).
49 Willcock (1964).

on particular moments of the Olympus' "history", and Hesiod presents his vision in a linear way, Homer shows the changes happening on Olympus through the perspective of the gods themselves, making them the narrators of their story. Because of that, it is not only the poet and the audience who observe the changes in the mythical world from an eagle-eye point of view, but the gods and the heroes also receive an awareness of the past, which can affect their choices and behaviours. The events of cosmic significance receive thus a unique personal level.

Bibliography

Alden, M. (1996), "Genealogy as Paradigm: The example of Bellorophon", *Hermes* 124: 257–263.
Alden, M. (2000), *Homer Beside Himself. Para-Narratives in the* Iliad, Oxford.
Alden, M. (2017), *Para-Narratives in the 'Odyssey': Stories in the Frame*, Oxford.
Allan, W. (2006), "Divine Justice and Cosmic Order in Early Greek Epic", *JHS* 126: 1–35.
Andersen, Ø. (1981), "The 'Mortality' of Gods in Homer", *GRBS* 22: 323–327.
Andersen, Ø. (1993), "Myth, Paradigm and 'Spatial Form'", in J. Bremer, I.J.F. de Jong and J. Kalff (eds.), *Homer: Beyond Oral Poetry*, Amsterdam: 1–13.
Andersen, Ø. (1997), "Diomedes, Aphrodite and Dione. Background and Function of a scene in Homer's *Iliad*", *C&M*: 25–36.
Aronen, J. (2002), "Genealogy as a form of mythic discourse. The case of the Phaeacians", in S. Des Bouvrie (ed.), *Papers from the First International Symposium on Symbolism at the University of Tromsø*, June 4–7: 89–111.
Austin, N. (1966), "The Function of Digression in the '*Iliad*'", *GRBS* 7: 295–312.
Bakker, E. (2008), "Epic Remembering", in E. Mackey (ed.), *Orality, Literacy, Memory in Ancient Greek and Roman World*. Mnemosyne Supplements 298, Leiden/Boston: 65–78.
Ballabriga, A. (1990), "Le dernier adversaire de Zeus: le mythe de Typhon grecque archaïque", *RHR* 207: 3–30.
Biaise, F. (1992), "L'Épisode de Typhée dans la Théogonie d'Hésiode (v. 820–885): la stabilisation du monde", *REG* 105: 349–70.
Blickman, D. (1987), "Styx and the Justice of Zeus", *Phoenix*: 341–355.
Chaudhuri, P. (2014), *The War with the God. Theomachy in the Imperial Poetry*, Oxford.
Eliade, M. (1969), *Images and Symbols*, (trans. P. Mairet), New York.
Elmer, D. (2012), *The Poetics of Consent: Collective Decision Making and the* Iliad, Baltimore.
Fränkel, H. (1960), *Wege und Formen frühgriechischen Denkens*, Munich.
Grethlein, J. (2006), *Das Geschichtsbild der Ilias. Eine Untersuchung aus phänomenologischer Perspektive*, Göttingen.
Grethlein, J. (2008), "Memory and Material Objects in the *Iliad* and the *Odyssey*", *JHS* 128: 27–51.
Griffin, J. (1977), "The Epic Cycle and the Uniqueness of Homer", *JHS* 97: 39–52.
Griffin, J. (1978), "The Divine Audience and the Religion of the *Iliad*", *The Classical Quarterly* 28: 1–22.
Griffin, J. (1986), "Homeric Words and Speakers", *JHS* 106: 36–57.

Grube, G. (1951), "The Gods of Homer", *Phoenix* 5 (3/4): 62–78.
Heiden, B. (2008), *Homer's Cosmic Fabrication: Choice and Design in the* Iliad, New York.
Howald, E. (1924), "Meleager und Achill", *Rheinisches Museum für Philologie* 73: 402–425.
de Jong, I. (1988), "Homeric Words and Speaker", *JHS*: 188–189.
de Jong, I. (2007), *Time in Ancient Greek Literature*, Leiden.
Kakridis, J.Th. (1930), "Die Niobesage bei Homer: zur Geschichte des Griechischen παράδειγμα", *RhM* 19: 113–122.
Kakridis, J.Th. (1949), *Homeric Researches*, Lund.
Lateiner, D. (2002), "Pouring Bloody Drops (*Iliad* 16.459): The Grief of Zeus", *Colby Quarterly* 38: 42–61.
Lattimore, R. (1951), *The Iliad of Homer*, Chicago.
Levy, H. (1979), "Homer's Gods: a Comment on their Immortality", *GRBS* 20: 215–218.
Louden, B. (2006), *The* Iliad: *Structure, Myth and Meaning*, Baltimore.
Lopez-Ruiz, C. (2014), "Greek and Canaanite Mythologies: Zeus, Baal, and their Rivals", *Religion Compass* 8: 1–10.
Minchin, E. (2012), 'Memory and memories: personal, social, and cultural memory in the poems of Homer', in F. Montanari, A. Rengakos and C. Tsagalis (eds.), *Homeric Contexts: Neoanalysis and the Interpretation of Oral Poetry*. Trends in Classics Supplementary Volumes, Boston.
Porter, A. (2014), "Reconstructing Laomedon's Reign in Homer: Olympiomachia, Poseidon's Wall and the Earlier Trojan War", *GRBS* 54: 507–26.
Raaflaub, K. (2000), "Poets, lawgivers, and the beginnings of political reflection in archaic Greece", in C. Rowe & M. Schofield (eds.), *The Cambridge History of Greek and Roman Political Thought*, Cambridge: 23–59.
Segal, C. (1974), "*The Homeric Hymn to Aphrodite*: a Structuralist Approach", *CW* 67: 205–212.
Smith, P. (1981), *Nursling of Immortality: A Study of the Homeric Hymn to Aphrodite*, Frankfurt am Mein.
Slatkin, L. (1986), "The Wrath of Thetis", *TAPhA* 116: 1–24.
Slatkin, L. (1991), *The Power of Thetis. Allusion and Interpretation in the* Iliad, Berkeley.
Steiner, D. (2001), *Images in Mind: Statues in Archaic and Classical Greek Literature and Thought*, Princeton.
Strauss Clay, J. (1989), *The Politics of Olympus. Form and Meaning in Major Homeric Hymns*, Princeton.
Strauss Clay, J. (1993), "The Generation of Monsters in Hesiod", *CPh* 88: 105–116.
Strauss Clay, J. (2003), *Hesiod's Cosmos*, Cambridge.
Strauss Clay, J. (2011), "The Homeric Hymn as Genre", in A. Faulkner (ed.), *The Homeric Hymns: Interpretative Essays*, Oxford: 232–253.
Willcock, M. (1964), "Mythological Paradeigma in the *Iliad*", *The Classical Quarterly* 14: 141–154.
Whitman, C. (1970), "Hera's anvils", *HSPh* 74: 37–42.
Yasumura, N. (2011), *Challenges to the Power of Zeus in Early Greek Poetry*, London.

Part III: **Female Memory**

Katharine Mawford
The Manipulation of Memory in Apollonius' *Argonautica*

Abstract: Over the course of Book 3 of the *Argonautica*, Apollonius' Medea is manipulated into falling in love with and aiding Jason through the joint efforts of Hera, Aphrodite, and Eros. This manipulation takes place successively, beginning with Eros' love spell which simultaneously burns away Medea's own wishes and instils in the heroine a deep and destructive love for Jason. At the centre of Eros' spell is an attack on Medea's memory; memory also plays a central part in Medea's grappling with her decision to help Jason. This paper presents a re-examination of the manipulation of Medea and Apollonius' characterisation of his heroine in light of the poet's use of memory as a narrative device. Through this, Medea is first divested of her agency and, eventually, reclaims this with an active and conscious wielding of her own memory, a striking act of metapoetic awareness which brings her closer to other epic heroes and heroines, and one which ties closely into the *Argonautica*'s inter- and intra-textual makeup.

1 Introduction

Scholarship on the character of Medea in the *Argonautica* has primarily focused on three areas: her relationship with Jason and her love – or lack thereof – for the hero; her role in the murder of Apsyrtus; or the virgin/witch dichotomy seemingly inherent to her character.[1] Certainly, her characterisation does depend to some extent on each of these factors, and the heroism (or failed heroism) of Jason also plays a part in this.[2] However, it is Medea's memory that forms the focus of this paper. Her memory, as I shall show, is a further important element of Apollonius'

I am very grateful to Julene Abad Del Vecchio, Katherine Molesworth, William Mundy, and my co-editor Eleni Ntanou for their help with drafts of this chapter, and for my time spent at Fondation Hardt in March 2019, in whose library crucial edits to this chapter were made. The Greek text has been taken from the Loeb editions, and the translations given, unless otherwise stated, are my own. The commentaries I have used, Richard Hunter's *Apollonius: Argonautica* (Cambridge, 1989) and Francis Vian's *Argonautiques: chant III* (Paris, 1961) will be referred to in the following pages as Hunter and Vian.

1 See, e.g. Phinney Jr (1967), Byre (1996).
2 Cf. Jackson (1992), Hunter (1988).

https://doi.org/10.1515/9783110728798-008

epic, one which plays a crucial role in her transition from innocent young girl to fratricidal woman³ and which merits closer attention; as we shall see, Medea's (lack of) control over her memory is an essential device used by the poet to punctuate her developing characterisation in Book 3. Memory is of central importance to Apollonius' epic and it is the narrator's memory which frames the whole narrative at the start of Book 1:

> Ἀρχόμενος σέο, Φοῖβε, παλαιγενέων κλέα φωτῶν
> μνήσομαι
>
> A.R. 1.1–2
>
> Beginning with you, Phoebus, I shall remember the famous acts of men born long ago.

Naturally, any orally recounted story demands the memory of its teller, yet here the prominence of the Muse expected in the Greek epic tradition is reduced.⁴ Unlike the Homeric narrator, the *Argonautica*'s narrator is inspired by Apollo – and this narrator is not a vehicle for the Muses' song, as is explicitly the case in the Homeric works and the *Theogony*.⁵ Instead, like the narrator of the *Homeric Hymn to Apollo*,⁶ who begins his narration with an emphatic declaration of memory: μνήσομαι οὐδὲ λάθωμαι Ἀπόλλωνος ἑκάτοιο ('I will remember and not forget far-shooting Apollo', v.1), Apollonius' narrator emphasises his own ability to remember through his prominent use of the first person μνήσομαι, v.1.2.⁷ With this statement Apollonius' narrator secures his agency in the context of narration and his control over the story, pronouncing that the narrative is to be relayed by means of his *own memory* (inspired, rather than told by, his divine benefactor), and thus the epic relies on and cements the narrator's agency and voice. In fact, the prominence of Apollonius' self-insertion not only 'foregrounds the consciousness of the poet,'⁸ but in fact does so even over his subject matter. Apollonius' narrator

---

3 See Ngan in this volume for a discussion of Medea's memory in Seneca.
4 This is not uncommon to Hellenistic poetry, however; we might compare Callim. *Aet.* 1.22–30 or Lyc. 1–12. See Fantuzzi/Hunter (2014) 3, McNelis/Sens (2016) 5; cf. further Helen's statement in *Od.* 4.240: πάντα μὲν οὐκ ἂν ἐγὼ μυθήσομαι οὐδ' ὀνομήνω, which takes a similarly authorial stance.
5 *Il.* 1.1: μῆνιν ἄειδε θεά; *Od.* 1.1: ἄνδρα μοι ἔννεπε, μοῦσα; Hes. *Theog.* 1: μουσάων Ἑλικωνιάδων ἀρχώμεθ' ἀείδειν.
6 On the *Hymn*'s narrator and his place in the Delian maidens' song, see, e.g., Calame (2011) esp. 351–2.
7 By invoking memory, of course, Apollonius recalls Mnemosyne, the mother of the Muses (Hes. *Theog.* 53–5), and therefore their role in epic song (22–8), yet the Muses are still denied an explicit role in this epic's telling.
8 Fantuzzi/Hunter (2004) 91, cf. 95.

is both omniscient and omnipotent over his narrative; simultaneously reliant on and diverging from the Homeric narrator.

Furthermore, the epic relies – as do the Homeric works – on the cultural memory of the audience. Without this, references, allusions and the wider mythology would lose their significance.[9] Particularly in the telling of the *Argonautica*, the narrative is framed implicitly as an exchange of memory between the narrator and the audience: an exchange which we shall see mirrored later on in exchanges between Medea and Jason. Memory is not simply used by Apollonius as a means of constructing epic, however; it is thematised in the poet's characterisation of Medea in Book 3 in her manipulation at the hands of Hera and Aphrodite. Memory thus operates on multiple levels within the epic, required for the creation of the poem (and the perpetuation of epic itself) and additionally crucial to the reader's understanding; it is also central within the poem to the depiction and relationships of its characters, as promised, threatened and compromised acts of remembering position the epic in relation to the *Odyssey* and simultaneously recall its narrative priority.

For the purposes of this discussion, I suggest that memory as a concept can be split into two distinct categories, active memory and passive memory, and encompasses one's own memory and one's position in the memory of others. This is the distinction between deliberately and consciously *remembering* events, people, or things, and *being reminded* or *made to remember*. Commemoration and retelling from memory both belong to active memory and denote agency of the person who remembers whilst being reminded entails a form of passivity. A further layer, that of *being remembered*, lies somewhere in between these poles. The telling of the *Argonautica*, then, is an instance of active memory use, one which speaks to the narrator's role and authority in the epic, and which shapes the relationship of the narrator to his characters and to his audience. We can also usefully apply these terms to a reading of Medea and her developing relationship with Jason in the *Argonautica*: as I shall show, the poet carefully interweaves instances of active and passive memory as a means of punctuating the heroine's developing characterisation as she falls in love with Jason, in order to emphasise the extent to which Medea is initially divested of her agency and yet – eventually – reclaims some control over her situation. Apollonius employs several significant intertextual links with Homeric epic to expand on his discourse of memory – these will also form part of my focus. It is my purpose here, with this

---

9 The audience or 'reader' of epic – indeed of any genre – must be an active participant in the narrative; ancient audiences were more practiced in responding to the demands of form. See, e.g. Iser (1991), Jauss (1982).

centrality of memory to the epic programme in mind, to explore the poet's use of memory in the *Argonautica* specifically as it relates to the characterisation and development of Medea in the course of Book 3, and to discuss its inclusion at significant narrative points relevant to Medea's development in this section. My focus here is on the poet's use of memory as a motif in four interrelated instances which together contribute to Medea's emerging characterisation and which – I shall suggest – show her transition from victim of manipulation to agent and wielder of memory. As I shall discuss, these instances are closely connected not only as components of Medea's characterisation, but also exist within a range of inter- and intratextual connections which situate Medea (and Jason) against other epic figures, and that memory is a crucial narrative device. By its analysis, we may reach a deeper understanding of Medea's psyche.

Thus, following and building upon previous scholarship,[10] I shall demonstrate that memory is used as a narrative device by which Medea is first manipulated (in the course of Eros' love spell, 3.275–98); then becomes aware of the consequences of her betrayal on her legacy (in her inner monologue, 3.791–4); is further deprived of her agency (by Hera's intervention, 3.809–21); and through which she finally reclaims her identity and gains agency (in her commands to Jason, 3.1069–71). The prominence of Medea's memory ties into the internal focus of the poem's third Book, in which Medea's psyche is investigated in a way that the narrator's is never considered,[11] allowing the reader to experience her motivations and thought processes closely. By looking at these events involving Medea's memory we can gain a deeper understanding of the extent to which she is affected by the actions of Hera, Aphrodite, and Eros, and find hints as to the dangerous figure she will become. Further, by considering the depiction of memory in these instances, I shall explore the intertextual background which informs Medea and Jason's interactions, and bring fresh context to the poet's use of Homeric intertexts.

My approach here will be split into two parts: first, I shall discuss the depiction of passive memory and how it relates to Medea's victimisation in the narrative, including the manipulation of her memory to engender forgetfulness and the removal of her agency. In the second, I shall turn my attention to a significant turning-point in Medea's characterisation, in which the heroine begins to use memory consciously and to her own advantage, and discuss how Apollonius employs this as a device to link her to other epic heroes and heroines. I shall consider these instances chronologically according to their appearance in the narrative:

---

10 E.g. Fantuzzi/Hunter (2004), Holmberg (1998), Knight (1995).
11 See Papadopolou (1997), cf. Toohey (1992).

this will allow for consideration of Medea's ongoing character development, rather than simply considering the nature of these episodes individually.

2 Eros' love spell

As is evident from the epic's beginning, the narrator is shown to have a beneficial relationship with Apollo which allows for the *Argonautica* to be told and is innately connected with the act of remembering. Medea, on the other hand, has no such luck in her relationship with Hera or with her memory – in fact, it is Hera's regard for Jason[12] which ensures Medea's lack of agency. This imbalance of control over one's memory creates a hierarchy of sorts between the narrator and his subjects, helpless by comparison, since – as is often the case for mortals – Medea is subject to the will of the gods and is unable to resist their control.[13] Hera's manipulation of Medea begins with Eros' love spell, which marks one of the most pivotal moments for the heroine's role in the narrative: being made to fall in love with Jason. This manipulation, intended to ensure Jason's success in his quest and carried out primarily by Aphrodite and Eros on the instruction of Hera, is the central event of Book 3. However, this intervention is not limited to the act of making Medea fall in love, but also involves the manipulation of her mind and, in particular, her memory.

> ἧκ' ἐπὶ Μηδείῃ· τὴν δ' ἀμφασίη λάβε θυμόν.
> αὐτὸς δ' ὑψορόφοιο παλιμπετὲς ἐκ μεγάροιο
> καγχαλόων ἤϊξε· βέλος δ' ἐνεδαίετο κούρῃ
> νέρθεν ὑπὸ κραδίῃ φλογὶ εἴκελον. ἀντία δ' αἰεὶ
> βάλλεν ἐπ' Αἰσονίδην ἀμαρύγματα, καί οἱ ἄηντο
> στηθέων ἐκ πυκιναὶ καμάτῳ φρένες· οὐδέ τιν' ἄλλην
> μνῆστιν ἔχεν, γλυκερῇ δὲ κατείβετο θυμὸν ἀνίῃ.
> 3.284-90

> He shot at Medea; speechlessness seized her heart. He darted back out of the high-roofed hall, elated, but the arrow burned deep within the girl's heart like a torch. She kept casting glances at the son of Aeson, and her wise thoughts drifted from her mind. She could not hold on to any other memory, as her heart flooded with sweet pain.

The effect of this spell, and one which is certainly crucial to its success, is that Medea's 'wise thoughts' (πυκιναὶ...φρένες, v.289) leave her, and she cannot 'hold

---
12 Hera holds Jason in 'unceasing regard' (τῷ νύ μοι ἄλληκτον περιτίεται): A.R. 3.61–74.
13 On the danger associated with mortal forgetfulness, see Morrison in this volume.

on to any other memory' but that of Jason (οὐδέ τιν' ἄλλην / μνῆστιν ἔχεν, vv.289–90). Eros' spell alters (or cements) Medea's future, but the depiction of memory loss shows the all-consuming nature of the spell, since the heroine's past is also affected. This, of course, is essential to the function of making Medea fall in love with Jason: since Hera's plan and Jason's success is dependent on Medea betraying her father (and, eventually, violently breaking with her family) the heroine must necessarily disregard or forget about her responsibilities and family ties. The significance of this effect is emphasised in Medea's later dilemma between her duty to and respect for her family, and her own reputation, against her love for Jason and desire to help him (3.751–69).

That Eros' manipulation of Medea's memory is central to his spell is emphasised by the prominence of μνῆστις, 'memory', at the beginning of v.290; the close positioning of this word for remembrance in the narrative at the same time as Medea's 'wise thoughts' abandon her indicates to the audience the simultaneity of these events. Without forgetting her wisdom, perhaps, Medea would not go on to betray her family; this fact reinforces the positive portrayal of Medea: she must be made to forget these ties rather than simply abandoning them.[14] Memory, therefore, is integral to Medea's characterisation here. Eros' spell not only results in the heroine falling in love with Jason but also results in some loss of self. Pindar also describes the spell's effect in this way, with Jason removing Medea's respect (αἰδώς) for her parents, and thus assuming a more active role in the assault:

λιτάς τ' ἐπαοιδὰς ἐκδιδάσκησεν σοφὸν Αἰσονίδαν,
ὄφρα Μηδείας τοκέων ἀφέλοιτ' αἰδῶ

Pyth. 4.217–18

and she taught the son of Aeson wisdom of prayers and incantations, so that he could take away Medea's respect for her parents.

This loss of memory and the subsequent betrayal will result in Medea's exile. Both Pindar and Apollonius thus invert the Homeric sense of memory loss; where in

---

14 This may be considered one of a variety of factors contributing to the initial portrayal of Medea's innocence, see Pavlou (2009). We find a similar connection between memory loss and forgetting one's family ties in the effects of Helen's drug in *Odyssey* 4.220–6, the effects of which are focused on one's family members: 'not if his mother and father lay dead, nor if in front of him men should kill his brother or dear son with a sword' (οὐδ' εἴ οἱ κατατεθναίη μήτηρ τε πατήρ τε / οὐδ' εἴ οἱ προπάροιθεν ἀδελφεὸν ἢ φίλον υἱὸν / χαλκῷ δηιόῳεν); on this and the pains of remembering, see Morrison in this volume.

Homer memory loss is a threat to epic, seen – for instance – in the threat presented to *nostos* by the Lotus-Eaters,¹⁵ and thus also threatens the spread of *kleos*, Jason's quest *depends* on memory loss.¹⁶ Moreover, that Eros' spell results in loss of self for Medea is explicitly shown in the fire simile used to describe her state of mind. Fire imagery to describe love is also found elsewhere, for instance in Sappho fr. 31:¹⁷

> ἀλλὰ κὰμ μὲν γλῶσσά <μ'>ἔαγε, λέπτον
> δ' αὔτικα χρῷ πῦρ ὐπαδεδρόμηκεν,
> ὀππάτεσσι δ' οὐδ' ἒν ὄρημμ', ἐπιρρόμ-
> βεισι δ' ἄκουαι,
> κὰδ δέ μ' ἴδρως κακχέεται, τρόμος δὲ
> παῖσαν ἄγρει, χλωροτέρα δὲ ποίας
> ἔμμι, τεθνάκην δ' ὀλίγω 'πιδεύης
> φαίνομ' ἔμ' αὔτ[ᾳ.
>
> Sapph. fr.31.9–16

no: tongue breaks and thin / fire is racing under skin / and in eyes no sight and drumming / fills ears / and cold sweat holds me and shaking / grips me all, greener than grass / I am and dead–or almost / I seem to me. (trans. A. Carson, 2002)

Sappho's fire, unlike Apollonius', is 'subtle' (λεπτόν), although it has a similarly destructive and all-consuming effect centred on its victim's senses. Apollonius points forward to the negative repercussions of Medea's love, and employs the model of fire imagery to draw our attention to what is lost. Eros' spell results not in an enhancement to Medea's state of mind, but rather disrupts and damages it.

---

15 *Od.* 9.92–97. As the *nostos* is such a central theme of the epic, the prospect of forgetting one's desire to go home is clearly threatening, and by extension it puts at risk the composition and telling of epic itself; indeed, forgetting is crucial to the close of the epic at 24.482–6. See Fantuzzi-Hunter (2004) 118–19.
16 Cf. Aeneas' forgetfulness which causes the loss of Creusa (*nec prius amissam respexi animumve reflexi*, 'nor did I look back for her as she was lost, nor turn my mind backwards') at V. *A.* 2.740–3, a moment of forgetfulness which is essential to his quest to claim his kingdom and Lavinia (*regnumque et regia coniunx*, 2.783); this is matched by Cupid's erasure of Dido's memory of Sychaeus (*abolere Sychaeum*, 1.720).
17 Cf. Callim. *Epigr.* 44 and 45. Fire, of course, is also a prominent feature of Dido's love for Aeneas, e.g. at V. *A.* 1.713, 4.54, 4.101.

3 Medea's legacy (i)

Unlike those who taste the Lotus in the *Odyssey*, however, Medea is not yet ready to forget her home; in fact, Apollonius' next use of memory concerns Medea's own thoughts and concerns and shows that the process of memory loss depicted through the fire simile (that of Eros' spell and her love for Jason burning away other parts of her psyche) is not yet complete, and that the heroine is not yet fully under Hera's control. Following Eros' spell, Medea temporarily regains some autonomy as, faced with the decision between Jason and her family, the heroine wishes to kill herself (τεθναίην, v.789, 'may I die') and therefore avoid her role as pawn in Hera's plan by acting of her own volition. This decision and her internal struggle are prompted, in part, by concern for her reputation:

> ἀλλὰ καὶ ὧς φθιμένῃ μοι ἐπιλλίξουσιν ὀπίσσω
> κερτομίας· τηλοῦ δὲ πόλις περὶ πᾶσα βοήσει
> πότμον ἐμόν· καί κέν με διὰ στόματος φορέουσαι
> Κολχίδες ἄλλυδις ἄλλαι ἀεικέα μωμήσονται·
> 3.791–4

> But in future and even after I have died they will mock and smirk at me, and the whole city will announce my fate far and wide, and the Colchian women will spread my story on their lips everywhere as they go around criticising and insulting me.

Medea fears the future impact of her actions if she were to help Jason, that despite her death the women of Colchis would criticise her in future (ὀπίσσω); this carries echoes of heroic fame but with a decidedly negative outcome, a legacy over which she will have no control.[18] Here, Medea's connection to her family and country is further established as she fears particularly that the story will be carried by people of her city.[19]

The use of μωμήσονται ('criticise') here in combination with the action of telling Medea's story is in effect quite similar to the narrator's declaration at the epic's opening: these Colchian women will become narrators themselves and ones who have the ability to spread a story far and wide. This story, however, will

---

[18] Compare, for example, the concerns and ability of heroes or heroic men to alter or tell their story after death, such as Agamemnon or Elpenor in the *Odyssey*. Medea, rather, would be more like the women of Odysseus' catalogue, silent and unable or unwilling to take agency.

[19] This is one of several instances in which Medea's situation parallels that of Nausicaa in *Odyssey* 6. See Knight (1995) esp. 230–40. Euripides' Medea voices a similar fear that she will be criticised by the Corinthian women (E. *Med.* 214–15): Κορίνθιαι γυναῖκες, ἐξῆλθον δόμων / μή μοί τι μέμψησθ'.

not be kind to Medea. Her fear of a legacy over which she will not be able to exert any control may be read as a metapoetic one, caused by an awareness of the role of memory in fame, rumour and, by extension, poetry. This awareness links Medea to the Iliadic Helen, whose expression of concern for the Trojan women's words (Τρῳαὶ δέ μ' ὀπίσσω / πᾶσαι μωμήσονται, *Il.* 3.411–12, 'all the Trojan women will criticise me in future') finds an echo in Medea's words, and who shows a striking metapoetic understanding of the poem's composition and her role in the epic context:[20]

οἷσιν ἐπὶ Ζεὺς θῆκε κακὸν μόρον, ὡς καὶ ὀπίσσω
ἀνθρώποισι πελώμεθ' ἀοίδιμοι ἐσσομένοισι.
Il. 6.358–8

Zeus has set out a terrible fate for us, so that in the future we may be songs for men to come.

In Helen's view, the current sufferings (κακὸν μόρον), will be replaced in the future by songs which will guarantee her lasting memory[21] – quite the opposite of Medea's fear that her sufferings and even death arising from love of Jason will result in future scorn. The two women are further linked by their relationship with a foreign man, and in this connection we may indeed locate the source of Medea's fear: to be thought of as a quasi-Helen.[22] This identification with Helen in the mind of the reader will be taken to its full, dark potential later in the murder of Apsyrtus. Medea, who fears the negative memories of her fellow women and thus fears to act, will eventually commit far greater crimes than the Iliadic Helen ever does.

4 Hera's intervention

Medea's concern for her own reputation or memory, however, cannot be allowed to derail Hera's plan, so naturally the goddess acts to ensure her success. In the

---

20 Cf. Benardete (1997) 27–29 and Graziosi (2013) 22: 'Helen is the character who comes closest to sharing the perspective of the poet on the Trojan War,' despite her human limitations.
21 Cf. the preservative power of epic song as described in Pindar's sixth *Nemean*, vv.29–30: παροιχομένων γὰρ ἀνέρων / ἀοιδαὶ καὶ λόγοι τὰ καλά σφιν ἔργ' ἐκόμισαν, 'when men have passed on, songs and stories preserve their glorious deeds'.
22 Helen, however, is concerned with her reputation among unspecified 'men to come' (ἀνθρώποισι ... ἐσσομένοισι), as opposed to Medea's fear of the Colchian women's malicious rumours; this is natural since Helen has already left her home.

midst of this dilemma, Medea is struck again, not by a love spell, but by an intense fear of Hades:[23]

> ἵετο δ' ἥ
> γε φάρμακα λέξασθαι θυμοφθόρα, τόφρα πάσαιτο·
> ἤδη καὶ δεσμοὺς ἀνελύετο φωριαμοῖο
> ἐξελέειν μεμαυῖα, δυσάμμορος. ἀλλά οἱ ἄφνω
> δεῖμ' ὀλοὸν στυγεροῖο κατὰ φρένας ἦλθ' Ἀίδαο·
> ἔσχετο δ' ἀμφασίῃ δηρὸν χρόνον. ἀμφὶ δὲ πᾶσαι
> θυμηδεῖς βιότοιο μεληδόνες ἰνδάλλοντο·
> μνήσατο μὲν τερπνῶν, ὅσ' ἐνὶ ζωοῖσι πέλονται,
> μνήσαθ' ὁμηλικίης περιγηθέος, οἷά τε κούρῃ·
> 3.806-14

> She longed to pick out the life-destroying drugs to eat, and she was already undoing the clasps of the chest in her eagerness to take the out the potions, but suddenly a deadly fear of hateful Hades came into her mind, and for a long time she was held speechless. Around her appeared all of life's lovely cares. She remembered the pleasures which exist for the living and she remembered her great happiness with her friends, just like a girl would.

Against this fear, happy memories (μνήσατο...τερπνῶν) flood around Medea. This combination of fear and happiness – specifically remembered happiness – is enough to make Medea forget her decision to die and fall in line with Hera's plan to assist Jason. These memories of the past act to distract Medea from her imagined future memory of the Colchian women and to prevent the heroine from using her own φάρμακα against herself. Again, Apollonius emphasises the importance of remembering to this episode by the repetition and emphatic positioning of μνήσατο at the beginning of vv.813-14.

These memories and fears are not a natural reaction to her planned suicide, however; nor is the effectiveness of this tactic undermined by Medea's indecision (shown explicitly at 3.766-69: ἄλλοτε μέν ... ἄλλοτε δ' οὔ ... αὐτίκα δ' οὔτ'). Rather, Medea had all but resolved herself to her suicide by this point. By the time she is struck with these memories, Medea had already (ἤδη) taken out the chest of drugs and begun to open it. She is then tormented for an extended period of time (δηρὸν χρόνον) and changes her mind (μετάτροπος, v.818). All this, we discover after she has put the chest down, was caused by Hera (Ἥρης ἐννεσίῃσι,

---

[23] Phinney Jr (1967) 339-40 suggests that Apollonius depicts Medea's fear and love alternately – here, however, the fear of Hades and happy memories of her childhood seem to appear simultaneously.

v.818).[24] The manipulation of Medea's memory is essential to her giving in; while Medea had some degree of free will after Eros' spell and enough concern for her family and responsibilities to attempt to avoid betraying them, after Hera's second, direct intervention the heroine's only thought is of Jason:

ἐέλδετο δ' αἶψα φανῆναι
ἠῶ τελλομένην, ἵνα οἱ θελκτήρια δοίη
φάρμακα συνθεσίῃσι καὶ ἀντήσειεν ἐς ὠπήν.
πυκνὰ δ' ἀνὰ κληῖδας ἐῶν λύεσκε θυράων,
αἴγλην σκεπτομένη·
       3.819–23

She longed for rising dawn to appear quickly, so that she could give him the promised enchanting drugs and meet him face-to-face. Time and again she undid the bolts on her doors, looking for daylight.

Medea's desire for the new day both reverses her intended suicide and echoes this,[25] creating a ring composition in this episode which is additionally bookended by the depiction of Medea picking up and putting down the chest, and in her parallel actions of unlocking the chest (δεσμοὺς ἀνελύετο φωριαμοῖο, v.808) and the doors (κληῖδας ἐῶν λύεσκε θυράων, v.822). The chest is symbolic both of Medea's indecision – she could use the drugs either to end her life or to help Jason – and of her power in terms of spell casting. Positioned as it is in the narrative, it additionally becomes symbolic of Medea's power to self-determination.

This memory-focused attack differs from Eros' in several significant ways. That Hera acts directly here, rather than through Eros, and that we see memories added rather than removed (cf. Eros' spell above), are two factors which might influence the success of this attempt to manipulate Medea, who retained sufficient independence or free will following Eros' spell to question whether she should aid Jason and the potential repercussions of this act. Moreover, unlike the fire which rages inside Medea after Eros' attack that shows not only the destructive nature of the spell but also indicates the speed with which Medea's mind is taken over, Hera's new manipulation involves a longer process. Through this attack, Medea puts aside the instruments of her power (which make her a threat to

---

[24] The same expression in used in Callim. *Dian.* 108 to describe Hera's machinations of Heracles' labours. Cf. Vian *ad loc.*
[25] This links back to her previous eager desire to commit suicide at vv.806–9, discussed above. Vian *ad* 3.824 comments on the high level of realism in this depiction of Medea's *'attente'*.

social order); her loss of agency is further emphasised by the narrator's characterisation of the witch as an ordinary girl, 'she remembered... just like a girl would' (μνήσαθ' ... οἷά τε κούρη, v.814). However, these memories, as I have established, do not arise naturally but rather from Hera's direct intervention, and thus the use of οἷά τε κούρη throws into sharp relief the artificiality of the episode. Medea is certainly a κούρη when persecuted by Hera, but in no way are we to understand that this could be a situation in which a typical κούρη might find herself.[26]

The artificial alteration of Medea's memory is, therefore, the final part of her subjugation at Hera's hands – following the spell she had become a pawn in the goddess' plan, but it is only after her memory is affected a second time that Hera's control is cemented. Apollonius' apparent fixation with memory here is not unique, of course, nor is it strange that he depicts memory as a method of manipulation and a marker of agency and autonomy. The connection between one's own memory and identity, and between loss of memory and loss of self or agency is also thematised in the *Odyssey* where, in addition to the harmful effect of the Lotus, a further threat to memory and selfhood arises on Circe's island. While the men Circe has turned to pigs still have their human minds, it is only when this transformation occurs that we realise that the same may have happened to the animals Odysseus' companions meet when they arrive on Circe's island (10.212–19). This ambiguity lends Circe's island a further threat – perhaps, once, those animals were human too – certainly, we should not believe that this is the first time Circe has transformed men who intrude on her island.[27]

These episodes in the *Argonautica* depict a Medea who is not in control of her own memory or legacy, although we see that she is certainly aware of and to some extent motivated by it. She is, ultimately, subject to the will of Hera, whose manipulation depends on the alteration of Medea's mind and selfhood, particularly that related to her memory. Medea's understanding of events is thus altered in a manner comparable to that found in tragedy, for instance the sensory manipulations performed on Euripides' Herakles or Sophocles' Ajax. Although Medea's literal vision is not affected, her perception of her own memory is the site of Hera's attack, and this parallel invites the audience to consider the often horrific outcomes of such divine manipulation (which may be found in the murder of

---

[26] Hera's intervention and the companions Medea remembers as a result of it recall Athene's far more gentle manipulation of Nausicaa in *Od.* 6.21–40.
[27] On the hierarchy of these animal forms, see Vidal-Naquet (1986) 22–3. Cf. Apollonius' description of Circe's 'Empedoclean' animals at 4.672–81, creatures which hint at primordial times and therefore collapse time, but which are not transformed men: see Knight (1995) 188–9.

Apsyrtus). I suggest that Apollonius here draws on tragic themes to present a Medea far removed in agency from her Euripidean counterpart, as I shall explore in more depth below. Medea is clearly depicted as a pawn of the gods here, and it is the manipulation of her memory which removes the heroine's agency and leads to greater pathos from the audience.

5 Medea's legacy (ii): Medea as narrator

However, while it seems that Hera has succeeded in obliterating Medea's resistance, Apollonius is not finished with Medea's memory yet; I shall now turn my attention to the final passage to be discussed here – one which represents another turning point for Medea's characterisation, as the poet finally uses the motif of memory to allow Medea to regain some of her autonomy. As we have seen, Medea is firmly established as a character who is concerned with her reputation and fame, at least with avoiding reproaches. Shortly after Hera derails Medea's planned suicide with an attack on her memory, the heroine returns to her concern for her reputation, but this time with the ability (or at least the desire) to regain some control.

The episodes discussed above, and indeed Book 3 in general, present us with a detailed internal view of Medea's mindset. We are left in no doubt that she is aware of the future and, to the extent she can be, of her role in this (vv.791–4). In this way, she takes on some typically heroic characteristics.[28] After Medea helps Jason (an action which, as we have seen above, is in no way Medea's own decision), the heroine turns her attention once again to her reputation and future memory. Aware that should her intervention allow Jason to escape successfully, her reputation would indeed suffer as she feared earlier, Medea asks him to relate the story of her help to others, using language reminiscent of that of the poet at the epic's opening:

> μνώεο δ', ἤν ἄρα δή ποθ' ὑπότροπος οἴκαδ' ἴκηαι,
> οὔνομα Μηδείης· ὣς δ' αὖτ' ἐγὼ ἀμφὶς ἐόντος
> μνήσομαι.
> 3.1069–71

> But remember, if you ever do return to your home, the name of Medea: equally, I shall remember you, although you will be far away.

---

28 On this see, e.g., Holmberg (1998).

This request (μνώεο) echoes that of Hypsipyle to Jason earlier in the epic (1.896–7), potentially foreshadowing Jason's abandonment of Medea and suggesting his lack of commitment to her through the close alignment of Hypsipyle and Medea's respective situations,[29] but Medea's request places emphasis on her name and on the reciprocal nature of the proposed exchange.[30] In effect, therefore, this is a request for Medea's *kleos* to be spread[31] – this request, along with the Argonauts' reliance on her help (which continues as she defeats the serpent guardian of the fleece and, later, Talos) supports the establishment of her heroic status since with this request she solidifies her place in future retellings of Jason's quest. Memory does not necessarily equate to retelling, of course, but from the *Argonautica*'s opening lines the act of remembering is so closely related to the telling of epic itself that the two concepts are almost interchangeable. When read against the narrator's opening address to Apollo, Medea's command to Jason acts as an extension of the connection between remembering and retelling and establishes a metaliterary connection between narrator and character: Jason is to be the narrator of her story, while Medea, like the narrator, will remember Jason.

This attempt to mitigate her negative fame in Colchis not only reinforces Medea's awareness of the future, but is also figured as an exchange, comparable to those in the *Odyssey* between Menelaus and Telemachus (4.589–92),[32] or Nausicaa and Odysseus (8.457–68). Unlike Menelaus' sending-off of Telemachus, however, which places gifts on one side of the exchange, and Telemachus' memory of Menelaus (and, presumably, a favourable report of his hospitality) on the other,[33] Medea's exchange with Jason is figured as a mutual remembering. The drugs and advice which Medea has given Jason at the beginning of this episode (3.1013–14ff) are not mentioned, and thus her sending-off of Jason breaks

---

29 Hypsipyle appears more accepting that Jason will not return (vv. 894–5), and despite her reluctance for Jason to leave (which aligns Hypsipyle with Calypso) their farewell scene is short and relatively uncomplicated in contrast to Jason and Medea's; see Knight (1995) 33, 241.
30 Vian *ad* 1070 notes that this is the first time that Medea names herself before Jason: this turning point in her characterisation and agency is firmly connected with the declaration of her identity.
31 Hunter *ad loc.* notes that the inclusion of Ariadne as an *exemplum* also influences this desire to be remembered: while Medea is not yet ready to leave Colchis with Jason (cf. 3.1107–8), her dependence on Jason is firmly established here. This theme is further picked up in Jason's use of ἐπιλήσεσθαι ('forget', 3.1080) in his reply to Medea.
32 Although Medea herself rejects the idea of φιλοξενίη between their families at 3.1108.
33 Helen, too, gives Telemachus a gift of a *peplos* to remember her by (τοῦτο δίδωμι, μνῆμ' Ἑλένης χειρῶν, *Od*. 15.125–6, 'I give you this, as a reminder of the hands of Helen). As Grethlein (2008) 37–8 notes, these gifts are explicitly tied to memory, and function as objects of commemoration, with emphasis placed on their temporal dimension.

away from the Homeric mould. A closer parallel exists in Nausicaa's parting words to Odysseus in *Odyssey* 8:[34]

χαῖρε, ξεῖν', ἵνα καί ποτ' ἐὼν ἐν πατρίδι γαίῃ
μνήσῃ ἐμεῦ, ὅτι μοι πρώτῃ ζωάγρι' ὀφέλλεις
Od. 8.461–2

Goodbye, stranger, and afterwards even in your homeland may you remember me, since you owe me first the safety of your life.

Nausicaa's previous help of Odysseus is neatly summed up in the term ζωάγρια,[35] 'life-debt', while the emphasis is placed on Odysseus' remembering of her (μνήσῃ), a more direct command than Menelaus' request, and one which provides a model for Medea's command to Jason. Like Nausicaa, Medea commands Jason to remember her, but states that she will remember him in turn, the words μνώεο and μνήσομαι placed close together and emphatically at the start of lines 1069 and 1071. Here, we see Medea become an active user of memory, a fact which is striking against both the Homeric model and the previous episodes involving the manipulation of her memory. Through this assertion, she reclaims some of the agency she has lost in the episodes discussed above, declaring (in a manner echoing the narrator's voice at v.1.2) that she will create her own memories, as well as ensuring her reputation.[36] This intratextual link with the narrator's opening declaration, moreover, allows Medea a chance of life beyond Jason's departure, figuring her not only as an active user of memory, but as a potential narrator herself.

However, behind this exchange of memory lies the exemplum of Ariadne, forgotten by Theseus on their return from Crete – a detail notable in its absence, as Jason neglects to mention this to Medea when she asks him to recount the tale (vv.1074–6). Here, the reader's understanding of the myth – which was certainly known to Apollonius[37] – emphasises the insecurity of Medea's position and creates a tension by contrast with her request. In a sense fitting this tension, Jason

---

[34] Nausicaa's words to Odysseus also lie behind Aeneas' parting statement to Dido at V. A. 4.333–6; see Hunter in this volume.
[35] This word has few attestations and occurs just once in each of the Homeric epics; in the *Iliad* it is used by Hephaestus to describe his debt to Thetis (18.406–7). It is also used by Herodotus (3.36.5) and Callmachus (fr. incert. 516) with the meaning of a ransom.
[36] On the hierarchical nature of memory in the *Iliad* in particular, see Kostecka in this volume.
[37] The story is provided by the narrator at 4.423–34. On this theme in the *Argonautica*, see especially Jackson (1999), and see Weber (1983) on the temporal distortions at play between the

accepts Medea's memory exchange, yet his response is framed in terms of forgetting rather than remembering:

> καὶ λίην οὐ νύκτας ὄίομαι οὐδέ ποτ' ἦμαρ
> σεῦ ἐπιλήσεσθαι, προφυγὼν μόρον, εἰ ἐτεόν γε
> φεύξομαι ἀσκηθὴς ἐς Ἀχαιίδα, μηδέ τιν' ἄλλον
> Αἰήτης προβάλῃσι κακώτερον ἄμμιν ἄεθλον.
> 3.1079–82

> I truly do not think I will ever, night or day, forget you, if I evade death, if I really get away to Achaea safely, and if Aeetes does not set some even worse trial before us.

This departure from terms of remembering is not accidental; Jason's agreement does not, I suggest, encompass the retelling which is an explicit aspect of Medea's request, particularly when one considers the parallel of Ariadne's myth which is presented to the reader. This exchange invites the reader to recall Medea and Jason's *agon* in Euripides' tragedy, a parallel which might lead us to read Jason's response above as one foreshadowing his actions toward Medea later on. Euripides' Medea states her role in helping Jason (*Med.* 475–90), to which Jason responds by attributing the help she gave to Aphrodite and Eros, removing Medea's agency and any need for reciprocity (vv.522–531).[38] Moreover, as with Medea's proposed reciprocal exchange, Jason's answer recalls the instances given above in the *Odyssey*. The mention of 'night or day' (νύκτας ... οὐδέ ἦμαρ) recalls Menelaus' 'remember me all your days' (ἐμέθεν μεμνημένος ἤματα πάντα, *Od.* 4.592) and Odysseus' reply to Nausicaa.[39] However, it is in Odysseus' words that we find the strongest hint that Jason's reply is not quite fitting for Medea's request.[40] I give Odysseus' reply to Nausicaa in full for comparison:

> Ναυσικάα θύγατερ μεγαλήτορος Ἀλκινόοιο,
> οὕτω νῦν Ζεὺς θείη, ἐρίγδουπος πόσις Ἥρης,
> οἴκαδέ τ' ἐλθέμεναι καὶ νόστιμον ἦμαρ ἰδέσθαι·
> τῷ κέν τοι καὶ κεῖθι θεῷ ὣς εὐχετοῴμην
> αἰεὶ ἤματα πάντα· σὺ γάρ μ' ἐβιώσαο, κούρη.
> *Od.* 8.464–8

---

voyages of the Argonauts and Medea's relationship with Theseus in Apollonius, Callimachus, and Catullus.
38 On this speech and Medea's characterisation in Euripides play, see Gill (1998) 154–74.
39 Cf. Hunter *ad loc.* Fantuzzi/Hunter (2004) 94.
40 Fantuzzi-Hunter (2004) 121 present Jason's reply as equivalent to Odysseus'; I suggest rather that we should read Jason's promise as inherently deficient.

Nausicaa, daughter of great-hearted Alcinous, now may Zeus, loud-thundering husband of Hera, grant that I come to and one day see again my homeland: then even there I will pray to you as a god for all my days, for you have saved my life, girl.

Unlike Jason's reply, which omits Medea's name in favour of 'you' (σεῦ, 1080), a notable absence considering her specific request which emphasised her name, Odysseus' promise includes a full address to Nausicaa and reaffirms her aid, thus neatly and satisfactorily concluding their association.[41] It is unsurprising, then, that Medea seems unconvinced by Jason's promise and repeats her commands shortly afterwards, this time reminding Jason that she has helped him at the cost of betraying her parents: 'remember me, and I shall remember you, too, in spite of my parents' (μνώεο, σεῖο δ' ἐγὼ καὶ ἐμῶν ἀέκητι τοκήων / μνήσομαι, 3.1110–11). Furthermore, she expands on her previous request and responds to Jason's word choice by threatening that if she hears a rumour that Jason has forgotten her (ὅτ' ἐκλελάθοιο ἐμεῖο, v.1112), she will remind him of his debt to her (μνήσω ἐμῇ ἰότητι πεφυγμένον, v.1116), a threat reminiscent of Medea's reproach of Jason in Euripides' play,[42] and which plays on each's respective word choice in their promises to reinforce a connection. Here we see an indication of Medea's future and the lengths to which she will go to secure her legacy, but one which is again centred on memory and reputation. Certainly, this response is strong enough to provoke Jason to present the possibility of their eventual marriage (v.1128: λέχος), an offer which he had avoided in the promise not to forget her, above.[43] However, Jason appears now to recognise Medea's awareness of memory and her reputation, and here furthers his previous statements by promising that she will be honoured like a goddess (οἱ δέ σε πάγχυ θεὸν ὣς πορσανέουσιν, 3.1124), thus reminding the reader once again of Odysseus' promise to Nausicaa.

Finally, let us turn briefly back to Medea's connection with Helen and Circe in the Homeric poems. I have already discussed above how as a female character showing an apparently extra-textual awareness of future events and of the process of 'story' telling (in the form of rumour or report), Medea resembles Helen in Book 6 of the *Iliad*. However, Helen's words in the *Iliad* are simply a metapoetic comment on her understanding – Helen knows that the events will form the songs of future generations, but while her understanding of the nature of orality is more explicit than Medea's, Helen does not act to ensure her place in this tradition

---

41 Knight (1995) 241 comments on the awkwardness of length, by contrast, of Jason and Medea's exchange.
42 Hunter *ad loc.*
43 See Jackson (1992) esp. 158 on the role of necessity in Jason's actions here (and later, in marrying Medea).

(aside from her initial resistance to Aphrodite's plan, *Il.* 3.411–12).⁴⁴ In fact, while the Iliadic Helen is concerned and aware of the future and preservation of memory, in *Odyssey* 4 she possesses drugs which remove pain, anger, and negative memories which she uses on Menelaus and Telemachus:

> αὐτίκ' ἄρ' εἰς οἶνον βάλε φάρμακον, ἔνθεν ἔπινον
> νηπενθές τ' ἄχολόν τε, κακῶν ἐπίληθον ἁπάντων
> *Od.* 4.220–1

> Straightaway she put a drug into the wine which they were drinking, one which removes pain and anger, and brings forgetfulness of all bad things.

Similarly, as mentioned above, Circe's magic may in some way contribute to forgetfulness of self and resulting loss of identity, although this is left quite ambiguous. There seems to be some – by no means exclusive – connection here between female characters, particularly those with potential magical knowledge, and memory. Medea, however, does not use her magic for forgetfulness in Apollonius' epic, but rather to ensure her fame: if Jason escapes safely and victoriously as a result of her magic, and Medea is unable to follow, she will see to it that he tells her story. Unlike Helen, Medea acts to preserve her future reputation and her place in the epic narrative itself in commanding Jason to remember her, as we saw above. It is significant, then, that it is Hera, a female goddess, who manipulates Medea's memory in order to gain control of the heroine – especially since Medea, in light of Helen and Circe's acts above, could well be a potential threat to others in this way.

6 Conclusion

Throughout Book 3 of the *Argonautica*, Apollonius' Medea is a character shaped by her memories and her awareness of the past and future, a characteristic which establishes a striking parallel with the Iliadic Helen, allowing Medea not only a metapoetic awareness but the desire to shape her future reputation. Whether her memory is controlled or manipulated by others, or reclaimed by the heroine, Medea's personal memories form an important part of her characterisation. Moreover, this motif is used explicitly to show development in Medea's character arc.

---

44 Helen does, however, become a literal weaver of poetry (and her own story) in *Iliad* 3.125–8, as she depicts the battles fought on her behalf (ἔθεν εἵνεκ'), before performing her *teichoskopia*: on this, see Elmer (2005).

Over the course of Book 3, Medea undergoes a full transformation as her command to Jason at lines 1069–71 shows a desire to preserve her life and reputation, as well as an engagement with her own memory, a stark comparison to her earlier thoughts of suicide and the shame which would last even beyond her death to become her legacy. The heroine thus develops from a largely passive victim of Hera's manipulation to a figure who, in her reclaimed agency over both her own memory and that of others, casts herself as an active user of memory, paralleling the role and language of the epic's narrator. Throughout, despite Hera's manipulation, Medea retains her understanding of her role in future memory, similarly to Helen in the *Iliad*. In light of the parallels both to Hypsipyle and Nausicaa, the latent and ominous parallel with Ariadne, and to displays of heroic desire for remembrance, whether this is Menelaus' treatment of Telemachus or Odysseus' parting words to Nausicaa, Medea's active request for a place in Jason's memory allows the heroine to regain some of the empowerment lost at Hera's hands and solidifies her heroic status.

Bibliography

Baragwanath, E. (2008), *Motivation and Narrative in Herodotus*, Oxford.
Benardete, S. (1997), *The Bow and the Lyre: A Platonic Reading of the* Odyssey, Lanham/London.
Byre, Calvin S. (1996), "The Killing of Apsyrtus in Apollonius Rhodius' *Argonautica*", *Phoenix* 50 (1): 3–16.
Calame, C. (2011), "The Homeric Hymns as Poetic Offerings", in A. Faulkner (ed.), *The Homeric Hymns: Interpretative Essays*, Oxford: 334–358.
Elmer, D. (2005), "Helen Epigrammatopoios", *Classical Antiquity* 24: 1–39.
Fantuzzi, M./R.L. Hunter (2004), *Tradition and Innovation in Hellenistic Poetry*, Cambridge.
Gill, C. (1998), *Personality in Greek Epic, Tragedy, and Philosophy*, Oxford.
Graziosi, B. (2013), "The Poet of the *Iliad*", in A. Marmodoro & J. Hill (eds.), *The Author's Voice in Classical and Late Antiquity*, Oxford: 9–38.
Grethlein, J. (2008), "Memory and Material Objects in the *Iliad* and the *Odyssey*", *The Journal of Hellenic Studies* 128: 27–51.
Hunter, R.L. (1987), "Medea's Flight: The Fourth Book of the *Argonautica*", *The Classical Quarterly* 37 (1): 129–39.
Hunter, R.L. (1988), "'Short on Heroics': Jason in the *Argonautica*", *The Classical Quarterly* 38 (2): 436–53.
Hunter, R.L. (1989), *Apollonius:* Argonautica Book 3, Cambridge.
Holmberg, I.E. (1998), "Μῆτις and Gender in Apollonius Rhodius' *Argonautica*", *Transactions of the American Philological Association (1974-)* 128: 135–59.
Iser, W. (1991), *The Act of Reading: A Theory of Aesthetic Response*, Baltimore/London.
Jackson, S. (1992), "Apollonius' Jason: Human Being in an Epic Scenario", *Greece & Rome* 39 (2): 155–62.

Jackson, S. (1999), "APOLLONIUS' "ARGONAUTICA": The Theseus / Ariadne Desertion." *Rheinisches Museum für Philologie*, Neue Folge, 142 (2): 152–157.
Jauss, H.R. (1982), *Toward an Aesthetic of Reception*, (trans. T. Bahti), Minneapolis.
Knight, V. (1995), *The Renewal of Epic*, Leiden.
McNelis, C./A. Sens. (2016), *The Alexandra of Lycophron. A Literary Study*, Oxford.
Papadopoulou, T. (1997), "The Presentation of the Inner Self: Euripides' *Medea* 1021–55 and Apollonius Rhodius' *Argonautica* 3, 772–801", *Mnemosyne* 50 (6): 641–664.
Pavlou, M. (2009), "Reading Medea through Her Veil in the *Argonautica* of Apollonius Rhodius", *Greece & Rome* 56 (2): 183–202.
Phinney Jr, E. (1967), "Narrative Unity in the *Argonautica*, the Medea-Jason Romance", *Transactions and Proceedings of the American Philological Association* 98: 327–341.
Toohey, P. (1992), Ἀκηδείη and Ἔρως in Apollonius of Rhodes (*Arg.* 3.260–298)", *Glotta* 70: 239–247.
Vian, F. (1961), *Argonautiques: chant III*, Paris.
Weber, C. (1983), "Two Chronological Contradictions in Catullus 64", *Transactions of the American Philological Association (1974–2014)* 113: 263–271.

Sophie Ngan
Bound to Break Boundaries: Memory and Identity in Seneca's *Medea*

Abstract: In this chapter, I consider memory in Seneca's *Medea* on both extra-dramatic and intra-dramatic levels, to show that Medea's identity as a transgressive figure cannot be changed, because of both the plot structure of the Medea myth and the gendered structures of Medea's Romanised dramatic universe. As a character more generally, Medea is transgressive due to her divine lineage, her Eastern origins, her supernatural powers, and her infanticide. Throughout the course of the play Seneca's Medea inadvertently multiplies these transgressions as she tries, unsuccessfully, to alter her transgressive identity and regain her status as Jason's wife.

I first discuss how Medea appropriates the masculine discourses of epic and beneficence, in order to manipulate collective memory and reclaim her marital identity. By presenting herself as an epic hero who has earned Jason as booty through her heroic deeds, and by describing her deeds as favours to Jason, Medea claims her identity as Jason's wife. However, Medea's attempts to manipulate memory fail; Jason's and Creon's perceptions of her remain unchanged, and her disruption of the norms of these masculine discourses makes it clear that her gender prevents her from appropriating them successfully. Thus, Medea is forced to turn to her memories of her own literary and personal past, calling on her reputation as inspiration for how she should behave. Acting in accordance with her criminal past, Medea kills the children she and Jason share in order to jointly avenge the divorce and reclaim her marital status. Medea is forced to commit infanticide by both the tragic structures of her past and the gendered structures of her world, which prevent her from engaging in masculine discourses. This action, which is unavoidably entangled with her femaleness and maternity, confirms not only Medea's status as a transgressive figure, but also the gendered hierarchies positioning her as a transgressive woman.

I would like to thank Dr Erica Bexley, Esther Meijer and J.L. Watson, who have read and commented on this chapter at various stages of its creation. I am indebted to Martina Astrid Rodda, whose knowledge of Greek literature I have mined. Thanks are also due to Katharine Mawford and Eleni Ntanou for their editorial input. The texts have been taken from Oxford Classical Texts editions, apart from that of the *De Beneficiis*, which is from Hosius' 1914 Teubner. All translations are my own.

https://doi.org/10.1515/9783110728798-009

1 Memory, Identity, Medea

It is well known that "literary memory," in the form of intertextual references to earlier versions of the Medea myth, is an integral part of Seneca's retelling and of his characterisation of Medea; as Wilamowitz comments: 'This Medea has read Euripides.'[1] Medea's literary self-awareness is evident in her nominal exclamations which bookend the development of Medea's character throughout the play. During her conversation with her nurse after the prologue, she proclaims her intent to manifest her identity as "Medea" (*Med.* 171):

> NVT. Medea –
>   ME. fiam.
>
> NU. Medea –
>   ME. I will become her.

Towards the end of the play, in the moment when Medea debates whether to kill her children, her earlier proclamation is fulfilled (*Med.* 910):

> ME. Medea nunc sum.
>
> ME. Now I am Medea.

Medea's aspiration to "become Medea" and her claim to "be Medea" are, inevitably to an audience aware of her rich literary heritage, self-conscious references to the most defining act of her literary past, the murder of her own children.[2] The palimpsestic nature of Seneca's play and his Medea's literary self-awareness have engendered readings of Seneca's *Medea* which focus on Seneca's engagement with his literary predecessors.[3] Whilst Seneca's play cannot be separated from the

---

[1] Wilamowitz-Moellendorff (1919) III.162: 'diese Medea hat Euripides gelesen'. Likewise, Littlewood (2004) 269 notes: 'In drama, where no words happen but that a character speaks them, literary self-consciousness is an aspect of characterization.' As Boyle (2006) 332 notes on Senecan tragedy in general: 'Beneath each Senecan tragedy are a host of subtexts – Greek and Roman, Attic, Hellenistic, republican, Augustan, and early imperial – clarifying and informing their discourse.' See Boyle (2014) cvii–cxviii on the metatheatricality of Medea's self-awareness.
[2] For further discussion of Medea's self-naming, see Segal (1982) 241–243; Boyle (2014) cix–cxii. The extra-textual awareness of female figures is also touched upon by Mawford in this volume.
[3] Some studies (e.g. Mayer (1990); Roisman (2005)) directly compare Seneca with his predecessors, highlighting parallels and divergences. These have developed into examination of how Seneca engages with literary tradition, e.g. Hinds (2011) explores further how the post-Ovidian poetic landscape of Seneca's time affects his writings. As Boyle (2006) 338 notes: 'The "anxiety

literary tradition it follows, my aim is to bring focus to the personal identity of Seneca's Medea as well.[4] By considering these two perspectives as different, but not necessarily mutually exclusive, I draw attention to the importance of the intra-dramatic gendered forces which shape Seneca's Medea, as complementary to the extra-dramatic literary forces on the play.[5]

Just as the role of memory has been important in constructing identity in both modern theories of identity and studies of Roman antiquity, memory is also integral to both the intra-dramatic and extra-dramatic levels on which Medea's identity is constructed.[6] What is key to the identity Medea constructs intra-dramatically is the specifically female status of wife. In Seneca's contemporary Roman context, a woman's social and legal identity would be constituted in terms of her father or husband.[7] Moreover, it was through identities within the social setting of the family, those of wife and mother, that women were commemorated and remembered.[8] Medea constructs her own identity both through literary, intertextual memory and, as I focus on in this chapter, through memory internal to the dramatic universe of the play.

The joint literary and personal aspects of Medea's use of memory to construct her own identity are highlighted in her prologue, a self-addressed monologue in which she exhorts herself to action (*Med.* 48–50):

>   levia memoravi nimis:
> haec virgo feci; gravior exurgat dolor:
> maiora iam me scelera post partus decent.

---

of influence" ... which dominates the behaviour of characters such as Phaedra, Hippolytus, Atreus, Thyestes, Aegisthus, Oedipus, Jocasta, Agamemnon, Helen, Medea mirrors Seneca's own anxiety before the determining literary past and prescriptive parental figures of the Graeco-Roman poetic tradition.' On Medea in particular, Trinacty (2014) (esp. 93–126) highlights how allusions to different Ovidian works coincide with Medea's different roles, interpreting these as Seneca's exploration of how an author navigates their literary heritage.

4 See Bexley (2016), a study which likewise moves scholarly discussion away from Medea's literary identity, evaluating 'the self-conscious behaviour of Seneca's Medea with reference not only to meta-theatre and literary precedent, but also to Stoic ideals of personal constancy' (32).
5 For other treatments of memory as jointly metaliterary and internal to narrative poetry, see Burke-Tomlinson, Mawford and Ntanou in this volume.
6 Modern theories of identity highlight its narrative construction through memory (e.g. Brockmeier and Carbaugh (2001); Nichols (2017)). Likewise, the role of memory in constructing identity in the Roman world has been much discussed (e.g. Gowing (2005); Galinsky (2014)).
7 On the dependence on men for social identity, Hallett (1973) 106: 'a woman's social class and social acceptability were determined by the man in her life.' See also: Pomeroy (1975) 149–189.
8 On which, see Flower (2002); Larsson Lovén (2011).

> I have recalled things too trivial; I did these things as a maiden. Greater grief rises up; greater crimes befit me after giving birth.

Just before these lines, Medea has recounted the various crimes she committed to reach Corinth (*Med.* 44–48); here she describes these as *levia* and exhorts herself to *maiora scelera*. These words, *levia* and *maiora*, are used to contrast themes and behaviour appropriate to, on the one hand, Medea's changing generic identity within literary tradition, and, on the other hand, the older age of Seneca's Medea. The word *maiora* in particular recalls the word *maius* in the closing line of *Heroides* 12, Ovid's elegiac epistle from Medea to Jason (*Her.* 12.212):

> nescio quid certe mens mea maius agit.
>
> Certainly, my mind rouses something greater.

This line itself is a reference to Ovid's generic escalation from elegiac epistles to his lost tragedy *Medea*, mapping the language of magnitude to genre as Ovid did himself.[9] Seneca's reference to *Heroides* 12 alludes to Medea's literary baggage. Seneca, like Ovid, seeks to transcend the elegiac *levia* of the *Heroides*, by presenting her tragic *maiora*, weighty themes more suitable for tragedy.[10] It is also worth noting, here, that tragedy is not the only "weighty" genre. Epic is likewise characterised by its magnitude from the Hellenistic period onwards (Call. *Aet.* fr. 1), with a variety of adjectives indicating largeness;[11] in Book 3 of the *Odes*, Horace uses the adjective *magnus* to refer to epic themes (*Carm.* 3.3.72), the positive form

---

[9] Ovid's previous use of this language in *Am.* 3.1.23–24: *tempus erat thyrso pulsum graviore moveri; / cessatum satis est: incipe maius opus* (It was time that you were moved, struck by a greater *thyrsus*. There has been enough delay: begin a greater work); as discussed by Trinacty (2014) 99–100. Hinds (1993) 34–43 discusses the (potential) interactions between Ovid's *Heroides* 12 and lost tragedy *Medea*. On the specifically generic implications of this line and the associations of *maior* with tragedy, see Barchiesi (1993) 343–345; Hinds (1993) 41–43, (2011) 22–23. Hinds (2011) 22 in particular notes: 'the end of Medea's epistle to Jason, *Heroides* 12, operates as a self-conscious metapoetic trailer, not just to the bloody Corinthian revenge immediately beyond the end of that epistle, but to the specific tragic text immediately beyond the end of that epistle; in other words, *Heroides* 12 is cast by Ovid as a "prequel" to his own Medea-tragedy.'

[10] For further discussion of Medea's literary recollection in Seneca, see Trinacty (2007), (2014) 95–126. Trinacty (2014) 99–100: 'Medea strives throughout the work to perform "greater" crimes and transcend her previous Ovidian representations.' This kind of palimpsestic claim to surpass a predecessor is also discussed by Burke-Tomlinson in this volume, with reference to Ovid. On generic interplay, see also Ntanou in this volume.

[11] E.g. *grandis* (Hor. *Carm.* 1.6.9), *gravis* (Prop. 1.9.9., Ov. *Am.* 1.1.1, Ov. *Met.* 3.366, 10.150).

of the comparative *maior* which Medea uses in her self-exhortation. Medea's *maiora* are not only a metapoetic comment on her generic elevation to tragedy, but also foreshadow her use of epic discourse, which I shall show she employs.

Within the context of Seneca's play, the words *levia* and *maiora* also refer to specific actions within the life of the character Medea, actions by which she defines her own identity. Medea contrasts her earlier crimes, described as minor (*levia*), with her plans to commit more serious crimes, *maiora scelera*. By associating her status as a *virgo* with *levia*, and her maternal role *post partus* with *maiora*, Medea highlights how her own personal ageing parallels the escalation of her crimes.[12] Thus, the imagery of growth works on the literary level of generic transcendence, as well as on the internal narrative level of ageing and more extreme transgressions which are appropriate for Medea's older age; genre, personal identity, and scale of transgression are interconnected through the rhetoric of growth. From the perspective of literary allusion, *maiora* are more generically suitable for a tragic (versus elegiac) Medea, whereas within the play, *maiora* are preferred for an older Medea. Therefore, the Senecan Medea's identity is constructed through the opposition between her (literary and biographical) pasts and presents, meaning that memory plays an important role in Medea's identity on both extra-dramatic and intra-dramatic levels.

Having established that memory and identity are closely linked for Medea as a character in Seneca's play with both a literary past and personal past, I now consider why identity is so important to Medea. As noted above, it is well known that Medea's awareness of her identity stands in for Seneca's awareness of the literary tradition preceding him. I show that it is important to consider, in addition, Medea's awareness of her identity from within the play itself, since this awareness is closely linked to the fragility of her identity within the Romanised social world of the play, as she navigates the changes in her status after her divorce. My interpretation of the connection between Medea's marital status and identity draws on both Guastella's observation that 'the divorce strips away the meaning of everything that the *virgo* Medea did in order to become the *coniunx/mater*', and Walsh's identification of Medea's identity crisis between past and present selves.[13]

---

12 Cf. Hine (2000) 120: 'M.'s obsession with making sure her behaviour in the current situation will match her behaviour in the past.' Medea's identity as a maiden is also explored in Apollonius' *Argonautica*, opposed to her identity as a witch, on which see Mawford in this volume.
13 Guastella (2001) 200; Walsh (2012) 71–73.

The closing lines of Medea's prologue, which continue to reiterate the links between Medea's life events and identity, draw attention to the importance of her marital status to her identity (*Med.* 52–55):

> paria narrentur tua
> repudia thalamis. quo virum linques modo?
> hoc quo secuta es. rumpe iam segnes moras:
> quae scelere parta est, scelere linquenda est domus.

> May your divorce be told of together with your marriage. In what way will you leave the man? In the same way you pursued him. Now break off lazy delays. A household which was begotten in crime should be left in crime.

The interconnected increase of Medea's age and crimes is reinforced by the parallels she makes between her marriage and divorce, events which have effected significant changes to her identity. The equivalence of *repudia* and *thalamis*, the coordination of *quo modo ... hoc quo*, and the repetitive structure of Medea's final line highlight the parallels between Medea's divorce and her marriage, which occur under the same criminal conditions, because of the same repeated *scelera*. This final line indicates a further parallel in Medea's conception of her marriage and divorce and, consequently, their importance to her identity. The verb *linquo*, meaning "to leave", can be used poetically to refer to dying as leaving life.[14] The repetitive phrasing of *scelere parta est* and *scelere linquenda est* coincides with the conceptual parallel of marriage as the birth of a household and divorce as its death. This quasi-biological conceptualisation of marriage and divorce emphasises their importance as the beginning and ending of Medea's wifehood, and consequently implies the importance of marital status itself to Medea.

The disruptive effects of Jason's divorce from Medea are clear from her response to the chorus' wedding song, which signifies Jason's remarriage to Creusa and solidifies Medea's loss of marital identity (*Med.* 116–120):

> occidimus: aures pepulit hymenaeus meas.
> vix ipsa tantum, vix adhuc credo malum.
> hoc facere Iason potuit, erepto patre
> patria atque regno sedibus solam exteris
> deserere durus?   120

---

14 See, for example, Verg. *Aen.* 3.140, 10.856. On the use of *linquo* for death, see also *OLD* 1033 s.v. "*linquo*" 1c, *TLL* 7.2.2 s.v. "*linquo*" 1461.6–20.

> I am ruined. The wedding song has struck my ears. I myself still scarcely believe so much evil. Could Jason do this, with my father, fatherland and kingdom torn away, could the harsh man leave me alone in a foreign land?

The primacy of social, familial identities for women within a Roman context, mentioned above, is reflected in Medea's exclamation of despair (*occidimus*), which highlights her instability due to Jason's divorce from her. Her dependence on social relations to male figures is emphasised by the repetition of words indicating paternality, *patre patria*, directly adjacent without an intervening conjunction. However, Medea experiences an extra level of complication, making marital status doubly important for her identity. Not only has she lost Jason himself, but she also specifies that she lacks a father and homeland to return to. Unlike a typical Roman woman, Medea cannot return to her birth family after her divorce.[15] Her description of herself as *sedibus solam exteris* emphasises her vulnerability in its word order, with Medea (*solam*) surrounded by a foreign land, Corinth (*sedibus exteris*). After her divorce, Medea is left as a lone woman with no familial connections, a condition compounded by both the unfamiliarity of the land to her and her status as an outsider within.[16]

Therefore, Medea cares about how she is remembered not only because she recalls her identity from literary past, but also because she, as a woman within the dramatic fabric of Seneca's play, has lost her identity as Jason's wife and has little other social capital within Corinth. Medea's self-awareness of her own identity is a result of not only external literary knowledge, but also the loss of her status as Jason's wife, which consequently exposes the fragility of her social identity within the world of the play.

Having highlighted the connection between memory and identity, and having shown why memory and identity are important to Seneca's Medea on both intra-dramatic and extra-dramatic levels, in the remainder of this chapter I address Medea's attempts to reconstitute her marital identity through the employment of different modes of remembering. As well as constructing her self-identity through her own memories, Seneca's Medea manipulates the memories of other characters and groups in order to construct a narrative in which she has the status of Jason's wife. Medea's focus is on the memories of the Corinthians and Creon

---

15 Hine (2000) 120: 'What particularly distinguishes M.'s situation from that of the Roman wife, however, is that the divorced Roman women could always return to her father, or her nearest male relative … but M. has nowhere to go.' On the effects of divorce in Rome, see Treggiari (1991) 466–467.
16 Betrayal of family are also of concern to Apollonius' Medea, as discussed by Mawford in this volume.

(which I refer to as collective memory), and Jason's memories of her.[17] In sections 2 and 3, I show that, in order to manipulate the memories of these two groups, Medea appropriates the discourses of epic remembrance and beneficence respectively, two modes of remembering touched upon in Medea's first two speeches in the play.

However, Medea's appropriation of these two modes of remembering later in the play constitutes transgression, firstly in the fact that she, as a woman, appropriates masculine discourses, and secondly in the way in which she interacts with the norms of these discourses.[18] The latter of these serves to reinforce the former, proving it is impossible for a woman, within this dramatic universe, to engage in masculine discourses without revealing her gender through her misunderstanding of these discourses. Like other women in Greco-Roman mythology who transgress into male spheres, Medea is unsuccessful in manipulating Creon's and Jason's memories in order to reclaim her identity as Jason's wife.[19] This failed appropriation of aspects of masculinity highlights, within Seneca's dramatic universe, the location of gender boundaries and the negative consequences for women transgressing those boundaries.[20]

Having failed to alter others' memories of her, Medea, as I discuss in section 4, embraces her past crimes, remembering the criminal reputation of her literary and personal pasts, and fulfilling it by killing her children in Jason's presence. Medea's transgressions of gender are an extension of her transgressive identity more generally, as a foreigner in Corinth, with her divine lineage from the Sun giving her supernatural abilities, and with her eventual infanticide.[21] On an extra-

---

[17] I use the term "collective memory" to refer to the specific kind of "collective memory" that Assmann (1995) 125–127 classifies as "communicative memory" – memory constructed in relation to a group. Specifically, my use of the term denotes the shared memories of the Corinthians (the chorus and Creon) about Medea. On the identification of the chorus with the Corinthians, see Boyle (2014) 135–136; Mazzoli (2014) 562.
[18] Gendered transgressions by women are also discussed by Burke-Tomlinson (Pasiphäe's sexual transgression) and Ntanou (Galatea's transgression as a female narrator within masculine genres) in this volume.
[19] The (attempted) manipulation of memory by characters is also discussed by Mawford in this volume.
[20] One example of a woman transgressing into male discourse is Ovid's Byblis, who uses the aesthetics of Roman elegy in her failed attempts to justify her incestuous desire for her twin brother Caunus (Ov. *Met.* 9.450–665); discussions of this episode: Raval (2001); Mayor (2017) 223–234. The use of artistic product to keep women within their bounds is not an unfamiliar one; for example, Rabinowitz (1993) 14 writes: 'Euripides may indeed "invent woman" and "reverse traditional representations," but ultimately he recuperates the female figures for patriarchy.'
[21] Jonhnston (1997) 7–9 and Graf (1997) 38–39 note Medea's transgressive characteristics.

dramatic level, the mythological structures of Medea's literary memory and her literary identity as a transgressive figure cannot be changed. On an intra-dramatic level, Medea's failed alteration of memory, due to the transgression of the gendered norms of her Romanised world, confirms the gendered structures which shape that world, thereby reinforcing Medea's already transgressive identity.

2 Epic Memory

In this section, I discuss how epic memory[22] is implicated in Medea's construction of her identity at the start of the play. I then show how Medea appropriates epic memory in her interactions with Creon, in order to reclaim her marital identity; however, as highlighted in the second half of this section, the gendered incongruity of Medea's adoption of this masculine discourse is evident from the inconsistencies between her self-portrayal and others' perceptions of her.

The closing lines of Medea's prologue foreshadow her use of epic discourse to relate her present to the future, a mode of remembering both metaliterary and personal. As noted by Trinacty, the verb *narro* (*Med.* 52) has a metaliterary function; by using this verb, Medea assumes an authorial role, taking control of her own destiny and writing her eponymous tragedy with the knowledge of her literary past.[23] This verb also introduces how Medea employs memory within the play, indicating her adoption of epic *kleos*, the preservation of heroic deeds for posterity, as a mode of her own memorialisation.[24] Whilst the verb *narro* does not have the immediate epic recognisability of *cano*, it does have epic connotations, as highlighted by its use in Virgil's *Aeneid*, where it refers not to the epic song of the bard, but the recounting of heroic and anti-heroic acts in a less formal sense.[25] This verb is used of Aeneas' narration of his own deeds:

---

[22] Whilst Medea adopts other themes of epic, such as martial imagery, my focus is on epic memory. For Medea's engagement with other epic themes, see, for example, Walsh (2012) 82–83 on Medea's engagement with heroic ethos. In the different context of Apollonius' *Argonautica*, Mawford in this volume discusses the similar themes of Medea's concern for her reputation, aim to confer *kleos* on herself, and self-fashioning as an epic hero.
[23] Trinacty (2014) 94.
[24] On *kleos* in Homeric epic as the glory conferred on a hero through his deeds recorded by the epic poet, see Nagy (1999) 17.
[25] Whilst there is not sufficient space to fully discuss the issue of the performance of Seneca drama, it is important to note here the potential for performance and, consequently, the additional metadramatic force of Medea's spoken exhortation to continue being spoken about. On

> sic pater Aeneas intentis omnibus unus
> fata renarrabat divum cursusque docebat.
>
> *Aen.* 3.716–717

Thus, father Aeneas alone, with everyone attentive, told of the fates of the gods and explained his course.

> Iliacosque iterum demens audire labores
> exposcit pendetque iterum narrantis ab ore.
>
> *Aen.* 4.78–79

Again, maddened, she [Dido] demands to hear the Trojan hardships and again hangs onto the lips of the one narrating.

In both these cases, the verb *narro* (and the etymologically related *renarro*) refers to Aeneas' narration of his journey from Troy to Carthage, an act of narration mirroring Odysseus' narration of his journey from Troy to Phaecia.[26] This verb, therefore, has epic range, used of the narration of the deeds of an epic hero within an epic poem.

The verb *narro* can also be used of anti-epic deeds, as in Pyrrhus' and Turnus' respective addresses to their victims before they die (*Aen.* 2.547–550; 9.741–742):

> referes ergo haec et nuntius ibis
> Pelidae genitori; illi mea tristia facta
> degeneremque Neoptolemum narrare memento.
> nunc morere.

And so you will report these things and go as a messenger to my father, son of Peleus. Remember to tell him of my wretched deeds and his ignoble Neoptolemus. Now die!

> incipe, si qua animo virtus, et consere dextram,
> hic etiam inventum Priamo narrabis Achillem.

Come then, if there is any courage in your heart, and face my right hand. You will tell Priam that an Achilles has also been found here!

In both instances, the speakers use the verb *narro* to instruct their victims-to-be to tell of their deeds in the Underworld. Just as in Homeric epic, *kleos* allows the

---

performance and Senecan drama, see, for example: Boyle (1997) 3–12; Harrison (2000); Kohn (2013).
26 Clausen (2002) 58; Heyworth and Morwood (2017) 21.

hero's reputation to transcend their absence in death, the act of narration, indicated by *narro*, transcends the anti-hero's absence from the Underworld.[27] This verb, therefore, refers to the reporting of heroic and anti-heroic deeds in an epic context, which results in the transmission of a hero's, or anti-hero's, reputation.[28] In this sense, Medea uses the verb *narro* at the start of the play to exhort that her (anti-)epic deeds are reported as evidence of her reputation in spite of her absence from Corinth after her divorce from Jason.

The suggestion that Medea's reputation is epic in its mode of transmission is fulfilled in her interactions with Creon, as she uses epic memory in her attempts to alter her reputation. In their quasi-*agon*, in which she entreats him to return Jason, Medea fashions herself as an epic hero, an inversion of others' memories of the Argonautic journey. As McAuley notes, 'she speaks as if she were Achilles, bringing back spoils from war, keeping only Jason for herself'.[29] In addition to the parallels noted by McAuley, I highlight that the Achillean self-characterisation by Medea is particularly evident in her claim to have single-handedly saved all the Argonauts, which echoes Achilles' speech on the depreciation of his role in the Trojan expedition (*Med.* 225–235 cf. *Il.* 9.321–337):

> ... solum hoc Colchico regno extuli,   225
> decus illud ingens Graeciae et florem inclitum,
> praesidia Achivae gentis et prolem deum
> servasse memet. munus est Orpheus meum
> ...
> geminumque munus Castor et Pollux meum est.   230
> ...
> vobis revexi ceteros, unum mihi.   235

I brought back only this one thing from the Colchian kingdom: that great glory of Greece, the famous bloom, the shields of the Achaean race, the offspring of the gods – I myself saved them. My gift is Orpheus... and Castor and Pollux my twin gift... For all of you I brought back the rest of them, just one for me.

οὐδέ τί μοι περίκειται, ἐπεὶ πάθον ἄλγεα θυμῷ
αἰεὶ ἐμὴν ψυχὴν παραβαλλόμενος πολεμίζειν.

---

27 On the immortalising function of *kleos*, see Nagy (1999) 174–209.
28 Compare also with Juno's use of this verb of Hercules' reputation at *Her. F.* 37–40: *qua Sol reducens quaque deponens diem / binos propinqua tinguit Aethiopas face, / indomita virtus colitur et toto deus / narratur orbe.* (Wherever the sun, leading back and taking away the day, touches the twin Ethiopian tribes with its close torch, his unassailable courage is revered and he is told of as a god throughout the whole world.)
29 McAuley (2016) 215.

> ...
> ὣς καὶ ἐγὼ πολλὰς μὲν ἀΰπνους νύκτας ἴαυον, 325
> ἤματα δ' αἱματόεντα διέπρησσον πολεμίζων
> ἀνδράσι μαρνάμενος ὀάρων ἕνεκα σφετεράων.
> δώδεκα δὴ σὺν νηυσὶ πόλεις ἀλάπαξ' ἀνθρώπων,
> πεζὸς δ' ἕνδεκά φημι κατὰ Τροίην ἐρίβωλον·
> τάων ἐκ πασέων κειμήλια πολλὰ καὶ ἐσθλὰ 330
> ἐξελόμην, καὶ πάντα φέρων Ἀγαμέμνονι δόσκον
> Ἀτρεΐδῃ·
> ...
> ἄλλα δ' ἀριστήεσσι δίδου γέρα καὶ βασιλεῦσι,
> τοῖσι μὲν ἔμπεδα κεῖται, ἐμεῦ δ' ἀπὸ μούνου Ἀχαιῶν 335
> εἵλετ', ἔχει δ' ἄλοχον θυμαρέα. τῇ παριαύων
> τερπέσθω.

> There is no gain for me, when I suffer pains in my heart, always risking my life in war... Thus, I spent many nights without sleep, and made many days blood-red in battle, fighting men for the sake of their wives. I plundered twelve cities of men with ships, I claimed eleven by foot in fertile Troy; from all these cities I took many good treasures, and, bringing them back, I gave them to Agamemnon, son of Atreus... He gave some of the treasures as prizes to the chiefs and kings, and for those men the gifts are set, but from me alone of the Achaeans he has taken; he has my pleasing concubine. Let him delight in lying beside her.

Although the two speeches differ in their purposes – Medea attempts to persuade, whilst Achilles rebukes Odysseus' persuasion – comparison highlights how Medea's self-fashioning as an epic hero functions as one of the persuasive strategies she uses to reclaim her marital status.

Medea, like Achilles, emphasises the solo nature of her achievements. In both speeches, the protagonists use first person pronouns to set themselves apart from others (e.g. *Med.* 228: *memet, meum* cf. *Il.* 9.321: μοι). Through the juxtaposition of their plurality against her singularity, Medea, like Achilles, draws attention to the vastness of her heroic deeds; the many cities Achilles has plundered correspond to the many Argonauts Medea has saved. The multiple terms of status used to describe the Argonauts further underline their plurality, thereby drawing attention to Medea's heroism, since she, alone, has saved not just many men, but many heroes.[30] Just as Achilles provided Agamemnon with κειμήλια, Medea offers *munera*, in the form of the objectified Argonauts, to Creon and the Corinthians. Moreover, like Achilles has been slighted by Agamemnon's snatching of Briseis, Medea has been slighted by Creon's adoption of Jason as his son-in-law.

---

[30] For discussion of Medea's use of these terms, see: Hine (2000) 141. For the Roman terminology of status in general, see: Lendon (1997) 272–274.

Medea, therefore, presents to Creon a narrative of gender reversal, in which her deeds are heroic and Jason is the reward she deserves for those deeds

The inversion of genders in the Achilles-Medea, Briseis-Jason parallels coincides with Medea's inversion of the collective memory of the Argonautic expedition. When attempting to persuade Jason of her ability to protect him, Medea proposes a contest with Creon, in which he will be the prize (*Med.* 517–518):

> certemus sine,
> sit pretium Iason.

> Let us contest, and let the prize be Jason.

Medea confirms her self-characterisation as an epic hero by applying the militaristic verb *certo* to herself.[31] Yet, Medea's objectification of Jason contradicts the chorus' descriptions of her, highlighting the discrepancy between her perspective and that of others.[32] The chorus has previously described Medea as a *pretium*, the same word she uses of Jason (*Med.* 518), as part of the reward for the Argonautic voyage (*Med.* 361–364):

> quod fuit huius pretium cursus?
> aurea pellis
> maiusque mari Medea malum,
> merces prima digna carina.

> What was the prize of this journey? The golden fleece, and Medea, a greater evil than the sea, a reward worthy of the first ship.

Medea's status as a *pretium*, shared with the golden fleece, indicates the chorus' perception of Medea as property; likewise, the alliterative application of *merces* to Medea highlights her objectification by the chorus.[33] By transferring the term *pretium* from herself to Jason, Medea inverts her and Jason's roles in the collective memory of the Argonautic myth, whilst also inverting the gendering of normative epic roles, presenting Jason as property and herself as the warrior who has earned him. This objectification of the person claimed as the epic prize has parallels with

---

31 For the military connotations of *certo*, see *TLL* 3 s.v. "*certo*" 897.40–898.74, *OLD* 304 s.v. "*certo*" 2: 'to contend in battle, fight'; e.g. Verg. *Aen.* 10.355.

32 Such selective remembering by characters is also discussed by Burke-Tomlinson in this volume.

33 Littlewood (2004) 153 on Medea as property vs. participant. See Traina (1979); Segal (1982) on terms alliterating with Medea's name: *mater, malum, monstrum*.

Briseis' explicit objectification as a γέρας in the *Iliad*, highlighting further the reversal of normative gender roles in epic.[34] By presenting Jason, rather than herself, as the prize for an epic conquest, Medea claims to have earned him as her husband, like Achilles and Jason earnt Briseis and Medea respectively. The contrasting applications of *pretium*, to Jason by Medea and to Medea by the chorus, highlight the discrepancy between how Medea presents herself and how others perceive her.

From Creon's unchanged perception of Medea as a monstrosity, it is clear that Medea fails to alter collective memory through the appropriation of epic discourse. The first time Creon describes her to his attendants, he draws attention to her transgressive lineage and deeds (*Med.* 179–181, 190–191):

> Medea, Colchi noxium Aeetae genus,
> nondum meis exportat e regnis pedem?
> molitur aliquid: nota fraus, nota est manus.
> ...
>   vade veloci via
> monstrumque saevum horribile iamdudum avehe.

> Medea, harmful offspring of Colchian Aeëtes, does she not yet take her feet from my kingdom? She plans something. Her crime is known, her hand is known... Go by a swift path, take away, at last, the savage, terrible monster.

His first reference to her by a patronym highlights his "othering" of her, through drawing attention to her non-Greek heritage from Colchis and her divine lineage from the Sun via her father Aeëtes. He explicitly describes her as a *monstrum*, also applying the adjectives *saevus* and *horribilis* to her, as a result of her past deeds, which he refers to negatively as *fraus* (crime), and orders her to leave his kingdom.

After her attempted persuasion by means of epic memorialisation, Creon's view of Medea remains unchanged from his very negative description of her (*Med.* 266–269):

> tu, tu malorum machinatrix facinorum,
> cui feminae nequitia, ad audendum omnia
> robur virile est, nulla famae memoria,
> egredere...

> You, you deviser of evil deeds, who have the wickedness of a woman, the manly strength to dare everything, and no care for your reputation, leave...

---

34 E.g. *Il.* 1.184–185.

He still orders her to leave Corinth (*avehe*, *egredere*), and he still recalls her deeds as crimes. Creon's clarification that Medea's deeds are *mala facina* highlights the fact that what she considers to be heroic deeds, he remembers not as heroic, or even neutral actions, but as crimes.[35] From Creon's perspective, Medea's unheroic actions show that she does not care about her *fama*, her "reputation" with particularly epic connotations.[36] Thus, Medea's appropriation of epic memory, her attempt to claim Jason by changing others' memories of her criminal deeds into memories of heroic deeds, fails.

Medea's unsuccessful appropriation of epic discourse is distinctly gendered. To further emphasise Creon's negative perception of Medea, a feminine form of *machinator*, a noun typically used of male inventors or craftsmen, is used. This is the only place in extant Latin literature where this noun is found, highlighting that Medea is so shocking that novel vocabulary which transforms masculine words must be used to describe her.[37] The gendered aspect of Medea's transgression is further emphasised by the ambiguities of *Med*. 267–68; it is possible to punctuate after *nequitia* (as Zwierlein's text printed here) or after *omnia* to give: *cui feminae nequitia ad audendum omnia, / robur virile est*.[38] The acts Medea has committed, of daring everything, are ambiguously associated with both female wickedness and male strength. The moral contrast between *nequitia* and *robur* highlights that daring is positive in men and negative in women, thereby drawing attention to Medea's own ambiguous gendering and the moral judgement of audacity relative to gender. That Creon denounces Medea with these words shows both that her crossing of gender is transgressive and that there is a double standard at play here.

Medea's and Achilles' shared statuses as liminal figures, yet differing reputations, highlight the ramifications of Medea's gender. Both have divine lineage, which separates them from humans, and both undergo gender reversal. Medea's inversion of normative genders, through her analogy of herself with Achilles and Jason with Briseis, recalls Achilles' cross-dressing in the pre-*Iliad* myths of the epic cycle, most well known from Statius' *Achilleid*.[39] However, unlike Achilles,

---

35 The word *facinus* can refer to either a deed or a crime: *OLD* 667 s.v. "*facinus*" 1 'a deed, act', 2 'a misdeed, crime, outrage'.
36 See Hardie (2012), esp. 78–125.
37 *TLL* 8 s.v. "*machinatrix*" 16.80–81: as the feminine form of *machinator*; it only occurs here in Seneca's *Medea*.
38 E.g. Boyle (2014) punctuates after *omnia* which would result in the alternative translation 'who has the womanly wickedness to dare everything, manly strength, and no care for your reputation', attributing such boldness to *robur virile*, instead of to *feminae nequitia*.
39 On this, see Heslin (2005); McAuley (2010).

whose cross-dressing does not negatively affect his heroic status, and whose divine lineage contributes to his heroic status, Medea's crossing of gender boundaries is not accepted, and her divine heritage turns her into a monstrosity.[40] Medea is like Achilles; she is of divine lineage, is stripped of her rightful reward, which she deserves due to her heroic deeds, and crosses gender boundaries. However, because of her difference in gender from Achilles, it becomes clear that whilst Medea's actions are acceptable and even commendable for a man, they are transgressive when performed by a woman.

Medea's transgressions of epic memory are, therefore, manifold: she inverts the gender of the epic hero and the the prize for epic conquest, and she commits transgressive deeds which necessarily could not be considered positive due to her gender. Medea's use of epic memory is transgressive in a further, gendered sense. Despite her engagement with epic reputation, Medea diverges from the generally masculine concerns of epic, differing from male epic protagonists both in gender and in wanting to be remembered in an epic mode not for martial deeds, but for deeds associated with her marital status.[41] On the one hand, like Euripides' Phaedra, who is highly concerned with being remembered for her honour in marriage, Medea wants to be remembered for the acts of marriage and divorce, distinctly female means of commemoration, since a woman's social status, as daughter, wife, and mother, was integral to her social identity.[42] On the other hand, however, unlike Phaedra, there is nothing honourable about the criminal acts with which Medea associates her marriage and divorce. Thus, Medea's remembrance is marked by transgressions; Medea transgresses the bounds of her gender not only in her criminality, but also in her adoption of the epic mode, which she also transgresses by using epic ideology towards un-epic ends.[43]

3 Beneficent Memory

I now move on to discuss how Medea attempts, unsuccessfully, to manipulate Jason's memory by appropriating the discourse of beneficence. The structure of

---

[40] On Achilles' divine lineage and heroism, see Slatkin (1991) 89–96; Nagy (1999) 158–167.
[41] McAuley (2010) 37: 'the primary importance of heroic, warrior masculinity to Roman male identity and society is affirmed again and again by Roman poets, orators and historians.'
[42] E.g. E. *Hipp.* 419–423.
[43] Likewise, Medea uses Stoic ideas towards un-Stoic ends: see Bartsch (2006) 255–58; Star (2006).

this social institution of gift-exchange was integral and specific to the contemporary social context of Seneca's time.⁴⁴ Thus, I consider the material from the *De Beneficiis* as part of not only the philosophical context, but also the Roman social context relevant to Seneca's *Medea*.⁴⁵ I begin by showing the relevance of beneficence to Medea's interactions with Jason. I then highlight Medea's transgressions of beneficent discourse, which constitute her failed appropriation. Just as Medea engages with epic discourse but violates its norms, she also appropriates and disrupts the discourse of the social institution of beneficence.

Medea's interaction with beneficence is signalled towards the beginning of the play, in her response to Jason's remarriage (*Med.* 120–22):

> merita contempsit mea   120
> qui scelere flammas viderat vinci et mare?
> adeone credit omne consumptum nefas?

> Has he disregarded my services, he who had seen fire and sea overcome my crime? Does he think now all my wrongdoing has been used up?

Medea's vocabulary in this passage has resonances with that of Seneca's *De Beneficiis*. She refers to the deeds she has done for Jason as *merita*, a word frequently used throughout the *De Beneficiis* of the services done for another; similarly, the word *munus*, which Medea uses in her speech to Creon (*Med.* 228, 230), also appears throughout the *De Beneficiis*.⁴⁶ Her use of the verb *contemno*, in combination with *merita*, to describe Jason's devaluation of her deeds highlights how Medea quantifies her actions, thus incorporating the quasi-financial aspect of gift-exchange into her conception of her relationship with Jason.⁴⁷

---

44 See Griffin (2013), esp. pp.7–15.
45 The relationship between Seneca's tragedies and philosophical writings has been much discussed. For an overview, see Hine (2004); Ker (2009) 128. For examples of how Senecan philosophy has been applied to the tragedies, see: Rosenmeyer (1989) (cosmology); Nussbaum (1997), Schiesaro (2003) (passions); Busch (2009), Wray (2009), Bexley (2016) (selfhood).
46 Seneca uses *munus* (*Med.* 142) throughout the *De Beneficiis* to refer generically to gifts bestowed on another (e.g. *Ben.* 1.1.4, 1.1.9), and *merita* (*Med.* 120) to refer to services committed for another (*Ben.* 1.1.8, 1.5.2).
47 Seneca notes that he uses financial language metaphorically (*Ben.* 4.12.1): *cum creditum dicimus, imagine et translatione utimur ... cum dico creditum, intellegitur tamquam creditum* (When we say "loan", we use an image and a metaphor ... when I say "loan", it is understood as if a loan). Seneca often differentiates gift-exchange from financial exchange, e.g. at *Ben.* 1.2.4: *turpis feneratio est beneficium expensum ferre* (It is shameful lending to enter a benefit into one's accounts). As Griffin (2013) 39 notes: 'Though Seneca often discusses the exchange of benefits in

Medea's speech here also foreshadows her manipulation of Jason's memory via beneficent discourse. The verb *consumo*, which, like *contemno*, suggests Medea's quantification of her deeds, is used in the *De Beneficiis* in negative relation to memory (*Ben.* 12.1–2):

> Ingratos quoque memoria cum ipso munere incurrit, ubi ante oculos est et oblivisci sui non sinit, sed auctorem suum ingerit et inculcat... Apud paucos post rem manet gratia; plures sunt, apud quos non diutius in animo sunt donata, quam in usu. Ego, si fieri potest, **consumi** munus meum nolo; extet, haereat amico meo, convivat.

> Remembering rushes upon ungrateful men with the gift itself, when this gift is before the eyes and does not allow itself to be forgotten, but thrusts and forces its giver upon the receiver... Amongst few men, gratitude remains after the fact. There are many amongst whom gifts are in the mind no longer than in use. I, if it is possible, do not want my gift to be used up. Let it be visible, let it stick to my friend, let it live with him.

A *consumptum munus* can no longer incite the memory and, thus, neither the gratitude of its receiver. At the most basic level of beneficent exchange, memory is essential; as Seneca notes, ingratitude, the most common vice and the root of all other vices, results from forgetfulness (*Ben.* 3.1.3):[48]

> ingratissimus omnium, qui oblitus est.

> The most ungrateful of all is he who forgets.

Therefore, from Medea's perspective, Jason's judgement that her *nefas* is *consumptum*, like a *consumptum munus* within Seneca's philosophy of social exchange, implies that he does not remember her deeds for him. In her interactions with Jason, Medea's persuasive strategy centres upon reminding him of her services to him, for which, she argues, he owes her the status of wife.[49]

---

metaphorical terms drawn from credit and debt ... he is concerned throughout his treatise to distinguish sharply between the two kinds of exchange.'

48 See Griffin (2013) 25. At *Ben.* 1.1.1, Seneca states that there is no vice *frequentius* (more common) than ingratitude. On ingratitude as the root of all other vices, see *Ben.* 1.10.4: *erunt homicidae, tyranni, fures, adulteri, raptores, sacrilegi, proditores; infra omnia ista ingratus est, nisi quod omnia ista ab ingrato sunt, sine quo vix ullum magnum facinus adcrevit.* (There will be murderers, tyrants, thieves, adulterers, rapists, sacrilegious men, traitors; below all these is the ungrateful man, except all these vices are from the ungrateful man, without which scarcely any great crime grows.)

49 With reference to Apollonius' *Argonautica*, Mawford in this volume also discusses Jason's forgetfulness of Medea's deeds and her threat to make him remember.

For Medea, Jason's ingratitude goes hand in hand with his forgetfulness of her deeds, thus indicating to her his rejection of her as wife. In her speech to Jason, after addressing him as *ingratum caput*, she proceeds to remind him at length of everything she did for him (*Med.* 465–466, 482):

> ingratum caput,
> revolvat animus igneos tauri halitus
> ...
> redde supplici felix vicem.
>
> Ungrateful man, let your mind wind back to the fiery breath of the bull ... Repay a suppliant, fortunate man.

Whilst not strictly a verb of remembering, *revolvo* does have this semantic potential, especially in reference to the list of past events which follows this verb in *Med.* 466–477.⁵⁰ The coincidence of recalling her deeds to Jason, reminding him of them, and describing him as *ingratus*, highlights how Medea adopts the social institution of beneficence as a means of persuasion. The verb *reddo*, which Medea uses here, is frequently used throughout the *De Beneficiis* to refer to the repayment of a favour.⁵¹ Therefore, by reminding him of everything she has done for him, for which he should be grateful, and by entreating him to repay her, Medea demands that he recognise her as his wife.

The deeds Medea reminds Jason of are not only her personal memories, but also, unavoidably, her poetic memories.⁵² In particular, Medea's description of Jason as *ingratus* recalls Ovid's *Heroides* 12, from Medea to Jason, the only poem of the collection which contains the word *ingratus*.⁵³ Ovid's Medea, similarly, recalls her deeds in response to Jason's ungratefulness towards them (*Her.* 12.21):

> Est aliqua ingrato meritum exprobrare voluptas.
>
> It is some pleasure to make my service a matter of reproach to an ungrateful man.

The earlier focus of the Senecan Medea on her services to Jason (*Med.* 120) and her accusation of his lack of gratitude recalls Ovid's Medea. The weight of poetic

---

50 *OLD* 1649 s.v. "*revolvo*" 2c: 'to go back over (past events, etc.) in thought or speech'. Hinds (2011) 27–28 also takes *revolvat animus* to refer to remembering.
51 E.g. *Ben.* 1.1.1, 1.1.3, etc.
52 See, for example, Hinds (2011) 27–28 for how Seneca, in this passage, recalls Ovid's *Heroides* 12 and *Metamorphoses* 7.
53 As noted by Hinds (1993) 33; Boyle (2014) 252.

recollection enhances the contrast between her remembrance of her own personal deeds, and Jason's forgetfulness of them (*Med.* 560–562):

> discessit. itane est? vadis oblitus mei
> et tot meorum facinorum? excidimus tibi?
> numquam excidemus.

> He has left. Is that it? Do you go, forgetful of me and my many deeds? Are we lost to you? We will never be lost.

Despite Medea reminding Jason of her services to him, Jason actively forgets them, emphasised by Medea's use of two verbs (*obliviscor* and *excido*).[54] Moreover, Medea equates Jason's forgetfulness of her deeds with forgetfulness of her, highlighting the link between her identity and the deeds she committed. This link is also clear from Medea's exploitation of the slippage between *facinus* as deed and as crime to jointly explain that, by committing crimes, she has experienced the loss of her natal family and, consequently, the loss of her identity as daughter and sister, and that, through deed, she has provided favours to Jason, for which she demands repayment through the status of wife. Her betrayal of her father and murder of her brother, acts committed in order to marry Jason, are now losses from which Medea has gained nothing since Jason has divorced her.[55]

However, by recalling her favours to Jason, and by demanding repayment through reminding him of them, Medea distorts the norms of beneficent exchange, according to Seneca's treatise. Whilst Jason should remember the benefits bestowed upon him, Medea, as the benefactor, should forget the benefits she has bestowed (*Ben.* 2.10.4):

> haec enim beneficii inter duos lex est: alter statim oblivisci debet dati, alter accepti numquam.

> This is the law of benefits between two people: one should immediately forget that it has been given, the other should never forget that it has been received.

---

54 On *excido* as a verb of forgetting ("to fall from memory"): *OLD* 634 s.v. "*excido*¹" 9b; *TLL* 5.2 s.v. "*excido*" 1239.6–1240.2. See the use of *excido* to refer to forgetfulness causing ingratitude at *Ben.* 1.2.5: *ingratus est adversus unum beneficium? adversus alterum non erit; duorum oblitus est? tertium etiam in eorum, quae exciderunt, memoriam reducet.* (Is he ungrateful towards a single benefit? He will not be towards another. Has he forgotten two? A third will lead his memory back to those which fell from him.)
55 Guastella (2001) 200.

Medea also fails to partake in ideal beneficent exchange when she demands Jason repay the favour, if Seneca's advice is applied (*Ben.* 1.1.3):

> Nec facile dixerim, utrum turpius sit infitiari an repetere beneficium.
>
> I would not easily say whether it is worse to repudiate the favour or ask for it back.

Medea's transgression of ideal beneficent exchange is compounded by her transgression of gendered behaviour. Like the discourse of epic heroism, the institution of beneficence also constitutes a masculine discourse. Whilst, in theory, women and slaves could participate in beneficence, its socialising function, in forming the bonds of *amicitia*, nevertheless makes it a masculine discourse in practice;[56] as Griffin discusses, beneficence functioned to create social bonds between *alieni* and was typically practised between social equals.[57] *De Beneficiis* 1.12.2 (quoted above) highlights this socialising function of beneficence; Seneca hopes that a gift keeps him in his friend's mind, with the specific reference to *amicus meus*, confirming that beneficence usually strengthens the bonds of specifically male friendship. Therefore, by even implicating marital status within beneficent exchange, Medea disrupts the norms of beneficence, as well as the norms of marital union.[58]

---

56 As in other contexts (e.g. Seneca, *Ad Marciam.* 16.1), men and women in the *De Beneficiis* are considered to have equal capacity for virtue (*Ben.* 3.18.2): *nulli praeclusa virtus est; omnibus patet, omnes admittit, omnes invitat, et ingenuos et libertinos et seruos et reges et exules; non eligit domum nec censum, nudo homine contenta est* (Virtue is closed off to no one; it lies open to all, it admits and invites everyone, freeborn men, freedmen, enslaved people, kings, and exiles; it does not choose lineage and property, it is content with the bare man). On the equal capacity of women and men for Stoic virtue, see also: Asmis (1996); Mauch (1997) 13–20; Gloyn (2017) 18, 89–94.

57 On the socialising function of beneficence, see: Griffin (2013) 25–29. See also *Ben.* 3.18.1: *beneficium esse, quod alienus det (alienus est, qui potuit sine reprehensione cessare)* (A *beneficium* is what a stranger gives – a stranger is someone who could hold it back without reproach). On the practice of beneficence between equals, see Griffin (2013) 11: 'both [Seneca and Cicero] are primarily interested in liberality and gratitude, as practised between social equals and those who are to be treated as social equals.'

58 Medea's disruption of marital norms is also evident in how she describes her dowry of lost homeland and relatives (*Med.* 486–489). The dowry, which should unite the families of husband and wife, is instead destructive, and paid by Medea herself, instead of her father. Medea also conflates her language of loss and beneficent exchange with the concept of the dowry which she demands to be returned (*Med.* 488–489). For further discussion of Medea's marriage and dowry, see: Abrahamsen (1999) 113; Guastella (2001) 206–208; McAuley (2016) 215–216.

Medea's multifaceted transgression of beneficent discourse – her female focus, her reminding of Jason, her criminal deeds – coincides with the failure of this mode of persuasion. Despite her reminders, Jason nevertheless forgets her deeds; Medea fails to reclaim her status as wife. Therefore, like Medea's engagement with epic memory, her use of beneficent memory is transgressive of the norms of beneficent discourse and of gendered behaviour. Just as Medea fails, on an intra-dramatic level, to rewrite Creon's and Jason's memories of her past deeds, she also fails to rewrite the memories of her literary past.[59] Unable to change memories of her past, Medea embraces them, alluding, at *Med.* 562, to the preservation of her legacy through her unforgotten (and unforgettable) deeds, to which I now turn.

4 Remembering Medea

In the final scene of Seneca's *Medea*, Medea returns to the memories of her own past, recalled in her prologue speech, to (re)construct her identity (*Med.* 905–910):

> en faxo sciant 905
> quam levia fuerint quamque vulgaris notae
> quae commodavi scelera. prolusit dolor
> per ista noster: quid manus poterant rudes
> audere magnum, quid puellaris furor?
> Medea nunc sum; crevit ingenium malis. 910

> I will make them know how trivial and how commonplace the crimes which I granted were; through those my grief was rehearsed. What greatness could untrained hands, or the rage of a girl, dare? Now I am Medea; my nature has grown with evils.

Referring to her past deeds as *levia*, Medea recalls not only the deeds, but also her prologue speech where the opposition of *levia* and *maiora* foreshadowed her infanticide (*Med.* 48). By the end of the play, Medea fulfils her earlier claims: her *levia* have grown into the *magnum* which she is about to commit, and she, declar-

---

59 Hinds (2011) 28: "'Can you still not remember (as a husband, as a reader …) all that I am to you, how the *topoi* of our story are shaped? Well then, let me repeat the lesson, and perhaps this time it will stick.'" Moreover, as Curley (2013) 180 notes, Medea's literary past forms 'a master Medea code' which, by Seneca's time, made Medea's tragic mythology inescapable.

ing *Medea nunc sum*, has fulfilled her reputation in both literary and intra-dramatic senses, becoming the infanticidal witch known from Euripides' play and from her murder of her own brother, which foreshadows the death of a father's child.[60]

The verb *proludo* (*Med.* 907) draws attention to the contribution of Medea's earlier deeds to her later crimes; as Boyle notes, the metatheatrical connotations of this verb suggest that Medea's earlier crimes were a rehearsal for her infanticide.[61] Medea makes sure to perform the murder of their second child in front of Jason, having killed the first without his presence (*Med.* 992–994; 1001):

> derat hoc unum mihi,
> spectator iste. nil adhuc facti reor:
> quidquid sine isto fecimus sceleris perit.
>
> This one thing was lacking for me, that man as spectator. I think nothing of what has already been done; whatever crime I did without that man is ruined.
>
> hic te vidente dabitur exitio pari.
>
> This one too will be given to death with you watching.

The absence of Jason from the murder of the first child (*sine isto*) is rectified in the killing of the second (*te vidente*). In her authorial persona, Medea requires an audience, a *spectator*, in Jason, to witness her work; yet in her intradramatic characterisation as a woman who wants to be remembered, Medea must also be seen in order to generate the memory of herself, her own reputation. After killing their children, Medea's identity as Jason's wife now converges with her reputation as murderess, as she leaves Jason, reclaiming her marital status (*Med.* 1020–1021):

> lumina huc tumida alleva,
> ingrate Iason. coniugem agnoscis tuam?
>
> Lift up your swollen eyes, ungrateful Jason. Do you recognise your wife?

Medea again accuses Jason of ingratitude. However, instead of reminding him of her favours to him, she has taken away the children she bore for him; thus, Medea's commitment of infanticide is highly transgressive and gendered as female

---

[60] As Guastella (2001) 214–215 notes, Medea's murder of her brother, like the murder of her children, is an injury against a father.
[61] Boyle (2014) 355.

through her now paradoxical maternity.[62] The epic remembrance of Medea converges with tragic recognition as she forces Jason to acknowledge her as his wife through the use of a rhetorical question (*coniugem agnoscis tuam?*). Within the play, it seems, Medea has succeeded in her mission; she has taken control of her reputation and regained her marital identity, leaving Jason with nothing except the memory of his wife and children in the final words she speaks to him. However, in order to do so, she could not appropriate masculine discourses; the only successful way of doing so was destroying her own children, the concrete evidence of her marital status, indicating both the female failure to engage with masculine discourses, and Medea's transgressive femininity. Jason's parting words to her point out that her terrible crimes have separated her from society (*Med.* 1026–1027):[63]

> Per alta vade spatia sublime aetheris,
> testare nullos esse, qua veheris, deos.
>
> Go through the high expanse of the lofty sky. Bear witness that there are no gods where you go.

Medea escapes into the sky, from which even the gods are absent, signifying her rejection from and of human society. However, even in the act of escape, Medea is trapped by her literary past, riding the chariot of the Sun, emulating her Euripidean predecessor (E. *Med.* 1321–1322).

5 Conclusion

As shown in sections 2 and 3, Medea's attempts to appropriate the masculine discourses of epic and beneficence, to assume an authorial role by changing the memories of her past, fail because of the tragic structures of her literary past and the crimes of her personal past. Moreover, Medea's failure to use masculine dis-

---

[62] As McAuley (2016) 227 notes: '[Seneca] constructs a Medea whose motherhood is not antithetical but ontologically central to her infanticide, intimating the horrifying possibility that this is not only the most monstrous, but also the most maternal of crimes.'
[63] See Fitch and McElduff (2002) 20 for an alternative reading of this line, that there are no gods absolutely. Both readings are available and emphasise how shocking Medea's infanticide is. A similar detachment of transgressive women from mortal society is also discussed by Burke-Tomlinson in this volume.

courses coincides with her transgression of gendered behaviour by even appropriating them, and with her transgression of their norms, thus indicating that female engagement with masculinity is inherently impossible. In light of her failure, as I discussed in section 4, Medea embraces her past, and creates her identity based on a female sphere of action, motherhood, and its antithesis, infanticide. However, Medea's extreme and female act causes her to be rejected from society; she is trapped into infanticide by the tragic structures of her literary past, as well as the gendered structures of her Romanised dramatic world which prevented her from claiming her identity legitimately and forced her to kill her own children to be recognised as Jason's wife. By focusing specifically on gendered discourses, I have shown that, whilst Medea can seemingly have agency over her literary and social identity, ultimately, she cannot successfully manipulate either literary memory or gendered hierarchies.

Bibliography

Abrahamsen, L. (1999), "Roman Marriage Law and the Conflict of Seneca's *Medea*", *Quaderni Urbinati di Cultura Classica* 62: 107–121.

Asmis, E. (1996), "The Stoics on Women", in J.K. Ward (ed.), *Feminism and Ancient Philosophy*, London: 68–92.

Assmann, J. (1995), "Collective Memory and Cultural Identity", *New German Critique* 65: 125–133.

Barchiesi, A. (1993), "Future Reflexive: Two Modes of Allusion and Ovid's *Heroides*", *Harvard Studies in Classical Philology* 95: 333–365.

Bartsch, S. (2006), *The Mirror of the Self: Sexuality, Self-Knowledge, and the Gaze in the Early Roman Empire*, Chicago.

Bexley, E. (2016), "Recognition and the Character of Seneca's *Medea*", *Cambridge Classical Journal* 62: 31–51.

Boyle, A.J. (1997), *Tragic Seneca: an Essay in the Theatrical Tradition*, London.

Boyle, A.J. (2006), *An Introduction to Roman Tragedy*, London.

Boyle, A.J. (2014), *Medea*, Oxford.

Brockmeier, J./D.A. Carbaugh (eds.) (2001), *Narrative and Identity: Studies in Autobiography, Self and Culture*, Amsterdam.

Busch, A. (2009), "Dissolution of the Self in the Senecan Corpus", in S. Bartsch & D. Wray (eds.), *Seneca and the Self*, Cambridge: 255–282.

Clausen, W. (2002), *Virgil's* Aeneid: *Decorum, allusion, and ideology*, München.

Curley, D. (2013), *Tragedy in Ovid: Theater, Metatheater, and the Transformation of a Genre*, Cambridge.

Fitch, J.G./S. McElduff (2002), "Construction of the Self in Senecan Drama", *Mnemosyne* 55: 18–40.

Flower, H.I. (2002), "Were Women Ever 'Ancestors' in Republican Rome?", in J.M. Højte (ed.), *Images of Ancestors*, Aarhus: 159–184.

Galinsky, K. (ed.) (2014), *Memoria Romana: Memory in Rome and Rome in Memory*, Ann Arbor.
Gloyn, L. (2017), *The Ethics of the Family in Seneca*, Cambridge.
Gowing, A.M. (2005), *Empire and Memory: the Representation of the Roman Republic in Imperial Culture*, Cambridge.
Graf, F. (1997), "Medea, the Enchantress from Afar: Remarks on a Well-Known Myth", in J.J. Clauss & S.I. Johnston (eds.), *Medea: Essays on Medea in Myth, Literature, Philosophy, and Art*, Princeton: 21–43.
Griffin, M.T. (2013), *Seneca on Society: a Guide to* De Beneficiis, Oxford.
Guastella, G. (2001), "*Virgo, Coniunx, Mater*: The Wrath of Seneca's Medea", *Classical Antiquity* 20: 197–220.
Hallett, J.P. (1973), "The Role of Women in Roman Elegy: Counter-Cultural Feminism", *Arethusa* 6: 103–124.
Hardie, P.R. (2012), *Rumour and Renown: Representations of Fama in Western Literature*, Cambridge.
Harrison, G.W.M. (ed.) (2000), *Seneca in Performance*, London.
Heslin, P.J. (2005), *The Transvestite Achilles: Gender and Genre in Statius'* Achilleid, Cambridge.
Heyworth, S.J. & J. Morwood (2017), *A Commentary on Vergil,* Aeneid *3*, Oxford.
Hinds, S. (1993), "Medea in Ovid: Scenes from the Life of an Intertextual Heroine", *Materiali e Discussioni per l'Analisi dei Testi Classici* 30: 9–47.
Hinds, S. (2011), "Seneca's Ovidian Loci", *Studi Italiani di Filologia Classica* 9: 5–63.
Hine, H.M. (2000), *Medea*, Warminster.
Hine, H.M. (2004), "*Interpretatio Stoica* of Senecan Tragedy", in M. Billerbeck & E.A. Schmidt (eds.), *Sénèque Le Tragique*, Geneva: 173–220.
Johnston, S.I. (1997), "Introduction", in J.J. Clauss & S.I. Johnston (eds.), *Medea: Essays on Medea in Myth, Literature, Philosophy, and Art*, Princeton: 3–17.
Ker, J. (2009), *The Deaths of Seneca*, Oxford.
Kohn, T.D. (2013), *The Dramaturgy of Senecan Tragedy*, Ann Arbor.
Larsson Lovén, L. (2011), "The Importance of Being Commemorated: Memory, Gender and Social Class on Roman Funerary Monuments", in H. Whittaker (ed.), *In Memoriam: Commemoration, Communal Memory and Gender Values in the Ancient Graeco-Roman World*, Newcastle-Upon-Tyne: 126–143.
Lendon, J.E. (1997), *Empire of Honour: The Art of Government in the Roman World*, Oxford.
Littlewood, C.A.J. (2004), *Self-Representation and Illusion in Senecan Tragedy*, Oxford.
Mauch, M. (1997), *Senecas Frauenbild in den philosophischen Schriften*, Bern/Frankfurt am Main.
Mayer, R.G. (1990), "*Doctus* Seneca", *Mnemosyne* 43: 395–407.
Mayor, J.M.B. (2017), *Power Play in Latin Love Elegy and its Multiple Forms of Continuity in Ovid's* Metamorphoses, Berlin.
Mazzoli, G. (2014), "The Chorus: Seneca as Lyric Poet", in G. Damschen & A. Heil (eds.), *Brill's Companion to Seneca*, Leiden: 561–574.
McAuley, M. (2010), "*Ambiguus Sexus*: Epic Masculinity in Transition in Statius' *Achilleid*", *Akroterion* 55: 37–60.
McAuley, M. (2016), *Reproducing Rome: Motherhood in Virgil, Ovid, Seneca and Statius*, Oxford.
Nagy, G. (1999), *The Best of the Achaeans: Concepts of the Hero in Archaic Greek Poetry*, Baltimore.

Nichols, S. (2017), "Memory and Personal Identity", in S. Bernecker & K. Michaelian (eds.), *The Routledge Handbook of Philosophy of Memory*, New York: 169–179.
Nussbaum, M. (1997), "Serpents in the Soul: A Reading of Seneca's *Medea*", in: J.J. Clauss & S.I. Johnston (eds.), *Medea: Essays on Medea in Myth, Literature, Philosophy, and Art*, Princeton: 439–483.
Pomeroy, S.B. (1975), *Goddesses, Whores, Wives and Slaves: Women in Classical Antiquity*, London.
Rabinowitz, N.S. (1993), *Anxiety Veiled: Euripides and the Traffic in Women*, Ithaca.
Raval, S. (2001), "'A Lover's Discourse': Byblis in *Metamorphoses* 9", *Arethusa* 34: 285–311.
Roisman, H.M. (2005), "Women in Senecan Tragedy", *Scholia* 14: 72–87.
Rosenmeyer, T.G. (1989), *Senecan Drama and Stoic Cosmology*, Berkeley.
Schiesaro, A. (2003), *The Passions in Play: Thyestes and the Dynamics of Senecan Drama*, Cambridge.
Segal, C. (1982), "*Nomen Sacrum*: Medea and Other Names in Senecan Tragedy", *Maia* 34: 241–246.
Slatkin, L.M. (1991), *The Power of Thetis: Allusion and Interpretation in the* Iliad, Berkeley.
Star, C. (2006), "Commanding *Constantia* in Senecan Tragedy", *Transactions of the American Philological Association* 136: 207–244.
Traina, A. (1979), "Due Note a Seneca Tragico", *Maia* 31: 273–276.
Treggiari, S. (1991), *Roman Marriage: Iusti Coniuges from the Time of Cicero to the Time of Ulpian*, Oxford.
Trinacty, C. (2007), "Seneca's *Heroides*: Elegy in Seneca's *Medea*", *The Classical Journal* 103: 63–78.
Trinacty, C. (2014), *Senecan Tragedy and the Reception of Augustan Poetry*, New York.
Walsh, L. (2012), "The Metamorphoses of Seneca's Medea", *Ramus* 41: 71–93.
Wilamowitz-Moellendorff, U. von (1919), *Griechische Tragödien*, Berlin.
Wray, D. (2009), "Seneca and Tragedy's Reason", in S. Bartsch & D. Wray (eds.), *Seneca and the Self*, Cambridge: 237–254.

Eleni Ntanou
Audita mente notaui: (Meta)memory, Gender, and Pastoral Impersonation in the Speech of Ovid's Galatea

Abstract: This chapter explores the Nereid Galatea's recollection and re-performance of the Cyclops' serenade for her in Ovid's epic, the *Metamorphoses* through the lenses of the mechanics of memory, gender, and generic interaction. I will suggest that Galatea's dynamic recreation of the traditional myth of her interaction with Polyphemus parallels the modern notion of the malleability of memorisation, as theorised in cognitive studies. The idea that all recollections are subject to altering and revisions every time they are retraced and retold is integrally linked with another significant aspect of this chapter, intertextuality, the memory of other genres and texts in the *Metamorphoses*. The Cyclops Polyphemus' serenade for Galatea was introduced into pastoral in Theocritus' *Idylls* and had become a standard theme of pastoral in post-Theocritean poetry, both Hellenistic and Roman.

Nonetheless, the performance of the Cyclops' song is striking not only for its transference into a new generic context, that of epic, but also for its re-enactment by Galatea. In pastoral poetry, the Nereid Galatea is repeatedly presented as paradigmatically alien to pastoral, belonging to the sea, which is often depicted as the 'other' of the pastoral world. In a stark upturn of the masculine poetics of both epic and pastoral, the *Metamorphoses* strikingly offers a voice to Galatea by presenting her as the controller of the memory and the narrator of the Cyclops' story. Galatea's female memory and voice clash with the male centred-worlds of both epic and pastoral poetry and thus simultaneously irrupt into both genres. In bringing to sharp focus issues of genre and gender and their reprisal in the *Metamorphoses*, Galatea's memory and repetition of the Cyclops' story and song can be read as a substantial case-study for Ovid's innovative epic poetics.

In the thirteenth book of Ovid's epic poem,[1] the *Metamorphoses*, readers find their expectations disrupted, as the narrative of Aeneas' wanderings is continuously revised as well as being interrupted by embedded stories.[2] Among the stories which interrupt the so-called 'little *Aeneid*' (*Met.* 13.623–14.582) of the *Metamorphoses*,[3] where the background of Virgilian epic poetry is mostly at work, are the lengthy love stories of Scylla and Galatea. Typically mentioned as the love-object of the Cyclops Polyphemus, Galatea's narrative voice is unattested before the *Metamorphoses* and is probably an Ovidian invention. By having the Nereid Galatea recount Polyphemus' passionate love for her to Scylla and recite the Cyclops' rambling serenade in its entirety from memory, the episode brings the issue of memory centre-stage. In the present chapter, I will explore Galatea's astonishing memory-skills and striking narratorial role, showing how these contribute to the episode's clash with its ostensibly stern-epic framework.

The approach to the Cyclops and Galatea episode suggested in the present chapter builds on the recent evolution of memory studies. Starting early in antiquity, in the synergy between the poet and the Mnemonides Muses, the notion of the close bond between literature and memory has been attracting growing interest recently, promoted by the rapid advances in the study of memory. For classical studies, in particular, the concern with memory is by no means new, as the notion of collective memory,[4] memorialisation, and 'poetic memory' – to allude to Conte's famous study[5] – are concepts that have been studied for many decades now. However, the dramatic increase in the study of memory in recent years, designated as the 'memory boom',[6] has led to the development of memory studies as

---

[1] Even though the epic character of the *Metamorphoses* is accepted today by most critics, there has been a long discussion over what kind of epic the *Metamorphoses* is, and the very 'epicness' of the poem has been contested in scholarship. Heinze (1919) famously supported the poem's epic character, contrasting it to the *Fasti*, opposed by Little (1970) and Knox (1986) 2. After Heinze, the reading of the *Metamorphoses* as an epic was significantly defended by Otis (1970). A more modern, genre-based study of the *Metamorphoses* as an epic poem was offered by Hinds (1987). For a very recent and detailed study of the *Metamorphoses* as an epic poem, see Sharrock (2019).
[2] For the love tales interrupting the narrative of Aeneas' wanderings, see Nagle (1988). For Ovid as an 'interpreter' of *Aeneid* 3 in *Metamorphoses* 13.623–14.582, see Casali (2007). See also Papaioannou (2005). For the *Metamorphoses* as constantly challenging the reader's perception of epic, see Sharrock (2019).
[3] For the term, see Papaioannou (2005).
[4] For the evolution of the study of collective memory from Halbwachs' conceptualisation of collective memory to recent years, see Russell (2006). See also Nora (1989) and Assmann (1995).
[5] See Conte (1986). Cf. Hinds (1998) 14–15.
[6] For 'memory boom', see Simine (2013) 14–19.

a rapidly growing, diverse and interdisciplinary field.[7] Memory studies theory offers new interpretative tools for the study of memory across a broad range of disciplines. Classics has already followed suit with fruitful studies, applying various different approaches to the multifarious phenomenon of memory. The following collected volumes on memory in ancient thought and literature have substantially promoted the discussion of memory in Classical studies: Galinsky (2014) explores the memory of Rome mainly from a historical perspective;[8] Mackay (2008) studies the correlation between memory and the study of orality and literacy in Ancient Greek and Roman texts. Castagnoli and Ceccarelli (2019) have edited a volume offering new ways into the phenomenon of memory by applying interdisciplinary memory theory tools to texts, which range from the Archaic period to Late Antiquity. Furthermore, the study of cognition is gaining growing interest over the last years in the field of Classics. Among the fundamental subjects of cognitive studies explored in classical texts is, of course, memory: *Cognitive Classics*[9] showcases a more rigid application of memory studies theory stemming from neuroscience and psychology.[10] In the present chapter, I will build on the above approaches and examine Galatea's recollections through three main lenses: the mechanics of memory, intertextuality and memory, and gendered memory.

The traditional hypothesis that memories are transferred into long-term memory storage, where they are consolidated and from where they can be retrieved intact when necessary, has been revised by modern neuroscience and cognitive studies. The latter compellingly argue for the dynamic quality of remembering:[11] every time memories are reactivated, they are subject to revision and recreation. Instead of merely recapitulating our memories, we reconstruct them while we reflect on them.[12] I shall argue that the Galatea episode is deeply concerned with the mechanics of memory. Ovid's Galatea dynamically recreates the Cyclops' song and even reflects on the cognitive process of memorialisation. The Galatea story can be read as paralleling the modern conception of the malleability of memory by showcasing how memories of previous texts function into a

---

[7] For an introduction to modern memory studies, see Roediger/Wertsch (2008); Keightley/Pickering (2013). See also Pethes (2019), who focuses particularly on cultural memory studies.
[8] See also Galinsky & Lapatin (2016) on cultural memory in Rome.
[9] I borrow the term from the homonymous OUP series, see Grethlein, Huitink & Tagliabue (2019).
[10] See especially Easterling & Budelmann (2010).
[11] See Kitamura *et al.* (2017) 43–56; Hunsaker/Kesner (2017) 57–80; Easton/Eacott (2008).
[12] See Cuc *et al.* (2007).

new whole through the act of re-membering. In mentally re-synthesising previous poetry, Galatea can be read as a counterpart of both the writer and the reader of the *Metamorphoses*.[13]

The idea of repetition as a creative process, enabled in the Galatea episode through memory, is one that Ovid often explores throughout his corpus. The relatively recent edition of a volume on Ovidian repetition, edited by Fulkerson and Stover (2016), has shown how Ovid systematically explores the creative potential of repetition on both an inter- and an intra-textual level. I will here build on this theory, suggesting that memory is a fundamental way into Ovidian repetition. I will argue that Galatea's anamnesis and 'repeat performance' of the Cyclops' song challenge the epic character of the *Metamorphoses* by mobilising new takes on characters and themes of previous literature.

The story of Polyphemus, Galatea, and Acis that Ovid's Galatea recounts constitutes both a thematic and a generic digression from the main narrative, of Aeneas and the Trojans' travel towards Italy:[14] for most readers of the *Metamorphoses*, the Polyphemus episode is considered to be the quintessential 'pastoral' episode of the poem.[15] The reference to the Cyclops Polyphemus invites the reader to remember an emblematic epic encounter of the *Odyssey*, that between Odysseus and the Cyclops. The *Metamorphoses*, however, subverts the mnemonic cue as instead of re-enacting Odysseus' encounter with the Cyclops, an episode which is touched upon later in the poem,[16] the poem centres on the Cyclops' passion and serenade for Galatea, a theme patently at odds with the typical scope of epic poetry. I will suggest that the story is doubly subversive, both by its very theme and by the fact that it is recalled and retold by a marginalised female character.[17]

By the time Ovid composed the *Metamorphoses*, Polyphemus' song for Galatea had become a standard myth and theme of pastoral poetry. Polyphemus features twice in Theocritus' bucolic poems. In *Idyll* 11, Theocritus picks up the Cyclops' love for Galatea, possibly attested first in Philoxenus' dithyramb *Cyclops* or *Galatea* (beginning of 4th c. BCE),[18] and revisits the Cyclops' connections with

---

13 For the selection involved in readerly practice, see Sharrock (2000) esp. pp. 21–38.
14 See above, n. 2.
15 For a discussion of the dialogue of genres in the Polyphemus episode, see Farrell (1992). See also Barchiesi (2006).
16 For a discussion of the Cyclops' two occurrences in the poem in view of each other, see Papaioannou (2005) 96–8.
17 For Ovid and the marginalised figures of the Ovidian corpus, see Fulkerson (2016). On the interplay among gender, generic *decorum* and memory, see also Nghan in this volume.
18 See Creese (2009) 563; Mack (1999) 51. For Polyphemus before Theocritus, see also Gutzwiller (2006).

shepherding as known already from Homer. It is only through song that the Cyclops alleviated his erotic pain for Galatea, as Theocritus advises his friend Nicias, in the framing of the *Idyll* (*Id.* 11.1–4, 17–18, 80–1). In effect, the reinvented figure of Polyphemus in the *Idylls* symbolises the generic interplay between Theocritus' hexameter poems and Homeric epic poetry.[19] In place of the violent Cyclops of Homeric epic, Theocritus presented a young Cyclops on the verge of adulthood and indifferent to his shepherding duties on account of his unrequited passion for the sea-nymph Galatea, a reconstruction that the *Metamorphoses* revisits and inverts anew for the purposes of epic.

In Theocritus' *Idyll* 6, the story of the Cyclops and Galatea forms part of the amoebaean song exchange between the poet-herdsmen Damoetas and Daphnis.[20] By having Damoetas appropriate the voice of the Cyclops in his performance, Theocritus constructs the shepherding Cyclops as a mythical predecessor of the poet-herdsmen.[21] The tone of *Idyll* 6 is markedly different from *Idyll* 11, as the two protagonists have exchanged roles. Polyphemus is this time portrayed as indifferent to Galatea, a stance that is later shown to be an act on Polyphemus' part in order to conquer the Nereid,[22] who now becomes the one pursuing the Cyclops. Moreover, unlike Polyphemus in *Idyll* 11, who is aware that his ugliness may repel the Nereid (*Id.* 11.30–3), the Polyphemus of *Idyll* 6 displays a narcissistic self-admiration for his own image, as reflected on the surface of the sea, and stresses the beauty of his features, καὶ καλὰ μὲν τὰ γένεια, καλὰ δέ μευ ἁ μία κώρα,/ ὡς παρ' ἐμὶν κέκριται, κατεφαίνετο..., ('my beard seemed beautiful, my one eye seemed beautiful too, in my judgment', *Id.* 6.36–7).[23]

Despite his overriding importance for the construction of the bucolic myth in Theocritus, the Cyclops is nowhere mentioned in Virgil's pastoral collection, the *Eclogues*. Nonetheless, the song for Galatea is repeatedly evoked and re-enacted in the *Eclogues*, thus turning Polyphemus into an absent presence in Virgilian pastoral poetry.[24] *Eclogue* 2 markedly replays the song of the amorous Cyclops but

---

19 See Payne (2007) 67–71; Kania (2016) 30–1; Heerink (2015) 78–80.
20 The poem is set earlier in the collection but was possibly composed after *Idyll* 11, as Gutzwiller (1991) 67 and Hunter (1999) 244–5 suggest.
21 For Polyphemus as part of the pastoral myth and a 'comic counterpart' of Daphnis, see Bernsdorff (2006) 186; Hunter (1999) 248.
22 See Payne (2007) 97; Hunter (1999) 245. It is not clear whether Galatea's love interest in the Cyclops is real or Polyphemus' own fantasy, see Fantuzzi (2012) 293.
23 See also Hardie (2002) 164–5 for the possible associations between the myths of Narcissus and Polyphemus. For a discussion of the evolution of the Cyclops' figure in Moschus, see Fantuzzi (2012) 292 and Hubbard (1998) 38–9.
24 Cf. Hutchinson (2007) 29.

substitutes the Cyclops' invitation of the nymph Galatea to the pastoral world with the amorous poet-herdsman Corydon's invitation of the city-boy Alexis. By doing so Virgil 'corrects' the innate incongruities in the depiction of the monstrous Cyclops as a poet-herdsman and 'distils' the pastoral genre.[25]

The association between the serenade for Galatea and memory is more prominent in *Eclogue* 7, in which the play with identity and the Cyclopisation of Corydon also resurface. The song of Polyphemus forms part of Thyrsis' amoebaean exchange with Corydon, who nevertheless does not fully identify with the Cyclops, but maintains his own identity as Corydon, when he invites the Nereid Galatea to join him (*Nerine Galatea, thymo mihi dulcior Hyblae...si qua tui Corydonis habet te cura, uenito*, 'Galatea, Nereus' daughter, sweeter to me than the thyme of Hybla...if you care at all for your Corydon, come', *Ecl.* 7.37–40). The entire amoebaean singing contest of *Eclogue* 7, in which the serenade for Galatea in *Eclogue* 7 is set, is retold by the herdsman Meliboeus from memory, as the narrative frame highlights (*Haec memini, et uictum frustra contendere Thyrsin*, 'These I remember, and the conquered Thyrsis striving in vain', *Ecl.* 7.69).[26] Meliboeus' reflection of Corydon's victory in the song contest serves to inscribe internally Corydon's identity as an established figure for the entire pastoral community (*ex illo Corydon Corydon est tempore nobis*, 'from that time on it is Corydon, Corydon for us', *Ecl.* 7.70). Thus Meliboeus' individual memory of the song explains – whilst at the same time constructing – the prominence and renown of Corydon in the shared and cultural memory of the Virgilian poet-shepherds.[27]

The interplay among intertextual, personal, and cultural memory is perhaps nowhere more prominent in Virgilian pastoral poetry than in *Eclogue* 9. Two shepherds discuss the threat to the pastoral world from violence and war.[28] The younger herdsman, Lycidas, asks the older one, Moeris, to perform a song. Although the poet-shepherd Moeris starts singing the serenade for Galatea, he declares his difficulty in remembering how the serenade goes (*si ualeam meminisse*, 'if I could remember it', *Ecl.* 9.38) and manages to perform the song only partially. Only a few lines later, Moeris repeats the mourning over the loss of his memory, which directly affects his ability to perform songs (*...saepe ego longos,/ cantando puerum memini me condere soles./ nunc oblita mihi tot carmina...*, 'I remember

---

[25] See DuQuesnay (1979) 38.
[26] For *Idyll* 7, see. For the reading of the *Eclogues* through the lens of social memory, see Meban (2009).
[27] For pastoral poetry's internal construction of its myth, see Hunter (1999) 6.
[28] See also Hardy (1990), who connects the threat of war in *Eclogue* 9 to Roman history and politics.

myself as a boy, often hiding long summer days with my singing. Now I have forgotten so many songs', *Ecl.* 9.51–3).

The reference to Moeris' memory underlines the play with the inter- and intra-textual memory in the repetitions of this pastoral classic.[29] I will try to show how the *Metamorphoses* will pick up and reactivate the association between the serenade for Galatea and memory. The invitation for Galatea to join the pastoral world in *Eclogue* 9, *huc ades, o Galatea* ('come here, Galatea', *Ecl.* 9.39), looks back at the Cyclopised Corydon's invitation to Alexis into the pastoral world in *Eclogue* 2, *huc ades, o formose puer* ('come here, beautiful boy', *Ecl.* 2.45), thus joining the two different Virgilian repetitions of the Cyclops' song together.[30] While the mention of Galatea gestures towards the Cyclops' serenade and the lines that Moeris sings are a reworking of *Idyll* 11.42–8, Virgil omits any explicit reference to the Cyclops from Menalcas' song, leaving it ambiguous whether it is Polyphemus or Corydon who calls for Galatea.[31]

However, it is Moeris' failure to remember that is particularly striking,[32] as the encounter and exchange of song are central premises of the pastoral fiction which is standardly pre-existing and *re*produced for performance in the poem.[33] Anamnesis and the repetition of songs and song contests are building blocks of the fantasy of the pastoral meta-world.[34] The entire pastoral world is presented as being built upon the memory of its heroes, myths, and songs, which are presented as part of the poet-herdsmen's cultural memory.[35] Both the Hellenistic pastoral poet Theocritus and Virgil deploy the explicit repetition of songs, so as to establish within their poetry a past for their lesser-known characters, the herdsmen, as skilled singers. Pastoral performances have a built-in past story and re-performing functions as a mythopoetic procedure. In Theocritus' *Idyll* 1 a goatherd urges the shepherd Thyrsis to sing a song entitled 'the sufferings of Daphnis' in the way

---

29 For the theory of intratextuality, see Sharrock (2000).
30 Cf. Virg. *Ecl.* 7.9.
31 Cf. Coleman (1977) 265.
32 For memory and the pose of orality in *Eclogue* 9, see also Breed (2006) 17–24; Hardy (1990); Alpers (1979) 142–3. See also Meban (2009), who connects forgetting and silencing to civil discourse and the political framework of the *Eclogues*.
33 See Karakasis (2011) 7. See also Alpers (1983) on 'pastoral convention'.
34 See Breed (2006) 88–94, Fantuzzi (2006) 237–41. Iser (1993) 48–51 suggests that anamnesis and repetition merge the worlds of fiction and reality in Sannazaro's pastoral romance, *Arcadia*.
35 As has been rightly pointed out, the notions of presence and absence and memory and nostalgia are fundamental in pastoral. See Hardie (2002) 20–2. For memory as shaping collective as well as individual memory, see Castagnoli & Ceccarelli (2019) 1–42.

that he did when he competed against a rival, named Chromis (*Id.* 1.19–25).³⁶ In effect, the first song we read in *Idyll* 1, a poem later regarded as the beginning of pastoral poetry,³⁷ is already a repetition, already a memory.

Thus Moeris' loss of memory in the *Eclogues* threatens the continuation of the herdsmen's orally-based repertory. Virgilian pastoral poetry systematically gestures towards the tension between the fiction of the poet-herdsmen's oral performances and the written text in which these performances are enclosed.³⁸ The near oblivion of an emblematic pastoral song, such as the serenade for Galatea, challenges the basis of the pastoral fiction, which relies heavily on the herdsmen's performances that construct and internalise the pastoral world and its shared memories.

The *Metamorphoses* plays out the Galatea serenade's associations with memory anew. As I will show, the sustained concern for memory in the Ovidian version of the serenade for Galatea lends itself to a new approach through the use of modern memory theory concepts. Memory in the *Metamorphoses* is also intricately related to Ovid's predilection for repetition. As the recent theorising of Ovidian repetition has shown, the systematic use of the trope of repetition in Ovid's poetry is operative on various different levels.³⁹ In a marked inversion from Virgilian pastoral, in which Polyphemus is never mentioned, Ovid reclaims 'the serenade for Galatea' for the Cyclops as well as for Galatea herself. I will argue that the originality of the Cyclops' episode in the Ovidian epic substantially rests on its novel focalisation from the perspective of the Cyclops' love-interest, Galatea. Instead of having the Cyclops perform his song in the dramatic present of the poem, the *Metamorphoses* has the nymph Galatea reperform Polyphemus' song from memory. Galatea's narratorial role is unparalleled in all of the attested references to the Nereid before Ovid. By becoming the narrator and the controller of the memory of Cyclops' story and song, the *Metamorphoses*' Galatea restages and

---

36 As Hunter (1999) 6 points out, '*Idyll* 1 conjures up a pre-existing tradition, while itself founding such a tradition'.
37 Pastoral is more clearly conceptualised as constituting a new genre in post-Theocritean poetry, see Alpers (1996) 153; Bernsdorff (2006); Coleman (1977) 2; Hardie (1998) 6.
38 See Kania (2016) 111–55 and Breed (2006) 81–3 and *passim*.
39 See Fulkerson/Stover (2016). The employment of the creative potential of repetition in Ovid is, of course, already explored in the pivotal study of Sharrock (1994), which focuses mainly on *Ars Amatoria* 2.

revises the previous renditions of her story.⁴⁰ I will suggest that this upturn is even more arresting as both epic and pastoral are genres primarily focusing on male characters and viewpoints.

Ovid sets Galatea's extensive female narrative where the background of Virgilian epic poetry is most powerfully at work, in the 'little *Aeneid*' of the *Metamorphoses*. Epic poetry is primarily a masculine genre, where female speeches often constitute 'dangerous voices' to the heroic and masculine code of epic.⁴¹ If Virgil's *Aeneid* 'constructed (and deconstructed) the ideal of Roman masculinity',⁴² Ovid devotes an extensive part of his 'little *Aeneid*' to a female speech, thus rendering Galatea's narrative all the more dangerous precisely through its position. In place of battles and epic *nostoi*, we get Galatea's erotic adventures caught in a triangle between Polyphemus and her beloved, the young boy Acis. Ovid draws attention to the feminine voice through the very situation and the strongly female context where the speech is delivered, while Scylla was combing Galatea's hair (*Met.* 13.738–9).

Galatea's memory in the context of her discussion with Scylla points to the memory studies notion of 'discursive memory'.⁴³ According to this notion, no memory is 'purely individual',⁴⁴ but rather, when a memory is specifically recalled into a discursive context, this interaction significantly affects the reconstruction of the recollection.⁴⁵ As Erll aptly points out, collective memory is an 'operative metaphor', which transposes the cognitive act of remembering onto the level of an entire community.⁴⁶ Individual memories and the cognitive process in turn are closely linked to a cultural framework: far from being a datum which is simply recalled, brought out of the storehouse of fixity, every narrative of a memory is recreated and altered, depending on the context of its reperformance. What triggers Galatea's recollection is precisely Scylla's narrative of her suitors, ... *elusos iuuenum narrabat amores* ('she was narrating the deceived loves

---

40 For epic as a masculine genre, see Sharrock (2002) and Keith (1999). For the primacy of male voices in pastoral, see Keith (2009) 366–7. Salzman-Mitchell (2007) approaches Galatea's narrative as a form of resistance towards the male-centred presentation and reading of women in Roman love elegy and in several stories from the *Metamorphoses*.
41 For the challenge of female voices in epic, see Hinds (2000); Holst-Warhaft (1992) *passim* (esp. pp. 3–6); Keith (1999).
42 Sharrock (2002) 104.
43 For discursive memory, see Brown/Reavey (2013).
44 See Pickering/Keightley (2013) 7.
45 See Brown/Reavey (2013) 49.
46 See Erll (2008) 4.

of the young men', *Met.* 13.737). In response to Scylla, Galatea highlights how different was the outcome of the rejection of her own suitor, Polyphemus (*Met.* 13.740–1). Thus, the recreation and retelling of Galatea's memory within a conversational setting in the *Metamorphoses* can be read as a paradigm of the interrelation between interaction and the meta-cognitive formation of memories, studied by discursive psychology.

The fact that Galatea's narrative is a 'repeat performance'[47] invites the reader to think about how this repetition functions in the poem. Galatea's narrative is marked by the use of the participle *repetens* 'repeating', a term drawing attention precisely to the acts of recapping and remembering (*talibus adloquitur repetens suspiria dictis*, 'with such words she spoke, repeating her sighs', *Met.* 13.739). The repetition and altering of memory, when set in a new context, are very close to the modern understanding of intertextuality, in which the new context is, in fact, a new text. The dialogic aspects of intertextuality are introduced by Bakhtin's theory of the polyphony of the novel[48] and Kristeva's pivotal conception of the text as a 'mosaic of quotations'.[49] The reference to the acts of remembering and repeating by characters, who either appear ignorant or display metaliterary self-consciousness or even both, often functions as a marker for the reader calling for their intertextual and intratextual memory.[50]

The mention of repetition and memory interwoven with the serenade for Galatea strongly gestures towards Virgil's *Eclogue* 9. As already mentioned, the poet-herdsman Moeris questioned his ability to remember the serenade for Galatea in its entirety (*si ualeam meminisse*, 'if only I could remember it', *Ecl.* 9.38) and is able to sing only an excerpt from the song. He prefaced the song with a *litotes* as one not unrenowned, *neque est ignobile carmen* ('and it is not an unrenowned song' *Ecl.* 9.38). This characterisation of the love song for Galatea suggests elevated undertones, which point to the epic origins of the Cyclops. Moreover, the mention of the song's renown gestures towards the in-world prominence of the song for Galatea for the poet-herdsmen as well as signalling its literary repetitions throughout pastoral poetry.[51]

---

47 I am borrowing Fulkerson & Stover's (2016) term here.
48 Bakhtin (1984).
49 Kristeva (1986) 37.
50 See Hinds (1998) *passim* on how terms related to the lexicon of memory are connected to intertextuality, esp. 11–15.
51 Cf. Papanghelis (2006) 390.

Both the *Eclogues*' Moeris and the *Metamorphoses*' Galatea are examples of what modern literature theorists term 'fictions of memory', the mimesis of a character attempting to remember something.[52] Unlike the Virgilian herdsmen of *Eclogue* 9, however, Ovid's Galatea strongly asserts her ability to remember (13.788–9) and manages to deliver Polyphemus' longwinded song from memory. In displaying astounding memory skills, Galatea is cast in the role of a bard. As Assmann notes, before the development of writing, there were trained 'ancient carriers of memory', such as priests and bards, who aimed at verbatim transmission of knowledge and whose memory was 'used as a 'database' in a sense approaching the use of writing'.[53] Ovid's Galatea is cast in a bard-like role, presenting the ability to perform from memory like a specialised 'carrier of memory', an idea permeating both pastoral and epic poetry, which both systematically act out the pretence of oral performance and of singing from memory.[54]

More than that, Galatea is involved in an act assimilating what modern memory theorists term as 'meta-memory', a subdiscipline of metacognition, which studies how people observe and self-reflect on their memory.[55] In a display of metamemory, Galatea not only remembers but also expounds on the process of memorialisation. In a palpable metaphor of the cognitive mechanisms by which individual memory functions, Galatea assimilates the act of remembering to drinking in every word of the song with her ears (...*auribus hausi | talia dicta...*, 'drank in with my ears such words', *Met.* 13.787–8).[56] Her active involvement in remembering is also suggested in Galatea's claim that she has noted everything she heard in her mind (*auditaque mente notaui*, 'and noted the things I heard in my mind', *Met.* 13.788). Through her memory, Galatea presents herself as creating an inner depository of song, which she may now employ for her reperformance. *Notaui* also echoes *Eclogue* 5 (... *et modulans alterna notaui*, 'and noted in couplets while setting them to music', *Ecl.* 5.14), in which noting down a pastoral song, in that case physically, points to and conflates the inherent tension of pastoral between the written poems and the fiction of oral performances. Galatea's assimilation of remembering to writing suggests a fundamental concept of intertextuality, the function of the text as a palpable mnemonic space. This parallel-

---

52 For 'fictions of memory', see Neumann (2008).
53 See Assmann (2008) 114.
54 For orality in epic, see Heubeck, West & Hainsworth (1988); Clark (2004); Depew/Obbink (2000). For the pretence of orality specifically in the *Metamorphoses*, see Wheeler (2000). For orality in Virgilian pastoral, see Breed (2006) 91–6.
55 For metamemory, see Dunlosky/Tauber (2016); Koriat (2007); Flavell (1979).
56 For the phrase, see also *Met.* 14.309; Virg. *Aen.* 4.359.

ism between memory and writing also points to the malleability of memory: similarly to writing, remembering is a creative process, and all recollections are subject to altering and revisions every time they are retraced and retold.[57]

In a now classic article on the *Metamorphoses*, Farrell used the Polyphemus episode as a case study for the 'dialogue of genres' in the *Metamorphoses*.[58] Indeed, although one can read numerous allusions to Hellenistic and Virgilian pastoral poetry, alongside epic and elegiac *topoi*, throughout the Ovidian version of the Cyclops' song, it is also significantly different from its counterparts.[59] Unlike *Idyll* 11, Ovid's Galatea stresses the savagery of the Cyclops that Theocritus had strongly downplayed. Although the Theocritean Polyphemus is savage in that he is not sophisticated, he is depicted as harmless. His boorishness is deployed by Theocritus to create a comic effect through the incongruity of this portrayal and Polyphemus' artistic endeavours. Hence the repeated mention of Polyphemus' ferocity (*feros...uultus*, 'fierce face' 13.767; *feritas*, 'savagery', 13.768; *ferus*, 'savage', 13.780)[60] stands in contrast with Galatea's previous statement that the amorous Cyclops had forgotten his savage ways and foreshadows the violence that Polyphemus displays at the end of the Ovidian episode.

Another significant distinction in Galatea's account of the story is the role of her beloved, Acis, who is absent in all the other attested versions of the story.[61] While the Theocritean Cyclops and the Cyclopised Corydon conclude their serenades with the hope that they will find another beloved (εὑρησεῖς Γαλάτειαν...ἄλλαν, 'you will find another Galatea' *Id.* 11.76; *inuenies alium...Alexin*, 'you will find another Alexis' *Ecl.* 2.73), Ovid's Cyclops refers to the other lover that Galatea *already* has. In sharp contrast to Galatea's claims that she sticks to the 'original song', as fixed in her memory, Galatea's version of the Cyclops' serenade significantly exceeds *Idyll* 11 in terms of length: in place of the sixty lines of the song in Theocritus, Ovid gives a Cyclopean song of eighty-one lines.[62] In differing significantly from its Theocritean and Virgilian counterparts, Galatea's narration of the Cyclops' story and song acts out the process of intertextuality and highlights the dynamic character of both the text and memory.

In mentally rewriting the Cyclops' song, Galatea is arrestingly cast in the role of an effective poet-herdsman in that she manages to deliver, without failure, a

---

[57] For the concept, see Keightley & Pickering (2012) 1–10 and *passim*.
[58] See Farrell (1992).
[59] See Barchiesi (2006) and Farrell (1992).
[60] Cf. Hopkinson (2000) 216; Farrell (1992) 243.
[61] For Acis as an Ovidian invention, see Griffin (1983) 192; Mack (1999) 54.
[62] See also Barchiesi (2006) 416.

prolonged pastoral serenade. Although appearing as the recipient and the love object of a pastoral song rather than directly in the role of a poet-herdsman, Galatea emerges as an expert in mnemotechnics and seems to be able to participate in an intricate process of orally performing the Cyclopean song.[63] By having Galatea explicitly ingest the Cyclops' song, the *Metamorphoses* acts out pastoral roleplaying. The impersonation of a mythical character is a *topos* of pastoral singing performances. Already, in *Idyll* 1, Thyrsis takes on the role of Daphnis and performs a substantial part of the song of the archetypical bucolic hero in direct speech (*Id.* 1.115–18). Assuming specifically the persona of Polyphemus is also a pastoral *topos*.[64] In *Idyll* 6, in response to Daphnis' song, who is now brought to the dramatic present of the poem, Damoetas plays the part of the Cyclops, thereby reinventing and fictionalising the Cyclops anew.[65] In the *Metamorphoses*, it is Galatea who takes on the role and voice of the Cyclops in the fashion of pastoral singers. Furthermore, the notion of remembering as a shared co-operative process, performed among women, matches the joint creative process in the amoebaean singing of the male herdsmen. The *Metamorphoses* replays the iconic pastoral *topos* of the encounter, dialogue, and song exchange between male herdsmen in the encounter and sharing of stories and songs between female characters.

The Cyclops, however, is not just a mythical persona that Galatea can adopt in her performance, as happens in pastoral impersonations, but forms part of her own story, her internal narrative, a fact which becomes critical at the end of the song. For Galatea, the memory of the song is not part of cultural memory and an oral tradition but is rather projected as personal, rather than collective, traumatic memory.[66] Moreover, unlike, the external narrator and audience of *Idyll* 11 (Theocritus and Nicias) and the internal singers of *Idyll* 6, who belong to a different era from that of the Cyclops, Galatea is directly affected by the Cyclops story and even by the Cyclops' song. In sharp contrast to the consolatory effect that the song has had on the Cyclops at the end of *Idyll* 11, where the ability of the song to tame erotic pain is the explicit moral of the poem (*Id.* 11.1–3, 17–18, 80–1), in the

---

63 For another case of mnemotechnics and quoting from memory, see Haley in this volume.
64 For the Cyclops as a pastoral role, see Breed (2006) 35; Hubbard (2008) 101–2.
65 See Payne (2007) 96.
66 For a recent discussion of the notions of individual and collective memory and the complex relationship between the two, see Castagnoli/Ceccarelli (2019) 3–8. For traumatic memory, see Kansteiner/Weilnbock (2008).

Metamorphoses, there is a strong sense that the very act of singing fuels Polyphemus' wrath (13.865–9), thus prompting his assumption of a role characterised by a violence associated with epic.

The wrath of Achilles serves as the driving force of the *Iliad*, and Juno's *ira* sets the *Aeneid* in motion. Likewise, the blazing wrath of Ovid's Cyclops suggests the return to epic teleology. Projecting in his mind not only the beauty of the pastoral world but also Galatea reciprocating Acis' love, Ovid's Cyclops burns with jealousy. Near the end of his song the Cyclops says that he feels like Aetna has been transferred into his chest (*Met.* 13.868–9), a phrase which functions as a marker for the return of Polyphemus to his epic past.[67] Although Sicily is particularly affiliated to the pastoral genre[68] and Aetna figures already in Theocritus' *Idyll* 1 as the birthplace of Thyrsis (Θύρσις ὅδ' ὡξ Αἴτνας, 'This is Thyrsis of Aetna', *Id.* 1.65), the imagery of the fire ingested by Polyphemus is a far cry from the pastoral world and signals the return of the Cyclops to epic violence.[69] Of course, the mention of burning love points to the elegiac *topos* of *eros* as fire, which takes on epic dimensions here. We could also detect a humorously hyperbolic reworking of Sappho 31's famous fire imagery in the *uror enim, laesusque exaestuat acrius ignis* ('for I burn, and wounded, a fire rages more fiercely', *Met.* 13.867). The encoding of generic stances is notable here: *exaestuat acrius ignis* is a monstrous mutation of Catullus' 'slender flame' (*tenuis...flamma*, Cat. 51.9–10) that enacts the overwriting of lyric/pastoral delicacy by epic bombast.

Being pulled away from the pastoral world by his extreme erotic passion, Ovid's Polyphemus, the last pastoral singer of the *Metamorphoses*,[70] replays the role of Virgil's Gallus, who famously surrenders to love and leaves the pastoral world, *omnia uincit Amor: et nos cedamus Amori* ('Love conquers all, let us too yield to Love', *Ecl.* 10.69). The allusion to the last poem of Virgil's pastoral collection signals the end of the pastoral songs of the *Metamorphoses*, which will be achieved here through a return not to elegiac love but to epic violence, as the Cyclops brutally kills Acis. But even at this tragic climax of her recollection, Galatea arrestingly appears to be concerned anew with the process of storing into memory, as she notes that she was able to see everything, *Talia nequiquam questus (nam cuncta uidebam) / surgit...* ('Having lamented with such words in vain

---

[67] See Tissol (1997) 121–2 for the anticipation of violence on the verbal level before moving on to the physical.
[68] For Sicily's pastoral connotations, see Hutchinson (2013) 176–9.
[69] Farrell (1992) 258 rightly notes the reversal of *Idyll* 11.47–8, where the Cyclops displays Aetna's cool water among other pastoral allurements.
[70] The Cyclops offers the last extensive quasi-pastoral performance in the *Metamorphoses*. Cf. Barchiesi (2006).

(for I was seeing everything), he rose', *Met.* 13.870–1). As previously she confirmed her auditory record of the song (*auribus hausi*, 'drank in with my ears', *Met.* 13.787), Galatea now highlights her autopsy of the events she remembers.[71] By declaring that she was an eyewitness to the events she recounts, Galatea suggests her reliability as a narrator, as eyewitness testimonies were traditionally considered to be the most trustworthy in antiquity.[72] All the same, this mention functions as a readerly reminder that the story is, in fact, filtered through a different viewpoint, that of the Nereid and the memory is staged anew, leading to a necessary alteration and revision of the events recorded.

The *Metamorphoses* creates an interplay between memory and oblivion.[73] Despite Galatea's meta-cognitive comments, the reader is systematically conditioned to 'forget' who is narrating it. When Galatea gets to the part where she retells the song of the Cyclops, there is a sense of a remarkable degree of identification between her voice and that of the Cyclops, substantially achieved through the absence of any apparent narratorial comments and the use of direct speech throughout the re-performance of the serenade. Moreover, the intertexts of the Theocritean soliloquy of the Cyclops and the soliloquy of his Virgilian double, Corydon, may affect our reading of the Cyclops' song in the *Metamorphoses*. Most scholars focus on the figure of the Cyclops and almost completely pass by the fact that it is Galatea who retells the Cyclops' serenade in Ovid.[74] This is significantly due to the fact that we, as readers of *Idyll* 11 and *Eclogue* 2, are quite likely set up to read the Cyclops' song, almost like overhearing his performance and nearly forgetting Galatea's role as the deliverer of the song, in sharp contrast to the fact that we are told from the very beginning that the song of the Cyclops is retold by Galatea.

Pastoral erotic monologues typically remain unheard, aside of course from the sympathetic landscape. As Payne points out, 'the singers of Theocritus' monologue poems do not seem to be in communication with their intended audience. Rather, as they sing, they become their own audience, telling stories in which they fashion an imaginative escape from the desire that led them to sing in the first place'.[75] In *Idyll* 11, the Cyclops sings 'by himself' (αὐτός, *Id.* 11.14) and there is no sign of Galatea entering the scene at any point the scene or listening to the

---

71 Cf. Tissol (1997) 108.
72 See Squire (2015); De Jong (2004) 273–6. See also Hunter (1982) 57.
73 For the complex of memory and oblivion in the *Metamorphoses*, see also Burke-Tomlinson's discussion of the Pasiphae myth in the Ovidian epic in this volume.
74 For a notable exception, see Salzman-Mitchell (2007).
75 Payne (2007) 93.

song that the Cyclops performs. By having Polyphemus perform a monologue in *Idyll* 11, Theocritus gestures towards the Cyclops' affectionate speech to his ram in the *Odyssey*. As the Homeric Cyclops imagines that the ram participates in his grief for the loss of his eye, the scenario of the Nereid reciprocating Polyphemus' affection seems rather like wishful thinking and the Nereid never appears physically in the poem. Thus, the objects of both his affectionate speeches, Galatea and the ram, seem – at least from the perspective of the reader – equally unresponsive. Likewise, in *Eclogue* 2, Corydon's solitude during his performance is underlined in the frame of the poem (*solus*, 'alone', *Ecl.* 2.4). Virgil's Corydon is a double of Polyphemus and of Callimachus' elegiac Acontius grieving alone in the woods.[76]

By contrast, in the *Metamorphoses*, it is as if the reworkings and the multiple literary invitations to join him functioned like a charm spell, for Ovid's Galatea finally joins the Cyclops in his recitation. Galatea is both present and absent from the scene of Polyphemus' performance, for as she says, while the Cyclops was singing, she was hiding under a rock (*Met.* 13.786–8). In hindsight, the *Metamorphoses* affects our reading of previous poetry and suggests that Galatea may have always lain hidden somewhere during the Cyclops' pastoral performances listening to the serenade for her. Although the Cyclops complains in his song that Galatea is 'deafer than the sea' (*surdior aequoribus*, *Met.* 13.804), Galatea listens to his song very attentively. The fact that the Cyclops' song catches her attention, even though she was lying together with Acis (*Met.* 13.787), suggests that Galatea was more interested in the Cyclops than she admits.[77] This Galatea bears something from the wooing Galatea of *Idyll* 6 or the Galatea who reciprocates the Cyclops' love, as she is occasionally depicted in Roman art.[78]

Although in the *Metamorphoses* the story and song of Polyphemus are presented as Galatea's individual memory, we should keep in mind the discursive framework in which it is set. By staging the memory in front of an audience, Galatea has the power to perform what Mackay describes as a being a key aim of public reperformances, that is to define how the story 'should be remembered'.[79] By making Galatea not simply part of Polyphemus' internal audience but the con-

---

[76] For the affinity between Corydon and Callimachus' Acontius, see Kenney (1983).
[77] See also Hardie (2015) 333 and Mack (1999) 55–6, who note that, as in the case of Odysseus, Galatea's reliability as a narrator of her own story of her encounter with Polyphemus is questionable.
[78] See *LIMC* (Suppl.) p. 1017 s.v. 'Polyphemos'.
[79] Mackay (2008) 3.

troller of the memory, Ovid pushes pastoral beyond its usual boundaries. Although not promoting the classical ethos of *uirtus* through military achievements as epic, the pastoral world is, like epic, male-centred. The poet-herdsmen who engage in amoebaean competitions or soliloquies are almost exclusively men.[80] Women typically figure either as the love objects of the pastoral poet-singers or as roles to be acted out during the herdsmen's singing performances. In Virgil's reworking of Theocritus' 'urban' *Idyll* 2 in *Eclogue* 8, Theocritus' witch is 'pastoralised', and her speech has turned into a role performed by Damon in his singing competition against Alphesiboeus. Thus, Galatea's repetition of the Cyclops' song is arresting when viewed against pastoral poetry. Although Galatea claims that she is retelling the Cyclops' song, rather than delivering a fully autonomous performance, this repetition re-enacts and perverts the poet-herdsmen's re-performances of songs from the pastoral repertory.

In recent years, several researchers of memory studies have concentrated on the gendering of memory.[81] The study of the interrelationship between gender and memory has been analysed in terms of neurofunctional differences in the function of memory across genders.[82] Most gendered memory works, however, have been duly concerned with the gendering of cultural memory. Ann Reading notes that, given that recording a memory is a selective, creative process, this very selection of memories is often affected by the difference in cultural norms across different genders. The common marginalisation of women in records of ancient history exemplifies how memory is tied up with, culture, and gender.[83] The concept of gendered memory could be usefully applied to the reading of Galatea's individual recollection. The idea that traditionally in history 'women and women's stories are easily forgotten'[84] is, in typical Ovidian fashion, simultaneously confirmed and reversed. Galatea manages to narrate her recollections in an extensive narrative and we are made to *listen* to the song through her listening to it. The challenge of imagining how she heard what she heard becomes part of the dynamics of pastoral memorialisation. It is not just female narration that becomes important here, but female listening. Her narratorial control, however, is nearly forgotten whilst reperforming the Cyclops' song.

---

80 A rare exception to this norm is the bucolic *Idyll* 27, which features a female shepherdess, Acrotime, who engages in a dramatic exchange with Daphnis.
81 See Reading (2016); Jacobs (2008); Hill, Laird & Robinson (2014).
82 See Hill, Laird & Robinson (2014); Kramer *et al.* (2003).
83 See Reading (2016) 24 ff.
84 Reading (2016) 24. See also Jarratt (2002).

The reconstruction of Galatea as a counterpart to poet-herdsmen fails to fit pastoral norms squarely not only because of her gender but also because of the Nereid's traditional role in pastoral poetry. In Hellenistic pastoral poetry, Galatea is marked as a figure paradigmatically alien to the pastoral world: the sea, her normal realm, is typically constructed within pastoral as the 'other' of the pastoral countryside.[85] Polyphemus' song precisely emphasises the attractions of the pastoral world in an attempt to entice her to leave the sea for the countryside. In Virgil's *Eclogues*, Galatea occurs in contexts highly reminiscent of the Cyclops' serenade but also starts acquiring a story of her own, which is not immediately linked to the Cyclops. There is a sense that in her occurrences aside from the serenades, she is now a more integral part of the pastoral world. In *Eclogue* 1, a Galatea is mentioned as the beloved of Tityrus. Unlike the unattainable lover Alexis, Tityrus says that Galatea was his girlfriend before Amaryllis, *postquam nos Amaryllis habet, Galatea reliquit* ('after Amaryllis took hold of me, Galatea left me', *Ecl*. 1.30). The identity of this Galatea is ambiguous: are we to understand her as the Theocritean Nereid, who is mentioned in *Eclogue* 7 (*Nerine Galatea*, *Ecl*. 7.37) or is she a different character with the same name?[86] Moreover, is the change of Tityrus' beloved from Galatea to Amaryllis in *Eclogue* 1 to be understood programmatically for the changed themes and tone of Virgilian pastoral? Clausen proposes that 'Galatea and Amaryllis must be, as Tityrus had been, slaves, *conseruae*'.[87] In *Eclogue* 3, Galatea is portrayed as the *lasciua puella* (3.64) – the term is a significant link to the promiscuous elegiac beloveds – who throws apples to the herdsman Damoetas and then hides under the willows (3.64–5). Kania suggests the 'possibility of a more distinctly Virgilian Galatea' in the *Eclogues*.[88]

But even though Virgil opens up the potential of a Galatea separate from the Cyclops in the *Eclogues*, the Virgilian Galatea never gets an independent voice. It is in the *Metamorphoses* that Galatea is bestowed for the first time with a voice of her own and is set as a focaliser and narrator of the Cyclops story.[89]

By having Galatea retell an emblematic pastoral song, Ovid brings her more energetically into the pastoral world and renders her a counterpart to the pastoral poet herdsmen. Yet pushing pastoral too far away from its boundaries, Galatea's voice proves a 'dangerous voice' to pastoral singing and gives the deathblow to

---

85 See Mosch. fr 1 (Gow). See also Frederick (2011) 75–6.
86 Cf. Kania (2016) 26.
87 Clausen (1994) 44. See also Paschalis (2008).
88 Kania (2016) 28. The name Galatea is also often attributed to Pygmalion's ivory beloved, which seems, however, to be a much later addition to the myth, see Law (1932).
89 See also Tissol (1997) 113.

pastoral song in the *Metamorphoses*. Indeed, this will be the last quasi-pastoral song of the *Metamorphoses*. Unlike the *Eclogues*, where oblivion threatens the continuation of the pastoral fiction, in the *Metamorphoses* it is Galatea's memory and control over the pastoral song which threaten and, ultimately, metamorphose the 'pastoral world' of the Ovidian epic.

In conclusion, the interaction between Galatea's individual memory and the intertextual memory of an iconic pastoral song can be read as paralleling the modern concept of the dynamic character of memory. Galatea's recollection of the Cyclops' story and song showcases how the *Metamorphoses* rewrites and employs the overriding generic self-obsession of pastoral poetry and its tendency to create its own fiction internally, significantly through the means of singing performance and repetition. Similarly to how individual memory contributes to self-understanding, the narrative of Galatea's memory in the *Metamorphoses* is employed as a means of reconstructing her character in literature and of challenging the previous generic and gender dynamics of the Cyclops and Galatea story. By bringing into sharp focus issues of genre and gender, Galatea's anamnesis and re-performance of the Cyclops' song can be fruitfully read as a substantial case-study for the *Metamorphoses*' redeployment of previous poetry and its innovative epic poetics. In clashing with the male-centred worlds of both epic and pastoral poetry, Galatea's new role as the controller of memory, one that is highlighted through metamemorial comments, simultaneously erupts into both genres. Remembering, rather than forgetting, the serenade emerges as a new danger of a pastoral world, which is now integrated and partakes of the realm of the epic world of the *Metamorphoses*.[90]

Bibliography

Alpers, P.J. (1979), *The Singer of the Eclogues: A Study of Virgilian Pastoral*, Berkeley.
Alpers, P.J. (1983), "Convening and Convention in Pastoral Poetry", *New Literary History* 14: 277–304.
Alpers, P.J. (1996), *What is Pastoral?*, Chicago.
Assmann, J. (1995), "Collective Memory and Cultural Identity", *New German Critique* 65: 125–133.

---

[90] Special thanks are due to Prof. Alison Sharrock, Dr. Thomas Phillips and my co-editor Katharine Mawford for their invaluable comments. I would also like to thank the audience of the University of Manchester, where an early version of this paper was given (AMPAL 2018, 'Memory and Commemoration').

Assmann, J. (2008), "Communicative and Cultural Memory", in A. Erll & A. Nünning (eds.), *Cultural Memory Studies: Media and Cultural Memory*, Berlin/New York: 109–18.

Bakhtin, M. (1984), *Rabelais and His World*, (Translated by H. Iswolsky), Bloomington.

Barchiesi, A. (2006), "Music for Monsters: Ovid's *Metamorphoses*, Bucolic Evolution and Bucolic Criticism", in M. Fantuzzi & T.D. Papanghelis (eds.), *Brill's Companion to Greek and Latin Pastoral*, Leiden/Boston: 403–25.

Bernsdorff, H. (2006), "The Idea of Bucolic in the Imitators of Theocritus, 3rd–1st century B.C.", in M. Fantuzzi & T.D. Papanghelis (eds.), *Brill's Companion to Greek and Latin Pastoral*, Leiden/Boston: 167–208.

Breed, B.W. (2006), *Pastoral Inscriptions: Reading and Writing Virgil's* Eclogues, London.

Brown, S.D./P. Reavey (2013), "Experience and Memory", in E. Keightley & M. Pickering (eds.), *Research Methods for Memory Studies*, Edinburgh: 45–59.

Budelmann, F. (2010), "Bringing Together Nature and Culture: On the Uses and Limits of Cognitive Science for the Study of Performance Reception", in E. Hall & S. Harrop (eds.), *Theorising Performance: Greek Drama, Cultural History and Critical Practice*, London: 108–22.

Budelmann, F./P. Easterling (2010), "Reading Minds in Greek Tragedy", *G&R* 57: 289–303.

Casali, S. (2007), "Correcting Aeneas's Voyage: Ovid's Commentary on *Aeneid* 3", *TAPhA*: 181–210.

Castagnoli, L./P. Ceccarelli (eds.) (2019), *Greek Memories: Theories and Practices*, Cambridge.

Clark, M. (2004), "Formulas, Metre and Type-Scenes", in R. Fowler (ed.), *The Cambridge Companion to Homer*, Cambridge: 117–38.

Clausen, W.V. (1994), *A Commentary on Virgil*, Eclogues, New York.

Coleman, R. (1977), *Vergil's* Eclogues, Cambridge.

Conte, G.B. (1986), *The Rhetoric of Imitation. Genre and Poetic Memory in Virgil and Other Latin Poets*, Ithaca (NY).

Creese, D. (2009), "Erogenous Organs. The Metamorphosis of Polyphemus' *Syrinx* in Ovid, *Metamorphoses* 13.784", *CQ* 59: 562–77.

Cuc, A. et al. (2007), "Silence is not Golden: A Case for Socially Shared Retrieval-Induced Forgetting", *Psychological Science* 18: 722–33.

Depew, M./D. Obbink (eds.) (2000), *Matrices of Genre: Authors, Canons, and Society*, Cambridge (MA)/London.

Dunlosky, J./S.U.K. Tauber (eds.) (2016), *The Oxford Handbook of Metamemory*, Oxford.

DuQuesnay, I.M. Le M. (1979), "From Polyphemus to Corydon: Virgil, *Eclogue* 2 and the *Idylls* of Theocritus", in D. West & T. Woodman (eds.), *Creative Imitation and Latin Literature*, Cambridge: 35–70.

Easton, A./M. Eacott (2008), "A New Working Definition of Episodic Memory: Replacing 'When' with 'Which'", in E. Dere, A. Easton, L. Nadel and J. Huston (eds.), *Handbook of Episodic Memory*, Amsterdam: 185–96.

Erll, A. (2008), "Cultural Memory Studies: An Introduction", in A. Erll & A. Nünning (eds.), *Cultural Memory Studies: Media and Cultural Memory*, Berlin/New York: 1–16.

Fantuzzi, M. (2012), "Achilles at Scyros and One of His Fans: The *Epithalamium of Achilles and Deidameia* (*Buc. Gr.* 157–8 Gow)", in M. Baumbach & S. Bär (eds.), *Brill's Companion to Greek and Latin Epyllion and Its Reception*, Leiden/Boston: 283–308.

Fantuzzi, M./T.D. Papanghelis (eds.) (2006), *Brill's Companion to Greek and Latin Pastoral*, Leiden/Boston.

Farrell, J. (1992), "Dialogue of Genres in Ovid's 'Lovesong of Polyphemus' (*Metamorphoses* 13.719–879)", *AJPh* 113: 235–68.

Flavell, J.H. (1979), "Metacognition and Cognitive Monitoring: A New Area of Cognitive–Developmental Inquiry", *American Psychologist* 34: 906–11.
Frederick, J. (2011), *Virgil's Gardens. The Nature of Bucolic Space*, London.
Fulkerson, L. (2016), *Ovid: A Poet on the Margins*, London/New York.
Fulkerson, L./T. Stover (eds.) (2016), *Repeat Performances: Ovidian Repetition and the Metamorphoses*, Madison/London.
Galinsky, K./K. Lapatin (2016), *Cultural Memories in the Roman Empire*, Los Angeles.
Grethlein, J./L. Huitink/A. Tagliabue (eds.) (2019), *Cognitive Classics: Experience, Narrative, and Criticism in Ancient Greece*, Oxford.
Griffin, A.H.F. (1983), "Unrequited Love: Polyphemus and Galatea in Ovid's *Metamorphoses*", *G&R* 30: 190–7.
Gutzwiller, K.J. (1991), *Theocritus' Pastoral Analogies: The Formation of a Genre*, Madison.
Gutzwiller, K.J. (2006), "The Herdsman in Greek Thought", in M. Fantuzzi & T.D. Papanghelis (eds.), *Brill's Companion to Greek and Latin Pastoral*, Leiden/Boston: 1–23.
Hardie, P. (1988), "Lucretius and the Delusions of Narcissus", *MD* 20/21: 71–89.
Hardie, P. (2002), *Ovid's Poetics of Illusion*, Cambridge.
Hardie, P. (2015), *Ovidio: Metamorfosi, Vol. VI, Libri XIII-XV*, Milan.
Hardy, R.B. (1990), "Vergil's Epitaph for Pastoral: Remembering and Forgetting in *Eclogue* 9", *SyllClass* 2: 29–38.
Heerink, M. (2015), *Echoing Hylas. A Study in Hellenistic and Roman Metapoetics*, Madison.
Heinze, R. (1919), *Ovids elegische Erzählung*, Leipzig.
Heubeck, A./S. West/J.B. Hainsworth (1988), *A Commentary on Homer's* Odyssey. *Vol. 1, Books I-VIII*, Oxford.
Hill, A./A. Laird/J. Robinson (2014), "Gender Differences in Working Memory Networks: A Brain Map Meta-Analysis", *Biol Psychol.* 102: 18–29.
Hinds, S. (1987), *The Metamorphosis of Persephone: Ovid and the Self-Conscious Muse*, Cambridge.
Hinds, S. (1998), *Allusion and Intertext: Dynamics of Appropriation in Roman Poetry*, Cambridge/New York.
Hinds, S. (2000), "Essential Epic: Genre and Gender from Macer to Statius", in M. Depew & D. Obbink (eds.), *Matrices of Genre: Authors, Canons, and Society*, Cambridge (MA)/London, 221–44.
Holst-Warhaft, G. (1992), *Dangerous Voices: Women's Laments and Greek Literature*, London/New York.
Hopkinson, N. (2000), *Ovid.* Metamorphoses *Book XIII*, Cambridge.
Hubbard, T.K. (1998), *The Pipes of Pan. Intertextuality and Literary Filiation in the Pastoral Tradition from Theocritus to Milton*, Ann Arbor.
Hunsaker, M./R. Kesner (2017), "Unfolding the Cognitive Map: The Role of Hippocampal and Extra-Hippocampal Substrates Based on a Systems Analysis of Spatial Processing", *Neurobiol Learn Mem.* 147: 90–119.
Hunter, R.L. (1999), *Theocritus: A Selection. Idylls 1, 3, 4, 6, 7, 10, 11 and 13*, Cambridge/New York.
Hunter, V.J. (1982), *Past and Process in Herodotus and Thucydides*, Princeton.
Hutchinson, G.O. (2007), "The Monster and the Monologue: Polyphemus from Homer to Ovid", in P.J. Finglass, C. Collard & N.J. Richardson (eds.), *Hesperos: Studies in Ancient Greek Poetry Presented to M.L. West on His Seventieth Birthday*, Oxford, 22–39.
Hutchinson, G.O. (2013), *Greek to Latin. Frameworks and Contexts for Intertextuality*, Oxford.

Iser, W. (1993), *The Fictive and the Imaginary. Charting Literary Anthropology*, Baltimore.
Jacobs, J. (2008), "Gender and Collective Memory: Women and Representation at Auschwitz", *Memory Studies* 1: 211–15.
Jarratt, S.C. (2002), "Sappho's Memory", *Rhetoric Society Quarterly*: 11–43.
Kania, R. (2016), *Virgil's Eclogues and the Art of Fiction: A Study of the Poetic Imagination*, Cambridge.
Kansteiner, W./H. Weilnboeck (2008), "Against the Concept of Cultural Trauma or How I Learned to Love the Suffering of Others without the Help of Psychotherapy", in A. Erll & A. Nünning (eds.), *Cultural Memory Studies: Media and Cultural Memory*, Berlin/New York: 229–40.
Karakasis, E. (2011), *Song Exchange in Roman Pastoral*, Berlin/New York.
Keightley, E./M. Pickering (2012), *The Mnemonic Imagination: Remembering as Creative Practice*, New York.
Keightley, E./M. Pickering (eds.) (2013), *Research Methods for Memory Studies*, Edinburgh.
Keith, A. (1999), "Versions of Epic Masculinity in Ovid's *Metamorphoses*", in P. Hardie, A. Barchiesi and S. Hinds (eds.), *Ovidian Transformations: Essays on the* Metamorphoses *and Its Reception*, Cambridge, 214–39.
Keith, A. (2009), "Sexuality and Gender", in P.E. Knox (ed.), *A Companion to Ovid*, Oxford: 355–69.
Kenney, E.J. (1983), "Virgil and the Elegiac Sensibility", *ICS* 8: 44–59.
Kitamura, T. *et al.* (2017), 'Engrams and Circuits Crucial for Systems Consolidation of a Memory', *Science* 356: 73–8.
Knox, P.E. (1986), *Ovid's* Metamorphoses *and the Traditions of Augustan Poetry*, Cambridge.
Koriat, A. (2007) 'Metacognition and Consciousness', in P.D. Zelazo, M. Moscovitch and E. Thompson (eds.), *The Cambridge Handbook of Consciousness*, Cambridge: 289–325.
Kramer, J.H. *et al.* (2003), 'Distinctive Neuropsychological Patterns in Frontotemporal Dementia, Semantic Dementia, and Alzheimer Disease', *Cognitive and Behavioral Neurology* 16: 211–18.
Kristeva, J. (1986), *The Kristeva Reader, Edited by Moi, T.*, New York.
Law, H.H. (1932), "The Name Galatea in the Pygmalion Myth", *CJ* 27: 337–42.
Little, D.A. (1970), "Richard Heinze: Ovids elegische Erzählung", in E. Zinn (ed.), *Ovids Ars amatoria und Remedia amoris. Untersuchungen zum Aufbau*, Stuttgart: 64–105.
Mack, S. (1999), "Acis and Galatea or Metamorphosis of Tradition", *Arion* 6: 51–67.
Mackay, A. (2008), "Introduction", in A. Mackay (ed.), *Orality, Literacy, Memory in the Ancient Greek and Roman World: Orality and Literacy in Ancient Greece, Vol. 7*, Leiden/Boston: 1–8.
Meban, D. (2009), "Virgil's *Eclogues* and Social Memory", *AJPh* 130: 99–130.
Nagle, B.R. (1988), "A Trio of Love-Triangles in Ovid's *Metamorphoses*", *Arethusa* 21: 75–98.
Neumann, B. (2008), "The Literary Representation of Memory", in A. Erll & A. Nünning (eds.), *Cultural Memory Studies: Media and Cultural Memory*, Berlin/New York: 333–44.
Nora, P. (1989), "Between Memory and History: Les Lieux de Mémoire", *Representations* 26: 7–24.
Otis, B. (1970), *Ovid as an Epic Poet*, Cambridge.
Papaioannou, S. (2005), *Epic Succession and Dissension: Ovid, Metamorphoses 13.623–14.582 and the Reinvention of the Aeneid*, Berlin/New York.
Papanghelis, T.D. (2006), "Friends, Foes, Frames and Fragments: Textuality in Virgil's *Eclogues*", in M. Fantuzzi & T.D. Papanghelis (eds.), *Brill's Companion to Greek and Latin Pastoral*, Leiden/Boston: 369–402.

Paschalis, M. (2008), "Tityrus and Galatea (Virgil, *Eclogue* 1): An Expected Relationship", *Dictynna* 5.
Payne, M.E. (2007), *Theocritus and the Invention of Fiction*, Cambridge.
Pethes, N. (2019), *Cultural Memory Studies: An Introduction*, Cambridge.
Reading, A. (2016), *Gender and Memory in the Globital Age*, London.
Roediger, H.L./J.V. Wertsch (2008), "Creating a New Discipline of Memory Studies", *Memory Studies* 1: 9–22.
Russell, N. (2006), "Collective Memory before and after Halbwachs", *The French Review* 79.4: 792–804.
Salzman-Mitchell, P.B. (2007), "Reading Resistance in the Galatea Episode of Ovid's *Metamorphoses*", *Myrtia* 22: 117–37.
Sharrock, A. (2000), "Introduction", in A. Sharrock & H. Morales (eds.), *Intratextuality. Greek and Roman Textual Relations*, Oxford/New York.
Sharrock, A. (2002), "Gender and Sexuality", in P. Hardie (ed.), *The Cambridge Companion to Ovid*, Cambridge: 95–107.
Sharrock, A. (2019), "Ovid's *Metamorphoses*: The Naughty Boy of the Graeco-Roman Epic Tradition", in C. Reitz & S. Finkmann (eds.), *Structures of Epic Poetry. Volume 1: Foundations*, Berlin/Boston: 275–316.
Simine, S.A. (2013), *Mediating Memory in the Museum: Trauma, Empathy, Nostalgia*, London.
Squire, M. (2015), *Sight and the Ancient Senses. The Senses in Antiquity*, London/New York.
Tissol, G. (1997), *The Face of Nature: Wit, Narrative, and Cosmic Origins in Ovid's Metamorphoses*, Princeton.
Wheeler, S.M. (2000), *Narrative Dynamics in Ovid's* Metamorphoses, Hildesheim.

Part IV: **Oblivion**

Hannah Burke-Tomlinson
Ovid's Labyrinthine *Ars*: Pasiphae and the Dangers of Poetic Memory in the *Metamorphoses*

Abstract: Allusions to Pasiphae and her infamous, bestial lust for the Cretan bull are scattered throughout Ovid's *Metamorphoses*. Yet the Cretan queen and her man-made 'metamorphosis' into a wooden heifer by Daedalus is strikingly denied explicit narrative exploration in Ovid's epic. Ovid's fragmentary presentation of Pasiphae in the *Metamorphoses* in various mythical narratives, via the memories of internal narrators, invites metapoetic interpretation concerning the established scholarly reading of Ovid's epic as a labyrinthine text. By extending this metapoetic reading and mobilising Conte's critical concept 'poetic memory', it can be discerned that the *Metamorphoses* is not only akin to the Cretan labyrinth with regards to its bewildering narrative structure but also, like the mythical structure crafted by Daedalus, contains dangerous monuments to female, sexual *furor*. Analysis of instances in which the dangerous paradigm of Pasiphae pervades Ovid's epic reveals that Pasiphae's legacy of erotic *furor* elucidates anxieties concerning the presentation of mythical Cretan women in Roman epic. This chapter argues that the anxieties excited by poetic commemorations and the memory of Pasiphae's grotesque sexuality necessitate the figure's artistic confinement. This artistic confinement is provided by Ovid's labyrinthine epic *ars*, which allows for a controlled display of the spectacle of the Cretan queen's sexual *furor* by way of small-scale allusions.

I would like to thank Sebastian Matzner for his supervision and thoughtful advice whilst initially developing this line of argument. I would also like to express my gratitude to the organisers and attendees of AMPAL 2017, where an incipient version of this chapter was presented. I am grateful to Elaine Sanderson, Rioghnach Sachs, Grace Emmett and especially to the volume co-editors Katharine Mawford and Eleni Ntanou for offering their time and helpful comments on earlier versions of this chapter.

1 Introduction

Pasiphae's erotic passion for the Cretan bull, and its monstrous consequences, fired the Roman imagination.[1] The prurient fascination with this tale found cultural expression in ancient Rome in a number of forms, perhaps the most striking of these being through the violent re-enactment of the myth in the form of grotesque amphitheatrical spectacle. Martial and Suetonius both attest that this 'fatal charade' – to borrow Coleman's terminology for public *munera* ('spectacles') in which mythical narratives were dramatised through role-play – faithfully recreated Pasiphae's copulation with the bull by presenting a captive woman (possibly condemned *ad bestias*) in the guise of the Cretan queen encased in a wooden heifer (Mart. *Spect.* 6, Suet. *Ner.* 12).[2] Suetonius also recounts that the emperor Galba capitalised upon this cultural interest by (somewhat dubiously) tracing his *gens*' illustrious ancestry back to Pasiphae through his maternal line and proudly displayed his *stemma* in his atrium (Suet. *Galb.* 2).[3] The myth likewise found cultural expression in the visual

---

1 For an overview of treatments of this myth (as well as the myths of other literary Cretan women) in ancient Greek poetry, and for details about the influence this Greek tradition had on the subsequent Roman fascination with Cretan women, see Armstrong (2006) 7–16. Cf. Franco (2017) 49–52 who analyses the prevalence of eroticised language and metaphors used to conceptualise interspecies relationships in ancient Greek and Roman sources. Franco notes that it is precisely the consequences of Pasiphae's interspecies relationship with the Cretan bull (namely the birth of the Minotaur) which marks this eroticised relationship as a negative one: 'interspecies attraction could only be positively "eroticised" as long as it did not mess up the blood heritage. Of course, the case of a god in animal disguise is different: this type of hybridisation was thought of as "progressive" and acceptable, giving birth to semi-divine offspring [...] cases of proper fertile zooerastia, such as Pasiphae and Polyphonte, resulted in a bloody wild offspring (the Minotaur, Agrius and Oreius respectively).'
2 Coleman (1990) 63–4, 67–70. Coleman further suggests that Martial's allusion to the staging of the myth recalls two scenes from Apuleius' *Metamorphoses*: namely, Apul. *Met.* 10.22 and 10.29. In the first instance, a wealthy woman desires and copulates with Lucius whilst he is still in his asinine form. In this passage, Lucius explicitly equates the woman's bestial desire with that of Pasiphae. In the second, a woman has been condemned *ad bestias* and her intended punishment is that she will be forced into intercourse with an ass, which is, in fact, the metamorphosed Lucius. Cf. Coleman (1990) 64, n. 177 and Franco (2017) 49 who each note that Martial's description of the re-enactment of this myth in the opening lines of the epigram – *Iunctam Pasiphaen Dictaeo credite tauro:* | *vidimus* ('Believe Pasiphae mated with the Dictaean bull; we have seen it') – mobilises the ambiguity of the word *iunctam* in such a way that it could either connote sexual intercourse or else indicate that the woman was in fact physically tied onto the bull.
3 It is notable that in this *vita* Suetonius makes no reference to Pasiphae's bestial desire, rather she is simply identified as the wife of King Minos (*Pasiphaam Minonis uxorem*). Galba's paternal ancestry is less ambivalent and claims descent from Jupiter, perhaps in an attempt to supersede the

arts and poetry.⁴ It is, for instance, famously commemorated in Book 6 of Vergil's *Aeneid*, in which the ekphrastic depiction of the friezes on the temple doors of Cumaean Apollo, created by Daedalus, presents Pasiphae's cruel love (*crudelis amor*; Verg. *Aen.* 6.24) as the pinnacle of Cretan erotic transgression (Verg. *Aen.* 6.14–33, 45–60);⁵ a presentation that is somewhat at odds with the poet's strikingly sympathetic portrayal of the Cretan queen in *Eclogue* 6.⁶ The longest extant Latin account of the Cretan queen's infatuation with the bull appears in the first book of the *Ars Amatoria* (Ov. *Ars am.* 1.289–326). Here Ovid rejects the *pathos*-suffused approach of Vergil's sixth *Eclogue* in favour of a ludic treatment of the Greek myth that exploits amatory, elegiac motifs to highlight the irrationality of Pasiphae's desire.

Comparatively, the absence of this myth in Ovid's *Metamorphoses*, a text largely inspired by erotic violence, taboo and transgression, is conspicuous.⁷ In fact, the epic's unifying theme of metamorphosis highlights this pointed omission. Although Pasiphae's is a false and temporary metamorphosis, it still displays the formulaic progression of other metamorphoses associated with erotic misdemeanours, in which an individual driven by desperation and overwhelming passion is transformed accordingly. Intriguingly, this particular myth also subverts the pattern of divine agency and causation typically associated with Ovidian metamorphoses. This fact is highlighted through the revelation that Pasiphae's 'transformation' into a wooden heifer, in order to abet her sexual *furor* ('passion', 'madness'), is engineered through Daedalus' mortal, artistic ingenuity

---

Julio-Claudian claims to Venus as a divine ancestor by way of Aeneas. On Galba's *stemma* Pasiphae appears not as a paradigmatic instance of female sexual *furor* but rather as someone who, by way of both their own ancestry and marriage to a son of Jupiter, has multiple connections with divine figures.

4 On the representation of Pasiphae in ancient Roman visual culture, see Papadopoulos (1994) 193–200 in particular and Newby (2016), who incorporates discussions of Pasiphae in conjunction with her broader examination of Greek myth in Roman art. Cf. Bergmann (2017) 203–4, 230–2 on the representation of Pasiphae and other female mythological figures in the paintings from the Villa of Munatia Procula.

5 Cf. Verg. *Aen.* 6.445–51 in which Pasiphae features in a catalogue of women (including her daughter Phaedra and the recently deceased Dido) consumed by cruel love even in death, who roam the Mourning Fields of the Underworld.

6 On the sympathy elicited for Pasiphae in Vergil's sixth *Eclogue* and how this contrasts with Ovid's treatment of the same myth in the *Ars Amatoria*, see Armstrong (2006) 169–86.

7 The lack of an extended narrative exploration of the Pasiphae myth by Ovid has been briefly noted by scholars. See, for instance, Blumenfeld-Kosinski (1996) 308–9 who analyses how the 'meagre allusions' to Pasiphae scattered throughout the *Metamorphoses* are transformed into a lengthier narrative in the medieval *Ovide moralisé*. Armstrong (2006) 137, n. 71 similarly comments in a footnote that '[t]he involvement of Pasiphae and Ariadne in the Labyrinth's story is emphatically underplayed' by Ovid, who rather focuses primarily upon the figure of Daedalus.

(Ov. *Met.* 8.133–4; 9.738–44) – an act that parallels Ovid's own capacity as a poet to engender transformation by way of his poetic *ars* ('art'). Furthermore, the aggressive and grotesque nature of Pasiphae's sexual misconduct would seem to lend itself especially to Ovid's particular preoccupation in the *Metamorphoses* with mythological narratives in which women are either subjected to or implicated in the perpetration of sexually motivated acts that defy Roman cultural norms, as well as Ovid's interest in and representation of dissident gender performances and sexualities in his corpus more broadly.

Despite being denied her own extended narrative within the *Metamorphoses*, Pasiphae, who embodies transgressive female sexuality, nevertheless emerges as a fragmentary – yet present – figure whose tale is similarly lacunose in its narrative presence. Scattered references to Pasiphae appear in the words of internal narrators who recall and allude to specific aspects of her mythological narrative and legacy. The memories of these internal narrators enable Pasiphae, and the sexual *furor* she embodies, to persistently pervade the narratives of both the epic as a literary spectre (through what Conte terms 'poetic memory') and in the personal narratives of individual characters who recall their 'lived experiences' ('personal memory').[8] This chapter assesses the function and meaning of Pasiphae's lacunose narrative presence in the *Metamorphoses* and argues that Conte's notion of 'poetic memory' offers a productive lens through which to consider this aspect of Ovid's epic project. After first outlining the allusions to Pasiphae in Ovid's epic, I then discuss how the recurring intrusion of the Pasiphae myth marks it as a malevolent, cautionary paradigm. I argue that the myth functions in a comparable way to the House of Atreus in Homer's *Odyssey*, as a lingering subtext that threatens to overwhelm the poetry within which it is contained. I will further contend that the nature of Ovid's epic poem, with its interwoven myths and polyphonic narratives, evokes both the structure and function of Daedalus' labyrinthine structure. Just as the Daedalian labyrinth contains a testament to Pasiphae's sexual *furor* (namely, the Minotaur whose existence attests to the consummation of her bestial passion), so too Ovid's labyrinthine epic functions as a prison for the memory of Pasiphae and the transgressive sexuality and femininity that she embodies. The myth of Pasiphae thus emerges as the repressed core of the text, which, despite its periodic reoccurrence, is artfully contained by Ovid's poetry. I propose further that the Pasiphae myth can act as a frame for reading the way in which Ovid takes on the challenge of representing and controlling irrepressible female passion through the labyrinthine nature of

---

[8] Cf. Armstrong (2006) 61 for the principle of 'personal memory'. These concepts are discussed in greater detail below.

the *Metamorphoses*: Pasiphae, and the Cretan emblem of female erotic misdemeanour she comes to personify, *is* successfully repressed. Thus, Ovid's poetic *ars* surpasses that of the mythological paradigm of Daedalus, the master craftsman, and that of his immediate Roman epic predecessor Vergil, who likewise negotiates the emblem of the labyrinth in the *Aeneid*.

2 Pasiphae: the Cretan paradigm

At the outset of Book 8 of his epic poem, Ovid recounts how the Megarian princess Scylla betrayed her father, Nisus, and her city by removing an apotropaic lock of hair from her father's head and offering it to the invading King Minos of Crete, in an attempt to seduce him. Minos' outraged response to this offering exposes the naivety of Scylla's actions, and in the aftermath of her treachery she first laments her unreciprocated passion before offering a particularly vehement diatribe against Minos. Embedded within Scylla's intradiegetic narration is another mythological narrative pertaining to deviant female behaviour and one that Minos would likely rather forget: namely, that of his wife Pasiphae and her passion for the Cretan bull.[9] Over the course of her tirade, Scylla situates the Cretan queen within the context of her sexual misdemeanours and, in so doing, explicitly characterises Pasiphae in terms of immorality and deception:

> te vere coniuge digna est,
> quae torvum ligno decepit adultera taurum
> discordemque utero fetum tulit. ecquid ad aures
> perveniunt mea dicta tuas, an inania venti
> verba ferunt idemque tuas, ingrate, carinas?
> iam iam Pasiphaen non est mirabile taurum
> praeposuisse tibi: tu plus feritatis habebas.

---

9 I use the terms 'intradiegetic' and 'extradiegetic' throughout this chapter as a means of distinguishing between narrators and audiences that feature either within or outside of the diegetic frame of Ovid's poem. On these theoretical terms, see Genette (1980). The internal narrators who reflect upon Pasiphae's sexual *furor* over the course of this chapter could be further distinguished through the appellation of either homo- or heterodiegetic narrator. Scylla and Iphis act as heterodiegetic-intradiegetic narrators, since they are both internal narrators who recount aspects of Pasiphae's mythology, whereas Hippolytus is a homodiegetic-intradiegetic narrator who is an internal narrator who recollects aspects of his own literary history by way of references to his earlier Euripidean incarnation. Barchiesi (2002) 184 notes the difficulty in apprehending 'any thematic or occasional motivation' for Ovid's use of either homo- or heterodiegetic narrative modes over the course of the *Metamorphoses*.

> She is a true mate for you who with unnatural passion deceived the savage bull by that shape of wood and bore a hybrid offspring in her womb. Does my voice reach your ears? Or do the same winds blow away my words to emptiness that fill your sails, you ingrate? Now, now I do not wonder that Pasiphae preferred the bull to you, for you were a more savage beast than he.[10]
>
> Ov. Met. 8.132-137

This condensed and elliptical account of Pasiphae's bestial desire and the ensuing birth of the Minotaur is notable for the constituent components of the mythic narrative that Scylla strategically elects to forget. Daedalus, the Athenian artificer to whom Ovid will soon turn in the ensuing Cretan narratives recounted in Book 8, is entirely absent from Scylla's intradiegetic narration. Instead only the wooden heifer is referenced – the artwork created by Daedalus that was so lifelike that it had the capacity to induce desire within the Cretan bull and thereby facilitated the conception of the Minotaur. Rather than emphasising the artistry of Daedalus' craftsmanship or its capacity to imitate nature, as Ovid will do in his subsequent description of the Cretan labyrinth, Scylla instead takes care to isolate Pasiphae's actions from any sphere of male influence. Her bestial desire and its consummation are presented as unabetted and lacking in the divine motivation supplied in other ancient narratives. The only possible motivation postulated by Scylla is that the bull proved a less savage alternative to Minos himself. As such, Pasiphae is presented as being entirely culpable for her actions. In so doing, Scylla casts Pasiphae as a paradigm of the *topos* of the Cretan woman, 'a cliché, operative at least from the fifth century BC, [which] sets among the ranks of disreputable females the Cretan woman who is incapable of controlling her desires, and whose reputation could easily taint those of her relatives.'[11]

Scylla's intradiegetic narration offers the first and lengthiest reference to Pasiphae in the *Metamorphoses*, after which point Pasiphae – and the monstrous female sexuality she embodies – fades from view. Subsequently, only two brief allusions to Pasiphae appear in Ovid's epic which similarly relegate Pasiphae's mythological narrative to the realm of memory and allusion. We next encounter Pasiphae in Book 9 where she is designated as the pinnacle of Cretan erotic misdemeanour during Iphis' lament about the supposed perversity of her own prodigious homoerotic desire for her female beloved, Ianthe. Iphis – who, like

---

10 Unless otherwise indicated, all translations of Ovid's *Metamorphoses* Books 1–8 are taken from Frank Justus Miller (1977; revised by G.P. Goold) and translations of Books 9–15 are taken from Frank Justus Miller (1984; revised by G.P. Goold).
11 Armstrong (2006) 109.

Pasiphae, is also (pointedly) a Cretan woman – reflects upon the monstrous female desire that has made Crete (in)famous:

> ne non tamen omnia Crete
> monstra ferat, taurum dilexit filia Solis,
> femina nempe marem. meus est furioisior illo,
> si verum profitemur, amor. tamen illa secuta est
> spem Veneris; tamen illa dolis et imagine vaccae
> passa bovem est', et erat, qui deciperetur, adulter.
> huc licet ex toto sollertia confluat orbe,
> ipse licet revolet ceratis Daedalus alis,
> quid faciet? num me puerum de virgine doctis
> artibus efficiet? num te mutabit, Ianthe?

Nevertheless, that Crete might produce all monstrous things, the daughter of the Sun loved a bull—a female to be sure, and male; my passion is more mad than that, if the truth be told. Yet she had some hope of her love's fulfilment; yet she enjoyed her bull by a trick and the disguise of the heifer, and it was the lover who was deceived. Though all the ingenuity in the world should be collected here, though Daedalus himself should fly back on waxen wings, what could he do? With all his learned arts could he make me into a boy from a girl? or could he change you, Ianthe?

Ov. *Met.* 9.735–44

Iphis here exhibits an acute degree of self-awareness of not only the ambivalent mythological heritage of Crete but also its association with extreme passions, particularly with regards to its women.[12] It is notable that, even in the context of Iphis' enumeration of paradigmatic instances of Cretan sexual perversity, Pasiphae's name is repressed here. The Cretan queen is only obliquely alluded to in the Latin, by way of her mythical ancestry, as *filia Solis* ('the daughter of the Sun') which foregrounds Pasiphae's separation from the mortal world and, possibly, its moral laws (Ov. *Met.* 9.736).[13] In spite of the monstrosity of Pasiphae's

---

[12] On characters' acute literary awareness and their implication within broader Greco-Roman literary traditions see in this volume Mawford's analysis of Apollonius Rhodius' Medea in the *Argonautica*, Ngan's study of Medea in Seneca's *Medea*, and Ntanou's examination of the Nereid Galatea in Ovid's *Metamorphoses*. For an overview of the ambiguities and paradoxes that characterise the land of Crete in ancient thought and myth, as well as the particular fascination Crete held in Roman culture see Armstrong (2006) 1–5, 12–6, 71–2, 300–1. See also Padel (1996) 77–8 on the association between Crete and eroticism, particularly violent female sexuality as perceived through the lens of the masculine eye.

[13] On the subject of endogamic relations amongst the gods, see Ov. *Met.* 9.497–501. In an attempt to validate her own incestuous desire for her twin Caunus Byblis looks to paradigms of male-sister relationships amongst the gods. In spite of her apparent self-delusion throughout

bestial passion, Iphis conceptualises her own same-sex desire for her beloved Ianthe as comparatively more deviant (*furiosior*), since female-female relationships contrastingly fail to abide by assumed gender binaries in ancient thought and, by extension, the phallocentric model of Roman sexuality.[14] Unlike Scylla, whose selective recollection of Pasiphae's mythological narrative omits Daedalus entirely, Iphis emphasises Daedalus' role in the deception of the Cretan bull and his other learned arts, which further serves to emphasise the perceived futility of Iphis' homoerotic desire. Pasiphae could hope, through Daedalus' artifice, to have her lust sated: *tamen illa secuta est | spem Veneris* ('Yet she had some hope of her love's fulfilment'; Ov. *Met.* 9.738–739). Iphis' *amor*, by contrast, is presented as being unintelligible to the intradiegetic narrator herself and as being so prodigious that it would elude even Daedalus' abilities. This is due to the fact that although Iphis herself has been raised to be performatively male both she and Ianthe are biologically female and thus necessarily passive according to Roman sexual paradigms, thereby precluding the possibility of 'normative' sexual fulfilment through penetration.[15] Iphis' recollection of the Pasiphae myth, like that of

---

this episode, Byblis nevertheless concludes that the gods are a law unto themselves and that mortal desires should not be measured against divine customs.

14 For the hegemonic, phallocentric model of Roman sexuality predicated upon the status of the elite male citizen, consult the studies undertaken by Richlin (1983), Walters (1997), Williams (2010), Masterson (2013), Rawles and Natoli (2013). The reference to gender binaries in the plural here is intended to denote the distinctions drawn in this phallocentric model between masculinity and femininity and corresponding binaries created between sexual activity versus passivity, penetration versus penetrated, and dominance versus submission.

15 Of all the Cretan women that populate Ovid's epic, Iphis' narrative is unique in that it ends in the miraculous transformation of Iphis into a biological male as a result of the divine benefaction of Isis, thereby allowing for Iphis' marriage to Ianthe to take place. This is likely due to the fact that Iphis' perspectives are consonant with Roman sexual mores, thereby distancing Iphis from such satirical figures as the *tribas*. The tribadic female is particularly grotesque in the Roman imagination as she assumes a penetrative, masculine role in sexual encounters. Iphis' lack of desire to attempt tribadic acts, or even being capable of conceiving of them, is explicitly stated prior to her soliloquy at Ov. *Met.* 9.724: *Iphis amat, qua posse frui desperat* ('Iphis loved without hope of her love's fulfilment'). This distinction between Iphis and tribadism is important, as it insists upon Iphis' passivity and, by extension, her *pudicitia*: this belies Iphis' ostensible, performative masculinity and rather points to her conformity to the sexual ideologies associated with her biological gender. Iphis evidently lacks the sexual aggression typically associated with the literary *topos* of the Cretan woman, who pursues the object of her desire and engages in sexually deviant acts despite the societal taboo and degradation it entails. On the figure of the *tribas*, see Hallett (1990) and Brooten (1996). See also Langlands (2006) who offers an insightful analysis of *pudicitia* as an ethical concept. Cf. Pintabone (2002) 278–9 for the reading that there is something potentially troubling about the ending to Iphis' narrative, particularly for a modern

Scylla, is highly selective; the birth of the Minotaur, the grotesque outcome of the interspecies union between Pasiphae and the bull, and the construction of the labyrinth are overlooked in favour of highlighting the beneficent (if problematic) actions of Daedalus in facilitating non-normative, female sexual desire.

Pasiphae is also alluded to with comparable ambivalence by the apotheosised Hippolytus (now Virbius) in Book 15. Hippolytus, consumed by the memory of his own prior misfortunes as recounted in Euripidean tragedy,[16] invokes Pasiphae's name through his allusion to her daughter Phaedra in which he utilises the matronymic *Pasiphaeia* (Ov. *Met.* 15.500). This prompt, when coupled with the aforementioned reference to Pasiphae in Book 9 as *filia Solis* ('daughter of the Sun'), alerts the audience to the inherited, seemingly inescapable sexually subversive legacy of literary Cretan women, to which not least the (quasi-)incestuous desire of Pasiphae's daughter, Phaedra, for her step-son attests.[17] Prior to this, Phaedra is simply referred to through the loaded term *noverca* ('stepmother'), recalling the declamatory stock type of the *saeva noverca* ('cruel stepmother').[18] Intriguingly, Phaedra's name is suppressed throughout Hippolytus' narration in a comparable manner to that of Pasiphae by Iphis in Book 9. As with Scylla and Iphis' respective recollections of the Pasiphae myth, Hippolytus' memories of the events that led to his death omit crucial details. There is, most notably, no reference to the Nurse who plays a central role in catalysing the tragic events of Euripides' extant *Hippolytus*. Watson argues that, rather than being omitted for the sake of poetic economy, the absence of the Nurse is for the purpose of augmenting Phaedra's guilt.[19] This is consonant with Scylla's characterisation of Pasiphae in Book 8, which similarly lays the blame squarely on a Cretan woman rather than considering any external factors that might mitigate her actions and desires.

This brief survey of the small-scale allusions to Pasiphae in Ovid's epic points to a number of intriguing similarities: firstly, all of these allusions to Pasiphae are made by intradiegetic narrators; Ovid does not, in his capacity as a poet, dedicate an extended narrative to Pasiphae in the *Metamorphoses*. As such, Pasiphae only

---

audience, as Iphis' former female identification may well problematise their seemingly beneficent masculine metamorphosis; there is, as Pintabone acknowledges, the unsettling notion that perhaps this *is* indeed a punishment, since Iphis' transformation marks the loss of the femininity with which s/he first identified.
16 Cf. Ov. *Met.* 15.500–505, which summarises the main plot of Euripides' extant *Hippolytus*.
17 Cf. Watson (1995) 111.
18 On this *topos* in Latin poetry, which owes much of its characterisation of the *saeva noverca* to the influence exerted by declamation, see Watson (1995) 92–222.
19 Watson (1995) 109–10.

emerges in the narrative by way of individual, focalised recollections of her mythic narrative and sexually subversive legacy. Secondly, all three intradiegetic narrators' recollections of Pasiphae are highly selective and omit specific and recognisable aspects of the mythological narrative surrounding Pasiphae's passion for the Cretan bull and its consequences.[20] These scattered references thus indicate that the figure of Pasiphae within Ovid's epic is one that exists largely in what Conte terms 'poetic memory'.[21] In his theoretical approach to the rhetorical function of literary allusion, Conte asserts that intertextuality allows for the enrichment of Latin literature through the evocation of an audience's memories associated with prior texts. Conte posits that allusion can only occur in a literary text if 'a sympathetic vibration can be set up between the poet's and the reader's memories when these are directed to a source already stored in both.'[22] Therefore 'poetic memory', by Conte's estimation, appears to exist by way of symbiosis; both the poet and the audience must be stirred to literary remembrance by way of allusion.[23] Poetic memory is clearly at play in all three allusions to Pasiphae. By way of their condensed narration and mobilisation of ellipsis, the three intradiegetic narrators' recollections of Pasiphae not only allow her to pervade Ovid's poetic narrative but also trigger the memories of an intertextually aware reader who is knowledgeable of the wider poetic and mythic traditions in which Pasiphae features and thereby capable of discerning the omissions within these allusions.

These allusions to Pasiphae in turn trigger the 'personal' memories of other characters within the epic, which encourages these figures to recall and respond to their 'lived' past. Elaborating upon the overlap between a character's 'personal' memory and a poet's employment of 'poetic' memory, Armstrong argues that

> The link between personal and poetic memory is stronger than one simply of shared vocabulary: an emphasis on the importance of memory on the narrated level shades into the poet/narrator's concern with his own literary memories. In this respect, the creator is not so very different from his creations, and is as profoundly aware of his poetic history as the characters are of their 'lived' past.[24]

---

[20] On the malleability of memories as theorised in cognitive studies and memorialisation as a dynamic and creative process in Ovid's *Metamorphoses*, see Ntanou in this volume. Discrepancies between the memories of various characters are also discussed by Ngan in this volume with regards to Seneca's *Medea*.
[21] Conte (1986) 23: Conte defines 'poetic memory' as a functional rhetorical matrix and constitutive element of poetic discourse, which contributes to poetic signification.
[22] Conte (1986) 35.
[23] Cf. Fowler (2000) 117 and Armstrong (2006) 22–3 for further reflections upon Conte's 'poetic memory'.
[24] Armstrong (2006) 22–3.

Memory can thus be seen to have a subversive role in the *Metamorphoses* as it enables Pasiphae, and the sexual *furor* she embodies, to persistently pervade the narratives of both the epic as a literary entity ('poetic memory') and by way of the personal narratives of Minos, Scylla's internal audience, and Hippolytus ('personal memory') – both of whom are stirred to recall aspects of their own 'lived' mythic pasts in which Pasiphae figures, to varying degrees.[25] In its reliance upon 'poetic' and 'personal' memory and its insistent perforation of Ovid's epic narrative, the Pasiphae myth can be seen to act in a similar manner to the House of Atreus in Homer's *Odyssey*: both emerge as lingering subtexts that act as cautionary paradigms that threaten not only to pervade the text in which they are contained but, in so doing, to also overwhelm them. In order to more clearly establish the productive parallels that emerge between these mythic subtexts as they are presented in Homer and Ovid's epics, this discussion will now turn to a more detailed consideration of Agamemnon's *nostos* as it is presented in the *Odyssey* – a detour that will inform and enrich our understanding of the function of Pasiphae's lacunose presence in the *Metamorphoses*.

Agamemnon's tragic *nostos*, culminating in his death through the machinations of his wife Clytemnestra and her lover Aegisthus, is alluded to with alarming regularity within Homer's *Odyssey* (Hom. *Od*. 1.28–43; 1.298–300; 3.306–316; 11.405–435). Katz pertinently notes that these allusions, having been sung within the context of the oral poetry of the *Odyssey* itself, allow for their entrance within the epic tradition and thus threaten Odysseus' own *nostos*. The allusions to Agamemnon's fate thereby 'construct an authoritative account of *nostos* toward which the story of Odysseus' return is drawn in the ensuing books of the poem.'[26] This might be inferred from the numerous allusions made to the House of Atreus in respect to Odysseus' *nostos*: at the very outset of the epic Zeus relates Aegisthus' seduction of Clytemnestra to the other gods present at the counsel (Hom. *Od*. 1.28–43); Telemachus is repeatedly exhorted to look to the paradigm of Orestes, which invites the audience to recognise Telemachus' capacity for comparable retributive justice directed towards the suitors who threaten his family's wealth and honour (Hom. *Od*. 1.298–300; 3.306–16); and Odysseus encounters Agamemnon during his *katabasis*, which allows Agamemnon to relate his ignominious death at the hands of his wife and her lover upon his return to Mycenae (Hom. *Od*. 11.405–435). The *nekyia* scene is particularly telling in this respect; having

---

25 Cf. Armstrong (2006) 61 for the principle of 'personal memory'.
26 Katz (1991) 20.

first exhorted Penelope's virtue and chastity in comparison to Clytemnestra, Agamemnon then advises Odysseus to remain aware of the potential fate that could befall him on his return to Ithaca:

> ἄλλο δέ τοι ἐρέω, σὺ δ' ἐνὶ φρεσὶ βάλλεο σῇσιν·
> κρύβδην, μηδ' ἀναφανδά, φίλην ἐς πατρίδα γαῖαν
> νῆα κατισχέμεναι· ἐπεὶ οὐκέτι πιστὰ γυναιξίν.
>
> And put away in your heart this other thing that I tell you. When you bring your ship in to your own dear country, do it secretly, not in the open. There is no trusting in women.[27]
>
> Hom. *Od.* 11.454–456.

These allusions rouse both Odysseus' 'personal memory' and the audience's 'poetic memory' in a manner designed to provoke anxiety in both, as both literary and personal remembrance note the danger that parallels with the House of Atreus imply for Odysseus and for the narrative trajectory of the epic itself. These allusions to the House of Atreus create a 'process of manipulative narrative misdirection,'[28] which nonetheless threatens the *telos* of the text through the presence of a dangerous paradigm. The evocation of Pasiphae, and the female sexual *furor* of which she is paradigmatic, is similarly insidious in Ovid's *Metamorphoses* but is, as with the House of Atreus in Homer's *Odyssey*, circumscribed by poetic *ars*. Odysseus, unlike Agamemnon, is successfully reinstated within his kingdom, in spite of the variform mortal and divine machinations that beset his *nostos*. Pasiphae and the monstrous creature her aggressive sexuality births are similarly successfully contained and suppressed through poetic *ars*. The threat Pasiphae embodies, however, is less immediately self-evident than that posed by the paradigm of the House of Atreus in the *Odyssey*. I propose that the paradoxical eroticism of the literary figure of the Cretan woman, who is simultaneously enticing and abhorrent, poses a threat in its reception and the potential it has to incite dangerous imitation and reification.

3 Ovid's labyrinthine epic

It is significant that Ovid situates the construction of the labyrinth directly after Scylla's indictment of Pasiphae's sexual conduct and Minos' moral decrepitude. The revelation that knowledge about Pasiphae's bestiality, and the subsequent

---

[27] Translation taken from Lattimore (2007).
[28] Olson (1990) 63.

birth of the Minotaur, has spread beyond Crete provokes Minos to seek to contain this knowledge through Daedalus' greatest artistic enterprise: the labyrinth. The labyrinth has proven to be a fecund transhistorical metaphor that facilitates moments of self-reflection in literature about complex artistic processes.[29] The Daedalian labyrinth in Ovid's *Metamorphoses* is likewise suitably replete with poetological potential. In describing the complex construction of the Cretan labyrinth and its bewildering design in Book 8 of the *Metamorphoses*, Ovid likens its structure to the river Maeander. This is an original epic simile that equates the construction's winding course with comparable circuitous patterns found in the natural world:[30]

> non secus ac liquidus Phrygiis Maeandros in Arvis
> ludit et ambiguo lapsu refluitque fluitque
> occurrensque sibi venturas aspicit undas
> et nunc ad fontes, nunc ad mare versus apertum
> incertas exercet aquas: ita Daedalus implet
> innumeras errore vias vixque ipse reverti
> ad limen potuit: tanta est fallacia tecti.

> Just as the watery Maeander plays in the Phrygian fields, flows back and forth in doubtful course and, turning back on itself, beholds its own waves coming on their way, and sends its uncertain waters now towards their source and now towards the open sea: so Daedalus made those innumerable winding passages, and was himself scarce able to find his way back to the place of entry, so deceptive was the enclosure he had built.
>
> Ov. *Met.* 8.162–168

Ovid's description of the labyrinth here evokes the meandering structure of the *Metamorphoses* itself, as numerous scholars have noted.[31] The poem's similarly

---

[29] On the labyrinth as a metaphor, particularly in classical and early Christian literature, consult Reed Doob (1990) 64–91. There Reed Doob highlights three metaphorical usages of the labyrinth: the first is the labyrinth as a sign of complex artistry; the second is the labyrinth as a sign of inextricability and impenetrability; and the third is the labyrinth as a symbol of a difficult process, which often has a didactic function. See also Reed Doob (1990) 17–38 for an overview of the representation of labyrinths in the works of Pliny, Vergil, and Ovid. Cf. Armstrong (2006) 134 who likewise notes the self-reflexive quality of labyrinths in ancient literature.

[30] On the novelty of Ovid's use of the river Maeander as a metaphor to describe the labyrinth constructed by Daedalus in contrast to prior representations in the works of Homer, Catullus, and Vergil (all of whom describe the labyrinth by way of *ekphrasis*) see Armstrong (2006) 137. Cf. Pavlock (2009) 64.

[31] The structural similarities between the labyrinth, the river Maeander, and Ovid's epic have been noted by Armstrong (2006) 137–8, Weiden-Boyd (2006) 183–4, Barolsky (2007) 109–10, 115, and Pavlock (2009) 62, 65–6. Note also Lateiner (1984) 18 who suggestively describes the poem

teasing course subverts the expectations of a traditional ancient epic narrative, which, though by no means necessarily linear, typically follows a progressive narrative associated with the fate of the epic protagonist(s).[32] Ovid contrastingly employs polyphonic narratives in the *Metamorphoses* that confound the trajectory traditionally associated with epic protagonists and orchestrates heteroglossia by incorporating a range of genres within his poem,[33] including ones traditionally conceptualised in ancient Rome as *nugae* ('trifles') in contrast to epic.[34] One such instance of heteroglossia is evident in Ovid's use of water imagery as a

---

as being like a 'confusing tapestry' or a labyrinth after having analysed the representation of the artists Arachne and Daedalus in Ovid's epic. Cf. Weiden Boyd (2006) 171–203 for the suggestion that the labyrinth's construction in Book 8, at the very centre of Ovid's fifteen-book epic, 'creates a model for further reading' through the representation of Daedalus who at turns may be interpreted either as a parallel for the poet Ovid, who constructs his own poetic labyrinth, and for the reader, for whom he models 'the hermeneutic skills needed to understand the (narrative) journey' of Ovid's poem. Consult Janan (1991) 243 for the argument that the river Maeander is an artistic paradigm and organisational pattern for Book 9 specifically, as well as offering a sexual paradigm for the incestuous desire of the river Maeander's granddaughter Byblis for her twin Caunus recounted in Ov. *Met.* 9.446–665, since Byblis likewise turns inwards on herself in her rejection of exogamic relationships.

32 On the structure and narratological complexity of Ovid's epic, see Wheeler (2000), Barchiesi (2001) 49–78 and Barchiesi (2002) 180–99. Sharrock (2019) 277–8 has recently argued that of Ovid's generic transgressions and innovations in the *Metamorphoses*, the 'problem of continuity' created as a result of the poem's labyrinthine structure constitutes one of the most serious challenges to its classification as an epic poem, even as it makes claims for continuity as a *carmen perpetuum*. For further details about Ovid's engagement with and divergence from conventional epic *topoi*, see Sharrock (2019) 275–311.

33 Speaking of 'polyphonic narratives' here is both a literal acknowledgement of the numerous voices that Ovid incorporates within the complex narratological structure of the *Metamorphoses* and is also utilised in order to evoke Bakhtin's use of the term and consideration of the 'polyphonic' text in 'Discourse in the Novel'. Bakhtin's conception of polyphony is inherently democratic, in which the central tenet is that all utterances, however variable, are considered equal. Although Bakhtin notes that poetry has a tendency towards monoglossia, the *Metamorphoses*, with its interwoven myths and narratives, might well be considered to be polyphonic in its structure and to thereby orchestrate heteroglossia both by way of this narratological polyphony and through the incorporation of other genres. Cf. Barchiesi (2001) 49 who suggests that the *Metamorphoses* is not 'truly polyphonic'. Barchiesi posits that '[m]ore than polyphony one should speak of *polyeideia*, of multiformity, a term that seems to be foreshadowed by the *mutatae... formae* of *Met.* 1.1.' This assessment, however, seems to create an unnecessary distinction between polyphony and *polyeideia* which coexist and contribute to the complexity of Ovid's epic narrative.

34 Consult Fitzgerald (2019) 22 for details about how generic affiliations in Latin literature consistently characterise epic as the 'unmarked term' against which other genres often (pejoratively and passive aggressively) situate themselves. On Ovid's incorporation of multiple genres within his epic project see Ntanou in this volume.

means of conveying the structural complexity of Daedalus' artistic creation. This, in turn, recalls the polemical jargon of Callimachean aesthetic and stylistic principles propounded by the Latin love elegists, amongst others, in the Augustan period. The great, yet refuse-ridden Euphrates is utilised by Callimachus as a metaphor for the conventional and uninspired neo-Homeric epic abhorred by Apollo and, by extension, the poet himself in the *Hymn to Apollo*.[35] Ovid's Maeander is the antithesis of Callimachus' pedestrian Euphrates, with its playfulness and dynamic capacity to change direction unexpectedly and turn inwards upon itself.[36] Ovid's Maeander thereby emphasises the extent to which the *Metamorphoses* will confound epic expectations, not least by employing seemingly incompatible Callimachean and neoteric aesthetic principles within it. As well as facilitating metapoetic reflections and inter-generic fertilisation within Ovid's epic narrative, the polyphonic quality of the *Metamorphoses* simultaneously attests to the gargantuan aspirations of Ovid's epic project. The unifying theme of metamorphosis (which facilitates this polyphony in all its variations) is employed in order to narrate from the beginning of the world up until the poet's own lifetime (*ab origine mundi | ad mea perpetuum deducite tempora carmen*; Ov. *Met.* 1.3–4). The structural complexity of Ovid's poetic *ars*, with its narratological polyphony and incorporated genres, augments the bewildering nature of the *Metamorphoses* and points to its labyrinthine quality. Just as Daedalus constructs the Cretan labyrinth, so too Ovid creates a comparably labyrinthine epic.

The bewildering construction of the Cretan labyrinth threatens to overwhelm even the craftsman who created it: despite being a celebrated artisan (*ingenio fabrae celeberrimus artis*; Ov. *Met.* 8.159), Daedalus is scarcely able to retrace his own steps (Ov. *Met.* 8.168). Armstrong suggests that this points threateningly to the prospect of an artist becoming trapped or lost within their own work.[37] This invites comparison with the task of composing an epic poem, especially one as vast and complex as the *Metamorphoses*. I would add that Daedalus' confusion and the threat of misdirection within this construction gestures obliquely towards another attribute of the Cretan labyrinth that has been overlooked in prior discussions of the *Metamorphoses*-as-labyrinth. As well as serving as a paradigm of artistic accomplishment and complexity, the labyrinth is also primarily designed to function as a prison for the Minotaur born of Pasiphae's bestial passion. If Ovid's epic poem is a labyrinthine text whose structure and complexity mirrors

---

35 Callim. *Hymn* 2.108–9. Cf. Prop. 2.10.13. There the elegiac poet invokes the image of the Euphrates after claiming he will abandon elegiac poetry in favour of singing about epic themes.
36 Likewise noted by Armstrong (2006) 137 and Pavlock (2009) 64.
37 Armstrong (2006) 137–8.

Daedalus' creation, is it likewise simultaneously a self-referential artwork and a form of artistic imprisonment? If so, what precisely does Ovid's poem artistically contain and repress? The labyrinthine nature of the *Metamorphoses* invites metapoetic exploration by pursuing and extending this poetological analogy.

I contend that Ovid contains within his poetry an analogous 'Minotaur' to that produced by Pasiphae's bestial union: the 'Minotaur' at the heart of Ovid's labyrinthine poetry is female sexual *furor* embodied in the figure of Pasiphae, who is contained and repressed within the *Metamorphoses*. Thus, Pasiphae becomes more than merely a cautionary myth: through permeating numerous narratives, she becomes an emblematic paradigm of female sexual *furor,* an absent presence, which is repressed and held in check by Ovid's poetic *ars*. Armstrong, in her penetrating analysis of the representation of Cretan women in Latin literature, examines the incongruity that inherently problematises art, considered to be the epitome of civilised pursuits, containing wild and violent passions. She aptly compares the fascination that Pasiphae inspired in the Roman imagination to the cultural preoccupation with violent spectacle in the arena, which exemplifies that within civilisation lies the morbid yearning for its very antithesis.[38] Ovid engages with this culturally embedded preoccupation with transgression, particularly of a sexual nature, through his own poetic spectacle: his *ars* shapes a controlled display of Pasiphae's transgressive sexuality, which is safely circumscribed within the poetic confines that paradoxically display it. The success of this enterprise is evident in the increasingly oblique references to Pasiphae after Ovid's description of the construction of the labyrinth in the aftermath of Scylla's tirade, which points to the wider metapoetic agenda of the *Metamorphoses* itself as a labyrinthine text: it is an innovative, artistic means of repressing transgressive female sexuality, as embodied in the figure of the Cretan woman.

4 Artistic precedents: Vergil's *Aeneid* and Daedalus' creations

The potential of art to control and suppress violent eroticism, which both titillates and disgusts, exhibits cultural concerns about the poetic potential for morally dangerous receptions of poetic art. Aristotle's representation of poetry in the *Poetics* asserts that poetic art is the imitation of human nature (Arist. *Poet.* 1448a). This assertion, in Heath's estimation, reflects Aristotle's understanding of human

---

38 Armstrong (2006) 14.

nature as inherently inquisitive and imitative which is reflected in poetry itself (Arist. *Poet.* 1448b), and deemed by Aristotle to be 'an expression of a human instinct for mimesis.'[39] Despite being notoriously problematic to define, Aristotle's conception of mimesis nevertheless points to the significance of imitation as a crucial part of art and, if extended to refer to a reception-centred view of art, entails a certain anxiety. This interpretation, in conjunction with the Aristotelian focus on the mimetic quality of human nature, illuminates anxieties in Roman epic: namely, the potential for art, particularly poetic *ars*, to inspire corresponding morality to that it commemorates and portrays. This anxiety is apparent within the epic poetry of both Ovid and Vergil, both of whom negotiate the emblem of the Cretan labyrinth. As the perennial symbol of artistic mastery over the monstrous, the labyrinth as it is presented in Vergil and Ovid's epics signifies the dangers of art and, by extension, what it represses.

Vergil exemplifies this in the compelling quality attributed to Daedalus' artistic renderings of the myths associated with the royal house of Crete over Aeneas and his fellow Trojans in Book 6 of the *Aeneid*, which largely concern Daedalus' abetting of unnatural, female sexual desire. As Kirichenko highlights, 'these pictorial representations, despite their highly disturbing character, [...] amount to a visually coherent triumphal celebration of Daedalus' art':[40]

> contra elata mari respondet Cnosia tellus:
> hic crudelis amor tauri suppostaque furto
> Pasiphae mixtumque genus prolesque biformis
> Minotaurus inest, Veneris monumenta nefandae;
> hic labor ille domus et inextricabilis error;
> magnum reginae sed enim miseratus amorem
> Daedalus ipse dolos tecti ambagesque resolvit,
> caeca regens filo vestigia.
>
> Opposite, rising from the sea, the Cretan land faces this; here is the cruel love of the bull, Pasiphae craftily mated, and the mongrel breed of the Minotaur, a hybrid offspring, record of monstrous love; there that house of toil, a maze inextricable; but Daedalus, pitying the

---

39 Heath (1996) xiii.
40 Kirichenko (2013) 76. See also, Fitzgerald (1984) 54–5 who notes that Daedalus' part in the story of Pasiphae and the creation of the labyrinth is not mentioned by Vergil in this *ekphrasis*, indicating that Daedalus is exculpating himself in a revisionist version of his mythological past. This mirrors Ovid's pointed underplaying of Daedalus' role in Pasiphae's conception of the Minotaur in the *Metamorphoses*, discussed above.

princess's great love, himself unwound the deceptive tangle of the palace, guiding blind feet with the thread.[41]

Verg. Aen. 6.23–30

The captivating nature of the Vergilian *ekphrasis*, along with the transgressive female sexuality it depicts, is such that the Cumaean sibyl averts Aeneas' attention and so interrupts it (Verg. Aen. 6.37–9). It can be adduced from this instance that the sibyl's actions reflect this concern with the potential of art inspiring mimesis of the immoral passions it depicts within its audience.[42] Indeed, Vergil attests that the Trojans would have continued to stare at the friezes until the culmination of its narrative *telos* had the sibyl failed to intervene and divert their prurient attention from such *spectacula* ('spectacles'): *quin protinus omnia | perlegerent oculis* ('and all the tale throughout would their eyes have scanned'; Verg. Aen. 6.33–4). The depiction and commemoration of Pasiphae upon the temple frieze aptly demonstrates the potential of art to inspire dangerous mimesis, as the very image recalls the recurrent motif within the Pasiphae myth of the failure of artistic endeavours to repress sexual *furor*. The wooden heifer, devised by Daedalus to contain Pasiphae and allow her to consummate her desire for the Cretan bull, only temporarily contains the sexual *furor* she embodies as it enables a false metamorphosis. Pasiphae's body, itself metamorphic in its pregnant state, is similarly impermanent as it can only temporarily contain the Minotaur, which it ultimately bears forth. The impermanent containment offered by Pasiphae's pregnant body is attested to in the *Metamorphoses*, as Ovid implies that it is the revelation of the Minotaur upon its birth that testifies to Pasiphae's bestial union. This bodily impermanence is reflected in the language Ovid uses to relate the discovery of Pasiphae's bestial adultery: *creverat obprobrium generis, foedumque patebat matris adulterium monstri novitate biformis* ('But now his family's disgrace had grown big, and the queen's foul adultery was revealed to all by her strange hybrid monster-child'; Ov. Met. 8.155–6). Ovid's use of the verb *pateo* here, though not linguistically associated with birth, invites a semantic interpre-

---

41 Translation is taken from H. Rushton Fairclough (1999; revised by G.P Goold).
42 Cf. Kirichenko (2013) 86 whose analysis of pictorial images in Vergil's *Aeneid* partly concludes that the *Aeneid* 'self-reflexively encourages the recipient to construct his/her reading experience as a notional imitation of the encounters with visual images enacted within the narrative'. Although Kirichenko suggests that this experience is subsequently used to modify the extradiegetic audience's 'perception of empirically familiar visual images' the focus here upon imitation gestures towards the threat posed by Daedalus' Cretan friezes not only to the intradiegetic audience of Aeneas and his fellow Trojans, but to Vergil's extradiegetic audience also.

tation of its associations with exposure (including exposure to danger) and visibility as connoting birth.⁴³ The exposure of the Minotaur and the bestial union that produced it is associated with its visibility as it is expelled from Pasiphae's body: the pregnant body can thus only offer transient containment of female sexual *furor*.

In her extensive analysis of Vergil's representation of art throughout the *Aeneid*, Bartsch emphasises that the failure of art to contain destructive passions is a recurring motif, in which the 'viewer of artistic scenes of violence in particular suffers a kind of infection, as if he were driven to imitate *furor* in art by *furor* in life.'⁴⁴ Vergil negotiates the 'mimetic striving' of art and depicts the means by which they might paradoxically 'further the interests of violence even as they literally hold it in.'⁴⁵ In his representation of Daedalus' rendering of the Cretan labyrinth in the *ekphrasis* of the doors at the temple of Cumaean Apollo, Vergil presents artistic endeavour as being compromised as it is invariably breached, resulting in the disintegration of societal norms.⁴⁶ The figure of Pasiphae, and artistic representations of her bestial lust, likewise serve to highlight the mimetic potential of her moral decrepitude to inspire a corresponding *furor* in others. The mimesis and fascination that Cretan women inspire in those who gaze upon them arouse anxieties for the need of their suppression and containment within art, a requisite that is never quite realised in the *Aeneid*. The denial of a distinct narrative pertaining to Pasiphae and her sexual misdemeanour in the *Metamorphoses* assuages this Roman anxiety of the mimetic capacity of art. Unlike Vergil, Ovid's labyrinthine text allows for the repression of the figure of Pasiphae within art and precludes the potential for it to be breached. In this respect, Ovid both surpasses his Latin epic predecessor and counteracts the recurrent motif of impermanence regarding Pasiphae's artistic containment.

Moreover, the emblem of the labyrinth, particularly regarding Ovid's labyrinthine poetic *ars*, engages in poetic allusion that encourages comparison with Vergil's depiction of the labyrinth in the *ekphrasis* discussed above. Conte's theoretical perspectives concerning literary allusion are particularly pertinent to interpretations of Ovidian engagement with Vergilian modes of description. Poetic allusion, particularly in the case of the *Metamorphoses*, is more complex than a simple recollection of previous works, as the text situates itself in contrast with its epic predecessors in order to 'compete with the tradition recalled' which is

---

43 *OLD* 1440 s.v. *pateo* 4, 6.
44 Bartsch (1998) 334.
45 Bartsch (1998) 325–6.
46 Bartsch (1998) 324.

achieved through 'opposition or differentiation or a relationship merely of variation.'[47] Vergil's labyrinth, as mentioned previously, is frequently compromised in spite of being described as *inextricabilis* ('inextricable'; Verg. Aen. 6.27). The labyrinthine composition of Ovid's poetry, by contrast, resists this. Conte states that:

> In the art of allusion, as in every rhetorical figure, the poetry lies in the simultaneous presence of two different realities that try to indicate a single reality. The single reality can perhaps never be defined directly, but it is specific and is known to the poet.[48]

Though Conte tentatively refutes the logical fallacy that the existence of these variant poetic realities, which rely upon poetic remembrance of literary predecessors, invariably results in the ambition to supersede these predecessors,[49] I would suggest that in the case of Ovid's epic this interpretative strategy is invited. The Vergilian poetic 'reality' of the labyrinth as an artistic emblem that has the potential to be breached is discredited by Ovid's poetry, which is itself a labyrinth that resists encroachment upon its integrity. Rather than maintaining the Vergilian image of the labyrinth as an artistic emblem Ovid renders it poetic 'reality', and thus surpasses his epic predecessor with regards to artistic composition: Pasiphae, the very paradigm of Cretan female sexual *furor*, is artfully contained and thereby counteracts anxieties present in the *Aeneid* concerning its release. This metapoetic reading of the *Metamorphoses* as a labyrinthine text, in which Ovid contains his 'Minotaur' (transgressive female sexuality) results in poetic posturing that equates Ovid to the figure of Daedalus.[50] Thus, Ovid as artist seeks to surpass not only Vergil, his Latin epic predecessor, but also the mythical epitome of artistic ingenuity and *hubris*: Daedalus. This reading is in keeping with Barolsky's understanding of the *Metamorphoses* as Ovid's attempt to situate his poetry as the culmination of artistic endeavour:

> Sculpture, architecture, painting, weaving, handicraft, poetry, song, storytelling, and rhetoric are brought together in *Metamorphoses* in a prodigious synthetic art, of which Ovid is the ultimate author, the artist who embodies and unifies all of the arts. In short, Ovid as artist is the supreme hero of his own epic.[51]

---

47 Conte (1986) 36.
48 Conte (1986) 38–39.
49 Conte (1986) 38.
50 On Daedalus as a parallel of the poet Ovid, see Weiden Boyd (2006) 178–9 and Pavlock (2009) 61–88.
51 Barolsky (2007) 108. See also Leach (1974) 135 and Lateiner (1984) 18–9 who each argue that in spite of the persistent theme of artistic failure and the destruction of artists and/or artworks

Ovid achieves this pre-eminence in his innovative description of Daedalus' labyrinth, which not only serves to distance the *Metamorphoses* from the *Aeneid* but also displays the inadequacies of Daedalus' artistic ingenuity, which lies precisely in its impermanence.[52]

The delineation of the labyrinth in the *Metamorphoses* pointedly emphasises its association with nature, as can be inferred from the aforementioned epic simile likening it to the river Maeander. This association between Daedalus and nature highlights the flaw inherent to the craftsman's *ars*, since Ovid's *Metamorphoses* repeatedly attests to the insubstantiality of nature as depicted through the unifying theme of the epic: the metamorphosis of 'natural' forms. Daedalus' ingenious but ultimately ineffectual imitation of nature is apparent in the narrative of Daedalus and Icarus' tragic attempt to escape Crete in Book 8, pointedly related immediately after Ovid's account of the creation of the labyrinth. The labyrinth is an artistic contrivance designed for the express purpose of containing and suppressing female sexual *furor*, embodied in the figure of the Minotaur, yet is nevertheless repeatedly breached by the Athenian victims sacrificed to the creature and mastered by the contrivances of Ariadne and Theseus (Ov. *Met.* 8.169–173). The waxen wings that Daedalus creates in his attempt to escape his incarceration in Crete likewise underscore the artisan's incredible capacity to mimic nature. Upon recognising that although Minos rules over all things he has no power to control the air (*omnia possideat, non possidet aera Minos*; Ov. *Met.* 8.187), Daedalus sets about simulating wing-patterns that might be discerned from the natural world in order to escape from Minos' tyrannical power and so end his exile: *dixit et ignotas animum dimittit in artes | naturamque novat* ('So saying, he sets his mind at work upon unknown arts, and changes the laws of nature'; Ov. *Met.* 8.188–9); a line that conceptually mirrors Ovid's epic ambitions as outlined in the opening lines of the *Metamorphoses*.[53] Ultimately, however, this imitation of nature is revealed to be entirely superficial, as Icarus' subsequent *hubris* and death

---

in the *Metamorphoses* Ovid nevertheless emerges as a triumphant artist figure who does not share in the fate of other artists in his epic.

52 On the theme of artistic failure in the *Metamorphoses* consult the seminal studies of Leach (1974) 102–35 and Lateiner (1984) 13–8.

53 Ov. Met. 1.1–4: *In nova fert animus mutatas dicere formas | corpora; di, coeptis (nam vos mutastis et illas) | adspirate meis primaque ab origine mundi | ad mea perpetuum deducite tempora carmen!* ('My mind is bent to tell of bodies changed into new forms. Ye gods, for you yourselves have wrought the changes, breathe on these my undertakings, and bring down my song in unbroken strains from the world's very beginning even unto the present time.')

tragically exposes (Ov. *Met.* 8.225–235).⁵⁴ For Leach, Ovid's representation of the Daedalian labyrinth and the waxen wings 'suggest the artist's inability to predict or control the consequences of his own art.'⁵⁵ It is also notable that these narratives highlight Daedalus' inability to master nature. Moreover, nature, as established previously, is particularly transient with regards to the figure of Pasiphae; Daedalus' artistry similarly only allows for temporary metamorphosis and containment. Pasiphae is temporarily encased in a wooden heifer, which, as Scylla recounts, was so life-like that it 'deceived the savage bull' (*quae torvum ligno decepit adultera taurum*; Ov. *Met.* 8.132), yet she is ultimately released from its artistic confines. Though his artistry is capable of deceiving nature, Daedalus' craftsmanship cannot exert genuine mastery over nature and bestow the permanence that Ovid's poetry grants.

The futility of imitating nature is evident in both Vergil and Ovid's respective epics, as Pasiphae's own metamorphic, pregnant body provides impermanent containment of her sexual *furor*, for it ultimately releases the monstrous offspring that attests to her bestial union.⁵⁶ It is evident that even nature, which transcends

---

54 Cf. Dinter (2019) 101–2 for whom Daedalus' wings constitute an 'imperfect intermedial product [...] Although the manufactured wings resemble those of birds, they do not fully metamorphose into living, beating wings which would ostensibly have facilitated a more successful flight.'
55 Leach (1974) 118. Cf. Lateiner (1984) 17–18.
56 Ov. *Met.* 8.155: Pasiphae's adultery is 'exposed' in her offspring (*foedumque patebat | matris adulterium monstri novitate biformis*). Cf. Verg. *Aen.* 6.26: The Minotaur is a monument to *nefas* ('a forbidden deed or act', 'sin') and perverse eroticism: *Veneris monumenta nefandae*. A parallel for this aspect of the Pasiphae myth can be found in Orpheus' representation of the birth of Adonis as a result of the incestuous union between Myrrha and her father Cinyras at Ov. *Met.* 10.503–17. Myrrha's sexual *furor*, like Pasiphae's, defies metamorphic containment by way of her pregnant body as she too births a child that bears testament to the consummation of her taboo desires after she has been transformed into a myrrh tree. Yet Adonis is no monstrous Minotaur. Upon his birth Ovid describes Adonis' bodily beauty as recalling paintings of Cupids (*qualia namque | corpora nudorum tabula pinguntur Amorum, | talis erat*; 'for he looked like one of the naked loves portrayed on canvas.') Emeljanow (1969) 70 argues that the supernatural beauty Adonis possesses is indicative of the abnormality of his conception and birth, which is microcosmically representative of the unnaturalness that characterises love and sexuality in Book 10. I would argue further that Orpheus' detail equating Adonis' beauty to that of a painting is pointed; Myrrha's sexual *furor*, which is temporarily contained through her metamorphosis into a myrrh tree by an unidentified divine force, is successfully contained by Ovid within art: poetic *ars* renders Adonis, the manifestation of Myrrha's sexual *furor*, art. Thus Adonis, like the Minotaur, is contained by art in such a way that reflects the wider metapoetic striving of Ovid's labyrinthine text which is itself designed to contain and suppress deviant passions. For further details about the Myrrha narrative in Ovid's *Metamorphoses*, as well as for a discussion about how the focalisation of this

Daedalus' craftsmanship, only offers temporary metamorphosis and suppression of Cretan sexual *furor* as opposed to that offered by the poet which grants containment *ad perpetuum*. This is evident in Iphis' soliloquy later in the *Metamorphoses* in which she laments her lack of a Daedalus figure to assist her in deceiving the world of her biological gender. Iphis nevertheless acknowledges the futility of Daedalus' art which cannot confer genuine bodily metamorphosis:

> huc licet ex toto sollertia confluat orbe
> ipse licet revolet ceratis Daedalus alis,
> quid faciet? num me puerum de virgine doctis
> artibus efficiet?

> Though all the ingenuity in the world should be collected here, though Daedalus himself should fly back on waxen wings, what could he do? With all his learned arts could he make me into a boy from a girl?
> Ov. *Met.* 9.741–4.

The close association between *ars* and artifice within the *Metamorphoses* is well attested and appositely summarised by Barolsky, who notes the frequency with which 'Ovid transforms a detail of nature into the artifice of craftsmanship.'[57] This association is crucial to Ovid's depiction of Daedalus as a craftsman who strives to imitate nature, yet also one that acknowledges the limitations of his own art which fails to truly master the natural world, as in the aforementioned instance of the wooden heifer. The futility of Daedalus' art and the craftsman's introspective acknowledgement of his artistic limitations are apparent in his overwhelming jealousy of his nephew Perdix, whose story is incorporated within Ovid's aetiological tale of the partridge immediately following Icarus' untimely demise in Book 8.[58] Perdix was entrusted to Daedalus' tutelage, but upon discovering Perdix's artistic *ingenium* ('genius'), Daedalus, in an act of jealousy, sought to destroy him by hurling the child from the citadel of Minerva. However, Perdix was saved by the providence of the goddess Minerva and metamorphosed into the partridge (Ov. *Met.* 8.240–55). Ovid stresses in this narrative that Daedalus' envy is incited as a direct result of the child's mastery of the forms and structures

---

narrative through the intradiegetic narrator Orpheus distinguishes this treatment of the theme of incest from Ovid's representation of Byblis' desire for her twin Caunus at Ov. *Met.* 9.454–665, see Nagle (1983) 301–15.
57 Barolsky (2007) 110–1.
58 For Ovid's aetiological account of the partridge and Perdix's attempted murder by Daedalus, see Ov. *Met.* 8.236–259. On the interrelation between the tales of Daedalus and Icarus and Daedalus and Perdix, see Faber (1998) 80–9.

perceptible in the natural world, which inspires his inventions and attests to his superior genius (Ov. *Met.* 8.240–55). Perdix observes the natural world and imitates it in a manner that Daedalus can only strive to emulate, as evidenced in Perdix's invention of the common handsaw modelled on the patterns of bones he had observed on the spine of a fish:

> ille etiam medio spinas in pisce notatas
> traxit in exemplum ferroque incidit acuto
> perpetuos dentes et serrae repperit usum.
>
> This boy, moreover, observed the backbone of a fish and, taking it as a model, cut a row of teeth in a thin strip of iron and thus invented the saw.
>
> Ov. *Met.* 8.244–6

Although Padel rightly acknowledges that Daedalus' eminence as an artist is exhibited throughout ancient depictions of Cretan myth through his capacity to confuse the possibilities of the human body,[59] it is apparent that in the *Metamorphoses* Ovid presents his poetic art as being infinitely superior in contrast to that of the master craftsman. Daedalus' *ars* can only *imitate* nature, whereas Ovid's poetic *ars* allows for the *genuine* alteration of nature through metamorphosis, as exhibited in the case of Iphis whom the poet transforms into the male figure s/he has hitherto performed (Ov. *Met.* 9.786–91). Within this narrative, poetic art renders the 'natural' gender binary fluid and emphasises that genuine mastery over nature is the prerogative of the poet.

5 Conclusion

As this discussion of the *Metamorphoses* has outlined, Ovid mobilises 'poetic memory' to signal how his epic surpasses both poetic predecessors and mythical antecedents by way of his labyrinthine poetic *ars*. The superiority of Ovid's labyrinthine epic relies upon its perpetual containment and suppression of violent, female sexuality embodied in the figure of Pasiphae as the pinnacle of Cretan erotic misdemeanour. The labyrinth is not only a perennial symbol of self-referential artistry but also reflects the capacity of art to master and contain the monstrous. Both Vergil and Daedalus make manifest the Roman concern with the failure of art resulting in the violent release of the passions contained and

---

[59] Padel (1996) 81.

commemorated within it and in doing so attest to Ovid's artistic pre-eminence, as well as his capacity to more effectively assuage anxieties about the mimetic capacity of art. Artistic endeavour in both Vergil's epic and Daedalus' creations ultimately fail to contain Cretan sexual *furor*. Moreover, Ovid is capable of navigating his labyrinthine creation in a manner that Daedalus cannot, since the craftsman can barely retrace his own steps once he has completed his tortuous creation. Ovid presents himself, and his poetic art, as the culmination and pinnacle of poetic artistry that truly surpasses all prior craftsmanship and nature in its ability to successfully manage and suppress violent passions. It is, however, somewhat ironic that in order to express his artistic confinement of the figure of Pasiphae, the embodiment of ruinous, female sexual *furor*, in a compelling manner Ovid must allow her to pervade his work; although the poet does not make any references to Pasiphae himself, she nevertheless infiltrates the epic through the memories and intradiegetic narrations of Scylla, Iphis, and Hippolytus. It appears that to acknowledge the success of his poetic containment of female sexual *furor*, Ovid must commemorate Pasiphae's grotesque sexuality through a controlled artistic spectacle. This feature of Ovid's *ars* nevertheless alerts the audience to the potential this malicious paradigm has to overwhelm the labyrinthine contrivance of the *Metamorphoses*.

Bibliography

Armstrong, R. (2006), *Cretan Women: Pasiphae, Ariadne, and Phaedra in Latin Poetry*, Oxford.
Bakhtin, M.M. (1981), *Dialogic Imagination: Four Essays* (trans. M. Holquist), Austin.
Barchiesi, A. (2001), "Voices and Narrative 'Instances' in the *Metamorphoses*", in A. Barchiesi, M. Fox and S. Marchesi (eds.), *Speaking Volumes: Narrative and intertext in Ovid and other Latin poets*, London: 49–78.
Barchiesi, A. (2002), "Narrative technique and narratology in the *Metamorphoses*", in P. Hardie (ed.), *The Cambridge Companion to Ovid*, Cambridge: 180–199.
Barolsky, P. (2007), "Ovid's Protean Epic of Art", *Arion* 14 (3): 107–120.
Bartsch, S. (1998), "*Ars* And The Man: The Politics Of Art In Virgil's *Aeneid*", *Classical Philology* 93 (4): 322–342.
Bergmann, B. (2017), "The Lineup: Passion, Transgression, and Mythical Women in Roman Painting", *Eugesta* 7: 199–246.
Blumenfeld-Kosinski, R. (1996), "The Scandal of Pasiphae: Narration and Interpretation in the 'Ovide moralisé'", *Modern Philology* 93 (3): 307–326.
Brooten, B.J. (1996), *Love Between Women: Early Christian Responses to Female Homoeroticism*, Chicago.
Coleman, K.M. (1990), "Fatal Charades: Roman Executions Staged as Mythological Enactments", *The Journal of Roman Studies* 80: 44–73.

Conte, G.B. (1986), *The Rhetoric of Imitation: Genre and Poetic Memory in Virgil and Other Latin Poets* (ed. and trans. C. Segal), Ithaca.
Dinter, M.T. (2019), "Intermediality in the *Metamorphoses*", *Trends in Classics: Journal of Classical Studies* 11 (1): 96–118.
Emeljanow, V. (1969), "Ovidian Mannerism: An Analysis of the Venus and Adonis Episode in *Met.* X 503–738", *Mnemosyne* 22 (1): 67–76.
Faber, R. (1998), "Daedalus, Icarus, and the Fall of Perdix: Continuity and Allusion in *Metamorphoses* 8.183–259", *Hermes*, Bd., H. 1: 80–89.
Fitzgerald, W. (1984), "Aeneas, Daedalus and the Labyrinth", *Arethusa* 17 (1): 51–65.
Fitzgerald, W. (2019), "Claiming Inferiority: Weakness into Strength", in S. Matzner & S. Harrison (eds.), *Complex Inferiorities: The Poetics of the Weaker Voice in Latin Literature*, Oxford.
Fowler, D. (2000), *Roman Constructions: Readings in Postmodern Latin*, Oxford.
Franco, C. (2017), "Greek and Latin Words for Human-Animal Bonds: Metaphors and Taboos", in T. Fögen & E. Thomas (eds.), *Interactions between Animals and Humans in Graeco-Roman Antiquity*, Berlin/Boston.
Genette, G. (1980), *Narrative Discourse: An Essay in Method*, (trans. J.E. Lewin), Ithaca.
Hallett, J.P. (1992), "Female homoeroticism and the denial of Roman Reality in Latin Literature", in W.R. Dynes & S. Donaldson (eds.), *Homosexuality in the Ancient World*, London.
Heath, M. (1996), "Introduction", in M. Heath (ed), *Aristotle: Poetics*, London.
Janan, M. (1991), "'The Labyrinth and the Mirror': Incest and Influence in *Metamorphoses* 9", *Arethusa* 24 (2): 239–256.
Katz, M.A. (1991), *Penelope's Renown: Meaning and Indeterminacy in the Odyssey*, Princeton.
Kirichenko, A. (2013), "Virgil's Augustan Temples: Image and Intertext in the *Aeneid*", *The Journal of Roman Studies* 103: 65–87.
Langlands, R. (2006), *Sexual Morality in Ancient Rome*, Cambridge.
Lateiner, D. (1984), "Mythic and Non-Mythic Artists in Ovid's *Metamorphoses*", *Ramus* 13: 1–30.
Masterson, M. (2013), "Studies of Ancient Masculinity", in T.K. Hubbard (ed.), *A Companion to Greek and Roman Sexualities*, Chichester.
Nagle, B.R. (1983), "Byblis and Myrrha: Two Incest Narratives in the *Metamorphoses*", *The Classical Journal* 78 (4): 301–315.
Newby, Z. (2013), *Greek Myths in Roman Art and Culture: Imagery, Values and Identity in Italy, 50 BC-AD 250*, Cambridge.
Olson, D.S. (1990), "The Stories of Agamemnon in Homer's *Odyssey*", *Transactions of the American Philological Association* 120: 57–71.
Padel, R. (1996), "Labyrinth of Desire: Cretan Myth in Us", *Arion* 4 (2): 76–87.
Papadopoulos, J.K. (1994), "Pasiphae", in *LIMC*, VII.1: 193–200.
Pavlock, B. (2009), *The Image of the Poet in Ovid's Metamorphoses*, Wisconsin.
Pavlock, B. (2019), "Scylla as Spoiler in *Metamorphoses* 8", *Classical Philology* 114: 66–78.
Pintabone, D.T. (2002), "Ovid's Iphis and Ianthe: When Girls Won't Be Girls", in N.S. Rabinowitz & L. Auanger (eds.), *Among Women: From the Homosocial to the Homoerotic in the Ancient World*, Austin: 256–85.
Reed Doob, P. (1990), *The Idea of the Labyrinth from Classical Antiquity through the Middle Ages*, Ithaca.
Richlin, A. (1983), *The Garden of Priapus: Sexuality and Aggression in Roman Humour*, New Haven/London.

Sharrock, A. (2019), "Ovid's *Metamorphoses*: the naughty boy of the Graeco-Roman epic tradition", in C. Reitz & S. Finkmann (eds.), *Structures of Epic Poetry. Volume 1: Foundations*, Berlin/Boston.
Walters, J. (1997), "Invading the Roman Body: Manliness and Impenetrability in Roman Thought", in J.P. Hallett & M.B. Skinner (eds.), *Roman Sexualities*, Princeton: 29–44.
Watson, P.A. (1995), *Ancient Stepmothers: Myth, Misogyny & Reality*, Leiden/New York/Koln.
Weiden Boyd, B. (2006), "Two Rivers and the Reader in Ovid, *Metamorphoses* 8", *Transactions of the American Philological Association (1974–2014)* 136 (1): 171–20.
Wheeler, S.M. (2000), *Narrative Dynamics in Ovid's* Metamorphoses. *Classica Monacensia, Bd. 20*, Tübingen.
Williams, C.A. (2010), *Roman Homosexuality,* 2nd ed., Oxford/New York.

A.D. Morrison
Divine Memory, Mortal Forgetfulness and Human Misfortune

Abstract: Forgetting gods such as Artemis or Hera is dangerous. Oeneus' forgetfulness (*Il.* 9.537) in failing to sacrifice to her prompts her to send the Calydonian Boar against him, while Pelias' lack of concern for Hera (A.R. 1.14) eventually brings Medea to Thessaly as his killer (Pind. *P.* 4.250). The ease with which mortals can forget something as important as honouring a god, and the terrible consequences which can follow, reveal some key elements in specifically Greek conceptions of memory, failures of memory and their relationship to divinity and humanity. In the modern imagination control of what is forgotten and what remembered is often figured as a mark of the power governments or corporations have over the individual: 'the struggle of man against power is the struggle of memory against forgetting' (Kundera, *The Book of Laughter and Forgetting*, 1980). In antiquity, however, forgetfulness is all too human and all too possible, a natural human failing which can incur the blame of the gods. From one perspective the possibility of catastrophic forgetfulness is an expression of the widespread notion of the vicissitudes of human fortune (cf. e.g. Pind. *P.* 8.fin., Hdt. 1.5), but it is also revealing with regard to Greek conceptions of the divine, since Memory (Mnemosyne) is herself a goddess, and strongly associated through her daughters (the Muses) with a privileged group of mortals, bards or poets.

Ἄρτεμιν (οὐ γὰρ ἐλαφρὸν ἀειδόντεσσι λαθέσθαι)
ὑμνέομεν
                             Call. *H.* 3.1–2

'... it is no light thing', Callimachus declares at the beginning of the *Hymn to Artemis*, 'for singers to forget (λαθέσθαι) Artemis'. Forgetting can be dangerous for mortals: Oeneus' forgetfulness in failing to sacrifice to Artemis prompts her to send the Calydonian Boar against him,[1] while Pelias' lack of concern for Hera eventually brings Medea to Thessaly as his killer.[2] In the modern imagination control of what is forgotten and what remembered is often figured as a mark of the power governments or corporations have over the individual: 'the struggle of

---

[1] ἢ λάθετ' ἢ οὐκ ἐνόησεν, *Il.* 9. 537.
[2] οὐκ ἀλέγιζεν, A.R. 1.14; τὰν Πελίαο φόνον, Pind. *P.* 4.250.

https://doi.org/10.1515/9783110728798-012

man against power is the struggle of memory against forgetting', as Kundera famously puts it (*The Book of Laughter and Forgetting*, 1980). In the era of big data and tech giants, a 'right to be forgotten' has only recently been enshrined in European law, to enable an individual to exercise some control against powerful entities controlling what is remembered about them. In antiquity, however, forgetfulness is all too human and all too possible, a natural human failing which can incur the blame of the gods and bring catastrophic consequences for the mortals concerned. I aim here to investigate early Greek portrayals of the experience of forgetting in order to focus attention on those individual acts of 'catastrophic forgetting' and to examine the relationship of different types of forgetting to Greek conceptions of memory and what they can tell us about the relationship between forgetfulness and what it means to be human.

Recent work on memory in antiquity has established its social and collective dimensions,[3] emphasising in important ways its role as (among other things) a means for maintaining communal identity and reinforcing the norms of social conduct.[4] But what has received rather less sustained attention is the role that particular individuals' forgetting on specific occasions plays in the development of some key Greek narratives of various kinds, and what this can tell us about Greek ideas about the experience of forgetting and how it contributes to conceptions of humanity and morality.[5] The paradoxical power of poetry, which commemorates and preserves the memory of mythic events of the past, itself to bring about a more beneficent kind of forgetfulness in its audience will also be important,[6] since the experience of forgetting one's cares in listening to a song or

---

[3] For recent perspectives on memory and its functions in Greek and Roman culture respectively see the papers collected in Castagnoli/Ceccarelli (2019b) and Galinsky (2014).
[4] On 'social memory' in ancient Greece and its relationship to socio-political power see Price (2012). The concept of 'social' or 'collective' memory originates with Halbwachs (*mémoire collective*; see Halbwachs (1925), Olick (2008), Assmann (2011) 21–33). Concepts (and uses) of memory are strongly tied to the socio-cultural contexts in which they are found (and contribute to the development of the identities of the groups or communities in which they are found): see in general Assmann (1995), (2011) 13–141 and on the socio-cultural contexts of memory in Greek culture Simondon (1982), Detienne (1996), Bakker (2002), Vernant (2006), Assmann (2011) 234–67, Castagnoli/Ceccarelli (2019a). See also Nikkanen (2012) on the role of memory in promoting correct social conduct in Homer.
[5] There has been some work on the desirability and difficulties of forgetting by groups or communities: see e.g. Loraux (2002), Weinrech (2004), which includes a broad survey of forgetting in classical antiquity, Connerton (2008), Esposito (2008) and the suggestive comments on the social needs served by forgetting in Price (2012). On the impossibility of an art of forgetting for the individual see Eco (1988).
[6] Cf. e.g. Vernant (2006) 81, Detienne (1996) 81.

watching a tragedy can be profitably compared with the experience of 'catastrophic forgetting', which itself sometimes forms part of those narratives which allow us to forget our mortal troubles and concerns.

The dangers of forgetting are present even in the earliest Greek narratives, often with a focus on the consequences of the act of forgetting for the individual: in the *Iliad*, a crucial turning-point in the direction of the story of Achilles is the act of forgetfulness when Patroclus ignores his instruction not to continue towards Troy when he has driven the Trojans from the ships.[7] The Homeric narrator strongly marks this moment with a counterfactual conditional:

> εἰ δὲ ἔπος Πηληϊάδαο φύλαξεν
> ἦ τ' ἂν ὑπέκφυγε κῆρα κακὴν μέλανος θανάτοιο.
> *Il*. 16.686–7

> If he had observed the command of the son of Peleus, surely he would have evaded black death's evil fate.

But, of course, Patroclus does not observe the son of Peleus' command and therefore dies at the hands of Hector, an event which leads directly to the return of Achilles to battle and therefore the deaths of Hector and (though outside the main narrative of the poem itself), Achilles. The direction of the plot of the poem depends, then, on a crucial individual act of 'catastrophic forgetting'. Forgetfulness also plays an important role in the *Odyssey*, though with some key differences. Forgetting is a significant danger to Odysseus and his crew, one which threatens in particular to overwhelm their attempts to return home (*nostos*).[8] It is therefore particularly prominent in Odysseus' account of his wanderings in *Od*. 9–12, where we meet repeated opportunities for Odysseus and his crew to commit individual acts of forgetting which will have serious consequences for their futures. The effect, for example, of eating the lotus offered by the Lotus-eaters is to forget one's *nostos* (νόστου τε λαθέσθαι, *Od*. 9.97), while the drugs which Circe mixes into the drinks for Odysseus' crew cause forgetfulness of home (ἵνα ... λαθοίατο πατρίδος αἴης, *Od*. 10.236). The potential for forgetfulness to alter one's future is most significant, of course, for Odysseus himself: none of his companions (after all) makes it back home to Ithaca. As Simondon has argued,[9] Calypso offers him the opportunity to forget his mortal cares forever by becoming immortal, but this

---

7 See Minchin (2006) 12.
8 On the temptations of forgetting in the *Odyssey* see Simondon (1982) 136–40.
9 Simondon (1982) 139.

will also entail a forgetting of *nostos*, home and wife. Calypso sets up an opposition between Odysseus' desire to go 'home to your dear homeland' (οἶκόνδε φίλην ἐς πατρίδα γαῖαν, 5.204) and her offer of immortality with her (ἐνθάδε κ' αὖθι μένων σὺν ἐμοὶ τόδε δῶμα φυλάσσοις | ἀθάνατος τ' εἴης, 5.208–9),[10] telling him that if he knew the 'troubles' (κήδε', 5.207) which awaited him, he would remain with her, for all that he longs constantly for Penelope (τῆς αἰὲν ἐέλδεαι ἤματα πάντα, 5.210).[11] Choosing Calypso means forgetting Penelope and Ithaca, but also his mortal cares and griefs.

For Odysseus this forgetting of home is a road not taken, but catastrophic acts of forgetting are not uncommon in Greek myth:[12] perhaps the most familiar to modern audiences is the forgetfulness of Theseus which leads to the suicide of his father Aegeus. The best-known version is probably that in Catullus 64, in which Theseus' failure to hoist white sails indicating success instead of the black denoting his death at the hands of the Minotaur is portrayed as the revenge of Ariadne for her abandonment by Theseus (Cat. 64.202–6),[13] but the story of is clearly much earlier, since a fragment of Simonides (*PMG* 550) contains a version in which the sail marking success was crimson not white, while another makes it clear that Aegeus' death was the consequence of Theseus' forgetfulness (*PMG* 551). The key role of forgetfulness is emphasised in Plutarch's version through the repetition of the detail of the forgetting on the part of Theseus himself and his helmsman (ἐκλαθέσθαι μὲν αὐτόν, ἐκλαθέσθαι δὲ τὸν κυβερνήτην, *Thes.* 22),[14]

---

[10] 'Staying here you would live with me and be immortal'.
[11] 'For whom you long always every day'.
[12] There also exist what we might term 'conscious' or 'deliberate' acts of 'forgetting', such as that of Medea before killing her children (Eur. *Medea* 1246, 1248), or the watchman at start of Aeschylus' *Agamemnon* (*Ag.* 36), but these involve the conscious choice of the individual and are therefore clearly different from 'catastrophic forgetting' which is *not* intended by the person who forgets. In some myths *not* forgetting can also be catastrophic (see Minchin (2006) 14–15 on the Iliadic Achilles' inability to forget his anger and the death of Patroclus in the *Iliad*; Ajax in *Od.* 11 has not even forgotten his quarrel with Odysseus in the underworld: see Minchin (2006) 9–10). A similar inability to forget is also frequent in tragedy: cf. Electra in Soph. *Electra* (e.g. 482ff., 1248–50) and see in general Webb 2017: chs. 2 and 3 on refusing to forget in Sophocles' *Electra* and *Antigone*; on memory in tragedy see also Ceccarelli (2019), Popescu (2012), Scodel (2008). On 'deliberate forgetfulness' on the part of some characters in Herodotus see Hernández Garcés in this volume. The dangers of remembering are also illustrated by Anacharsis' fateful completion of his vow in Hdt. 4.76, which causes his death on his return to Scythia. On the complexities of memory and forgetting in the *Aeneid* see Most (2001).
[13] See also Plut., *Thes.* 17, 22; [Apollod.] *Epit.* 1.10, Paus. 1.22.4–5, Hyginus, *Fab.* 43, Diod. Sic. 4.61.5–8.
[14] 'he forgot himself and his helmsman forgot'.

while in Catullus Ariadne's pleas to the gods for vengeance (192–201) result in a clear moment of 'catastrophic forgetting':

> ipse autem caeca mentem caligine Theseus
> consitus oblito dimisit pectore cuncta,
> quae mandata prius constanti mente tenebat,
> dulcia nec maesto sustollens signa parenti
> sospitem Erectheum se ostendit visere portum.
> 207–11

> But Theseus himself, his mind covered in a blind fog, let go from his forgetful heart all the orders he had earlier held with constant mind and did not raise up the sweet signal to his mournful father to show he was sighting the Erecthean harbour safe and sound.

Here Theseus' mind is 'covered in a blind fog [*caligo*]' in an image for the experience of forgetting which recalls the λάθας ... νέφος ('cloud of forgetfulness', 45) which descends on the Heliadae in Pindar's *Olympian* 7, which means that they forget to take fire with them for their sacrifices on Rhodes. Although the consequences for the Heliadae are much less serious than for Theseus (or Aegeus), this cloud nevertheless comes upon them ἀτέκμαρτα ('without warning') and 'displaces out of their minds the straight road of duty' (παρέλκει πραγμάτων ὀρθὰν ὁδόν | ἔξω φρενῶν, 46–7), suggesting an externalised force which temporarily afflicts the mind with a species of blindness. Similarly in Catullus the cloud of forgetfulness causes Theseus to overlook those commands he had previously held so dear (64.209).

In Catullus the assent of the gods to Ariadne's desire for vengeance is explicit (*annuit invicto caelestum numine rector*, 204)[15] and a similar, though less explicit, attribution of an act of 'catastrophic forgetting' to the gods is found in the Herodotean account of the coming to power of Cyrus the Great. It is an act of forgetfulness which leads to the overturning of Median rule over the Persians with the catastrophic failure of Astyages to remember his earlier cruel treatment of Harpagus (λήθην ποιεύμενος τά μιν ἐόργεε, 'overlooking what he had done to him', Hdt. 1.127.2),[16] whom he appointed commander of his armies, thus ensuring the victory of Cyrus, who deposes him as king (Hdt. 1.127–30). Herodotus describes Astyages in his forgetfulness as θεοβλαβής, i.e. 'afflicted by gods'. In part such a description underlines the key role this plays in the history of the Persian empire,

---

15 'the ruler of the heavenly ones nodded with invincible will'.
16 See also on this passage Hernández Garcés in this volume.

but it is also important to note that the focus is here on the individual act of forgetting, with a sense that this disastrous action comes from a force external to the individual.

In general it appears that the possibility of catastrophic forgetfulness, and the sense that this can afflict an individual all of a sudden, as if impelled by an external force, is from one perspective an expression of the notion, widespread in Archaic and Classical Greek texts, of the vicissitudes of human fortune (cf. e.g. Pind. *P*. 8.92–6, Hdt. 1.5.4),[17] and the concomitant tragic worldview that mortals are not in full control of their destinies, but subject to the whims and caprices of the gods and other forces more powerful than they. It is no wonder, then, that Lethe ('Forgetfulness') is a daughter of Ἔρις στυγερή in Hesiod (*Theogony* 227) and named second after Toil (Πόνος) and alongside other personified afflictions such as Hunger, Sorrows, Fights, Battles, Murders, Killings, and so forth (227– 32).[18] There is good reason to think that catastrophic forgetting by individual mortals is central to the conception of Lethe as an affliction in this part of the *Theogony*, since there is a clear focus in this section of the poem on individual action, where Oath (Ὅρκος) is described as bringing the most suffering to mortals when an individual (τις), willingly swears a false oath (231–2).[19] As we have seen, forgetfulness too can be conceived of as bringing disastrous consequences on the individual.

Forgetfulness can, of course, also afflict larger groups of mortals and over longer periods than individual acts of forgetting. We have already touched above on the example of the Heliadae in Pindar's *Olympian* 7.[20] Elsewhere in Pindar we also find a pronounced stress on the possibility of a whole community forgetting even great deeds and significant achievements, as in *Isthmian* 4 where Poseidon stirs the sleeping fame of the Cleonymidae (ἐκ λεχέων ἀνάγει φάμαν παλαιὰν | εὐκλέων ἔργων· ἐν ὕπνῳ γὰρ πέσεν, 'he stirs the ancient fame of glorious deeds

---

17 ἐν δ' ὀλίγῳ βροτῶν | τὸ τερπνὸν αὔξεται· οὕτω δὲ καὶ πίτνει χαμαί, | ἀποτρόπῳ γνώμᾳ σεσεισμένον. | ἐπάμεροι· τί δέ τις; τί δ' οὔ τις; σκιᾶς ὄναρ | ἄνθρωπος ('in a brief moment men's delight flourishes, but it also falls in this way to the ground, shaken by a dire judgement. Short-lived creatures: what is someone? What is no one? Man is the dream of a shadow', *P*. 8.92–6), τὴν ἀνθρωπηίην ὦν ἐπιστάμενος εὐδαιμονίην οὐδαμὰ ἐν τὠυτῷ μένουσαν, ἐπιμνήσομαι ἀμφοτέρων ὁμοίως ('Thus, in the knowledge that human happiness never endures in the same place, I will mention both in the same way', Hdt. 1.5.4).
18 See Vernant (2006) 116. On Lethe as a divine power see Detienne (1996) 24–5.
19 Oath is also a child of Eris in the *Theogony*: see Loraux (2002) 123–37 on the harm which Oath can do.
20 On forgetting by communities see also n.5 above.

from its bed, for it had fallen asleep', 22–3). In the Pindaric worldview this potential forgetfulness is caused by the fact that mortals are by nature forgetful: ἀλλὰ παλαιὰ γὰρ εὕδει χάρις, | ἀμνάμονες δὲ βροτοί ('but ancient glory sleeps, and mortals are forgetful ...', I. 7.16–17). The only remedy for this is commemoration in song, by the grace of Mnemosyne:[21]

> ταὶ μεγάλαι γὰρ ἀλκαὶ
> σκότον πολὺν ὕμνων ἔχοντι δεόμεναι·
> ἔργοις δὲ καλοῖς ἔσοπτρον ἴσαμεν ἑνὶ σὺν τρόπῳ,
> εἰ Μναμοσύνας ἕκατι λιπαράμπυκος
> εὕρηται ἄποινα μόχθων κλυταῖς ἐπέων ἀοιδαῖς.
> N. 7.12–16

For without songs mighty brave deeds stay in deep darkness: for fine deeds we know of a mirror of only one kind, if thanks to bright-headbanded Memory, reward for toils is found in glorious songs.

The strong connection in early Greek texts between Memory and song is most clearly expressed in the genealogy of the Muses in Hesiod's *Theogony* (vv. 52–63), where they are the daughters of Mnemosyne, an image often taken up by other poets (e.g. *h.Merc.* 429–30),[22] not least Pindar (cf. e.g. *I.* 6.74–5, *Pae.* 6.54–6, 7b.15–16). The Muses' parentage (their father is Zeus) points to the collective, social nature of memory in Archaic Greece, which we have touched on above, wherein the Muses authorise and enable poetic narratives which allow communities to understand their relationship to the mythic past.[23] The poetry the Muses enable is more than merely a useful aide-memoire; rather, the songs in which mythic events are described (or epinician victories commemorated) themselves enact and make present the events or achievements they narrate.[24] The association of memory with the Muses also underlines the wider association of memory

---

21 Cf. *I.* 7.18–19, where what mortals forget is what is not preserved in song: ὅ τι μὴ σοφίας ἄωτον ἄκρον | κλυταῖς ἐπέων ῥοαῖσιν ἐξίκηται ζυγέν. See Agocs (2009) 53.
22 Cf. also *PMG* 941 (Muses as daughters of Μνάμα), Alcman *PMG* 8.9, Solon fr. 13.1–2 West. See West (1966) 174.
23 See Detienne (1996) 35–48, Agocs (2009) 35–8.
24 Bakker (2002) 67–71, Nikkanen (2012). As Bakker shows, it is such making present which is mobilised by hymnal declarations such as μνήσομαι at the beginning or end of *Homeric Hymns*: cf. e.g., *Hom. Hymn. Dem* (μνήσομα', v. 495), *Hymn. Hom. Ap.* (μνήσομαι οὐδὲ λάθωμαι, v. 1, μνήσομα', v. 546), *Hymn. Hom. Merc.* (μνήσομα', v. 580), *Hymn. Hom. Bacch.* (μνήσομαι, v.2). On the visual aspects of this making present in Homer see Clay (2011) 16–17.

with the divine and the reverse,²⁵ the association of forgetting with mortals and their need for the Muses to guarantee remembrance. The contrast between divine knowledge and mortal ignorance is starkest in *Iliad* 2, where the narrator addresses the Muses before the Catalogue of Ships:²⁶

ὑμεῖς γὰρ θεαί ἐστε πάρεστέ τε ἴστέ τε πάντα,
ἡμεῖς δὲ κλέος οἶον ἀκούομεν οὐδέ τι ἴδμεν
Il. 2.485–6

For you are goddesses and are everywhere and know everything, but we hear only report and do not know anything.

Moreover it is clear that the Muses' acts of 'remembering' (μνησαίαθ', 492) are indispensable to the narrator's success here:²⁷ he is unable to name the mass of troops 'unless' (εἰ μή, 491) the Muses recall them to his mind.

In Homer the Muses enable the enactment of epic κλέος in song, reflecting the wider socio-cultural conditions of communication in early Archaic Greece, but since memory can productively be viewed as a 'a function of a culture's dominant medium of communication',²⁸ as writing becomes more important in Greek culture in the late Archaic and into the Classical periods, writing comes to play an increasingly important role in notions of memory, both by encroaching on the role of the Muses as guarantors of the mythic narrative and as a defence against the mortal propensity to forget.²⁹ The situation is somewhat in flux in Pindar, where the poet can portray himself as having forgotten the song owed to the victor in *Olympian* 10 (ἐπιλέλαθ', v. 3), but can bid the Muse and Truth (Ἀλάθεια) 'read out to me' (ἀνάγνωτέ μοι, v. 1) the victor's name and use a 'correcting hand'

---

25 The gods 'never forget': cf. κείνη δ' οὐδέποτε σφετέρης ἐπιλήθεται ἕδρης (*Callim. Hymn* 4.233), with reference to Iris. They are also unmerciful to those who forget: alongside the generalised statement at *Callim. Hymn* 4 (Phoebus hates him who λάθηται Delos, v. 8) we should place the fates of Pelias and Oeneus at the hands of Hera and Artemis (see above).
26 The extent of the Muses' knowledge is also clear in the *Theogony*, where the Muses breathe into Hesiod αὐδὴν | θέσπιν (31–2) in order that he might sing of τά τ' ἐσσόμενα πρό τ' ἐόντα ('things that will be and things that were', 32), which closely resembles the Muses' own song to their father Zeus (εἰρεῦσαι τά τ' ἐόντα τά τ' ἐσσόμενα πρό τ' ἐόντα, 'telling of things that are and things that will be and those that were', 38). In Pindar's fragmentary *Paean* 8 Mnemosyne (or her daughters, the Muses) declare τά τ' ἐόντα τε κα[ὶ | πρόσθεν γεγενημένα ('things that are and those that were before', 83–4).
27 Bakker (2002) 71.
28 Bakker (2002) 67.
29 On the key role that writing plays in the development of cultural memory from a phase based on ritual repetition to one focused on textual interpretation see Assmann (2011) 70–110.

(ὀρθᾷ χερί, v. 4) in his aid, portraying the Muse as depending on writing to play a similar role as the guarantor of truth we can observe in Homer and Hesiod. Writing is also depicted as an aid to memory and defence against forgetfulness in texts such as *Prometheus Bound*:

> ἦν δ' οὐδὲν αὐτοῖς οὔτε χείματος τέκμαρ
> οὔτ' ἀνθεμώδους ἦρος οὔτε καρπίμου
> θέρους βέβαιον, ἀλλ' ἄτερ γνώμης τὸ πᾶν
> ἔπρασσον, ἔστε δή σφιν ἀντολὰς ἐγὼ
> ἄστρων ἔδειξα τάς τε δυσκρίτους δύσεις.
> καὶ μὴν ἀριθμόν, ἔξοχον σοφισμάτων,
> ἐξηῦρον αὐτοῖς, γραμμάτων τε συνθέσεις,
> μνήμην ἁπάντων, μουσομήτορ' ἐργάνην.
>
> PV 454–61

Nor did they possess any reliable marker of winter, blooming spring or fruit-bearing summer, but everything they did without a plan, until I revealed to them the stars' risings and settings, which are hard to make out. And I invented for them numbers, greatest of inventions, and combinations of letters, the means of remembering everything, the servant which is the mother of the Muses.

Here Prometheus is the inventor of (among other things) letters, which serve as a tool to support memory and enable poetry (μνήμην ἁπάντων, μουσομήτορ' ἐργάνην), in effect (as Ceccarelli has pointed out) usurping the role earlier played by the Muses.[30] In other texts the inventor of writing is Palamedes, and his innovation similarly enables or promotes memory (cf. γράμματά τε μνήμης ὄργανον, Gorgias, *Palamedes* DK B11a 30)[31] or counteracts forgetfulness, as in Euripides fr. 578.1 (where he boasts that he has established τὰ τῆς γε λήθης φάρμακ').[32]

The connections between both the Muses and writing with memory are different ways of dealing with the 'anxiety about forgetting' which Agocs identifies in Pindar's *Isthmian* 7,[33] but which is much more widespread in Greek thinking in the Archaic and Classical periods. It is apparent also in the devising of a system

---

30 Ceccarelli (2013) 66–7. See also Steiner (1994) 101 for writing as underpinning memory in these passages.
31 'letters, an instrument of remembering'. Cf. Pl. *Rep.* 522d.
32 'The remedy for forgetting'. See Ceccarelli (2013) 81–2. It is this conception of writing as an aide-memoire that Plato is exploiting in the *Phaedrus*: *Phaedrus* 274e-275a μνήμης τε γὰρ καὶ σοφίας φάρμακον, 274e, οὔκουν μνήμης ἀλλὰ ὑπομνήσεως φάρμακον, 275a (see Steiner (1994) 103–4, 115–16 on these passages and the way in which Plato is modifying common image of remembering as reading off one's internal tablets, as in O.10).
33 Agocs (2009) 53.

of mnemonics by Simonides (μνήμην πρῶτος ὃς ἐφρασάμην, Call. *Aet.* fr. 64.10 Pf.),³⁴ and prominently at the beginning of Herodotus, where he makes it explicit that his account has been written in order that τὰ γενόμενα ἐξ ἀνθρώπων do not become 'faded' or 'extinct' (ἐξίτηλα) through the effect of time (τῷ χρόνῳ) and that great and wondrous ἔργα are not 'without κλέος' (ἀκλεᾶ).³⁵ Such an anxiety about forgetting also lies behind declarations of the superiority as a form of commemoration of poetry as compared with other means of remembering or preserving human achievement, such as Simonides' aggressive criticism of the impermanence of physical monuments (λίθον δὲ | καὶ βρότεοι παλάμαι θραύοντι· μωροῦ | φωτὸς ἅδε βουλά, 'a stone even mortal hands can shatter: this is the opinion of a stupid man', *PMG* 581.5–7), against which we can contrast his poetic memorialisation of the dead at Thermopylae (*PMG* 531), which 'time which overcomes all will not destroy' (οὔθ' ὁ πανδαμάτωρ ἀμαυρώσει χρόνος, *PMG* 531.5) and Pindar's proud statement of the memorialising power of Pindaric song at the beginning of *Nemean* 5, to which he unfavourably compares statuary.³⁶

Across these different genres and periods, even with the gradual shift in the dominant medium of communication as the Classical period wears on, there is a general association of memory with what is positive (such as praise or life), and forgetting with what is negative (including silence and death).³⁷ But there is also a crucial exception to this widespread binary opposition: the crucial, welcome forgetfulness of cares which poetry or song can bring about, at least temporarily.³⁸ In the Hesiodic account of the birth of the Muses their role in providing this respite is explicit and underlined by a curious punning with their mother Mnemosyne's name:

---

34 'I who first devised a system of remembering'. Cf. καὶ τὴν μνημονικὴν δὲ τέχνην εὗρεν, 'he also invented the craft of recollection', *Suda* Σ 439 Adler.
35 For time as causing forgetfulness cf. Soph. fr. 954: χρόνος δ' ἀμαυροῖ πάντα κεἰς λήθην ἄγει ('time obscures everything and brings it to forgetfulness'. On the relationship between time and memory in Greek thinking see Castagnoli-Ceccarelli (2019a) 5–8.
36 The irony that the poet of mnemonics and commemoration should himself have his monument destroyed is exploited by Callimachus in fr. 64 Pf. of the *Aetia* (the Tomb of Simonides). See Morrison (2013).
37 See Detienne (1967) 21–4, Simondon (1982) 133–5, Detienne (1996) 48–9, Agocs (2009) 36. The associations of forgetfulness with silence are clear (for instance) at Pindar, *Nemean* 8.24–5. The usually positive associations of memory and the conversely negative associations of forgetting in contemporary culture have hampered the intellectual study of the latter in Connerton's view (2008 59).
38 See in general Simondon (1982) 131–3.

> τὰς ἐν Πιερίῃ Κρονίδῃ τέκε πατρὶ μιγεῖσα
> Μνημοσύνη, γουνοῖσιν Ἐλευθῆρος μεδέουσα,
> λησμοσύνην τε κακῶν ἄμπαυμά τε μερμηράων.
>
> Theog. 53-5

On Pieria Memory bore them, she who rules over Eleuther's hills, when she joined with their father, the son of Cronus, as the unmemory of evils and respite from cares.

The rare word for 'forgetfulness' λησμοσύνη (only otherwise found at Sophocles, *Antigone* 151 before Gregory of Nazianzus in the fourth century A.D.) is placed in the same metrical position as Μνημοσύνη in the preceding line and in apposition to the Muses in v. 53,[39] so that the word-play underlines the apparent paradox of Memory giving birth to forgetting (or 'unmemory', as I have translated it).[40] The power of the Muses here to allow mortals to escape their cares is also underlined elsewhere in the Hesiodic Hymn to the Muses: at vv. 102-3 someone listening to a poet inspired by the Muses 'forgets anxieties and does not remember cares at all' (δυσφροσυνέων ἐπιλήθεται οὐδέ τι κηδέων | μέμνηται).[41] The language used of the power of song to dismiss cares is reminiscent of that employed elsewhere of the similar capacity for respite from mortal concerns which can be offered by such things as sleep, wine or drugs.[42]

Wine, for instance, is able to bring about sleep and so forgetfulness of cares as well as itself relieving their troubles in Euripides' *Bacchae* (as Teiresias attempts to explain to Pentheus):[43]

> ὃ παύει τοὺς ταλαιπώρους βροτοὺς
> λύπης, ὅταν πλησθῶσιν ἀμπέλου ῥοῆς,
> ὕπνον τε λήθην τῶν καθ' ἡμέραν κακῶν
> δίδωσιν, οὐδ' ἔστ' ἄλλο φάρμακον πόνων.
>
> Bacch. 280-3

---

39 See West (1966) 175.
40 Cf. Detienne (1996) 81, Clay (2003) 68-9 on the Muses telling the truth but bringing forgetfulness.
41 See Clay (2011) 18 n. 9.
42 See Clay (2011) 18. For the soothing power of song see also Pind. fr. 124 ab S.-M. with Simondon (1982) 130.
43 On wine as a drug for forgetting in Greek and later poetry see Weinrech (2004) 16. Such a view of the effects of wine was not, of course, universal. As Dodds point out (1960 105) Eur. fr. 1079 contains an attack on the idea of wine as a palliative for cares, arguing instead that the only remedy is the comfort of a friend.

This relieves suffering mortals of their pain, when they take their fill of the juice of the vine and this gives sleep as the forgetfulness of the troubles of the day. There is no other remedy for toils.

Similarly, Orestes wakes from sleep in the *Orestes* and praises its abilities to bring out a much-needed forgetfulness of cares:

ὦ φίλον ὕπνου θέλγητρον, ἐπίκουρον νόσου,
ὡς ἡδύ μοι προσῆλθες — ἐν δέοντί γε.
ὦ πότνια Λήθη τῶν κακῶν, ὡς εἶ σοφὴ
καὶ τοῖσι δυστυχοῦσιν εὐκταία θεός.
Eur. Or. 211–14

O dear charm of sleep, ally against illness, how sweetly you came to me - and how timely. O lady Forgetfulness of evils, how wise a goddess you are and how often invoked by those who are ill-fortuned.

Here too the sense of forgetfulness as bringing relief or respite from one's cares is very clear; the word λήθη is in fact used once in Sophocles of a literal respite in a physical disease (*Philoctetes* 878). Particularly suggestive with regard to the effect of song in bringing about such emotional relief is the description of the effect of the drug Helen employs in *Odyssey* 4:

αὐτίκ' ἄρ' εἰς οἶνον βάλε φάρμακον, ἔνθεν ἔπινον,
νηπενθές τ' ἄχολόν τε, κακῶν ἐπίληθον ἁπάντων.
ὅς τὸ καταβρόξειεν, ἐπὴν κρητῆρι μιγείη,
οὔ κεν ἐφημέριός γε βάλοι κατὰ δάκρυ παρειῶν,
οὐδ' εἴ οἱ κατατεθναίη μήτηρ τε πατήρ τε,
οὐδ' εἴ οἱ προπάροιθεν ἀδελφεὸν ἢ φίλον υἱὸν
χαλκῷ δηιόῳεν, ὁ δ' ὀφθαλμοῖσιν ὁρῷτο.
Od. 4.220–6

So at once she threw a drug into the wine from which they were drinking, painless and without anger, bringing forgetfulness of all evils. Whoever drinks this, when it is mixed in the wine-bowl, would not shed a tear on his cheeks for that day, not even if his mother and father should die or if in front of him they should kill with bronze his brother or own son and he should see it with his own eyes.

Helen is prompted to add the drug to the wine because Menelaus' speech moves all those present to tears. In particular it is *remembering* which causes them to cry: Peisistratus, Nestor's son, is moved to tears by remembering his brother Antilochus, about whom he asks Menelaus (*Od.* 4.186–202). It is in the context of the power of memory to cause grief that we should see Helen's drug which causes forgetfulness to ease such emotional pain. Helen's drug brings about, like the

Muses in the *Theogony*, a forgetfulness of cares (κακῶν ἐπίληθον ἁπάντων, 4.221 ~ λησμοσύνην τε κακῶν, *Theog.* 55), but this is only temporary (ἐφημέριος, 4.223), as the forgetfulness the Muses bring is only an ἄμπαυμα, a respite (*Theog.* 55).[44] Moreover it permits those gathered at Sparta to participate in telling stories about the past, but without pain as before: when Helen has added the drug (αὐτὰρ ἐπεί ῥ' ἐνέηκε κέλευσέ τε οἰνοχοῆσαι, 4.233),[45] she explicitly suggests the telling of stories (ἦ τοι νῦν δαίνυσθε καθήμενοι ἐν μεγάροισι | καὶ μύθοις τέρπεσθε, 4.238–9).[46] Helen's drug draws attention, therefore, to the capacity of songs and stories to cause pain and remind one of one's cares.[47] Such grief from memory also therefore inverts the normally positive associations of memory (as the respite from cares of forgetfulness brought by the Muses inverts the usually negative associations of forgetting). In *Odyssey* 19 the disguised Odysseus asks Penelope not to enquire after his origins, because the memories stirred up will cause him pain:

μηδ' ἐμὸν ἐξερέεινε γένος καὶ πατρίδα γαῖαν,
μή μοι μᾶλλον θυμὸν ἐνιπλήσῃς ὀδυνάων
μνησαμένῳ· μάλα δ' εἰμὶ πολύστονος

Od. 19.116–18

Do not ask after my family and homeland, lest you fill my heart even more with griefs as I remember: I am a man of many sorrows.

Similarly Penelope herself is caused pain by the song of Phemius in Book 1 of the *Odyssey* (*Od.* 1.340–4), which causes her to remember (μεμνημένη, 1.343) Odysseus,[48] and Achilles and Priam in *Iliad* 24 are joined in lamentation as they each remember (τὼ δὲ μνησαμένω, 24.509) their lost or distant *philoi* (*Il.* 24.509–12). This capacity for memory to bring pain is related to the making present which is fundamental to the workings of memory in Homer,[49] but the connection between remembrance and suffering is deeper still in Homer, as we can see from those passages where it appears that the purpose of the events of Troy and their aftermath are to provide the raw material for songs recalling those events. Alcinous regards the gods as responsible for the fall of Troy and characterises their action as having been carried out *in order* to provide a subject for future song:

---

44 See on the forgetfulness of cares brought by the Hesiodic Muses Clay (2003) 68–9.
45 'And when she had put it in and ordered the wine to be poured ...'.
46 'Now sitting in the halls feast and take pleasure in stories'.
47 On the capacity of epic stories to cause pain when too close to the listener's personal experience see Clay (2011) 18.
48 See Minchin (2006) 5–6, Nikkanen (2012).
49 Nikkanen (2012) and see further Bakker (2002) and pp. 233–9 above.

> τὸν δὲ θεοὶ μὲν τεῦξαν, ἐπεκλώσαντο δ' ὄλεθρον
> ἀνθρώποις, ἵνα ᾖσι καὶ ἐσσομένοισιν ἀοιδή.
>
> *Od.* 8.579–80

> The gods carried this out and spun the destruction for men, so that there might be a song for those to come.

His is an outsider's perspective on the Trojan War; it is even more striking when Helen expresses a similar sentiment in her self-aware comment on the fate bequeathed to her and Paris:[50]

> οἷσιν ἐπὶ Ζεὺς θῆκε κακὸν μόρον, ὡς καὶ ὀπίσσω
> ἀνθρώποισι πελώμεθ' ἀοίδιμοι ἐσσομένοισι.
>
> *Il.* 6.357–8

> On whom Zeus has placed an evil fate, so that in later times we should be the subject of song for men to come.

But it is these very songs, the songs preserving the memory of grief and suffering of individuals such as Helen, which themselves can bring welcome forgetfulness of cares for their audiences. In the *Theogony* it is when an *aoidos* sings of the κλεῖα προτέρων ἀνθρώπων ('the glorious deeds of earlier men', *Theog.* 100) that he forgets his troubles and ceases to remember his cares (*Theog.* 102–3), while in a fragment of the comic poet Timocles' *Dionysiazousai*, the connection between watching the sufferings of others in tragic drama and the forgetting of one's own griefs is even clearer:

> ὁ γὰρ νοῦς τῶν ἰδίων λήθην λαβὼν
> πρὸς ἀλλοτρίῳ τε ψυχαγωγηθεὶς πάθει,
> μεθ' ἡδονῆς ἀπῆλθε παιδευθεὶς ἅμα.
>
> fr. 6.5–7 K.-A.

> For the mind gets forgetfulness of its own suffering and is bewitched through the suffering of someone else and it goes off happily as well as having been taught.

The mind here is 'bewitched'[51] on witnessing the suffering of someone else (ἀλλοτρίῳ): it is the alien nature of the pains witnessed in tragedy which is key to its effectiveness in making the viewer forget his or her own cares. The painful memories in the passages of Homer above are, in contrast, one's own: the subject

---

[50] See Kirk (1985) *ad loc.*, Minchin (2006) 7–8 on Helen's remarkable perspective on her own role in the *Iliad*.
[51] See Olson (2007) 170 who comments that ψυχαγωγηθείς 'hints at wizardry'.

in those cases is caused to remember the loss of or separation from a family-member, i.e. to relive a grief directly connected to them. It is the peculiar power of Helen's drug precisely to allow contemplation of memories connected with oneself without such pain. It is also worth comparing the experience of the relieving forgetfulness from song or tragedy with the catastrophic forgetfulness we examined above. In the notion of the mind being 'bewitched' by tragedy (Timocles fr. 6.6) and the immediate forgetting (αἶψ' ... ἐπιλήθεται, *Theog.* 102) which is caused by the *aoidos* singing of men's glorious deeds there is a sense of being acted on by an external force which is too powerful to resist, reminiscent of the immediate effect of the drug Helen administers to cause forgetfulness of cares in *Odyssey* 4, which is such that one would not even shed a tear on witnessing the murder of one's own brother or son. In this respect the beneficent forgetfulness of song closely resembles the power of catastrophic forgetfulness.

The forgetfulness of one's troubles which the Muses can inspire is only temporary, as we have seen, though the vehicle for this temporary oblivion of one's cares is the permanent remembrance in song of those of mythic figure such as Helen. Much of the complexity of the paradox of the poetry of memory assuaging grief through forgetfulness by commemorating suffering is captured by another of the dangers to his *nostos* which Odysseus undergoes in the *Odyssey*, the Sirens. The Sirens are a distorted reflection of the Muses (the daughters of Terpsichore, according to Apollonius of Rhodes, A.R. 4.895–6)[52] and offer Odysseus the temptation of their knowledge, their memory, not only of what has happened at Troy, but in particular what the Greeks and Trojans suffered:

ἴδμεν γάρ τοι πάνθ' ὅσ' ἐνὶ Τροίῃ εὐρείῃ
Ἀργεῖοι Τρῶές τε θεῶν ἰότητι μόγησαν,
ἴδμεν δ', ὅσσα γένηται ἐπὶ χθονὶ πουλυβοτείρῃ.
Od. 12.189–91

We know everything which the Argives and Trojans suffered at spacious Troy by the gods' will and we know everything which happens on the nourishing earth.

The knowledge (ἴδμεν) they offer strongly resembles the knowledge of the Hesiodic Muses (cf. ἴδμεν ... | ἴδμεν, *Theog.* 27–8), while their sweet voice (μελίγηρυν ἀπὸ στομάτων ὄπ', 12.187) is very similar to that of the man loved by the Muses in the *Theogony* (γλυκερή οἱ ἀπὸ στόματος ῥέει αὐδή, *Theog.* 97). Circe describes their effect as 'bewitching' (πάντας | ἀνθρώπους θέλγουσιν, *Od.* 12.39–40), as does Apollonius in the *Argonautica* (ἡδείῃσιν | θέλγουσαι μολπῇσιν, A.R. 4.893–

---

52 Cf. Detienne (1996) 81.

4), which in turn resembles the beneficent effect of song in making the listener forget his or her own cares. But in fact of course the Sirens do not offer either remembrance or beneficent forgetfulness: to surrender to their temptations is to give oneself up to the forgetfulness of death and the loss of one's *nostos* and *oikos*:[53]

> τῷ δ' οὔ τι γυνὴ καὶ νήπια τέκνα
> οἴκαδε νοστήσαντι παρίσταται οὐδὲ γάνυνται,
> ἀλλά τε Σειρῆνες λιγυρῇ θέλγουσιν ἀοιδῇ
> ἥμεναι ἐν λειμῶνι, πολὺς δ' ἀμφ' ὀστεόφιν θὶς
> ἀνδρῶν πυθομένων, περὶ δὲ ῥινοὶ μινύθουσι.
>
> *Od.* 12.42–6

... his wife and infant children do not stand next to him and celebrate his return home; rather, the Sirens bewitch him with clear song, sitting in a field, but around them is a great pile of the bones of rotting men and round them decays the skin.

The Sirens seem to offer in their 'clear song' knowledge reminiscent of that of the Muses and enchantment (θέλγουσιν) reminiscent of the Muses' own power to banish cares, but this merely disguises their destruction of *nostos* and the concomitant obliteration of *kleos* which failing to return home would mean for a hero such as Odysseus. As Jason worries in Book 2 of the *Argonautica*, losing one's *nostos* implies being forgotten:[54]

> εἰ δὴ μήτ' ὀλοοῖο μετὰ πτόλιν Αἰήταο
> ἔσσεται, ἠὲ καὶ αὖτις ἐς Ἑλλάδα γαῖαν ἱκέσθαι
> πετράων ἔκτοσθε, κατ' αὐτόθι δ' ἄμμε καλύψει
> ἀκλειῶς κακὸς οἶτος, ἐτώσια γηράσκοντας.
>
> A.R. 2.890–3

If we cannot come either to the city of deadly Aietes or again back to the land of Hellas through the rocks, right here an evil fate will cover us up without glory as we grow old to no purpose.

The effect of the Sirens' song is also in an important sense similar to an act of catastrophic forgetting: such is the power of their song that it overwhelms (as an external force) the memory of one's home and family and the desire to return to them, to the extent that even Odysseus is so enveloped by a desire to hear their song (and nothing else) that he commands his men to set him free (αὐτὰρ ἐμὸν

---

53 Cf. also A.R. 4.901–2, 916.
54 See (e.g.) Segal (1983) 39–40.

κῆρ | ἤθελ' ἀκουέμεναι, λῦσαί τ' ἐκέλευον ἑταίρους, *Od.* 12.192–3).⁵⁵ The Sirens at once express the overwhelming, quasi-divine force which forgetting can have in Greek mythic narrative and the complex connections of song, memory and suffering in the Greek imagination. It is fitting that Odysseus' own tale of the Sirens and the dangers they posed to his *nostos* should produce an effect similar to that attributed to their song (ὣς ἔφαθ', οἱ δ' ἄρα πάντες ἀκὴν ἐγένοντο σιωπῇ, | κηληθμῷ δ' ἔσχοντο κατὰ μέγαρα σκιόεντα, *Od.* 13.1–2)⁵⁶ and that it leads Alcinous to predict that Odysseus will finally attain his return home:

> ὦ Ὀδυσεῦ, ἐπεὶ ἵκευ ἐμὸν ποτὶ χαλκοβατὲς δῶ,
> ὑψερεφές, τῷ σ' οὔ τι παλιμπλαγχθέντα γ' ὀΐω
> ἂψ ἀπονοστήσειν
>
> *Od.* 13.4–6

> Odysseus, since you have come to my bronze-floored house with its high roof, I do not think you will be driven off course as you return home.

Odysseus' *nostos*, of course, is only brought about because of the repeated intervention of various gods, including Zeus, Athena, Hermes and Ino-Leucothoe. He only overcomes the dangers of the Sirens because of the advice of Circe. Here too there is a reminder of the danger of catastrophic forgetting for mortals: without the guidance and protection of the gods such as Odysseus enjoys, the power of Lethe to blind mortals can come suddenly upon any mortal. As Detienne has noted,⁵⁷ in the *Theogony* Lethe is implicitly juxtaposed with Nereus, the Old Man of the Sea, who is 'without lies' (ἀψευδέα) and 'truthful' (ἀληθέα) and 'does not *forget* [my italics] laws' (οὐδὲ θεμίστων | λήθεται, *Theog.* 235–6). But Nereus is a god, the eldest son of Pontus, whose unforgetting divine memory serves to underline that forgetfulness well deserves her place alongside Toil and Hunger as a quintessentially human affliction.

---

55 'My heart longed to listen and I ordered my companions to release me'. Cf. the similar effect of the Sirens' song on the Argonaut Butes at A.R. 4.912–19.
56 'So he spoke and all were silent, held bewitched in the shadowy halls'.
57 Detienne (1996) 65–6.

Bibliography

Agocs, P. (2009), "Memory and Forgetting in Pindar's Seventh *Isthmian* Ode", in L. Dolezalová (ed.), *Strategies of Remembrance: From Pindar to Hölderlin*, Newcastle: 33–92.
Assmann, J. (1995), "Collective Memory and Cultural Identity", *New German Critique* 65: 125–33.
Assmann, J. (2011), *Cultural Memory and Early Civilization*, Cambridge.
Bakker, E.J. (2002), "Remembering the God's Arrival", *Arethusa* 35: 63–81.
Ceccarelli, P. (2013), *Ancient Greek Letter Writing*, Oxford.
Ceccarelli, P. (2019), "Economies of Memory in Greek Tragedy", in P. Ceccarelli & L. Castagnoli (eds.) (2019b), *Greek Memories: Theories and Practices*, Cambridge: 93–114.
Ceccarelli, P./L. Castagnoli (2019a), "Introduction", in P. Ceccarelli & L. Castagnoli (eds.), *Greek Memories: Theories and Practices*, Cambridge: 1–49.
Ceccarelli, P./L. Castagnoli (eds.) (2019b), *Greek Memories: Theories and Practices*, Cambridge.
Clay, J.S. (2003), *Hesiod's Cosmos*, Cambridge.
Clay, J.S. (2011), *Homer's Trojan Theater*, Cambridge.
Connerton, P. (2008), "Seven types of forgetting", *Memory Studies* 1: 59–71.
Detienne, M. (1967), *Les maîtres de vérité dans la Grèce archaïque*, Paris.
Detienne, M. (1996), *The Masters of Truth in Archaic Greece* (trans. J. Lloyd), New York.
Dodds, E.R. (1960), *Euripides:* Bacchae, Oxford.
Eco, U. (1988), "An *Ars Oblivionalis*? Forget It!", *PMLA* 103: 254–61.
Esposito, E. (2008), "Social Forgetting: A Systems-Theory Approach", in A. Erll & A. Nünning (eds.), *Cultural Memory Studies: An International and Interdisciplinary Handbook*, Berlin: 181–91.
Galinksy, K. (ed.) (2014), *Memoria Romana: Memory in Rome and Rome in Memory*, Ann Arbor.
Halbwachs, M. (1925), *Les cadres sociaux de la mémoire*, Paris.
Kirk, G. (1985), *The* Iliad*: A Commentary* (vol. 1), Cambridge.
Loraux, N. (2002), *The Divided City: On Memory and Forgetting in Ancient Athens*, New York.
Minchin, E. (2006), "Can One Ever Forget? Homer on the Persistence of Painful Memories", *Scholia* 15: 2–16.
Morrison, A.D. (2013), "Speaking from the Tomb?: The Disappearing Epitaph of Simonides in Callimachus, *Aetia* fr. 64 Pf.", in P. Liddel & P. Low (eds.), *Inscriptions and their uses in ancient literature*, Oxford: 289–301.
Most, G.W. (2001), "Memory and Forgetting in the *Aeneid*", *Vergilius* 47: 148–170.
Nikkanen, A. (2012), "A Note on Memory and Reciprocity in Homer's *Odyssey*", in *Donum natalicum digitaliter confectum Gregorio Nagy septuagenario a discipulis collegis familiaribus oblatum* (https://chs.harvard.edu/CHS/article/display/4616).
Olson, S.D. (2007), *Broken Laughter*, Oxford.
Popescu, C. (2012), "Beneath the Root of Memory: The Engine of Recollection and Forgetfulness in the Tragedies about Orestes' Matricide", Diss., University of Texas-Austin.
Price, S. (2012), "Memory and Ancient Greece", in B. Dignas & R.R.R. Smith (eds.), *Historical and Religious Memory in the Ancient World*, Oxford: 15–32.
Scodel, R. (2008), "Social Memory in Aeschylus' *Oresteia*", in E.A. Mackey (ed.), *Orality, Literacy, Memory in the Ancient Greek and Roman World*, Leiden: 115–42.
Segal, C. (1983), "*Kleos* and its Ironies in the *Odyssey*", *AC* 52: 22–47.

Simondon, M. (1982), *La mémoire et l'oubli dans la pensée grecque jusqu'à la fin du Ve siècle avant J.-C*, Paris.
Steiner, D. (1994), *The Tyrant's Writ*, Princeton.
Vernant, J.-P. (2006), *Myth and Thought among the Greeks* (trans. J. Lloyd with J. Fort), New York.
Webb, C. (2017), "Looking back in anger: The dynamics of remembering and forgetting in the Sophoklean 'polis'", Diss., University College London.
Weinrech, H. (2004), *Lethe: The Art and Critique of Forgetting* (trans. S. Rendall), Ithaca, NY/London.
West, M.L. (1966), *Hesiod:* Theogony, Oxford.

Carlos Hernández Garcés
Forgetfulness as a Narrative Device in Herodotus' *Histories*

Abstract: This study posits that Herodotus' use of λήθη and its cognates serves a narrative purpose in the *Histories*. It also puts forward that an underlying conception of (good or bad) *judgement* as the negation of forgetfulness (ἀ-λήθεια) is operational in the text. This paper consists of a preliminary bird's-eye view of λήθη in the literary corpus prior to Herodotus' work and the subsequent analysis of the role of λήθη and λανθάνω in the *Histories*. It is divided up in three sections. In the first one I examine jointly the only two occurrences of λήθη in the *Histories*, which document the earliest attestations of mortals *wielding* forgetfulness (λήθην ποιεῖσθαι). Equivalent in form, they bring about critically dissimilar consequences depending on the rightness (or not) in the assessment of the concrete situation in which forgetfulness is exercised. Secondly, I delve into the verbal cognate λανθάνω. In keeping with the strand set by the distribution of λήθη, I postulate that failure to assess correctly a set of circumstances and *being deceived* by them signals ruin. Conversely, sound analysis of the context keeps individuals safe and may even bring benefits. Lastly, I inquire into the only two instances of the expression ἑκὼν ἐπιλανθάνομαι. Making one of the characters choose overtly what is to be remembered and what forgotten, in a properly historicising fashion, Herodotus makes visible his own hand in the composition of his work. In conclusion, I argue that the three cognates ultimately function as a narrative device with a threefold purpose: To buttress Herodotus' authority over the account of past events he is shaping; To further characterise some actors' discernment (or lack of it), to the extent of occasionally paralleling it to his own as historian; And to depict the Greeks as being on a higher intellectual echelon than the non-Greeks insofar as they use better judgement in decision-making, understood as a quality intrinsic to the kind of knowledge which has memory at its heart.

1 Introduction

The premise that forgetfulness is a constituent part of memory reverberates throughout specialised works on ancient Greek literature. It is a recurrent theme both in Bernhard van Groningen's argumentation for the overriding ascendency of the past in ancient Greek thought¹ and in Gordon Shrimpton's analysis of memory in the configuration of historical thinking.² Forgetfulness is, in tandem with memory, the core of Michèle Simondon's publication, which is the only in-depth study on the topic with a focus on Greek thought until the end of the 5th century.³ Similarly, Harald Weinrich's monograph centres on forgetfulness, only he offers a panoramic view of its role in Western thought.⁴ Generally speaking, memory studies have fostered an awareness of the importance of forgetfulness for individuals and collectives alike in the re-construction of the past.⁵ This also made its mark on trends in Classics. Studies on Greek historiography, particularly on Herodotus, are ever more prone to point out, directly or indirectly, the choices historians had to make in the selection of the events and narratives about the past to be embedded in the collective memory.⁶ And yet, memory continues to hog the limelight in defining history.⁷ This sidelines forgetfulness and the intricacies of its perception, its representation and its narrative use in the sources.

To begin with, can proactive forgetfulness function as something desirable in Greek literature?⁸ Oral poetry and the literary tradition which stemmed from it made of memory and commemoration ruling cultural principles.⁹ Based on that

---

1 Groningen (1953).
2 Shrimpton (1997).
3 Simondon (1982).
4 Weinrich (2004).
5 Halbwachs (1997), Assmann (2011), Erll (2011).
6 For Herodotus' choices cf. Fornara (1971) 36: "He adapted the techniques of the poets in order to give colour and life to an account which *by his own choice of subject* absolutely required them"; Luraghi (2007) 70: "Such a use of the past – autonomous and arbitrary... regulated... only by *the historian's individual choice* – is possible only under the conditions of a script culture, writing being the 'enabling factor' for the individual and critical approach to tradition". Luraghi (2007) 8. For the role of choice inside the narrative of the *Histories* cf. especially Baragwanath (2016) 29: "Most notable is *the articulation rather than elision of choices* that were open in the past about future courses of action". Baragwanath (2016) 32: "The scope of *available choices* is expressive and creates an implied narrative of possible future outcomes". For Herodotus' invitation for listeners/readers to make their own choices cf. Saïd (2002) 125: "... since Herodotus *leaves open the choice* between two explanations...". The emphasis is mine in every case.
7 Cf. notably Le goff (1992) xi: "memory is the raw material of history". Along similar lines, cf. Shrimpton (1997) 13: "This identification... calls attention to the importance of memory in the matrix of historical production". Cf. also Finley (1965).
8 Simondon (1982) 325 specifies that, for the Greeks, forgetfulness could be salutary in the result it produced but not in its nature. Simondon (1982) 51: « L'œuvre de Pindare seul offre des exemples d'une semblable inversion des effets de l'oubli ». Cf. nn. 11, 12.
9 Particularly so concerning history. Cf. Simondon (1982) 305, where she brings up the connection between wisdom and memory, as the former springs from the accumulation of experiences.

rationale, forgetting ranked among the most baneful prospects. Although valid by and large, there are exceptions to this rule of thumb. In Antiquity, like today, forgetfulness could perform as a safety valve, famously so in its association with wine.¹⁰ This typified the active use of one's faculties at the service of temporary oblivion of one's everyday concerns.¹¹ Alternatively, it could come about as the result of an unmanageable factor like the passage of time.¹² Indeed, only time had the capacity to dissolve the vividness of past afflictions into a state of well-nigh non-existence tantamount to forgetfulness.

In principle, forgetfulness could not be the result of human action. Prior to Herodotus' composition, it appears either as the subject of the sentence or as the object of an action carried out by the gods. The earliest occurrences of λήθη in the literary corpus feature it as an autonomous, semi-divine personification of forgetfulness. In the *Iliad* it only occurs once:

ἀλλὰ σὺ σῇσιν ἔχε φρεσί, μηδέ σε Λήθη¹³ / αἱρείτω εὖτ' ἄν σε μελίφρων ὕπνος ἀνήῃ
Hom. *Iliad* 2.33–34

Keep this thought in your heart then, let not Forgetfulness take you, after you are released from the kindly sweet slumber.¹⁴

---

10 Simondon (1982) 130–32.
11 Euripides *Bacchae* 279–83: ὅταν πλησθῶσιν ἀμπέλου ῥοῆς, / ὕπνον τε λήθην τῶν καθ' ἡμέραν κακῶν / δίδωσιν, οὐδ' ἔστ' ἄλλο φάρμακον πόνων. (When they are filled with the stream of the vine, and gives sleep as oblivion of the evils that happen by day.) Cf. Simondon (1982) 129–31.
12 Simonides' verses to the contrary in *PMG* fr. 531 represent but the confirmation of the general belief that time could destroy the memory of the past: ἐντάφιον δὲ τοιοῦτον εὐρὼς / οὔθ' ὁ πανδαμάτωρ ἀμαυρώσει χρόνος. (Such a funeral-gift neither mould nor all-conquering time shall destroy.) Pindar's verses in *Olympian* 2.16–18 reiterate this idea, with the addition that they bring the benign effects of forgetting into the light: ἀποίητον οὐδ' ἄν / χρόνος ὁ πάντων πατὴρ δύναιτο θέμεν ἔργων τέλος. (Not even Time, the father of all, could undo their outcome.)
13 The Oxford and Teubner editions write λήθη in lower case, but one may wonder whether Oblivion may be intended as a divinity. This would be in keeping with the personification found in Hesiod's *Theogony* and, more to the point, with Ὄνειρος (or Dream), which is clearly a god in the same passage of the *Iliad*. The capitalization of Forgetfulness in Lattimore's translation is also mine.
14 Whilst λανθάνω occurs frequently (97 times), this attestation of λήθη is a *hapax legomenon* in Homer. For forgetfulness in the Homeric poems, see Simondon (1982) 131–40 and Weinrich (2008) 13–16. Pindar *Nemean* 8.24: ἦ τιν' ἄγλωσσον μέν, ἦτορ δ' ἄλκιμον, λάθα κατέχει / ἐν λυγρῷ νείκει. (Truly, oblivion overwhelms many a man whose tongue is speechless, but heart is bold, in a grievous quarrel.) This passage underlines the advantage of the ability to express oneself well (rhetoric) over valour, which is a far cry from Homer's world. I thank Anastasia Maravela for pointing this out to me.

Hesiod provides us with Lēthē's genealogy, describing her as the offspring of Eris (or Strife). Among her numerous siblings, Hesiod lists Lies (Ψέυδεα), Disputes (Ἀμφιλλογίας), Lawlesness (Δυσνομίην) and Ruin (Ἄτην):

> αὐτὰρ Ἔρις στυγερὴ τέκε μὲν Πόνον ἀλγινόεντα / Λήθην τε Λιμόν τε καὶ Ἄλγεα δακρυόεντα
> Hes. *Theog.* 227–28

> Hateful Strife bore painful Toil, Forgetfulness,[15] Starvation and tearful Pain.

Looking beyond the Homeric poems and Hesiod, unless referred to as a source of comfort, the negative tinge of λήθη is easily detectable across works. It is also attested as the object (or the result) of an action linking directly with a divinity or a mythological figure.[16] In Theognis λήθη is not a goddess. Persephone, the poet says, dispenses forgetfulness among mortals:

> ἥτε βροτοῖς παρέχει λήθην βλάπτουσα νόοιο·
> Thgn. 1.705

> [Persephone] gives men forgetfulness by disconcerting the mind.

In Pindar most traces of personification and divine intervention seen in Hesiod have disappeared:

> λάθα δὲ πότμῳ σὺν εὐδαίμονι γένοιτ' ἄν
> Pind. *Ol.* 2.18

> But with a fortunate destiny forgetfulness may arise.

And also:

> ἐπὶ μὰν βαίνει τε καὶ λάθας ἀτέκμαρτα νέφος, / καὶ παρέλκει πραγμάτων ὀρθὰν ὁδὸν / ἔξω φρενῶν
> Pind. *Ol.* 7.45

---

15 West (1988) opts for rendering λήθη as "Neglect", thus anticipating later developments. The interpretation of λήθη (and its cognates) as "neglect" or "negligence" would gradually gain ground. In Xenophon it is its primary meaning. However, there is no need to take that step retrospectively when dealing with Homer's and Hesiod's works. In them, λήθη is still conceived of as the source (i.e. a divinity), not as the end result (i.e. human negligence).
16 For a fine-grained analysis of forgetfulness in *Ol.* 7, see Simondon (1982) 52–55. Cf. Weinrich (2008) 6.

But without warning some cloud of forgetfulness comes upon them and wrests the straight path of affairs from their minds.

As with Theognis (or Herodotus later on) Pindar links forgetfulness with a defective use of the mind. The difference lies in the origin: Theognis explains the resulting human negligence as coming from Persephone, Pindar as carried by a cloud and Herodotus as mortals' own doing, even if in accordance to divine design.

There are two exceptions to this pattern but they constitute but intermediate steps with reference to the twist it acquires in the *Histories*. In the first case, Pindar speaks of *taking* solace for the hardships of life from victory in athletic games. Theaios *obtains* forgetfulness – i.e. comfort – from his success at the Nemean games:

Οὐλία παῖς ἔνθα νικάσαις δὶς ἔσχεν Θεαῖος εὐφόρων λάθαν πόνων

Pind. *Nem*. 10.24

In which [games] Oulias' son, Theaios, was twice victorious and won forgetfulness of his bravely borne labours.

On one occasion, Alcimidas *thwarts* forgetfulness, as his victory breathes new life into the glory of his great-grandfather, Socleidas, the memory of whom was almost extinct:[17]

καὶ πεντάκις Ἰσθμοῖ στεφανωσάμενος, / Νεμέᾳ δὲ τρίς, ἔπαυσε λάθαν / Σωκλείδα

Pind. *Nem*. 6.19–21

... and by winning crowns five times at the Isthmus and three at Nemea, he ended the oblivion of Sokleidas.

A contemporary of Herodotus, Sophocles, also resorts on occasion to λήθη. In Philoctetes, it is beneficial, as it refers to a momentary alleviation of physical pain:

καὶ νῦν ἐπειδὴ τοῦδε τοῦ κακοῦ δοκεῖ / λήθη τις εἶναι κἀνάπαυλα δή

Soph. *Phil*. 877–78

Since some oblivion and release from my disease has come to me.

---

17 Cf. Simondon (1982) 120.

Λήθη is not a divinity here. Furthermore, Sophocles' formulation insinuates that the relief may not be real.[18] Injured, deserted, and alone for years on an island, what makes Philoctetes feel better is that Neoptolemus is willing to stay by his side despite the stench of his wound. In a pseudo-medical fashion, although his relief is in all likelihood psychological at root, the wretched man puts it down to a remission of his physical pain.

In the medical treatises λήθη is well attested.[19] In the Hippocratic corpus forgetfulness occurs in an entirely rationalised manner and never as a cure but as the regrettable consequence of an ailment. It is documented five times in total.[20] Twice in *Epidemics* book 3, first as part of a wider symptom picture:

περὶ δὲ τοὺς παροξυσμοὺς λήθη καὶ ἄφεσις καὶ ἀφωνίη

Hippoc. *Epid.* 3.3.6

And about the exacerbations there was loss of memory with prostration and speechlessness.

And secondly, explaining the obvious result from memory loss:

λήθη πάντων, ὅ τι λέγοι· παρεφέρετο

Hippoc. *Epid.* 3.3.17

Forgetfulness of everything he said; he was not himself.

In *Epidemics* book 7, that brief statement is further explained:

Λήθη δέ τις τοιαύτη· ἐρωτήσας, ὅ τι πύθοιτο, σμικρὸν, καὶ διαλιπὼν πάλιν ἠρώτα, καὶ ἔλεγεν αὖτις, ὡς οὐκ εἴη εἰρηκώς

Hippoc. *Epid.* 7.1.3

Loss of memory of this sort: he would ask something he wanted to know, subside awhile and ask it again, and repeat it as though he had not spoken.

---

18 The indefinite τις, in conjunction with the verb δοκεῖ, seems to slash the assertiveness of the statement.
19 Nutton (2004) 93 notes that "Herodotus' ways of thinking about historical processes… have strong parallels within the Hippocratic Corpus". Cf. Thucydides' use of the term in his description of the plague in 2.49.8: τοὺς δὲ καὶ λήθη ἐλάμβανε παραυτίκα ἀναστάντας τῶν πάντων ὁμοίως, καὶ ἠγνόησαν σφᾶς τε αὐτοὺς καὶ τοὺς ἐπιτηδείους (There were some also who, when they first began to get better, suffered from a total loss of memory, not knowing who they were themselves and being unable to recognize their friends.)
20 All rank amongst the earliest texts making up the Hippocratic corpus. Cf. Jones (1962) for the traditional dating and Lane Fox (2020) for a new proposal.

Lastly, there is one identical clarification found in two works, *Prorrhetic* and *Coan Prenotions*:

> Μετὰ ῥίγεος ἄγνοια, κακόν· κακὸν δὲ καὶ λήθη
> Hippoc. *Prorrh.* 1.64 / *Coac.* 6

> Loss of understanding in conjunction with chills is a bad sign; bad also is forgetfulness.

In no case do mortals *wield* forgetfulness.

2 Λήθη in respect of sound judgement

In the *Histories*, however, Herodotus enacts the deliberate use of forgetfulness on the part of human agents.[21] For that reason, zooming into the distribution and performative value of λήθη and its cognates in Herodotus' *Histories* can shed light on the mechanisms of historical thinking (and writing) in relation to the dawn of human responsibility in a fate-ridden worldview. It can also allow further monitoring of the variations in the conception of forgetfulness, as well as in the positive or negative shading conferred on it. Thirdly, it can bring to light yet another aspect of the historian's multihued toolkit for characterisation.[22]

Indeed, depending on how actors assess a critical situation, the outcome from the actions they undertake can oscillate from beneficial to deleterious. This applies not just to the characters directly involved in making a critical decision but principally to the people at whose head they stand: Whereas tragedy hinges on the individual's experience in agonising over a decision, in history the significance of the decision in finding *cause* or *responsibility* and the consequences which ensue for whole peoples become the locus.

In the *Histories*, the right employment of forgetfulness may alternately bring about a group's rise to power or the death knell of its political ascendency over others. At the level of the stories, λήθη emerges as a catalyst of an understanding of *(good) judgement* as the absence of *forgetfulness* (ἀ-λήθεια). That is to say, as an (adequate) interaction with one's surrounding based on the knowledge of it, which, in its turn, stems from the cultivation of memory. Shrimpton rightly throws into relief the underlying etymology of truth (ἀ-λήθεια) as the negation of

---

[21] Baragwanath (2012) 54.
[22] Cf. Bakker (2018).

forgetfulness,[23] as well as underscoring the strong ascendency this link had in historiography.[24]

Significantly, the only two occurrences of λήθη in the *Histories* overlap in their formulation. Taken in conjunction, they showcase that knowing use of forgetfulness in decision-making, as part and parcel of sound assessment – i.e. relying on memory – can be positive. Conversely, heedless forgetfulness foreshadows ruin. The first passage can be found at the beginning of the Cyrus *logos*, in the episode in which a series of dreams appear to the Median king, Astyages. The Persian *Magi* take these dreams to presage that the Median princess, Mandane, will beget a son who would overthrow her father Astyages (1.107–8). In order to avoid that outcome, he first sets out to betroth her to a Persian man. Though still a noble man, his being a Persian made him inferior in rank by default, which, Astyages conjectured, would nullify the chance of his progeny rising to power. After the birth of Mandane's first child, however, Astyages decides to have the baby exposed with a view to ensuring that the prophecy would not be fulfilled. The unsavoury task he entrusts to Harpagus, a relative of his. Harpagus, in his turn, foists it upon a shepherd, who takes pity on the baby and adopts him. When years later Cyrus' identity is finally revealed, his grandfather Astyages lets him live (1.120) but does not forgive Harpagus. As punishment, Astyages kills Harpagus' son, has the body cooked and serves his flesh as dinner to him (1.119). Swallowing the abuse in that moment, Harpagus will, in time, find the opportunity to

---

23 Shrimpton (1997) 7. Cf. West (1966) 231, where he asserts that "the meaning of the word may have been influenced by its often felt antithesis with ἀλήθεια". West (1966) 233 he presses the point further as he sees ἀλήθεια in *Theog.* 234 as being "contrasted with Λήθην in 227. ἀληθής, -εια are often thought of in this etymological way, and so associated with remembering".

24 West (1966) 63. Quite plausible though this might be, this correlation does not appear to be fully established in Herodotus, at least on a conscious level. As Nightingale suggests, this is a distinctly Platonic style of thinking that projects 'truth' as an absolute and alētheia will be the word that fulfils this function in philosophical discourse. I owe this remark to Duncan Kennedy, whom I thank for it. Overt association of truth with history writing sensu stricto is therefore better posited for later authors. As an example, see Baragwanath (2017) and Tamiolaki (2017) for truth in Xenophon and Lucian respectively.

get back at Astyages by inciting Cyrus to revolt. At that crossroads, Astyages' blindness (θεοβλαβής)[25] leads to an ill-fated decision:[26]

> ἀκούσας δὲ ταῦτα ὁ Ἀστυάγης Μήδους τε ὥπλισε πάντας, καὶ στρατηγὸν αὐτῶν ὥστε θεοβλαβὴς ἐὼν Ἅρπαγον ἀπέδεξε, λήθην ποιεύμενος τά μιν ἑόργεε
>
> Hdt. 1.127.2

> Once he had heard the news, Astyages armed all the Medes and, in his delusion, he appointed Harpagus as their commander in chief, brushing off what he had done to him.[27]

Although it does not suggest full active force, the Middle Voice ποιεύμενος does underline that the conscious involvement of an individual in what he or she does (or does not do) is important.[28] Without attributing full agency to him, the participle ποιεύμενος in these lines denotes awareness on the part of Astyages. This stresses his responsibility in what follows. By choosing to 'brush off' (λήθην ποιεύμενος)[29] the hideous reprisal he had inflicted on Harpagus, Astyages hands him the command of the army sent to fight Cyrus. Ruin obviously follows for Astyages and the Medes, as they become subject to their former servants, the Persians. In the closing lines of the story, Astyages tries to put the onus of the overturn upon Harpagus (1.129) but the narration subtly contradicts him.

Offsetting this instance, the same formulation recurs for the second and last time. At the hour of truth, when a decision must be made whether to engage in battle with the Persian fleet at Salamis, the Greek commanders cannot seem to

---

25 In the *Histories*, myth permeates history and vice versa. In his comment on Helen's presence in Egypt (2.120) Herodotus applies to Priam the term φρενοβλαβής, which is likely to reflect a rational development of θεοβλαβής. As opposed to that, he resorts to θεοβλαβής in order to characterise the poor decision-making of two historical figures, Astyages here and the Macedonian king in 8.137.4 (cf. Asheri (2011) 164). The tension which arises from the clash between asserting that Astyages' judgement was clouded by a god and the emphasis on his personal responsibility is poignant. See Morrison in this volume for the external influence on Astyages' decision. One of Herodotus' tours-de-force is that he drives the wedge of responsibility and cause (αἴτιος / αἰτίη) between fate and contingency.
26 Cf. Simondon (1982) 306, where, in her commentary on Plutarch's definition of memory and forgetfulness in *De tranquilitate animi*, she writes the following: « La mémoire, pour Plutarque, est la conscience du passé ; l'homme oublieux, par contre, est celui auquel le présent échappe et pour qui le passé n'a plus d'existence».
27 All translations of Theognis, Simonides and Herodotus are mine, except where noted. For the other works I have used the following translations: West's for Hesiod, Lattimore's for Homer, Race's for Pindar and Kirk's for Euripides.
28 Smyth (1920) 392.
29 For periphrases of ποιεῖσθαι with verbal nouns, see Smyth (1920) 391. Cf. Sleeman (2003) 225.

reach an agreement (8.78). In that critical moment, with the Persian threat looming large over them, Aristides proposes to Themistocles that, bitter enemies though they are (8.79.2), they 'put aside' their differences (λήθην ἐκείνων ποιεύμενος) in order to fight off the common enemy:

> ὑπὸ δὲ μεγάθεος τῶν παρεόντων κακῶν λήθην ἐκείνων ποιεύμενος ἐξεκαλέετο
>
> Hdt. 8.79.2

> [Aristides] called [Themistocles] out [of the conference venue][30] choosing to put their differences aside because of the scale of their present plight.

The ensuing collaboration between them will force the battle upon both opponents, to the advantage of the Greeks.[31] The two occurrences of λήθην ποιεῖσθαι are practically identical in the phrasing and in the intentionality behind the characters' respective decisions.[32] What sets them apart is the validity of the assessment leading to the decision. Whilst Astyages (non-Greek) greatly underrates the risk of appointing commander a man whom he had atrociously punished, Aristides and Themistocles fathom the dire straits in which the Greeks find themselves. The capacity to wield forgetfulness *knowledgeably* is therefore shown to be the trademark of sound political analysis.[33] Extrapolated to Herodotus' unabashed

---

30 Bowie (2007) 170 thinks Aristides "was not *in* the meeting" (my emphasis). Purvis agrees: "[Aristides] stood at the door of the council". Waterfield, however, leaves the spatial question open: "he presented himself at the meeting". At any rate, Aristides does speak to the assembled generals shortly after (8.81).
31 Bowie (2007) 168–69 underlines Themistocles' capacity to "listen to advice" and that the reconciliation is a positive "sign" heralding what is to come. However, at the end of the day it is Aristides who reaches out for Themistocles: οὗτος ὡνὴρ στὰς ἐπὶ τὸ συνέδριον ἐξεκαλέετο Θεμιστοκλέα (8.79.2). Interestingly, somebody's conduct in relation to an assembly coheres in its characterisation: Xerxes takes his preeminent seat: ἐπεὶ δὲ ἀπικόμενος προΐζετο (7.67.1); Themistocles leaves the assembly by stealth: λαθὼν ἐξέρχεται ἐκ τοῦ συνεδρίου (8.75.1); Aristides stands in front of it: οὗτος ὡνὴρ στὰς ἐπὶ τὸ συνέδριον (8.79.2).
32 Herodotus makes no distinction in his formulation. Astyages does not *fail to remember* what he had done to Harpagus, he simply does not consider it good enough a reason to mistrust Harpagus. I am grateful to Jenny Bryan for bringing this to my attention. It is not his *memory* that lets Astyages down but the conclusion he draws from the previous incidents between them, i.e. the *knowledge* he has (not) acquired from his experience.
33 Glaucus intentionally pretends to have forgotten (6.86c.1) the money a Milesian man had left deposited with him for safety, owing precisely to Glaucus' fame for honesty: οὔτε μέμνημαι τὸ πρῆγμα οὔτε με περιφέρει οὐδὲν εἰδέναι τούτων τῶν ὑμεῖς λέγετε (6.86b.2). (Neither do I recall this matter nor does anything you are saying bring about any knowledge of it.) Note that 'memory' (μέμνημαι) and 'knowledge' (εἰδέναι) interlock in this line. The oracle's subsequent

use of forgetfulness,[34] this explains why the historian uses this so overtly at the level of the composition, as will be argued below.[35]

3 Λανθάνω in respect of self-deception

A similar trend is traceable in Herodotus' use of λανθάνω. In negative terms, it appears notably in connection with Croesus and Cambyses in contexts in which failure to correctly interpret the circumstances leads to a tragic demise with catastrophic political consequences. Both cases involve fate in the unfolding of events. On the occasion of the farmers' plea for Croesus to send a hunting party led by his son Atys to rid them of a boar of gigantic size that is ravaging their crops, the king accedes to the request but refuses point blank to let Atys join the party. A dream had recently spoken to him in his sleep foretelling the death of his son and Croesus was adamant against letting him take any risks (1.38.1). Only when confronted with Atys' personal entreaty does Croesus yield. In his eagerness to participate in the hunt, Atys argues that the meaning of the dream had *escaped* Croesus:

τὸ δὲ οὐ μανθάνεις ἀλλὰ λέληθέ σε τὸ ὄνειρον, ἐμέ τοί δίκαιον ἐστί φράζειν

Hdt. 1.39.1

---

condemnation of his intended hoax moves Glaucus to 'remember' and to return the money. Doing the right thing rounds off the episode, which joins together memory, knowledge, good judgement (even if ultimately by divine intervention, Glaucus does take the step to ask for approval) and good action. Cf. Hornblower/Pelling (2017) 206 for Herodotus' take on the matter: "The focaliser is Hdt.".

34 Cf. fn. 57 below.
35 The point in time of these two opposing instances, both within Herodotus' account and within the chronology of the events narrated, should be carefully noted: Whilst the first passage, dealing with the fall of the Medes, comes early on in the narration (book 1), thus setting the tone of what wielding forgetfulness unadvisedly might bring about, the second one comes close to the end (book 8), which somehow balances things out by showing that propitious developments will follow from wielding forgetfulness wisely. The former signposts an end – i.e. τέλος – (the Medes') and the latter a beginning – ἀρχή – (Athens), which establishes a stark narrative chiasm between the disposition of the text and the events narrated in it in relation to λήθη.

> In what sense you are not grasping the meaning of the dream but it has escaped you,[36] it is just that I tell you.

The rawness in this scene will be accentuated when Atys' death becomes a *fait accompli* and Herodotus sets forth Croesus' line of thinking about the accidental murderer of his son in the following terms:

> διότι δὴ οἰκίοισι ὑποδεξάμενος τὸν ξεῖνον φονέα τοῦ παιδὸς ἐλάνθανε βόσκων
>
> Hdt. 1.44.2
>
> Because he [Croesus] had taken the stranger into his home without realising that he was tending to the killer of his son.

Predictably, the causal chain leading to this tragic episode remains inscrutable for the characters. From the oracle foreboding the expiry date of the Mermnad dynasty, of which Croesus was predestined to be the last ruler in Lydia (1.13), all coalesces for this outcome to take place.[37] However, insofar as he, Croesus, is depicted as empowered to make decisions, he is made accessory to the fulfilment of what fate had determined. In the affair of his son's death Croesus is doubly responsible for *failing to understand* or, rather, for *letting himself be misled*.

Similarly, in a flagrant case of self-delusion which is in keeping with the portrayal Herodotus makes of him throughout, Cambyses kills himself by accident.[38] The story goes that, soon after his foiled attack against the Ethiopians (3.25), celebrations erupt in Memphis. Cambyses takes them mistakenly as a manifestation

---

[36] Cf. Sleeman (2003) 177. See Morrison in this volume for forgetfulness in the analogous episode of the Calydonian Boar mentioned in the *Iliad*. According to the Homeric poem, Artemis sends the boar owing to a mortal's forgetfulness of his duties toward the goddess. That is to say, a mortal's forgetfulness lies at the *origin* of the problem. By contrast, in the *Histories* the focus shifts toward mortals' *responsibility* in failing to deal with the problem wisely.

[37] As Baragwanath (2020) 170 remarks, the Lydians had forgotten about the oracle. Cf. Pelling (2019) 270 fn. 42. Within the awakening to human responsibility the *Histories* bears witness to, might that be an intimation that events could have unfolded differently had they not forgotten? Pelling (2006) appends the layer of the readers' possible forgetfulness of this determining factor. For the Lydian dynasties in Herodotus, see Fehling (1990) 216–39 and Asheri (2011) 79–80. For some of the discussions on Croesus, see Miller (1963), Stahl (1975), Sage (1985), Chiasson (2003), Kindt (2006) and Pelling (2006).

[38] As Baragwanath (2020) 170 remarks, the Lydians had forgotten about the oracle. Cf. Pelling (2019) 270 fn. 42. Within the awakening to human responsibility the *Histories* bears witness to, might that be an intimation that events could have unfolded differently had they not forgotten? Pelling (2006) appends the layer of the readers' possible forgetfulness of this determining factor. For some of the commentaries dealing with this episode, see de Brown (1982), Lloyd (1988), Munson (1991) and Jong (2006).

of joy for his defeat and declares himself *undeceived* by what he deems a sham orchestrated by the Egyptian priests:

οὐ λήσειν ἔφη αὐτὸν εἰ θεός τις χειροήθης ἀπιγμένος εἴη Αἰγυπτίοισι

Hdt. 3.28.1

He said that it would not have escaped his notice if a tame god had arrived in Egypt.

In order to drive his point home, Cambyses slaughters the calf the Egyptians considered to be the god Apis reincarnated, in honour of whom the festivities were actually being carried out (3.29). Later on, Cambyses will end his days injured by his own hand in precisely the same spot where he had struck the fatal blow which had killed the god-calf (3.64.3). For Cambyses, as well as for Croesus, ruin ultimately sprouts from their own incapacity to assess their circumstances adequately. Even if they act in accordance with fate's design, they do so by means of their own (wrong) decisions.

Compare their faring with Amasis'. Although an ambiguous figure in the *Histories*, Amasis comes across as a man of considerable practical wisdom.[39] Crucially, his appraisal of reality in analogously key situations differs drastically from Croesus' and Cambyses'. A man of humble origin who rises to power, on one occasion his friends warn him against the life of debauchery he leads at night, despite his good handling of affairs in the daytime (2.173). Establishing a parallel with the danger of a bow snapping if it should be kept in tension at all times, he replies that also a person needs to slacken off in order not to lose his mind:

εἰ ἐθέλοι κατεσπουδάσθαι αἰεὶ μηδὲ ἐς παιγνίην τὸ μέρος ἑωυτὸν ἀνιέναι, λάθοι ἂν ἤτοι μανεὶς ἢ ὅ γε ἀπόπληκτος γενόμενος

Hdt. 2.173.4

Anyone dead-set on being always serious and never indulging in a measure of playfulness would imperceptibly slide into madness[40] or suffer a stroke.

Independent of the degree of agreement Amasis' words could engender in the listener, this statement contrasts Amasis' good practices in government with Cambyses' rule of terror. Within the logic of the story, Herodotus endorses Amasis' opinion, as he will soon after speak of Amasis' reign as the most prosperous period of Egypt (2.177.1). Unlike Croesus and Cambyses, Amasis neither *deceives himself* nor *lets himself be deceived* in relation to his political dealings. The

---

39 For Amasis in Herodotus, see Lloyd (1993) 211–14.
40 Waterfield's translation of λάθοι ἂν ἤτοι μανεὶς.

same can be said of Amasis' insightful reading of Polycrates' seeming unshakable prosperity as a harbinger of trouble. Due to a long string of military and political successes, Polycrates was in everybody's mouth (3.39). *Undeceived* by Polycrates' apparently interminable wave of prosperity and obliged by the ties of friendship (ξενίη) between them, Amasis shares with Polycrates his concerns about what he regards as excessively good fortune:

> καί κως τὸν Ἄμασιν εὐτυχέων μεγάλως ὁ Πολυκράτης οὐκ ἐλάνθανε, ἀλλά οἱ τοῦτ' ἦν ἐπιμελές
>
> Hdt. 3.40.1
>
> However, Polycrates and his long spell of good fortune did not confound Amasis but had him worried.

Even though Amasis perceives Polycrates' lucky streak as being double-edged and tells him as much, this does not help the Samian tyrant eschew his downfall (3.125.2). Nevertheless, Amasis has proven the soundness of his judgement again. And yet, Herodotus does not make him the subject of λανθάνω. Amasis does not allow himself to be fooled by the vicissitudes but he has no active (grammatical) involvement with regard to λανθάνω. That was the case with Croesus' lament for his son's killing. In those lines, Herodotus had made the Lydian king the subject of the verb: διότι δὴ οἰκίοισι ὑποδεξάμενος τὸν ξεῖνον φονέα τοῦ παιδὸς ἐλάνθανε βόσκων (1.44.2).[41] Croesus realises that, by taking in the man who would finally strike down his son Atys, he has inadvertently *tripped himself up*.

In Herodotus' later exposition of how Themistocles intentionally *deceives* the Greeks, the wording links with Croesus' wailing. When Eurybiades, the Spartan commander of the fleet sent to Artemisium to fend off the Persians, adamant against the appeals of the Euboeans, decides to fall back, the islanders turn to Themistocles (8.4). Only they do not so empty-handed and the Athenian accepts a bribe of thirty talents to talk the other generals into standing fast. For that purpose, Themistocles spends twelve talents to coax Eurybiades and Adeimantus the Corinthian, and keeps the rest. In one stroke, he deceives all and rakes it in:

---

[41] In like manner, Polycrates is the subject of ἐλάνθανε in 3.40.1. Like in the narration of Croesus' downfall, Herodotus seems to subtly make Polycrates partly responsible for his imminent ruin, as he is failing to assess where he really stands in the geopolitics of the Persian advance on Greece.

οὗτοί τε δὴ πάντες δώροισι ἀναπεπεισμένοι ἦσαν καὶ τοῖσι Εὐβοεῦσι ἐκεχάριστο, αὐτός τε ὁ Θεμιστοκλέης ἐκέρδηνε, ἐλάνθανε δὲ τὰ λοιπὰ ἔχων

Hdt. 8.5.3

So they were all persuaded with gifts and the Euboeans got their way, while Themistocles himself made a killing concealing that he had kept the rest [of the money].

Since the fight at Artemisium results in a standoff, Themistocles' selfish act cannot be said to be detrimental to the Greeks. Despite his dubious ways and goals, Themistocles, unlike Croesus (and Polycrates), is thus portrayed as capable of evaluating correctly the reality of the moment.⁴² Moreover, the participle λαθών seems to bear out the existence of a certain pattern in Herodotus' employment (and understanding) of λανθάνω. It occurs only twice in the *Histories*. First in connection with the fashion in which Themistocles sneaks out of the Assembly:

ἐνθαῦτα Θεμιστοκλέης ὡς ἑσσοῦτο τῇ γνώμῃ ὑπὸ τῶν Πελοποννησίων, λαθὼν ἐξέρχεται ἐκ τοῦ συνεδρίου

Hdt. 8.75.1

---

42 Weinrich (2008) 11f. discusses the anecdote reported by Cicero (*De Oratore* 2.74.299) about a hypothetical meeting between a man learned in the ways of mnemotechnics and Themistocles (cf. Simondon (1982) 181–88). In Cicero's work Themistocles is described as *doctus homo atque in primis eruditus*. In the *Histories* he is first introduced as follows: ἦν δὲ τῶν τις Ἀθηναίων ἀνὴρ ἐς πρώτους νεωστὶ παριών, τῷ οὔνομα μὲν ἦν Θεμιστοκλέης (7.143.1). (There was a certain Athenian man who had recently risen to the echelon of the leading citizens. He was called Themistocles.) A later passage sketches out Themistocles' reputation among the people: (8.110.1): ἐπειδὴ γὰρ καὶ πρότερον δεδογμένος εἶναι σοφὸς ἐφάνη ἐὼν ἀληθέως σοφός τε καὶ εὔβουλος. (For, though regarded as a knowledgeable man from before, he showed himself to be truly knowledgeable, and also well-advised.) 'In primis' in the first instance echoes ἐς πρώτους and 'eruditus' in the second mirrors σοφός. However, no mention of Themistocles as having a remarkably good memory can be found in Herodotus. One may wonder whether the ambiguity encapsulated in λανθάνω between 'deceive' and 'forget' may be behind Cicero's choice of Themistocles for this story. After all, what Cicero's Themistocles wishes for is a 'technique of forgetfulness' instead a 'technique of memory'. Though in Cicero this is conveyed by the verb *oblivisci*, which has given rise to expressions as *Ars oblivionalis* (Eco n.d.), the term 'lethotechnic' is also in circulation (Weinrich (2008) 12). The latter would fit Themistocles to a T, only it could be argued that not as a 'technique for forgetting' but as 'a technique for deception'. Likewise, one may wonder whether the adverb ἀληθέως qualifying σοφός in Hdt. 8.110.1 may contain a play on words tying in Themistocles' knowledgeability with 'non-forgetfulness' (*a-lētheiōs*) and, by extension, to his peerless flair for 'deception' (i.e. capacity for *wielding* 'forgetfulness'). See Hunter in this volume who remarks in connection with Cicero's story about Themistocles that "memory is a double-edged sword". Indeed, and so can forgetfulness be.

As his opinion was losing ground to that of the Spartans, Themistocles left the assembly by stealth.⁴³

And secondly shortly after in relation to Aristides eluding the Persian siege on his return from Aegina:

> ἐνθαῦτα ἔλεγε παρελθὼν ὁ Ἀριστείδης, φάμενος ἐξ Αἰγίνης τε ἥκειν καὶ μόγις ἐκπλῶσαι λαθὼν τοὺς ἐπορμέοντας· περιέχεσθαι γὰρ πᾶν τὸ στρατόπεδον τὸ Ἑλληνικὸν ὑπὸ τῶν νεῶν τῶν Ξέρξεω
>
> Hdt. 8.81.1

> Aristides then joined [the assembled commanders] and told them that he had barely managed to slip through the blockade, for the whole of the Greek navy was indeed surrounded by Xerxes' ships.

On Themistocles' initiative (8.80),⁴⁴ Aristides tries to persuade the Assembly by telling the truth of the situation (and of his escape): That they are surrounded and have no choice but to fight. The respective connotations of λαθών for Themistocles and Aristides are on opposite poles but in line with the profile delineated for each character in the overall narration: Although their separate and joined efforts contribute decisively to the Greek cause, Themistocles does so by *evading* the assembled Greeks, whereas Aristides does so by *evading* the enemy.⁴⁵

4 Ἐπιλανθάνω in respect of choice

Herodotus' narrative use of λήθη and λανθάνω to indicate sound or defective judgement when facing a given set of circumstances suggests a certain degree of awareness on his part, not least in the consistent distribution which reflects the Greeks' superiority over non-Greeks in this respect. However, this is not to say that Herodotus is following a predetermined plan in his use of this cluster of cognates. Absolute prefiguration would imply overmuch authorial intention from

---

43 Cf. fn. 31 above.
44 Cf. Bowie (2007) 170.
45 Also, Aristides' contribution in this context consists in lending his credibility to the task of convincing his fellow Greeks that the best course of action is to fight at Salamis. Therefore, he *tells the truth* of their situation to his fellow Greeks. As opposed to that, Themistocles' participation consists in tricking the Persians into engaging in the fight and in *not telling the truth* of why the Persian fleet has made the retreat impossible to his fellow Greeks.

the outset, whilst Herodotus' *research* (ἱστορίη) suggests a process. One admittedly defined from the start in its main guidelines but one in which the narrative and the interpretation emerge gradually. It is hardly possible to envisage how a complete interpretation can be wholly explicit to the author himself beforehand.[46] In Herodotus' case the historian surely *shapes* meaning but that is not analogous to saying that he *controls* meaning. Instead, it emerges as a heuristic, rather than an abstract, notion.[47] This study does not aim, therefore, at positing a fully predesigned use of λήθη and λανθάνω as a narrative device on the part of Herodotus.

That said, another cognate, ἐπιλανθάνω, also shows traces of a certain degree of intentional narrative use. In that respect, it arises as defining of the historian's task.[48] Saving from oblivion what the historian deems to be the height of human deeds is admittedly one of the unifying threads of Herodotus' work. It is indeed one of history's very *raisons d'être*. The historian must decide what is to be remembered and what is to be left to drift into oblivion. By the same token, *unveiling* the truth about the past is a constituent of the historian's trade, unpleasant though it may be at times.[49] Again, a pair of utterances coincides around this principle. One can be found at the level of the stories and the other at the level of the composition. Before zooming out to the latter, namely, the plane on which Herodotus applies it to his decision to discard a piece of information, let us take a look at what this means when inserted in a story. This, in its turn, requires a little contextualisation.

---

[46] The view Grethlein (2016) 59 explicates on the importance of the vantage points with regard to the selection and the arrangement of the material in giving the work its specific character is enlightening as long as it is not taken in absolute terms.

[47] When Solon tells Croesus to look towards the *telos* (1.32.9) the notion provides a way of thinking about events, not an answer. At the end of the day, this depends on the question asked and the story told.

[48] At bare minimum, commendation, memorialization and causation make up the staple ingredients of ancient history by and large. In this study the emphasis lies on the underside of memory, namely, forgetfulness. The didactic lode is a peculiarity especially operational in Herodotus. Cf. Raaulaub (in Foxhall) (2015) 195–96 and Lateiner (1989) 226. Cf. Murray (in Luraghi) (2007) 30: "This type of tradition can be regarded as the origin of our western style of history, with its rationalism, its emphasis on action in politics and war, and its obsession with decision-making and human causation". Memorializing – i.e. glorifying – any given narrative of the past is part and parcel of the process of history writing. Cf. Bowie (in Luraghi) (2007) 63 and Marincola (2012) 18. Cf. Nicolai (in Luraghi) (2007) 279 for the pitfalls of finding truth in the past and the rift between Herodotus and Thucydides on this score. Cf. Gerhke (in Luraghi) (2007) 309 for the invention of the past in intentional history contruction.

[49] Cf. Thomas (2000) 168–212. Cf. also Foucault (1983) for *parrhesia*, the duty to speak out and the dangers involved in it in Ancient Greece.

Herodotus engages frequently in dialogue with the Homeric poems. In that sense, the *Histories* plausibly contains an update of the disclaimer Phemius the singer issues in the *Odyssey* as to the alleged inappropriateness of his singing. Telemachus steps in twice to save the singer: Once when Penelope rebukes Phemius for singing the *nostoi*, the homecomings of the Greeks from Troy (*Od.* 1.347–50);[50] And once when Odysseus is on the verge of finishing off the singer for having entertained Penelope's brazen suitors during his absence (*Od.* 22.356). As the singer explains, however, the choice is not down to him: his fate lies in the hands of men stronger than him and he is therefore obliged to comply with their wishes (*Od.* 22.354).[51] In the *Histories* something similar can be seen when Artabanus (7.10a.1) and Artemisia (8.68a.1) excuse themselves on speaking against Xerxes' design to invade Greece and to attack at Salamis respectively. The difference is that the 'inferior' now not only dare to speak their mind but consider it their duty: They justify their boldness before the king of kings adducing that good decision-making cannot be achieved without a sound analysis of their situation. Both speeches include a *captatio benevolentiae* for the potentially unpleasant truths they are about to utter. Still, in possession of sound analytical skills, they are compelled to speak out. Likewise, a character in the *Histories* behaves fleetingly as a true historian in his use of ἐπιλανθάνω and loses his life by doing so.

A Persian nobleman, Prexaspes, reveals the farce of the false Smerdis, the usurper of the Persian throne, and he does so at the price of losing his own life (3.75.1–2). Refusing to tell the Persian people the lie that would legitimise the usurper, Prexaspes exposes him instead:

ὁ δὲ τῶν μὲν ἐκεῖνοι προσεδέοντο αὐτοῦ, τούτων μὲν ἑκὼν ἐπελήθετο

Hdt. 3.75.1

He deliberately ignored everything they had asked him to say.

After his speech, Prexaspes kills himself.[52] Since sound historicising, insofar as it implied saving unpleasant truths from oblivion, entailed risks, this can represent

---

50 Penelope would rather not hear about homecomings, as it reminds her of her husband, whence her fit of anger. However, Penelope's wish for Phemius not to bring Odysseus' absence to mind should not be mistaken for a longing for forgetfulness. Cf. Pulleyn (2019) 207.
51 Pulleyn (2019) 207.
52 Probably knowing the usurper would do the job for him if he did not do it himself. Even so, there is the query whether Prexaspes is trying to confer a higher degree of validity to his words by making them his last. In some countries a dying declaration could be accepted as evidence in criminal law in recent times. I owe this remark to Stephen Todd.

the historian's *apologia* of the historian's task.⁵³ This passage further draws the contours of *(good) judgement* as the negation of forgetfulness (ἀ-λήθεια). In addition to brushing aside the instructions he had received from the usurper, by recalling the Persian lineage from Achamenes down to Cyrus in his speech,⁵⁴ Prexaspes is said to let the truth *shine through*:

> διεξελθὼν δὲ ταῦτα ἐξέφαινε τὴν ἀληθείην, φάμενος πρότερον μὲν κρύπτειν (οὐ γάρ οἱ εἶναι ἀσφαλὲς λέγειν τὰ γενόμενα)
>
> Hdt. 3.75.2
>
> Then after going through all that he told the truth and explained he had kept it secret before because it was not safe for him to tell what had happened.

Prexaspes, performing as something of a Doppelgänger of Herodotus at the level of the stories, casts the lies into oblivion and brings the truth (of the political situation) into the light.⁵⁵ This leads to the second example of ἐπιλανθάνω making up the pair, now applied to the level of the composition. The formulation when Prexaspes opts for disclosing the truth mimics what Herodotus declares on one occasion about his decision to withhold information.⁵⁶ Herodotus phrases this notion in a variety of ways but only twice does he employ this construction (ἑκὼν

---

53 Like for Prexaspes, Herodotus' apparently self-imposed decision to admonish the Athenians against taking the wrong decisions in his own present entailed its own risks. Cf. Moles (in Bakker) (2002) 13–52 for post Persian War Athens.
54 Without the term being present, Prexaspes does an exercise in genealogy. Cf. Asheri (2011) 469: "[ἐγενεηλόγησε] belongs to the technical terminology of the early Greek genealogists". This way, he confers trustworthiness and authority to his confession. Cf. Thomas (1989) 173–95 for the moral role of ancestry in political claims. Cf. West (2005) 3–30. As is often the case, budding concepts are operational in Herodotus even if they remain untheorised. Hornblower and Pelling (2017) 129 remark concerning ἐπηγγείλατο καταγωγὴν καὶ ξείνια in 6.35.2 that "the offer included a bed for the night (καταγωγὴν), but ξείνια covers a good deal more". May that idea also apply to καταγωγὴν in respect to genealogy? Could Miltiades be giving an account of his genealogy in 6.35.2, in addition to offer lodgings? After all the term is first attested in the *Histories* and only at a later stage will it be overtly used for that purpose.
55 This shines a positive light on the character's discernment as well as it reflects positively on Herodotus. Cf. Bakker (in Ash) (2016) 60: "Cambyses praises his servant Prexaspes as a 'good man' (ἀνὴρ ἀγαθός, 3.63.3) for his investigation into the identity of Smerdis. Indeed he dies as a 'man of repute' (3.75.3) as he refuses to join the Magi and kills himself publicly".
56 A noteworthy rephrasing of this idea arises in Otanes' deliberate disregard of Darius' orders not to kill or enslave the Samians after taking the island: τουτέων μὲν τῶν ἐντολέων μεμνημένος ἐπελανθάνετο (3.147.1). (He knowingly ignored Darius' orders.)

ἐπιλανθάνομαι), and only once does he apply it to his own work.[57] It appears in the section devoted to Sastaspes' attempted circumnavigation of Libya. In passing, Herodotus mentions that a Samian man had become wealthy by stealing the money from a fugitive eunuch. Although he knows the name of the man, he states that he chooses to keep it to himself:[58]

> τὰ Σάμιος ἀνὴρ κατέσχε, τοῦ ἐπιστάμενος τὸ οὔνομα ἑκὼν ἐπιλήθομαι
>
> Hdt. 4.43.7
>
> A Samian man took all the money. I know his name, but I prefer not to call it to mind.

Herodotus often resorts to formal aspects in his choice of language to give credibility to characters at specific junctures. A character verbalising things in the same terms as Herodotus does elsewhere is, as a rule, indicative of good analytical skills being attributed to that character.[59] The quite disparate outcomes for two identically correct exercises in historicising underscore the superiority of the Greeks in this respect.[60]

---

57 Herodotus adduces the following reasons to cast a piece of information into oblivion: political caution (τοῦ ἐπιστάμενος τὸ οὔνομα οὐκ ἐπιμνήσομαι – 1.51.4; τοῦ ἐπιστάμενος τὸ οὔνομα ἑκὼν ἐπιλήθομαι – 4.43.7); avoidance of exaggeration (ἐξεπιστάμενος μνήμην οὐ ποιήσομαι – 1.193.4; τὸν γὰρ περὶ Ἀβάριος λόγον τοῦ λεγομένου εἶναι Ὑπερβορέου οὐ λέγω – 4.36.1); distaste for the topic (τὸν γὰρ περὶ Ἀβάριος λόγον τοῦ λεγομένου εἶναι Ὑπερβορέου οὐ λέγω; οὔ μοι ἥδιον ἐστὶ λέγειν – 2.46.2; ἀποκτείνας δέ μιν οὐκ ἀξίως ἀπηγήσιος Ὀροίτης ἀνεσταύρωσε – 3.125.3); avoidance of whistleblowing (τῶν ἐγὼ εἰδὼς τὰ οὐνόματα οὐ γράφω – 2.123.3); religious qualms (πλὴν ὅσον αὐτῆς ὁσίη ἐστὶ λέγειν – 2.171.1–2); lack of relevance (τὸ δ' ἔτι τούτων ἔλασσον ἀπιεὶς οὐ λέγω – 3.95.2); and common knowledge (ἐπισταμένοισι τοῖσι Ἕλλησι οὐ συγγράφω – 3.103.1).
58 Cf. Baragwanath (2012) 54 and n. 75.
59 Cf. Baragwanath (2012) 55: "Herodotus' characters use of the past serves rather as a foil that illuminates by contrast his own more critical and balanced practice". On this occasion, Prexaspes' use of the past in his analysis of the present illuminates the risks involved in speaking the truth when it might not sit well with those in power. That is, the Magi for Prexaspes, and the Athenian people as a whole for Herodotus.
60 Ἐπιλανθάνω occurs three more times. Twice it describes cowardly behaviour taken as 'forgetting' threatening words uttered prior to the fight (4.4.1, 4.125.5). Once it appears in the episode of the embassy of the Samian exiles at Sparta: οἱ δέ σφι τῇ πρώτῃ καταστάσι ὑπεκρίναντο τὰ μὲν πρῶτα λεχθέντα ἐπιλελῆσθαι, τὰ δὲ ὕστατα οὐ συνιέναι (3.46.1). (In the first audience [the Spartans] explained that they had *put out of their minds* the first part of the speech and could not make sense of the last part.) Translations overlook the tinge of agency which ἐπιλανθάνω seems to distil and render it "that they had forgotten".

5 Conclusions

The selection of what is to be remembered and what is to be thrown into oblivion is crucial in Herodotus' composition to an extent equitable to other historical works. The *Histories*, however, displays that process explicitly in what seems an attempt to buttress the historian's authority over the narration. However, the downsides of this narrative choice seem to have outweighed the perks already at an early stage, as stating that information was being withheld from the audience did not become common place in historiography. All the more reason to treasure Herodotus' *Histories*, as it offers a rare vantage point into a basic element from among the tricks of the trade he greatly helped to shape.

Good judgement and entrusting to oblivion what the historian deems unworthy of being remembered is one and the same thing in the *Histories*. Observation,[61] inquiry and sound judgement were the means to attain an accurate analysis of the political context. Additionally, daring to speak the truth about it required courage, since it was an action bound to be met with opposition. Moreover, the value Herodotus bestows upon this narrative device becomes clear from how it instils the narration. Characters that possess sound judgement and can assess their political circumstances correctly, who have the courage to express their view and the rhetoric skills to convey the message appropriately are depicted in a positive light which shines indirectly on the historian. The narrative use of λήθη and its cognates in Herodotus' *Histories* therefore serves a threefold purpose: it further pinpoints the historian's authority over the (re)construction of the past; it sheds light on yet another mechanism for characterisation in historical works;[62] and it underscores the sway that making adequate use of the faculty of memory held within the Greek worldview.

---

61 Cf. Rutherford (2013) 149–50 and 334–36 for *theōriā* in Herodotus. Rutherford (2013) 324 for the implicit connection between *theōriā* and *philosophein*, embodied notably in Solon's travels. Neither *alētheia* nor *philosophein*, or *historein*, for that matter, should be mistakenly identified with *(absolute, abstract) truth, philosophy* or *history (as intellectual disciplines)* respectively. The intellectual pursuits these last refer to will hatch as such at a later stage. Using them as categories of analysis for the *Histories* can only muddle things up.
62 Cf. Ash (2016).

Bibliography

Ash, R. (2016), *Fame and infamy: essays for Christopher Pelling on characterization in Greek and Roman biography and historiography*, Oxford.
Asheri, D./A. Lloyd/A. Corcella/O. Murray/A. Moreno (2011), *A commentary on Herodotus books I–IV*, Oxford.
Assmann, J. (2011), *Cultural Memory and Early Civilization: Writing, Remembrance, and Political Imagination*, Cambridge.
Bakker, E.J./I.J.F.de Jong/H. van Wees (2002), *Brill's companion to Herodotus*, Leiden.
Bakker, E.J. (2018), "Herodotus", in: K. de Temmerman & E. van Emde Boas, *Characterization in ancient Greek literature*, Leiden: 135–52.
Baragwanath, E./M. de Bakker (eds.) (2012), *Myth, Truth and Narrative in Herodotus*, Oxford.
Baragwanath, E. (2012), "The mythic plupast in Herodotus", in: G. Jonas & C. Krebs (eds.), *Time and narrative in ancient historiography: the 'plupast' from Herodotus to Appian*, Cambridge: 35–56.
Baragwanath, E. (2016), "Herodotus and the avoidance of hindsight", in A. Powell (ed.), *Hindsight in Greek and Roman History*, Swansea: 25–48.
Baragwanath, E. (2017), "Intertextuality and Plural Truths in Xenophon's Historical Narrative", in I. Ruffell & L. Hau (eds.), *Truth and history in the ancient world: pluralising the past*, New York: 155–171.
Baragwanath, E. (2020), "History, Ethnography and Aetiology in Herodotus' Libyan *logos*", *Histos* Supplement 11: 155–88.
Bowie, A. (2007), *Histories. Book VIII*, Cambridge.
Brown, T. (1982), "Herodotus' Portrait of Cambyses", in *Historia: Zeitschrift Für Alte Geschichte* 31 (4): 387–403.
Chiasson, C. (2003), "Herodotus' use of Attic tragedy in the Lydian logos", in *Classical Antiquity* 22 (1): 5–35.
Chiasson, C. (2012), "Myth and Truth in Herodotus' Cyrus Logos", in E. Baragwanath & M. de Bakker (eds.), *Myth, Truth and Narrative in Herodotus*, Oxford: 213–232.
Collingwood, R.G. (2005), *The idea of history*, Oxford.
Connerton, P. (2008), "Seven types of forgetting", in *Memory Studies* 1 (1): 59–71.
Dewald, C./J. Marincola (2012), *The Cambridge Companion to Herodotus*, Cambridge.
Eco, U. (1988), "An *Ars Oblivionalis*? Forget It!", *PMLA* 103: 254–61.
Erll, A. (2011), *Memory in culture*, Hampshire.
Fehling, D. (1990), *Herodotus and his 'sources': citation, invention, and narrative art*, Leeds.
Fentress, J./C. Wickham (1992), *Social memory*, Oxford.
Finley, M.I. (1965), "Myth, Memory, and History", in *History and Theory* 4 (3): 281–302.
Fornara, C.W. (1971), *Herodotus: an interpretative essay*, Oxford.
Foucault, M. (1983), *Discourse and Truth: the Problematization of Parrhesia: 6 lectures given by Michel Foucault at the University of California at Berkeley*, Berkeley.
Fox Lane, R. (2020), *The invention of medicine: from Homer to Hippocrates*, London.
Foxhall, L./H.J. Gehrke/N. Luraghi (2015), *Intentional History Spinning Time in Ancient Greece*, Stuttgart.
Grethlein, J. (2016), "Ancient Historiography and 'Future Past'", in A. Lianeri (ed.), *Knowing future time in and through Greek historiography*, Berlin: 59–78.

Grethlein, J./C. Krebs (2016), *Time and narrative in ancient historiography: the 'plupast' from Herodotus to Appian*, Cambridge.
Groningen, A. van. (1953), *In the grip of the past; essay on an aspect of Greek thought*, Leiden.
Halbwachs, M./G. Namer/M. Jaisson (1997), *La mémoire collective*, Paris.
Hornblower, S./C. Pelling (2017), Histories. *Book VI*, Cambridge.
Jones, H.S. (1962), *Hippocrates 1*, Massachusetts.
Jong, I. de (2006), "Herodotus on the Dream of Cambyses (*Histories* 3.30, 61–5)", in *Land of Dreams. Greek and Latin Studies in Honour of A.H.M. Kessels*, Leiden: 3–17.
Jong, I. de (2014), *Narratology and classics: a practical guide*, Oxford.
Kindt, J. (2006), "Delphic Oracle Stories and the Beginning of Historiography: Herodotus Croesus logos", *Classical Philology* 101 (1): 34–51.
Kirk, G. (1970), *The Bacchae*, Englewood Cliffs.
Le Goff, J. (1986), *Histoire et mémoire*, Paris.
Lateiner, D. (1989), *The historical method of Herodotus*, Toronto.
Lattimore, R. (1951), *The* Iliad, Chicago.
Lloyd, A. (1993), *Herodotus, book II commentary 99 – 182*, Leiden.
Lloyd, A. (1988), "Herodotus on Cambyses: some thoughts on recent work", in A. Kuhrt & H. Weerdenburg (eds.), *Achaemenid history 3, proceedings of the London 1985 Achaemenid History Workshop III*: 55–66.
Luraghi, N. (2007), *The historian's craft in the age of Herodotus*, Oxford.
Marincola, J. (2007), *A companion to Greek and Roman historiography*, Malden.
Miller, M. (1963), "The Herodotean Croesus", *Klio* 41: 58–94.
Munson, R. (1991), "The madness of Cambyses (Herodotus 3.16–38)", *Arethusa*, 24 (1) 43–65.
Nightingale, W. (2004), *Spectacles of Truth in Classical Greek Philosophy: Theoria in Its Cultural Context*, Cambridge.
Nutton, V. (2004), *Ancient medicine*, London.
Pelling, C. (2006), "Educating Croesus talking and learning in Herodotus Lydian logos", *Classical Antiquity* 25 (1): 141–177.
Pelling, C. (2019), *Herodotus and the Question Why*, Austin.
Powell, A. (2016), *Hindsight in Greek and Roman history*, Swansea.
Pulleyn, S. (2019), Odyssey 1, Oxford.
Raaflaub, K. (2014), *Thinking, recording, and writing history in the ancient world*, Chichester.
Race, W. (1997), *Pindar 1*, Cambridge, MA.
Race, W. (1997), *Pindar 2*, Cambridge, MA.
Ricœur, P. (2003), *La mémoire, l'histoire, l'oublie*, Paris.
Ruffell, I./L. Hau (eds.), *Truth and history in the ancient world: pluralising the past*, New York.
Rutherford, I. (2013), *State Pilgrims and Sacred Observers in Ancient Greece: A Study of Theoria and Theoroi*, Cambridge.
Sage, P. (1985), *Solon, Croesus and the theme of the ideal life*, Ann Arbor.
Saïd, S. (2002), 'Herodotus and tragedy', in E.J. Bakker, I.J.F. de Jong and H. van Wees, *Brill's companion to Herodotus*, Leiden: 117–48.
Sleeman, J. (2003), *Herodotus: book I*, London.
Shrimpton, G./K. Gillis (1997), *History and memory in Ancient Greece*, Montreal.
Simondon, M. (1982), *La mémoire et l'oubli: dans la pensée grecque jusqu'à la fin du Ve siècle avant J.-C. : psychologie archaïque, mythes et doctrines*, Paris.
Stahl, H. (1975), "Learning through suffering? Croesus conversations in the history of Herodotus", *Yale classical studies* 24: 1–36.

Strassler, R./A. Purvis (2009), *The landmark Herodotus: the Histories*, New York.
Tamiolaki, M. (2017), "Lucian on Truth and Lies in Ancient Historiography: The Theory and its Limits", in I. Ruffell & L. Hau (eds.), *Truth and history in the ancient world: pluralising the past*, New York.
Thomas, R. (1989), *Oral tradition and written record in classical Athens*, Cambridge.
Thomas, R. (2000), *Herodotus in context: ethnography, science, and the art of persuasion*, Cambridge.
Yates, F. (2001), *The Art of Memory*, London.
Waterfield, R./C. Dewald (2008), *The Histories*, New York.
West, M.L. (1966), *Theogony*, Oxford.
West, M.L. (1988), *Theogony and Works and days*, Oxford.
West, M.L. (2005), *The Hesiodic catalogue of women: its nature, structure, and origins*, Oxford.
Weinrich, H. (2004), *Lethe: the art and critique of forgetting*, Ithaca.

Part V: **Further Thoughts**

Richard Hunter
Memory and its Discontents in Ancient Literature

Abstract: Memory and its threatened loss is one of the great driving narratives and anxieties of our own age, and 'cultural memory' has become one of the most important organising themes for innovative literary, social and historical work in the humanities. In Classics there has been important work on, in particular, the Athenian memory of the Persian Wars in literature and art in the fifth and fourth centuries – the 'art' of public inscriptions as central to the organisation of memory has been very much at the forefront of this work, and perhaps above all on the culture of Greece under the Roman empire. This paper considers some of the manifold ways in which ancient literature uses the idea of memory.

Themes of the paper include *kleos* and memory as compensations for death, both in poetry and in beliefs concerning the afterlife, *anamnesis* and the representation of memory in Plato, memory as an intertextual trope in post-classical Greek and Latin literature, and memory as a narratological device, both in Homer and later poetry. If all narratives are, to some extent, exercises of memory, then memory can act as a powerful way in which poetry can evoke its own reception, and this idea will be illustrated from both Homer and Virgil. Another aspect of the connection between memory and representation is the idea of recognition, and this paper will also consider some aspects of recognition both in Homer and in Aristotle's discussion in the *Poetics*.

The organisers of the AMPAL conference on memory no doubt knew what they were doing when they invited a speaker who worries constantly that he is losing his. Or perhaps they knew that one of my favourite ancient proverbial sayings is 'I hate a drinking partner with a memory'. What matters, however, is that we recognise how important this subject is. Memory and its loss is in fact one of the great driving narratives and anxieties of our own age, and this has nothing to do with how many gigabytes of RAM your computer has. We all take our daily dose

---

This is a lightly amended (and shortened) version of a lecture given at the Manchester AMPAL conference in June 2018; I have resisted the temptation to add multiple footnotes, bibliography etc, as this would misrepresent the status and the purpose of this text. I should like to express my very warm thanks to the organisers of the AMPAL conference, and in particular to Kat Mawford, for the invitation to address the conference and for their hospitality in Manchester.

of Vitamin D in a desperate attempt to persuade the ghost of dementia to pass by our house and visit another, but we all sadly know those who have failed in the attempt. The awfulness of this illness has even spawned its own genre of jokes, just as the source of terrible fears (and indeed memories) so often does.

In some contexts memory is what we live by. Far from wanting to forget, we insist (and rightly so) that our children learn to remember wars and genocides, whereas Herodotus famously reports that the Athenians imposed a heavy fine upon Phrynichus because his drama on the capture of Miletus 'reminded them of their own misfortunes' and they appear to have tried to erase the 'memory' of the play itself (6.21). We have of course to learn to remember; young children who learn 'times tables' or (if any such children still exist) declensions of Latin verbs are learning a lesson even more important than how to add up or the morphology of the pluperfect subjunctive. Antiquity regarded Simonides of Ceos as the inventor of an art of memory (a kind of upmarket University Challenge), and his legacy lives on in all those newspaper and magazine advertisements which offer to improve your memory so that you no longer forget people's names; reading what is left of Simonides' poems would actually be a more useful occupation.

If memory loss has become one of the driving nightmares of our age, then memory has moved centre-stage in another way also. Although we might be tempted to associate the theme of memory in literature above all with Proust, 'cultural memory' has become one of the most important organising themes for innovative literary, social and historical work in the humanities; cultural studies in the last decades have in fact experienced what has been called (not, I am glad to say, by me) a 'mnemonic turn', just as Classics – so we are told – has been experiencing its own 'philological turn'. Paul Fussell's groundbreaking *The Great War and Modern Memory* was first published in 1975 and it launched an avalanche of important work on how the First World War is remembered in literature, film and monument; Fussell's book is deeply concerned with literature as one of the ways in which we try to come to terms with the horrific chaos of war, and to complement this there is already a very considerable filmic bibliography which might be labelled 'The Vietnam War and Modern Memory'. The turn can in fact be traced much further back, above all to Maurice Halbwachs' work on 'collective memory' from the 1920s on, work perhaps still more often cited than read. The avalanche of work is such that some have even warned of 'memory burnout', so all pervasive has the interest in social memory become. Students of ancient cultures, on the other hand, often look to the work of the Egyptologist Jan Assmann and those who have followed in his trail. In the Preface of his *Das kulturelle Gedächtnis* of 1992 (published in English in 2011), Assmann identified three factors which had contributed greatly to the importance of the theme of memory in cultural studies. First, the revolution in the electronic storage of data; second, the fact that something which was passing, namely old European culture, still lives on as a subject of memory and commentary; and finally, the fact that a generation which had witnessed (in Assmann's words) 'some of the most terrible crimes and catastrophes in the whole of human history' was dying out (and this of course is truer now than when Assmann wrote). Another way perhaps of putting this, although I am not sure that I would, is that the 'mnemonic turn' may be in part a reaction to post-modern flux.

Classics has of course not been immune from these developments; quite the opposite. If the story of the Athenian reaction to Phrynichus and his drama appears to be an attempt to prevent memory, Aeschylus' *Persians* survives as an early example of the literary activation of, and attempt to shape, memories of war. Aeschylus' picture of warfare, like Homer's, is utterly different from, say, that of most poetry and film about the First World War, but some of the same mechanisms may be identified. There has been important work on, in particular, the Athenian memory of the Persian Wars in literature and art in the fifth and fourth centuries, and the 'art' of public inscriptions as central to the organisation of memory, no less than Herodotus' *Histories*, has been very much at the forefront of this work. So too, very important work has recently been done on the role of public documents – and not just the A-list such as the Parian Marble and the Lindos Chronicle – in fashioning cultural and mythic memory, particularly in the Hellenistic and Roman periods. This epigraphic material throws a great deal of light on the literature of the periods, and it should move much closer to the centre of our concerns as students of ancient literature. No field of classical studies, however, has been so influenced by the mnemonic turn as that of the culture of Greece under the Roman empire; here again, literature, art and architecture all play major roles in both remembering and fashioning, almost we might say 'inhabiting' a classical past. It is writers such as Pausanias who have benefitted most from a new appreciation of the extraordinary project of memory which he, and those like him, both recorded and indeed shaped. Strabo awaits as perhaps the next major imperial figure who deserves his moment at the heart of literary study.

Let me, however, turn back to private memory, though much work shows that private and public are not a simple dichotomy in this area. Severe dementia is sometimes described as a kind of living death, but it may be thought that memory is all that the ghosts of *Odyssey* 11 have left (for some, at least, after they have drunk the blood can converse with Odysseus). The fear of disappearing from all human memory goes hand in hand with the fear of losing our own. *Kleos* may be seen in poetry as a way of dealing with the former fear; consider how powerfully Sappho twists the knife, with a memory of the fluttering ghosts of *Odyssey* 11:

> κατθάνοισα δὲ κείσηι οὐδέ ποτα μναμοσύνα σέθεν
> ἔσσετ' οὐδὲ †ποκ'† ὕστερον· οὐ γὰρ πεδέχηις βρόδων
> τῶν ἐκ Πιερίας· ἀλλ' ἀφάνης κἀν Ἀίδα δόμωι
> φοιτάσηις πεδ' ἀμαύρων νεκύων ἐκπεποταμένα.
> Sappho fr. 55 Voigt

But when you die you will lie there, and afterwards there will never be any recollection of you or any longing for you since you have no share in the roses of Pieria; unseen in the house of Hades also, flown from our midst, you will go to and fro among the shadowy corpses.

'There will be no remembering or longing (πόθα) for you': the lady will be as ἀφανής in death as she was in life. Contrast how Dionysus himself describes his sudden πόθος, what Romans would call *desiderium*, for the dead Euripides at the beginning of Aristophanes' *Frogs* (vv. 52–67). The most famous stanza of Laurence Binyon's 1914 poem, 'For the Fallen', is by no means just a modern version of the positive side of this, a compensatory offering to the English war-dead, but it is that also:

> They shall grow not old, as we that are left grow old:
> Age shall not weary them, nor the years condemn.
> At the going down of the sun and in the morning,
> We will remember them.

I might add that the final image of that poem in which the famous dead are compared to Night's stars also adapts a common enough ancient idea of what happens to our spirits after death; antiquity bites back wherever you look.

As for the second fear, that of having all our own memories wiped out (the resonance of the language of computer storage is not accidental) in death, a death which is literally Lethe, 'forgetfulness', a fear I think all but universal (except for Epicureans, of course), more than one alleviation was found in antiquity, but none perhaps speaks to us so hauntingly as the 'Gold Leaves', inscribed tickets-to-ride which the dead were to take to help them negotiate the passage to another world. One of the best known comes from Hipponion in Southern Italy and dates from c. 400 BC:

> Μναμοσύνας τόδε ἔργον. ἐπεὶ ἂν μέλληισι θανεῖσθαι
> εἰς Ἀίδαο δόμους εὐήρεας, ἔστ' ἐπὶ δεξιὰ κρήνα,
> πὰρ δ'αὐτὰν ἑστακυῖα λευκὰ κυπάρισσος·

ἔνθα κατερχόμεναι ψυχαὶ νεκύων ψύχονται.
ταύτας τὰς κράνας μηδὲ σχεδὸν ἐγγύθεν ἔλθῃς
πρόσθεν δὲ εὑρήσεις τᾶς Μναμοσύνας ἀπὸ λίμνας
ψυχρὸν ὕδωρ προρέον· φύλακες δὲ ἐπύπερθεν ἔασι,
οἳ δέ σε εἰρήσονται ἐνὶ φρασὶ πευκαλίμαισι
ὅττι δὴ ἐξερέεις Ἄιδος σκότος ὀρφνήεντος.
εἶπον· Γῆς παῖς εἰμι καὶ Οὐρανοῦ ἀστερόεντος·
δίψαι δ' εἰμ' αὖος καὶ ἀπόλλυμαι· ἀλλὰ δότ' ὦκα
ψυχρὸν ὕδωρ πιέναι τῆς Μνημοσύνης ἀπὸ λίμνης.
καὶ δή τοι ἐρέουσιν ὑποχθονίωι βασιλῆι·
καὶ δώσουσι πιεῖν τᾶς Μναμοσύνας ἀπὸ λίμνας
καὶ δὴ καὶ σὺ πιὼν ὁδὸν ἔρχεαι ἅν τε καὶ ἄλλοι
μύσται καὶ βάκχοι ἱερὰν στείχουσι κλεεινοί.

Orphicorum Fragmenta 474 Bernabé [1]

This is the work Memory. When you are about to die down to the well-built house of Hades, on the right there is a spring, by which stands a white cypress. Descending there, the souls of the dead seek refreshment. Do not even go near this spring! Ahead you will find from the Lake of Memory cold water pouring forth; there are guards before it. They will ask you, with astute wisdom, what you are seeking in the darkness of murky Hades. Say: "I am a son of Earth and starry Sky, I am parched with thirst and am dying; but swiftly grant me cold water flowing from the Lake of Memory to drink." And they will announce you to the chthonian king, and they will grant you to drink from the Lake of Memory. And you too, having drunk, will go along the sacred road on which other glorious initiates and bacchants make their way.

trans. F. Graf and S.I. Johnston, adapted

There can be no greater promise than the retention of Memory in the afterlife. The happy initiate chorus of Aristophanes' *Frogs* is in fact living the dream, along, as the Gold Leaf says, 'the road which other μύσται καὶ βάκχοι travel'. This was a powerful idea and a powerful consolation in antiquity. In a poem from Hellenistic Knidos a deceased wife is made to offer the widower left behind such a consolation:

οὐκ ἔπιον Λήθης Ἀιδωνίδος ἔσχατον ὕδωρ
  ὥς σε παρηγορίην κἂν φθιμένοισιν ἔχω,
Θεῖε, πλέον δύστηνε, γάμων ὅτι τῶν ἀμιάντων
  νοσφισθεὶς κλαίεις χηροσύνην θαλάμων.

SGO 01/01/07

---

[1] There are familiar problems of text, orthography and interpretation here, but none affect the simple use to which this text is here put.

I did not drink the water of Forgetfulness, the daughter of Aidoneus, so that even among the dead I might have you, Theios, as a consolation. You are more wretched [than I], as you are robbed of our unstained marriage and lament the widowing of our bed-chamber.

No husband could ask for more, or rather no husband could offer himself such (?? delusional) consolation as to imagine a wife who will never forget him even in death.[2]

No one in antiquity was more concerned with memory than Plato. In a famous passage of the *Phaedrus* the king of Egypt very politely dismisses Theuth's invention of γράμματα:

> ἐπειδὴ δὲ ἐπὶ τοῖς γράμμασιν ἦν, 'Τοῦτο δέ, ὦ βασιλεῦ, τὸ μάθημα,' ἔφη ὁ Θεύθ, 'σοφωτέρους Αἰγυπτίους καὶ μνημονικωτέρους παρέξει· μνήμης τε γὰρ καὶ σοφίας φάρμακον ηὑρέθη.' ὁ δ' εἶπεν· 'Ὦ τεχνικώτατε Θεύθ, ἄλλος μὲν τεκεῖν δυνατὸς τὰ τέχνης, ἄλλος δὲ κρῖναι τίν' ἔχει μοῖραν βλάβης τε καὶ ὠφελίας τοῖς μέλλουσι χρῆσθαι· καὶ νῦν σύ, πατὴρ ὢν γραμμάτων, δι' εὔνοιαν τοὐναντίον εἶπες ἢ δύναται. τοῦτο γὰρ τῶν μαθόντων λήθην μὲν ἐν ψυχαῖς παρέξει μνήμης ἀμελετησίᾳ, ἅτε διὰ πίστιν γραφῆς ἔξωθεν ὑπ' ἀλλοτρίων τύπων, οὐκ ἔνδοθεν αὐτοὺς ὑφ' αὑτῶν ἀναμιμνῃσκομένους· οὔκουν μνήμης ἀλλὰ ὑπομνήσεως φάρμακον ηὗρες. σοφίας δὲ τοῖς μαθηταῖς δόξαν, οὐκ ἀλήθειαν πορίζεις· πολυήκοοι γάρ σοι γενόμενοι ἄνευ διδαχῆς πολυγνώμονες εἶναι δόξουσιν, ἀγνώμονες ὡς ἐπὶ τὸ πλῆθος ὄντες, καὶ χαλεποὶ συνεῖναι, δοξόσοφοι γεγονότες ἀντὶ σοφῶν.'
>
> Plato, *Phaedrus* 274e–5b

> When they came to letters, "This invention, O king," said Theuth, "will make the Egyptians wiser and will improve their memories; for it is an elixir of memory and wisdom that I have discovered." But Thamus replied, "Most ingenious Theuth, one man has the ability to beget arts, but the ability to judge of their usefulness or harmfulness to their users belongs to another; and now you, who are the father of letters, have been led by your affection to ascribe to them a power the opposite of that which they really possess. For this invention will produce forgetfulness in the souls of those who learn to use it, because they will not practise their memory. Their trust in writing, produced by external characters which are no part of themselves, will discourage the use of their own memory within them. You have invented an elixir not of memory, but of reminding; and you offer your pupils the appearance of wisdom, not true wisdom, for they will read many things without instruction and will therefore seem to know many things, when they are for the most part ignorant and hard to associate with, since they are not wise, but only appear wise.
>
> trans. Fowler, adapted

Plato has his own fish to fry here, but we ought at least to acknowledge his prescience. Today we have our own ὑπομνήσεως φάρμακον (or rather φάρμακα) in tools such as Wikipedia and Siri; we have no need to remember – even the term

---

[2] On this poem cf. J. Hanink, 'The epitaph for Atthis: a late Hellenistic poem on stone' *Journal of Hellenic Studies* 130 (2010) 15-34.

'facial recognition' refers to our own faces – and so, as Plato predicted, there is everywhere 'forgetfulness ... through lack of exercise of memory' (μνήμης ἀμελετησία). We live in an age where very large numbers of people appear to believe (or act as though they believe) that events have no meaning – almost did not in fact even happen – unless they are captured in photographs on mobile phones; it may be that such photos are supposed to preserve and stimulate memories, but perhaps rather they have taken the place of memory. The cult of the selfie may be depressingly banal, but there are in fact huge questions here for classicists about such things as social memory in oral cultures, the transition to literacy, the role of public inscriptions in antiquity and, not least, the composition and transmission of the Homeric poems. Memory and memories are a very productive way of attempting to order our study of antiquity.

Students of ancient literature have in fact intensively discussed several aspects of memory in recent decades. Most familiar perhaps has been the concern, particularly in Latin studies, with the language of memory as an intertextual marker: 'to remember' is to remember and hence recall past texts. Stephen Hinds devoted the first chapter of his widely read *Allusion and Intertext* to such effects, which will forever be associated with the name of Gian Biagio Conte, one of the most influential critics of Latin poetry of the last fifty years. The pattern has long been identified in English poetry also, and of course it continues to flourish, even in perhaps unexpected places. Andrew Lloyd Webber's very familiar composition 'Memory' from the musical *Cats* draws on (indeed quotes) the poetry of that most famous of cat lovers, T.S. Eliot, whose feline poetry inspired the show; here memory is double edged, as indeed it already is in the ancient texts which have been so intensively studied. T.S. Eliot himself of course was no slouch at this game. Consider the final stanza of *Journey of the Magi*:

        All this was a long time ago, I remember,
And I would do it again, but set down
This set down
This: were we led all that way for
Birth or Death? There was a Birth, certainly
We had evidence and no doubt. I had seen birth and death,
But had thought they were different: the Birth was
Hard and bitter agony for us, like Death, our death.
We returned to our palaces, these Kingdoms.
But no longer at ease here, in the old dispensation,
With an alien people clutching their gods.
I should be glad of another death.

The final stanza clearly picks up the voice of some of Cavafis' extraordinary poetry about rulers of the later Roman empire facing change and internal unease: the memory of Eliot's *magus* is (again) an intertextual memory. For classicists memory is inextricably linked to the textual instantiation of memory, and from the earliest date poems may be presented, as we have seen in Eliot, as records of memory. When Eurycleia recognises Odysseus through his scar and the poet tells at length the story of how he acquired it, it is difficult not to see a kind of narrative elaboration upon the instantaneous memory of the aged nurse; as elsewhere too, Homer dwells at length upon what 'in real life situations' would be unspoken memories or regrets or fears.

All narrative is memory of a kind. Theocritus, *Idyll* 7 is just such a poem:

ἧς χρόνος ἁνίκ' ἐγών τε καὶ Εὔκριτος εἰς τὸν Ἅλεντα
εἵρπομες ἐκ πόλιος, σὺν καὶ τρίτος ἄμμιν Ἀμύντας.
Theoc. Id. 7.1–2

> There was a time when Eucritus and I were on our way from town to the Haleis, and Amyntas made a third with us.

Memory plays tricks, and perhaps very few today would regard Theocritus 7 as a faithful memory of 'what really happened'; it is not just Odysseus who has given first-person narration a rather shaky reputation as far as truth is concerned. As is well known, all manner of earlier poetry bubbles up through the narrator's reminiscences in *Idyll* 7 and, as he recalls the bucolic party with which they celebrated their arrival, he becomes explicitly conscious of that poetic heritage:

πάντ' ὦσδεν θέρεος μάλα πίονος, ὦσδε δ' ὀπώρας.
ὄχναι μὲν πὰρ ποσσί, παρὰ πλευραῖσι δὲ μᾶλα
δαψιλέως ἁμῖν ἐκυλίνδετο, τοὶ δ' ἐκέχυντο
ὄρπακες βραβίλοισι καταβρίθοντες ἔραζε·
τετράενες δὲ πίθων ἀπελύετο κρατὸς ἄλειφαρ.
Νύμφαι Κασταλίδες Παρνάσιον αἶπος ἔχοισαι,
ἆρά γέ πᾳ τοιόνδε Φόλω κατὰ λάινον ἄντρον
κρατῆρ' Ἡρακλῆι γέρων ἐστάσατο Χίρων;
ἆρά γέ πᾳ τῆνον τὸν ποιμένα τὸν ποτ' Ἀνάπῳ,
τὸν κρατερὸν Πολύφαμον, ὃς ὤρεσι νᾶας ἔβαλλε,
τοῖον νέκταρ ἔπεισε κατ' αὔλια ποσσὶ χορεῦσαι,
οἷον δὴ τόκα πῶμα διεκρανάσατε, Νύμφαι,
βωμῷ πὰρ Δάματρος ἁλωίδος; ἇς ἐπὶ σωρῷ
αὖτις ἐγὼ πάξαιμι μέγα πτύον, ἃ δὲ γελάσσαι
δράγματα καὶ μάκωνας ἐν ἀμφοτέραισιν ἔχοισα.
Theoc. Id. 7.143–57

Everywhere was the smell of rich harvest, the smell of gathered fruits. Pears rolled plentifully at our feet and apples by our side, and the branches weighed down with sloes were bent to the ground. Wine jars were opened which had been sealed for four years. Nymphs of Castalia who dwell on Mt. Parnassus, could it have been a bowl like this that old Chiron provided for Heracles in Pholus' rocky cave? Could it have been nectar like this which set that famous shepherd by the river Anapus dancing among his sheepfolds—the mighty Polyphemus, who used to pelt ships with mountains? Of such quality was the drink which you then mixed for us, Nymphs, by the altar of Demeter, goddess of the threshing floor. May I plant my great winnowing shovel in her heap of grain once more, while she smiles on us with favour, holding sheaves and poppies in her hands.

The fact that memory both fades and plays tricks makes appeal to it a very powerful rhetorical tool. In Book 9 of the *Iliad*, for example, before Odysseus begins to report Agamemnon's offer to Achilles, he recalls what Achilles' father, Peleus, said to his son as he was setting out for war:

ὦ πέπον ἦ μὲν σοί γε πατὴρ ἐπετέλλετο Πηλεὺς
ἤματι τῶι, ὅτε σ' ἐκ Φθίης Ἀγαμέμνονι πέμπεν,
'τέκνον ἐμόν, κάρτος μὲν Ἀθηναίη τε καὶ Ἥρη
δώσουσ' αἴ κ' ἐθέλωσι, σὺ δὲ μεγαλήτορα θυμὸν   255
ἴσχειν ἐν στήθεσσι· φιλοφροσύνη γὰρ ἀμείνων·
ληγέμεναι δ' ἔριδος κακομηχάνου, ὄφρά σε μᾶλλον
τίωσ' Ἀργείων ἠμὲν νέοι ἠδὲ γέροντες.'
ὣς ἐπέτελλ' ὃ γέρων, σὺ δὲ λήθεαι· ἀλλ' ἔτι καὶ νῦν
παύε', ἔα δὲ χόλον θυμαλγέα.
                    Il. 9.252–60

Ah, my friend, your father Peleus gave you instructions on that day when he sent you from Phthia to join Agamemnon: 'My child, Athena and Hera will grant you strength if they wish, but do you restrain the great-hearted spirit in your chest; generosity of mind is better; avoid strife which brings evil, so that the Argives, young and old, will show you more honour'. These were the old man's instructions, but you forget. But even now cease! Drop the anger which grieves the spirit.

From a modern perspective, we might say that Odysseus' report of Peleus' parting words is, given the purpose of his mission, just 'too good to be true', and we should note that by Book 9 we have had no previous indication that Odysseus was present on such an occasion. In Book 11 Nestor recalls the same event to Patroclus, and the words which he there ascribes to Patroclus' father are again exactly right for what Nestor wishes to convey to Patroclus (11.785–91); of Peleus' speech to Achilles he merely reports in indirect speech that Peleus told his son 'always to fight gloriously (ἀριστεύειν) and to be superior to all others' (11.784). The two passages are linked, not just by situation, but also by the verse with which the speaker turns back to his addressees, Achilles and Patroclus respectively:

> ὣς ἐπέτελλ' ὁ γέρων, σὺ δὲ λήθεαι. ἀλλ' ἔτι καὶ νῦν ...
> *Il.* 9.259, 11.790
>
> These were the old man's instructions, but you forget them. Even at this time, however ...

In a later poet, 'you forget' would almost certainly be taken as a self-conscious marker of the fact that the report which has just been given is at least in part fictitious ('you do not remember, because this never happened ...'), but modern commentators are divided as to how we are to interpret Odysseus' stratagem; too often the question asked is 'How true is this account?', as though there really was such an occasion 'in the real world' (cf. 18.324–7), rather than what is the effect and purpose of Odysseus' rhetoric. Achilles never mentions, let alone responds to, Odysseus' recall of Peleus' words, and it may be that such embedded speeches were already in early epic a recognised mode of persuasive speech, acknowledged by both speakers and addressees, in which 'documentary truth' was very much a secondary issue. We are, I think, somehow inclined to believe those who apparently have perfect recall: not always a wise attitude.[3]

Our own memories, of course, are one of our most powerful resources for both good and ill. We relentlessly torture ourselves with them. Consider Achilles at the start of *Iliad* 24:

> λῦτο δ' ἀγών, λαοὶ δὲ θοὰς ἐπὶ νῆας ἕκαστοι
> ἐσκίδναντ' ἰέναι. τοὶ μὲν δόρποιο μέδοντο
> ὕπνου τε γλυκεροῦ ταρπήμεναι· αὐτὰρ Ἀχιλλεὺς
> κλαῖε φίλου ἑτάρου μεμνημένος, οὐδέ μιν ὕπνος
> ᾕρει πανδαμάτωρ, ἀλλ' ἐστρέφετ' ἔνθα καὶ ἔνθα
> Πατρόκλου ποθέων ἀνδροτῆτά τε καὶ μένος ἠΰ,
> ἠδ' ὁπόσα τολύπευσε σὺν αὐτῷ καὶ πάθεν ἄλγεα
> ἀνδρῶν τε πτολέμους ἀλεγεινά τε κύματα πείρων·
> τῶν μιμνησκόμενος θαλερὸν κατὰ δάκρυον εἶβεν,
> ἄλλοτ' ἐπὶ πλευρὰς κατακείμενος, ἄλλοτε δ' αὖτε
> ὕπτιος, ἄλλοτε δὲ πρηνής· τοτὲ δ' ὀρθὸς ἀναστὰς
> δινεύεσκ' ἀλύων παρὰ θῖν' ἁλός·
> *Il.* 24.1–12
>
> Then was the gathering broken up, and the army scattered, each man to go to his own ship. The rest took thought for the pleasures of supper and sweet sleep; but Achilles wept, ever

---

[3] Some of this discussion is drawn from *The Measure of Homer* (Cambridge 2018) 145–6.

remembering his dear comrade, neither might sleep, that masters all, lay hold of him, but he turned him ever to this side or to that, yearning for the courage and valorous might of Patroclus, thinking on all he had wrought with him and all the woes he had borne, passing though wars of men and the grievous waves. As he remembered he wept copiously, lying now upon his side, now upon his back, and now upon his face; and then again he would rise upon his feet and roam distraught along the shore of the sea. (trans. Murray, adapted)

Achilles' memories of achievements in war will evoke for the audience memories of martial epic (whether or not we subscribe to the modern view that Patroclus may be an addition by Homer – whoever *he* was – to the cast of epic characters); memory here triggers intertextual memories (even in a purely oral culture).

Poems can look forward, as well as back, of course. When Aeneas seeks to encourage his crew after their landing on the African shore,

> 'o socii (neque enim ignari sumus ante malorum)
> o passi grauiora, dabit deus his quoque finem.
> uos et Scyllaeam rabiem penitusque sonantis   200
> accestis scopulos, uos et Cyclopea saxa
> experti: reuocate animos, maestumque timorem
> mittite: forsan et haec olim meminisse iuuabit.
> per uarios casus, per tot discrimina rerum
> tendimus in Latium, sedes ubi fata quietas   205
> ostendunt; illic fas regna resurgere Troiae.
> durate, et uosmet rebus seruate secundis.'
>
> Virg. *Aen.* 1.198–207

"O comrades—for ere this we have not been ignorant of misfortune—you who have suffered worse, this also god will end. You drew near to Scylla's fury and her deep-echoing crags; you have known, too, the rocks of the Cyclopes; recall your courage and banish sad fear. Perhaps even this distress it will some day be a joy to recall. Through varied fortunes, through countless hazards, we journey towards Latium, where fate promises a home of peace. There it is granted that Troy's realm shall rise again; endure, and live for a happier day." (trans. Fairclough),

we recognise that Virgil is (*inter alia*) predicting the future reception of his own poem. It will bring the pleasure, in Greek τέρψις, that listening to epic poetry is intended to create. If we are attuned to this, the unspoken but bitter irony that hangs over Aeneas' final speech to Dido will not escape us:

> tandem pauca refert : 'ego te, quae plurima fando
> enumerare uales, numquam, regina, negabo
> promeritam, nec me meminisse pigebit Elissae
> dum memor ipse mei, dum spiritus hos regit artus.'
>
> Virg. *Aen.* 4.333–6

At last he briefly replies: "I will never deny, Queen, that you have deserved of me the utmost you can set forth in speech, nor shall my memory of Elissa be bitter, while I have memory of myself, and while breath governs these limbs".[4]

Behind Aeneas' words lie Nausicaa's final words to Odysseus in the *Odyssey* and Hypsipyle's to Jason in Apollonius' *Argonautica*, but is there also a suggestion from Aeneas that he will in the future 'recall' Dido and Carthage and the means of that recall will be Virgil's *Aeneid* itself? Dido's wish for remembrance is of a quite different kind:

'spero equidem mediis, si quid pia numina possunt,
supplicia hausurum scopulis et nomine Dido
saepe uocaturum. sequar atris ignibus absens
et, cum frigida mors anima seduxerit artus,
omnibus umbra locis adero. dabis, improbe, poenas.
audiam et haec Manis ueniet mihi fama sub imos.'
                                Virg. *Aen.* 4.382–7

"Yet I trust, if the righteous gods have any power, that on the rocks midway you will drain the cup of vengeance and often call on Dido's name. Though far away, I will chase you with murky brands and, when chill death has severed soul and body, everywhere my shade shall haunt you. Relentless one, you will repay! I shall hear, and the tale will reach me in the depths of the world below!"

After Dido has responded with such open bitterness and has been carried out by servants, Aeneas is famously silent:

at pius Aeneas, quamquam lenire dolentem
solando cupit et dictis auertere curas,
multa gemens magnoque animum labefactus amore
iussa tamen diuum exsequitur classemque reuisit.
                                Virg. *Aen.* 4.393–6

But loyal Aeneas, though longing to soothe and assuage her grief and by his words turn aside her sorrow, with many a sigh, his soul shaken by his mighty love, yet fulfils Heaven's bidding and returns to the fleet.

What might Aeneas have said to console her? He would not – surely? – have told her that the gods bring suffering on mankind so as to provide material for epic song to be enjoyed in future generations. Well, perhaps. Homer at least can suggest that suffering is somehow designed to allow the production of song:

---

4 Translations of the *Aeneid* are those of Fairclough in the Loeb edition, sometimes adapted.

εἰπὲ δ' ὅ τι κλαίεις καὶ ὀδύρεαι ἔνδοθι θυμῷ
Ἀργείων Δαναῶν ἠδ' Ἰλίου οἶτον ἀκούων.
τὸν δὲ θεοὶ μὲν τεῦξαν, ἐπεκλώσαντο δ' ὄλεθρον
ἀνθρώποισ', ἵνα ᾖσι καὶ ἐσσομένοισιν ἀοιδή.

Od. 8.577–80

Tell me why you are weeping and why you lament in your spirit as you hear of the fate of the Argive Danaans and of Ilios. This the gods wrought, and spun destruction for men, that there might be a song for those yet to be born.

The thought, well attested in both Homeric poems, is here precisely intended by Alcinous as consolation to Odysseus, and that is why we might ourselves remember it as we wonder what on earth Aeneas might have said to Dido. The Homeric verses are a striking example of the prominence given to song in the *Odyssey*, which is of course importantly a poem of recollection and story-telling; without the remembrance of song, suffering has no status at all. Suffering becomes in recollection a source of pleasure, something which very greatly disturbed Plato and which Aristotle sought to explain as part of the pleasure appropriate to tragedy. At one famous moment of the *Odyssey* epic poetry, however, does not bring universal delight. As Demodocus sings of the fall of Troy and in particular of Odysseus' role in it, a subject which the disguised Odysseus himself had requested, Odysseus weeps, but not, it would seem, with pleasure, as he is compared to a woman bewailing her dying husband:

ταῦτ' ἄρ' ἀοιδὸς ἄειδε περικλυτός· αὐτὰρ Ὀδυσσεὺς
τήκετο, δάκρυ δ' ἔδευεν ὑπὸ βλεφάροισι παρειάς.
ὡς δὲ γυνὴ κλαίῃσι φίλον πόσιν ἀμφιπεσοῦσα,
ὅς τε ἑῆς πρόσθεν πόλιος λαῶν τε πέσῃσιν,
ἄστεϊ καὶ τεκέεσσιν ἀμύνων νηλεὲς ἦμαρ·   525
ἡ μὲν τὸν θνῄσκοντα καὶ ἀσπαίροντα ἰδοῦσα
ἀμφ' αὐτῷ χυμένη λίγα κωκύει· οἱ δέ τ' ὄπισθε
κόπτοντες δούρεσσι μετάφρενον ἠδὲ καὶ ὤμους
εἴρερον εἰσανάγουσι, πόνον τ' ἐχέμεν καὶ ὀϊζύν·
τῆς δ' ἐλεεινοτάτῳ ἄχεϊ φθινύθουσι παρειαί·   530
ὣς Ὀδυσεὺς ἐλεεινὸν ὑπ' ὀφρύσι δάκρυον εἶβεν.

Od. 8.521–31

This song the famous bard sang. But the heart of Odysseus was melted and tears wet his cheeks beneath his eyelids. And as a woman wails and flings herself about her dear husband, who has fallen in front of his city and his people, seeking to ward off from his city and his children the pitiless day; and as she beholds him dying and gasping for breath, she clings to him and shrieks aloud, while the foe behind her smite her back and shoulders with their spears, and lead her away to captivity to bear toil and woe, while with most pitiful grief her cheeks are wasted: even so did Odysseus let fall pitiful tears from beneath his brows.

trans. Murray, adapted

Alcinous identifies that it is ἄχος, not τέρψις, which Odysseus is feeling (vv. 540–3), but Homer (not untypically) leaves us to infer from the simile why Odysseus weeps. Aristotle, however, supplies an answer to which many, I guess, would assent; he is discussing types of recognition:

ἡ τρίτη διὰ μνήμης, τῷ αἰσθέσθαι τι ἰδόντα, ὥσπερ ἡ ἐν Κυπρίοις τοῖς Δικαιογένους, ἰδὼν γὰρ τὴν γραφὴν ἔκλαυσεν, καὶ ἡ ἐν Ἀλκίνου ἀπολόγῳ, ἀκούων γὰρ τοῦ κιθαριστοῦ καὶ μνησθεὶς ἐδάκρυσεν, ὅθεν ἀνεγνωρίσθησαν.

Aristotle, *Poetics* 1454b37–5a2

The third kind [of recognition] is due to memory, to showing distress on seeing something. An example of this is the scene in the *Cyprians* by Dicaeogenes; on seeing the picture he burst into tears: and again in the 'Tale of Alcinous', hearing the minstrel he remembered and burst into tears; and thus they were recognized.

Odysseus weeps, according to Aristotle, because he remembers.

Incidentally, this is one of those passages which shows just how fascinating and how frustrating the *Poetics* is (at least for us). We know nothing of Dicaeogenes' *Cyprians* (presumably a tragedy), but it seems entirely reasonable that a sudden unexpected sight of a painting could have awoken sad memories which led to a recognition: 'Why does this painting make you weep'? someone may well have asked. The case of Odysseus would in some respects be close to this. He weeps at Demodocus' song of the fall of Troy and Alcinous asks him to identify himself, tell his story and, specifically 'why do you weep when hearing of the fate of the Greeks and of Troy?' (8.577–8). It is that similarity which was probably foremost in Aristotle's mind; it is, moreover, very likely (however speculative this guess is) that Dicaeogenes' scene in fact alluded to, was itself a 'poetic memory' of, *Odyssey* 8. There are two very striking things, however, about this passage of the *Poetics*. One is the parallelism between 'seeing/looking at a painting' and 'listening to (the song of) a lyre-player'; the parallelism between a painted and a sung artefact and between seeing and hearing may be thought to suggest a view about aesthetic experience which would at least have surprised in an earlier age. But then Aristotle is always full of surprises. That music can lead to memory and recognition should be very familiar to anyone who has ever watched *Casablanca*. Looking ahead (of Aristotle, not *Casablanca*, that is), we might see here the seeds of a narrative such as the opening scene of the novel of Achilles Tatius, where emotional sighs induced by a painting lead to the telling of Clitophon's story, his *Odyssey* if you like. Secondly, Aristotle names neither Odysseus nor the character who wept in Dicaeogenes' play, but seems to assume (or does he?) that his audience (whoever they may have been) will know; well, Odysseus is easy – very few will have trouble identifying him – but how familiar was Dicaeogenes' play and were its character and this scene remotely as well known as Odysseus and the end of Book 8 of the *Odyssey*? Probably not, but this is an area where a certain caution is necessary. Aristotle bandies around many plays which are not much more than titles to us. Dicaeogenes was a tragedian of the late fifth – early fourth century. Beyond his place in the *Poetics*, the fact about him which is of greatest interest (in fact almost the only fact known about him) was that he wrote choral dithyrambs as well as tragedies; the matter is mentioned both in late lexicographers and in a fascinating and difficult passage of the fourth book of Philodemus, *On Poets*. Philodemus was responding to someone (perhaps indeed Aristotle) on the subject (to put it simply) of the place of lyrics in tragedy, and takes it for granted that Dicaeogenes was a bad and unsuccessful poet. We do not have to accept the rhetoric, but it is interesting to see here Dicaeogenes unfavourably compared to 'classics' of Greek lyric poetry, Pindar and Simonides. He was then certainly someone who, at least later, was very much not on the A-list. Was he already an also-ran when Aristotle cited him alongside Homer? Such questions speak to large issues of canon formation and the growth of critical practice in antiquity – and deserve a conference devoted to them.

In *De Oratore* 2.299 Cicero tells the story of the great Athenian politician Themistocles being approached by a very learned man (*doctus homo atque in primis eruditus*) who offered to teach him an *ars memoriae* which would allow him to remember everything; presumably at some point in the history of this anecdote that man had a name – and that (presumably) was Simonides. In any case, Cicero records Themistocles as observing in answer that that man would do him a greater favour if he taught him to forget what he wanted to forget rather than to remember. It would be interesting to speculate on the relationship between this anecdote and Plato's story of Theuth to which I alluded earlier (is Cicero's anecdote about memory itself an example of textual remembering?), but (for now) it is worth reminding ourselves, as the story of Themistocles reminds us, that memory is a double-edged sword. The mind's mechanisms for suppressing memory are a subject of very great interest to modern psychologists, but we all know that, however hard we cling to memories, an *ars obliuiscendi* would sell out in no time. Only politicians appear able instantly to forget what they would like to forget. Why we forget, when we do forget, is at least as interesting a subject as that of memory, and both memory and forgetfulness are used in ancient literature as narrative signs in contexts of potential multiple causation. Both the Cyclops and the Phaeacians seem to have 'forgotten' prophecies concerning their future.

Why did Theseus abandon Ariadne on Naxos? Was it simple forgetfulness (i.e. he woke up and forgot that his bride was sleeping beside him – it happens, I guess), or was this a divinely induced forgetfulness; if that god was Dionysus, are we 'really' to understand that Theseus had had too much to drink? The whole story seemed so improbable that more 'plausible' accounts also circulated – a storm in fact separated their ships etc. In the first book of Apollonius' *Argonautica* the Argonauts forget to take Heracles with them when they set off after a stop in Mysia: how on earth could you not realise that Heracles was not on board? Once again the narrative opens itself to multiple explanations, and the paths of memory and forgetting are central to the roads both taken and not taken. Memory and forgetfulness are in fact central, not just to how literature constructs its narratives, but to how writers and moralists reflect on what makes us human. 'Elephants never forget', but we do …

List of Contributors

Hannah Burke-Tomlinson is a PhD candidate in the Department of Comparative Literature at King's College London undertaking a doctorate in Classics and Comparative Literature. Her PhD thesis examines poetic representations of the male poet's body and masculinity as a nexus for metapoetic reflections in the works of major Augustan Latin and Romantic English poets, and her research interests include metapoetics, literary representations of masculinity in ancient and modern sources, gender criticism, literary theory, Augustan Latin poetry (especially Latin love elegy), and Romantic English poetry. She is the co-editor of a special edition volume of the journal *Preternature: Critical and Historical Studies on the Preternatural* focusing on the presentation of the uncanny in Classical antiquity, which is due to come out in 2021.

Kate Cook is a Teaching Fellow in Classics at Durham University. Her research interests are in gender and language in Greek tragedy, particularly praise and blame language, and Classical reception in video games. Kate is currently working on monographs on praise and blame for 'heroic' figures in Greek tragedy, and women in Greek Tragedy, and is co-editing a volume on the representation of women in Classical and Archaeological Video Games.

Elinor Cosgrave (she/her) is a PhD finalist at the University of Leeds, UK. Her research focuses on representations of Roman captive-taking. She is the co-creator of *Ancient Herstories*, a project which aims to research stories of lesser-known women of the ancient world, and ensure they are accessible to and shared with a non-specialist audience. In 2020, Elinor co-wrote an article on *Ancient Herstories* which was published in the *Journal of Classical Teaching*.

Maria Haley is an Honorary Research Fellow at The University of Manchester. Her research interests include fragmentary drama in Greece and Rome and the theme of feasting in Latin literature. She has published a review of Boyle's Thyestes in *The Journal of Roman Studies* (2019) in addition to "Teknophagy and Tragicomedy: The Mythic Burlesques of Tereus and Thyestes" in *Ramus* (2019). She is currently co-editing a volume on Tereus in Antiquity and will be contributing a chapter on the myth in comedy and Roman satire (2022); she is also preparing a monograph entitled *The Myth of Thyestes in Greece and Rome*.

Carlos Hernández Garcés received his PhD in Classics (Greek) at the University of Oslo and he is currently teaching Spanish at Southwest University of Science and Technology (Mianyang, Sichuan, China). He also took a Master's degree in Archaeology and Heritage Management from Alcalá University and has participated in several projects in Spain, Ireland and Greece, where he has often collaborated with the Norwegian Institute in Athens. He has contributed to the elaboration of two dictionaries (*Diccionario jurídico griego bizantino-español* and *Medicalia Online*) and he has published some book reviews, two English-Spanish translations and a survey on heritage management. His research interests include ancient historiography, historical narratives and archaeology. He is currently working towards the publication of a monograph entitled *Herodotus and the Emergence of Historical Discourse: The Development of Key Terms and Concepts*.

Richard Hunter is Regius Professor of Greek at the University of Cambridge and a Fellow of Trinity College. His research interests include Hellenistic poetry, ancient literary and cultural criticism and reception, and ancient drama. His most recent books include *Apollonius of Rhodes, Argonautica IV* (Cambridge 2015), *The Measure of Homer* (Cambridge 2018), and (with Rebecca Laemmle) *Euripides*, Cyclops (Cambridge 2020). Many of his essays are collected in *On Coming After: Studies in Post-Classical Greek Literature and its Reception* (Berlin 2008).

Katarzyna Kostecka is a PhD student in Ancient History at the University of Warsaw. She is interested in the questions of identity, mobility, and myth. She has published a paper entitled "Geographical mobility and the dynamics of the status of elite specialists" in the journal *Incidenza dell'Antico* (2019). Her current research focuses on the mythical genealogies of the Greek elite.

Katharine Mawford is an Honorary Research Fellow at the University of Manchester and a Classics teacher. Her research interests include shape-shifting, transformation, monsters, and magic in Greek myth and poetry, and the interrelation of myth and folktale. She is also passionate about increasing access to Classics and the ancient world, and is the co-lead of the Classics public engagement project *Athena's Owls*.

Andreas N. Michalopoulos is Professor of Latin at the National and Kapodistrian University of Athens. He has published extensively on Latin literature of the 1st centuries BC and AD (especially epic, elegy and drama), edited numerous volumes (more recently *The Rhetoric of Unity and Division in Ancient Literature*, (Berlin/Boston: De Gruyter 2021), with A. Serafim, F. Beneventano della Corte, and A. Vatri) and is the author of *Ancient Etymologies in Ovid's Metamorphoses: A Commented Lexicon* (Leeds: Francis Cairns Publications, 2001), *Ovid, Heroides 16 and 17: Introduction, Text and Commentary* (Cambridge: Francis Cairns Publications, 2006), and *Ovid, Heroides 20 and 21: Introduction, Text and Commentary* (Athens: Papadimas, 2013). His research interests include Augustan poetry, ancient etymology, Roman drama, the Roman novel, and the modern reception of classical literature.

A.D. Morrison is Professor of Greek at the University of Manchester, where he has taught since 2001. His books include *The Narrator in Archaic Greek and Hellenistic Poetry* (Cambridge, 2007), *Apollonius Rhodius, Herodotus and Historiography* (Cambridge, 2020) and (as co-editor) *Ancient Letters* (Oxford, 2007) and *Lucretius: Poetry, Philosophy, Science* (Oxford, 2013). Current projects include a commentary on Callimachus for the Cambridge Greek and Latin Classics series, a G&R New Survey on Hellenistic poetry and (since 2016) co-directing the AHRC project on Ancient Letter Collections.

Sophie Ngan is a PhD student at Durham University, with a thesis on gender construction in Seneca's dramatic and philosophical writings. More widely, her research interests include Latin literature, Roman philosophy, and gender and sexuality. She also works on receptions of the ancient world in video games, and is currently working on a piece concerning female characters in Argonautic games.

Eleni Ntanou is a Classics teacher and has worked as a lecturer of Latin language and literature at the National and Kapodistrian University of Athens. She is mainly interested in pastoral and epic poetry and, generally, the study of genre as well as gender in Augustan and Flavian literature. Her publications include: '*HAC Arethusa TENUS* (Ov. *Met.* 5.642): Geography and Poetics in Ovid's Arethusa' in Sharrock, A., Malm, M. & Möller, D., eds., 2020, *Metamorphic Readings. Transformation, Language, and Gender in the Interpretation of Ovid's Metamorphoses*, Oxford: 84-103; and '*Musae Ambo*: Pastoral Poetry in the Ovidian Contest between Muses and Pierides', *The Journal of Greco-Roman Studies* Vol. 59–3, 2020: 77–94. She is currently working on Calpurnius Siculus as well as on generic interactions in Ovid's *Metamorphoses*.

Sophia Papaioannou is Professor of Latin at the National and Kapodistrian University of Athens. Her research interests embrace Ancient Epic, Latin poetry and Roman Comedy, and ancient performance, and she has published many books and articles on these topics. Recent publications include: *The Ancient Art of Persuasion Across Genres and Topics*, Leiden 2019 (co-edited with Andreas Serafim and Kyriakos Demetriou); *Plautus' Erudite Comedy: New Insights into the Work of a Doctus Poeta*, Newcastle 2020 (co-edited with Chrysanthi Demetriou); *Intertextuality in Seneca's Philosophical Writings*, London 2020 (co-edited with Myrto Garani and Andreas Michalopoulos); and *Elements of Tragedy in Flavian Epic*, Berlin 2021 (co-edited with Agis Marinis). She is currently co-editing (with Andreas Serafim and Michael Edwards) the *Brill's Companion to the Reception of Classical Rhetoric*, and a book project that explores the reception of the Latin tradition in Nonnus' *Dionysiaca*.

Index Rerum et Nominum

Achilles 76, 130–2, 134, 136–8, 174–80, 206, 249–50, 301–3
Acis 13, 196, 201, 204, 206, 208
Artemis 35, 247, 254 n.25, 278 n.36
Cannae 103–9, 114–19
captivity 11, 103, 106, 112–15, 118–19, 305
comedy 6, 9, 21–3, 35, 37, 57 n.49, 61 n.57, 105
Daedalus 13, 219, 221–7, 231–43
Dido 151 n.16–17, 159 n.34, 174, 221 n.5, 303–5
elegy 6, 93–94, 96, 97–99, 172 n.20, 201 n.40
epic 2, 4, 5–6, 9, 12–13, 74–7, 145–9, 157–8, 162–3, 168, 173–80, 188, 194, 196–7, 201–4, 206, 209, 211, 222–4, 227–33, 235–9, 242–3, 303–5
epitaphios 9, 11, 71–3, 78 n.31, 82–6
exempla 106–7, 109–10, 118–19, 158 n.31, 159
exile 3 n.7, 9, 21 n.9, 63, 64 n.59, 89–96, 98–100, 150, 239
fabula palliata 21, 25–6, 33, 37, 104
forgetting
 –as a narrative tool 13, 94–8, 99, 269, 273–87
 –dangers of 13, 91–2, 247–52, 254–63
Galatea 13, 194–211, 172 n.18, 225 n.12
genre 4, 6, 8, 9, 10, 11, 14, 22 n.10, 43, 47, 56, 59, 72–3, 82–6, 104, 139, 168–9, 194 n.1, 198, 201, 204, 206, 211, 232–3, 294
Helen 5, 9 n.26, 146 n.4, 150 n.14, 153, 153 n.20 and 22, 158 n.33, 161–3, 162 n.44, 166–7 n.3, 258–61, 275
Heracles 73–9, 127–8, 130, 132, 134, 301
 –children of 11, 71–86
historiography 6, 57, 62, 268, 274, 287
Hypsipyle 158, 158 n.29, 163, 304
intertextuality 7, 147–8, 166–7, 195, 198, 202, 204, 211, 228, 299–300, 303
Jason 145, 147–55, 157–63, 168, 170–2, 175–89, 262, 304

kleos 9, 12, 72–8, 85, 151, 158 173–4, 262, 293, 295
labyrinth, the 13, 222–4, 230–4, 235, 237–40, 242–3
letters, epistles 89–100, 91 n.4, 92 n.11, 93, 255, 298
lyric poetry 77, 78 n.31, 206, 307
magic, spells 149–52, 155–6, 162, 208
Medea 12, 52–3, 60, 63, 145–63, 166–89, 225 n.12, 247, 250 n.12
memory
 –commemoration 1, 6, 9, 11, 14, 36, 71–88, 147, 158 n.33, 180, 219, 236, 253, 256, 268
 –exchange of memory 94–100, 147, 157–162, 182
 –loss (see forgetting)
 –mnemotechnics 6, 21, 26, 27 n.22, 32, 205, 281 n.42
 –pain of remembering 162, 258–9, 261
 –palaces of memory 27–8, 36
 –poetic 2–3, 73 n.13, 79, 194, 219–45, 306
 –social function of 3–5, 10–11, 20 n.2, 73, 89–102, 103–21, 123–41, 198 n.26, 248 n.4, 294, 299
 –urban (see topography)
Minotaur, the 220 n.1, 222, 224, 227, 231, 233–9, 240 n.56, 250
mythic past 123–41, 229, 253
narrator, narratorial role 13, 125–128, 134, 140, 146–149, 152, 156, 157–62, 163, 172 n.18, 193–4, 200, 205, 207, 208 n.77, 209–10, 219, 222, 223 n.9, 226–8, 240 n.56, 249, 254, 300
Nausicaa 152 n.19, 156 n.26, 158–161, 163, 304
nefas 91–2, 181–182, 240 n.56,
Odysseus 1–2, 76, 99, 126, 154 n.18, 156, 158–161, 163, 174, 176, 196, 208 n.77, 229–30, 249–50, 259, 261–3, 284, 295, 300–2, 304–7
Olympus 123–141
orality 161, 195, 199 n.32, 203 n.54

oral tellings 4–5, 146, 200, 205
Pasiphae 13, 172 n.18, 219–245
pastoral 13, 193–215
Penelope 1–2, 99, 230, 250, 259, 284
Polyphemus 13, 193–215, 301
power, dynamics of 12, 92, 94, 123, 127–9, 131–4, 137–9, 155–6, 162–3, 239, 247–8, 251–2, 257, 262, 264, 274, 278–9
praise poetry 71, 77–8, 82–5, 256,
rhetoric 43–67, 80, 82, 84 n.47, 85, 165–91, 228, 238, 269 n.14, 287, 301–2, 307

Thetis 128, 130, 132–5, 137, 159 n.35
topography 19–39
tragedy 6, 9–11, 43–67, 71–88, 165–91, 249, 250 n.12, 260–1, 274, 277, 305–7
TS Eliot 299–300
war
–Argive 80, 83, 85
–First Punic 107
–Second Carthaginian 29
–Second Punic 107
–Trojan 5, 123–41, 153 n.20, 260

Index Locorum

Accius
Atreus
fr. 8 Ribbeck	42
fr. 3 Ribbeck	50–2
fr. 5 Ribbeck	48, 55, 57
fr. 9 Ribbeck	56, 59
fr. 9a Ribbeck	56
fr. 14 Ribbeck	55
fr. 16 Ribbeck	52–3
fr. 18 Ribbeck	48, 49

Aeschylus
Prometheus Bound
454–61	255

Apollonius Rhodius
Argonautica
1.1–2	146
1.14	247 n.2
1.896–7	158
2.890–3	262
3.61–74	148 n.12
3.275–98	148
3.284–90	149–50
3.751–69	150
3.766–69	154
3.791–4	148, 152
3.806–14	154
3.806–9	155 n.25
3.809–21	148
3.819–23	155
3.1013–14	158
3.1069–71	148, 157
3.1079–82	160
3.1107–8	158 n.31
4.423–34	159 n.37
4.672–81	156 n.27
4.893–4	161–2

Aristotle
Poetics
1454b37–5a2	306

Callimachus
Aetia
64.10 Pf.	256
Hymns
3.1–2	247

Catullus
51.9–10	206
64.204	251
64.207–11	251
64.209	251

Cicero
De Divinatione
1.17	47
De Natura Deorum
3.26.68	52
De Officiis
1.28.97	55–56
3.32	107 n.27
De Oratore
1.5.18	45
2.299	307
2.353–4	5–6
2.359	46
3.58.217	53
3.58.219	51
Philippics
1.14.34	55
1.34	48
2.7	91 n.4
Pro Plancio
24.59	58–60
Pro Sestio
48.102	56–7
Tusculan Disputations
4.36.77	51–2
4.55	49

[Cicero]
Ad Herennium
3.16–24	27 n.22
3.16	28

3.16.28	45	892–3	81
3.22.37	45–6	901–9	81, 83
		919–27	81
Euripides		937	78
Bacchae		1018–19	80
279–83	269 n.11	*Medea*	
280–3	257–8	214–15	152 n.19
Fragments		1321–2	188
fr. 578.1	255	*Orestes*	
Heraclidae		211–14	258
23	75 n.18		
69	79	**Gellius**	
75	75 n.18	*Attic Nights*	
89	74	13.2.2	48
111–13	79		
120–9	79–80	**Gorgias**	
191–4	83	*Palamedes*	
198	82	DK B11a 30	255
202–4	74, 83		
244–5	82	**Herodotus**	
271	80 n.34	1.127–30	251
273	80 n.34	1.127.2	275
297–8	75	1.39.1	277–8
315	83	1.51.4	286 n.57
320–28	75–6	1.44.2	278, 280
329–332	76 n.21, 80	2.46.2	286 n.57
333–5	76 n.21	2.132.3	286 n.57
335	76	2.171–2	286 n.57
353–6	80	2.173.4	279
359	80, 83	3.28.1	279
362–80	80	3.40.1	280
436–7	77	3.46.1	286 n.60
461	80	3.63	285 n.55
463	80	3.75.1	284
510–11	82–3	3.75.2	285
513	82–3	3.95.2	286 n.57
534	77	3.103.1	286 n.57
554	77	3.125.3	286 n.57
563	77	3.147.1	285 n.56
588–9	77	4.36.1	286 n.57
623–4	77	4.43.7	286
632	75 n.18	6.35.2	285 n.54
636	75 n.18	6.86b.2	276 n.33
776	83	6.86c.1	276 n.33
778–83	80–81	7.67.1	276 n.31
792	78	7.143.1	281 n.42
859	78	8.5.3	281

8.75.1	276 n.31, 281–2	8.18–26	123
8.79.2	276	8.205–7	124, 138
8.81.1	282	8.209–11	124
8.110.1	281 n.42	8.579–80	260
Theogony		9.252–60	301
1	146 n.5	9.259	302
31–2	254 n.26	9.321–337	175
38	254 n.26	9.537	247 n.1
53–4	257	11.790	302
55	259	14.113	77 n.27
71–7	128	14.242–62	128
97	261	14.257–8	129
100	260	14.259–62	130
102	261	15.14–33	128
227	252	15.20–1	135
227–8	270	15.47–77	129
231–2	252	15.184–200	124, 128
235–6	263	15.187–93	123
617	133	16.686–7	249
713–21	129, 133	18.394–410	132
718–20	133	18.428–37	132
820–68	133 n.33	19.91–136	130
886–900	139	20.5–108	124
		21.379–80	124 n.5
Hippocrates		21.436–60	131
Coan Prenotions		21.444	131
6	273	21.462–5	124
Epidemics		24.1–12	302–3
3.3.6	272	24.509	259
3.3.17	272	*Odyssey*	
7.1.3	272	1.1	5
Prorrhetic		1.2	146 n.5
1.64	273	1.340–4	259
		2.276–7	76 n.24
Homer		4.220–6	150 n.14, 258
Iliad		4.220–1	9 n.26, 162
1.1	146 n.5	4.233	259
1.395–407	132	4.238–9	259
1.585–94	130, 135	4.239	9 n.26
2.33–4	269	4.589–92	158
2.485–6	254	5.204	250
2.491	254	5.207	250
2.492	254	5.208–9	250
6.357–8	153, 260	5.210	250
7.17–21	124	6.21–40	156 n.26
7.24–36	124	8.457–68	158
7.446–54	131, 135	8.461–2	159

8.464–8	160	**Orphicorum Fragmenta 474**	296–7
8.521–31	305–6		
8.577–80	305	**Ovid**	
9.82–97	2 n.4	*Ars Amatoria*	
9.92–7	151 n.15	1.289–326	221
9.97	249	3.1.23–4	168 n.9
10.97	9 n.26	*Epistulae ex Ponto*	
10.212–19	156	1.8.31–8	93
10.236	249	2.4	90, 99, 100
11.404–56	1 n.1	2.4.1–4	99
11.454–6	230	2.4.1–10	90
12.39–40	261	2.11	94, 100
12.42–6	262	2.11.1–6	94
12.189–91	261	3.8	98, 100
12.192–3	263	3.8.1–4	98
13.1–2	263	3.8.19–22	98–9
13.4–6	263	4.6	96–7, 100
15.125–6	158 n.31	4.6.41–4	96–7
19.116–18	259	4.6.45–50	96
19.392–466	126	*Heroides*	
23.202–6	1	12.21	183
24.482–6	151 n.15	12.212	168
		Metamorphoses	
Homeric Hymns		1.1–4	239 n.53
Homeric Hymn to Apollo		1.3–4	233
1	5, 146, 253 n.24	8.132	240
311–31	132	8.132–7	223–4
Homeric Hymn to Aphrodite		8.155	240 n.56
33–52	139	8.155–6	236
Homeric Hymn to Demeter		8.159	233
310–14	139	8.162–8	231
495	253 n.24	8.187	239
Homeric Hymn to Dionysus		8.188–9	239
2	253 n.24	8.244–6	242
Homeric Hymn to Hermes		9.724	226 n.15
580	253 n.24	9.735–44	225
		9.738–739	226
Horace		9.741–4	241
Carmina		13.737	201–2
3.30	2	13.739	202
		13.767	204
Livy		13.768	204
26.27.1–4	28–29	13.780	204
39.44	31 n.27	13.787–8	203
40.51	31 n.27	13.804	208
41.27.7	30 n.26	13.867	206
		13.870–1	206–7

15.871–9	3		*Captivi*	
Tristia			1–2	111, 112 n.5
3.11.65–8	97		25	111
4.3.23–4	99		259–62	115
4.5.17–20	96 n.36		318–23	117
5.4	96 n.32		690	119

Pindar
Isthmian
4.22–3	252–3
7.16–17	253
7.18–19	253 n.21

Nemean
3.36–7	75 n.18
6.19–21	271
6.26–8	83 n.45
7.12–16	253
8.24	269 n.14
10.24	271

Olympian
2.16–18	269 n.12
2.18	270
2.83	83 n.45
2.89–90	83 n.45
7.45	270–1
7.45–7	251
10.1	254
10.3	254

Paeans
8.83–4	254 n.26

Pythian
1.30–3	74 n.16
4.217–18	150
4.250	247 n.2
8.92–6	252 n.17

Plato
Phaedrus
274e–5b	298, 255 n.32

Plautus
Curculio
462	23
466–86	23–25
475	31
476	32

Plutarch
Theseus
22	250

Quintillian
De Oratore
1	44

Sappho
fr. 31.9–16	151
fr. 55	296

Seneca
Medea
48–50	167–8
52–5	170
116–20	170
120–2	181
171	166
179–81	178
190–1	178
225–35	175
267–81	79
266–9	178
361–4	177
465–6	183
482	183
517–18	177
560–2	184
905–10	186
910	166
992–4	187
1001	187
1020–1	187
1026–7	188

De Beneficiis
1.1.3	185
2.10.4	184
3.1.3	182
12.1–2	182

Index Locorum

SGO 01/01/07	297–8	**Virgil**	
		Aeneid	
Simonides		1.8	6
PMG		1.198–207	303
531	256, 269 n.12	1.713	151 n.17
581.5–7	256	2.547–50	174
		3.716–17	174
Sophocles		4.54	151 n.17
Fr. 954	256 n.35	4.78–9	174
Philoctetes		4.101	151 n.17
877–8	271	4.333–6	159 n.34, 303–4
		4.382–7	304
Terence		4.393–6	304
Adelphoe		6.14–33	221
572–85	33–6	6.23–30	235–6
Hecyra		6.24	221
439–43	33 n.33	6.33–4	236
		9.741–2	174
Theocritus		*Eclogues*	
Idylls		1.30	210
1.65	206	2.4	208
6.36–7	197	2.45	199
7.1–2	300	2.73	204
7.143–57	300–1	3.64	210
11.14	207	5.14	203
11.76	204	7.37	210
		7.37–40	198
Theognis		7.69	198
1.705	270	7.70	198
		9.38	198, 202
Thucydides		9.39	199
2.49.8	272 n.19	9.51–3	198–9
2.35.1–3	72 n.5, 74 n.17	10.69	206

Timocles
Dionysiazousai
fr. 6.5–7 K.–A.   260

Varro
De Lingua Latina
5.71   32 n.31
5.145   29 n.24
5.146–7   30
5.155   29 n.24
6.46   93 n.15
6.49   91 n.8

www.ingramcontent.com/pod-product-compliance
Lightning Source LLC
Chambersburg PA
CBHW020221170426
43201CB00007B/276